RUNNING COMMENTARY

RUNNING
COMMENTARY

**The Contentious Magazine That Transformed the
Jewish Left into the Neoconservative Right**

BENJAMIN
BALINT

PUBLICAFFAIRS
New York

Published in the United States by PUBLICAFFAIRS™,
a member of the Perseus Books Group.

Editorial production by the Book Factory.
Text design by Cynthia Young in Garamond Pro.

Library of Congress Cataloging-in-Publication Data
Balint, Benjamin Z., 1976–
    Running Commentary : the contentious magazine that transformed
    the Jewish left into the neoconservative right / Benjamin Balint.
    —1st ed.
        p. cm.
    Includes bibliographical references and index.
    ISBN 978-1-58648-749-2
    1. Commentary (New York, N.Y.)   2. Jewish periodicals—United
States—History—20th century.   3. Jews—United States—Intellectual life.
4. Jews—United States—Politics and government—20th century.
DS101.C63B35   2010
305.892'407305—dc22

                                                          2010005268

FIRST EDITION

10 9 8 7 6 5 4 3 2 1

TO ROMY

Seek the welfare of the city to which I have exiled you, and pray to the Lord in its behalf, for in its prosperity you shall prosper.

—JEREMIAH

Contents

Preface

BY VIRTUE OF THE ARTICLES they had shepherded into print and their long-cultivated habits of mind, the editors of *Commentary* magazine, the flagship of the neoconservatives, felt well equipped to respond to the attacks of September 11, 2001. On an old, seldom-used television set in the midtown Manhattan office, they watched as Jihadi hijackers, screamers of *Allahu akbar*, felled the Twin Towers, and the editors knew then that America's ten-year "holiday from history," as columnist Charles Krauthammer called it, was over. The cold war may have been history, but the modes of apprehension it had taught were very much alive. These men were confident that their prestigious magazine of opinion could offer—with a clarity long absent from American foreign policy—the most cogent ideological template for the post-9/11 reality. Their contentious, tough-minded monthly, which had for decades wielded an outsized influence on American politics and literature, had long put resolute faith in the fundamental goodness of American power and urged a greater expansiveness and assertiveness in its uses—a faith that would now be tested anew. Twenty months before that terrible day, *Commentary* had run a symposium on "American Power." The first of the contributors, published alphabetically, was Elliott Abrams, son-in-law of the former editor and soon to be tapped as an adviser on George W. Bush's National Security Council. "Preserving our dominance," Abrams wrote then, "will not only advance our own national interests but will preserve peace and promote the cause of democracy and human rights. Since America's emergence as a world power roughly a century ago, we have made many errors, but we have been the greatest force for good among the nations of the earth."[1]

This hadn't always been the magazine's credo. In the decades since *Commentary* came to life just after World War II, the magazine had abandoned the liberal anticommunism of the 1950s for a species of 1960s radicalism, which it in turn rejected for the neoconservative sensibility of the 1970s and after. Through both apostasies, the magazine's political passions endured, as did the polemical style in which these passions were so forcefully expressed. *Commentary*'s first editor, Elliot Cohen, presided over a group of defectors from socialism who articulated in the magazine's pages a strong case against

Communist tyranny. As he traveled the road of self-creation from Brooklyn obscurity to uptown respectability, Norman Podhoretz, the second editor, first steered hard left into fashionable 1960s radicalism, and then, in revulsion against the excesses of the politics with which he himself had flirted, he threw the tiller the other way and made his magazine host to the much-castigated neoconservative cold warriors. In veering into its neoconservative phase, Podhoretz's *Commentary* sharpened old divisions and created new ones as it helped advance the rise of a powerful new Right from the remains of the old Left and redefined the role of American power at the very time that power was reaching its zenith. The third editor, Neal Kozodoy, in filial fidelity to his predecessor, guided the neoconservatives from the cold war to the war on terror—from World War III to World War IV, as they would say—laying along the way the intellectual foundations for the Bush Doctrine and the wars in Afghanistan and Iraq, the country's biggest foreign ventures since Vietnam. A once marginal group of ex-leftists found that their ideas were extraordinarily relevant to the country at large. Their quarrels had foreshadowed larger political shifts; their ideas had become the politics of governments; their preoccupations had become the country's.

"A magazine is always a date, 'an issue,' a moment," literary critic Alfred Kazin once wrote in *Commentary*; "it is created out of an exacting sense of time." Throughout its long life, *Commentary* registered the life of its times. It looked intently at America, and it offered a running commentary, for lack of a better term, on the decisive moments in postwar American life: from the cold war and the lasting effects of Europe's totalitarianism on American politics, to Vietnam and the counterculture, to 9/11 and the war on terror. *Commentary*'s story, in other words, bears closely on the life of the nation during the last sixty years.

And yet this American drama was all the while enacted on a Jewish stage. *Commentary* was founded, after all, by the American Jewish Committee in 1945 "to meet the need for a journal of significant thought and opinion on Jewish affairs and contemporary issues." For the eloquence with which it did so, there was none to compare. The same magazine that would host the neoconservative ascendancy ran the early fiction of Philip Roth, Bernard Malamud, Saul Bellow, Isaac Bashevis Singer, and Cynthia Ozick, as well as the powerful literary criticism of Lionel Trilling, Alfred Kazin, and Irving Howe. In essays of the highest distinction, *Commentary* grappled with the Holocaust, the birth of Israel, and the Six-Day War. Its pages were the first in America to feature *The Diary of Anne Frank*. It published incandescent essays on Jewish theology by Gershom Scholem and on Jewish nationalism by Hannah Arendt, not to mention Norman Mailer's six-part series on Martin Buber's collection of Hasidic stories. Over time, the magazine, fascinating in itself, became one of the most important journals in Jewish history, an incomparable barometer of the climate Jews came to enjoy in America. *Commentary* was deeply representative in some respects and deeply unrepresentative in others, but either way it registered Jews' negotiations with America and the complications and conundrums thereof.

What did the magazine's political trajectory have to do with the curve of its Jewish arc? By what alchemy had a liberal magazine, founded by marginal, disaffected, ex-radical children of immigrants—alienated from the Jewish tradition and America alike—become the bible of neoconservatives? Therein hangs an unusual but most instructive tale.

PART I

Outsiders

Loneliness

Exiled, wandering, dumbfounded by riches,
Estranged among strangers, dismayed by the infinite sky,
An alien to myself until at last the caste of the last alienation.
—DELMORE SCHWARTZ, "ABRAHAM"

IMMIGRANTS

The Jewish encounter with America began with two dozen refugees setting foot in New Amsterdam, the city on the Hudson River soon to be renamed New York, in 1654. No red carpet greeted them. Governor Peter Stuyvesant wished these members of what he called "the deceitful race" and "blasphemers of the name of Christ" to leave. He was overruled by the directors at the Dutch West India Company in Amsterdam. The newcomers stayed and were soon joined by brethren who established communities in Philadelphia, Newport, Charleston, and Savannah.

A hundred or so American Jews fought in the Revolutionary War on behalf of a country unique in history, a country that from its very inception guaranteed the free exercise of religion. In the not-so-distant past, the Jews of Europe had lived at the whim of their hosts, who could—and did—revoke Jews' residential rights at any time. Jews had been expelled from Vienna in 1670 and from Prague in 1744. They were commonly seen—and saw themselves—as temporary settlers, as tolerated strangers. Resigned to political powerlessness, they learned to dwell in Jewish tradition itself, poet Heinrich Heine said, as a "portable homeland." George Washington, by contrast, assured the Jews of Newport that the U.S. government, dedicated to religious tolerance, "gives to bigotry no sanction, to persecution no assistance."

Though accepted as full citizens, Jews remained obscure in influence and small in number. Fewer than three hundred Jews lived in New York on the eve of the Revolution. Only 3,000 or so resided in the young republic by 1820—mostly descendents of the Jews expelled from Spain in the fifteenth century. Starting in the 1820s, however, after the "Hep! Hep!" riots terrorized the Jews of Central Europe, a wave of German-speaking Jewish immigrants fled from Bavaria, Prussia, and Posen. Some of these "German" Jews—such as the founders of Temple Emanu-El on Fifth Avenue—brought with them Reform Judaism. Discarding ritual requirements and ideas of ethnic distinctiveness, throwing off the yoke of the law, these immigrants preferred to see Judaism not as a body of revealed law but as a set of ethical teachings. This only eased their way into American society, and most acculturated fast. Some of the German Jews made it big: investment banker Marcus Goldman; retailer Benjamin Bloomingdale; Nathan Straus of Macy's; Levi Strauss, who patented "riveted clothing" and clothed America's westward pioneers in jeans; mining millionaire Meyer Guggenheim. By 1880, more than a quarter million Jews lived in the United States.

But this, in retrospect, would come to be seen merely as the first and smaller wave of immigration. Between 1881, when the assassination of Czar Alexander II roiled Russia, and 1924, when the U.S. National Origins Immigration (Johnson-Reed) Act stemmed the tide of immigrants, 2.5 million Jews from Eastern Europe—Yiddish-speakers from the shtetls of Russia, Galicia, Lithuania, Hungary, and Romania, the poorest and least educated of Europe's Jews—landed on American shores. Driven away from the old country by pogroms, persecution, and poverty, and drawn by the promise of prosperity in the *goldeneh medina* (the Golden Land, in Yiddish), they gave New York City the largest Jewish concentration of any city in history. By 1910, they made up a quarter of the city's dwellers. By 1915, 1.4 million Jews made their home in New York. And by the end of World War I, more Jews lived in New York City than in Western Europe, South America, and Palestine put together.

Needless to say, some Americans were no more pleased by this inundation than Stuyvesant had been two and a half centuries before. In 1921, Albert Johnson, chair of the House Immigration Committee, quoted the head of the U.S. Consular Service as complaining that the recent Polish Jewish immigrants were "filthy, un-American and often dangerous in their habits." Several years earlier, in *The Education of Henry Adams* (1918), the grandson of John Quincy Adams and great-grandson of John Adams had remarked on the threat the immigrants posed. "Not a Polish Jew fresh from Warsaw or Cracow—not a furtive Jacob or Ysaac still reeking of the Ghetto, snarling a weird Yiddish to the officers of the customs—but had a keener instinct, an intenser energy, and a freer hand than he—American of Americans."

Along with the peddlers, tailors, bookbinders, shoemakers, and silversmiths, the wave of Eastern European immigration carried ashore pious traditionalists who brought into the New World a reverence for study— rabbinic luminaries who would put their indelible stamp on religious life in the new country. The Orthodox among them started day schools (such as Yeshivah Torah Vadaath), yeshivas (such as the Rabbi Isaac Elchanan Theological Seminary), synagogues (such as the Eldridge Street synagogue), and newspapers (such as the *Yiddishes Tageblatt*). Hasidic rebbes recreated their communities in Boro Park, Williamsburg, and Crown Heights. Scholars such as Solomon Schechter and Louis Ginzberg imported their European erudition to the Jewish Theological Seminary, which opened its doors in 1887. Mordecai Kaplan, founder of Reconstructionist Judaism, immigrated in 1889. Bernard Revel, founder of Yeshiva College (later Yeshiva University), arrived in 1906.[1]

Still more numerous were the Jewish radicals who took to trade unions and socialism, men and women who pioneered the labor movement to relieve their bitter conditions in the sweatshops. Not all socialists in America were Jews, but Jews were disproportionately represented in the socialist ranks. After 1900, Jews predominated in socialist trade unions such as the International Ladies' Garment Workers' Union and the Amalgamated Clothing Workers of America. Jews Adolph Strasser and Daniel De Leon led the Socialist Labor Party. The Socialist Party, which broke away from the SLP, was led by Jews such as Morris Hillquit (born Moishe Hillkowitz) and Victor Berger, the first socialist congressman.[2] (The only other socialist congressman, a two-term representative from the Lower East Side named Meyer London, elected in 1914, 1916, and 1920, was also a Jew.) More than a third of the Communist Party membership in New York—concentrated in the upper Bronx—was Jewish. By 1917, the Yiddish socialist *Forward*, edited by an ex-yeshiva student named Abraham Cahan—nicknamed *Der Proletarisher Magid* (the proletarian preacher)—enjoyed 150,000 subscribers. It was joined in 1922 by a smaller Yiddish Communist paper, *Freiheit*.

Part of the Jewish Left consisted of intellectuals, many of whom would be driven even further to the Left by the Depression. Playwright and essayist Lionel Abel later quipped that New York City of the 1930s used to be the most interesting part of the Soviet Union, and indeed into the New

York of the Red Decade crowded a mixed multitude of crypto-Communists and Communist sympathizers, Stalinoids and Stalinophiles, Marxist mavericks and socialist schlemiels and parlor pinks. Stalinists may have dominated the Left, but because Marxist politics acted in those days like a theology, there was plenty of heresy and schism to go around. Now-forgotten factions and splinters of factions proliferated like breakaway Hasidic sects: Shachtmanites and Shermanites, Cannonites and Lovestoneites, Fieldites and Fosterites. The distinctions between them were usually apparent only to those on the inside, and a decade or two later few would remember the questions over which these factions had so bitterly divided. Finally, starting in the mid-1930s, these groups were joined by the Weimar émigré intellectuals, including Leo Strauss, Hannah Arendt, Herbert Marcuse, Max Horkheimer, and Hans Morgenthau—Hitler's gift to America.

YOUNG TROTS

Those who would midwife *Commentary* magazine into the world resembled nothing so much as a loosely knit, self-formed Family (as future paterfamilias Norman Podhoretz would call it), bound by a common language and frame of reference, a shared ordering of values, and an intense crisscrossing alertness to one another's judgments. These were kinsmen of a common cause, a common past, and a common set of ancestors. They practiced their hypercritical intellectual gamesmanship—a form of close infighting—*en famille*.

The Family for the most part emerged from the dissident, fiercely anti-Stalinist Trotskyists, a tiny minority even on the Left. Many had belonged to the Trotskyist Young People's Socialist League (YPSL), City College division. They had looked to Leon Trotsky (born Lev Davidovich Bronstein) as the "good" revolutionary: a founder of the Soviet state, theoretician of the Russian Revolution, leader of the Red Army, archinternationalist creator of the Fourth International (antagonist of Joseph Stalin's Third International, or Comintern), brilliant polemicist and writer of manifestos, a man intoxicated with politics who took literature with high seriousness. His example encouraged the Young Trots to feel like a small but potent ideological vanguard. (In 1917, after all, when Trotsky lived in New York for several months, there were only 40,000 Communists in a Russia of 70 million, and look what they wrought.) Like Trotsky, his American acolytes—revolutionaries duped by the revolution—loathed Stalin's dictatorial tendencies. Refusing to rationalize away Stalin's crimes as somehow necessary to the revolution, they insisted that Stalin had betrayed the revolution. Following Trotsky's example, too, the

Family theory-spinners learned to think hard about politics from an internationalist perspective—with great independence of mind and ideological fervor. They pored over the Trotskyist journal the *New International* and Trotsky's *Literature and Revolution* (1924); they talked incessantly about what had gone awry with Communism. Haunters of public libraries who got an education via the little magazines, seekers after coherence and comprehensiveness, they took *positions*. They staged debates—rhetorical jousts, really— at Irving Plaza off Union Square.

For formal education there was the City College of New York (CCNY). Many Family members—"sturdy sons of City College," as the school's alma mater song wishfully hailed its graduates—thought of the neo-Gothic perch overlooking Harlem as the Harvard of the proletariat. William Phillips (class of 1928), later an editor of *Partisan Review* and a contributor to *Commentary*, called City College "the poor boy's steppingstone to the world."[3] Being both free of quotas and free of tuition, City College was in the late 1920s and 1930s at least three-quarters filled with Jewish boys (the girls were at Hunter College, on East 68th Street).

Members of the Family's City College branch picked up a high combative style from an acerbic Minsk-born philosophy professor named Morris Raphael Cohen (class of 1900), who taught at CCNY from 1912 to 1938— the first Jew to join the philosophy faculty there. Cohen's witty Socratic style made him a popular teacher. According to the 1935 yearbook, "Dr. Overstreet may be chairman of the department, but to the cognoscenti there is but one God . . . and his prophet is Morris Raphael Cohen."[4] After class, and under its influence, Cohen's Trotskyist students spent brown-bagged lunchtimes in their alcove in the cafeteria of Shepard Hall debating the finer points of Charlie Marx's thought: Was the Soviet Union a degenerated worker's state? When would the class structure wither and a genuine proletariat emerge?

If these preoccupations now seem arcane, a more consequential question closed the Red Decade. Although most American Jews wholeheartedly supported American entry into World War II, the Young Trots opposed America's involvement, not because they were isolationists, but because they could not help seeing World War II as a war to extend capitalist domination. They wanted no part in a war between rival imperialisms.[5] They could not bring themselves to support a capitalist regime, even against Hitler. Nazism seemed to them just capitalism in extremis—fascism as the last, desperate convulsion of capitalism. "That the Nazis wanted to murder every Jew they could get their hands on was the last thing about Nazism that interested us," said Milton Himmelfarb (CCNY 1938), later a *Commentary* contributing editor. "For us the big question, the question that called forth all our dialectical virtuosity, was, Is Nazism the final stage of capitalism?"

MARXMANSHIP

Politics was the Family's alpha and omega, a master light of all its seeing. Saul Bellow, who would head the novelist branch of the Family, used to say he first heard of V. I. Lenin and Trotsky "in the high chair while eating my mashed potatoes." Daniel Bell (CCNY 1939), destined for prominence as a sociologist at Columbia and Harvard, had joined YPSL at the precocious age of thirteen. At fourteen, future literary critic Irving Howe (CCNY 1940) had joined a YPSL circle in the East Bronx.

In such company it was nearly impossible to remain a noncombatant. To be liberal was considered wishy-washy; to be Republican, unthinkable. "If there were any Republicans at City," Irving Kristol (CCNY class of 1940 and later a *Commentary* editor) said, "and there must have been some, I never met them, or even heard of their existence." Outside the Family, there was, in the 1930s, a smattering of Jewish anti-Communists, including Eugene Lyons and Isaac Don Levine. But if in the Family politics was everything, Marxist socialism was politics, a style of perception entire unto itself. Marxism offered a comprehensive theory of history, a coherent view of human experience, an ebullient and tantalizing purity of purpose.

The Family's radicalism was, as they used to say, overdetermined; it drew from several sources, each of which would have been sufficient alone. As if it weren't enough that they were Jews and intellectuals, they were also prodigal sons of working-class immigrant families, intimates of poverty and prejudice. These young men, whom we shall meet later as adults, had grown up in tough neighborhoods in Brooklyn and the Bronx. Sidney Hook (City College 1923), a son of a garment worker, had grown up in a Williamsburg tenement slum. Lionel Trilling's father was a tailor, and his father-in-law, an immigrant from Poland, made straw braid. Irving Howe's father peddled linens door to door, and Clement Greenberg's worked as a necktie wholesaler. Irving Kristol's father, who worked in the clothing business, suffered several bankruptcies. "We were poor," Kristol said, "but then everyone was poor, more or less." Nathan Glazer (CCNY 1944), the youngest of seven kids, was born in East Harlem and raised in the East Bronx, where his father spent his days bent over a sewing machine. When the young Glazer later got an editorial job at *Commentary*, wielding his blue pencil over manuscripts, his proud if uncomprehending mother could only tell her friends, "My Nathan is in the pen line."

In the 1930s, dreams of a classless society answered Depression anxieties and immigrant disorientations both. The Zionists and the Orthodox separatists had their answers; the Jewish socialists had another, which involved an escape from the barbarisms of capitalism and an entry into the wider family of humanity. As far as the Family was concerned, capitalism was not just unviable and unjust; it was also through. The Family felt especially drawn to socialism's moral concern. Its dramatic doctrine—its collective hope for humankind—offered rootless radicals the exhilaration of replacing Jewish parochialism with universalism, the relief of transposing loyalty from nation to class. Trying to dissolve the indissoluble, they looked to socialist universalism as a means to transcend religious distinctions and to escape Jewish difference into a higher allegiance, in which the relevant distinction was no longer between Jew and goy, but between worker and capitalist. This universalism would allow them, command them even, to overcome their origins, to become men of broad sympathies, to make them, to use Shelley's line, "equal, unclassed, tribeless, and nationless"—citizens of the world.

Before World War II, then, Marxism, with its calls for social justice, acted upon the Family like a substitute faith, enthroning Man in God's place. Its dogma of progress through class struggle offered a secularized account of collective redemption. "We'd read *Kapital* the same way we read *Humash* [Pentateuch]," Daniel Bell remembered. "Line by line." Irving Howe said that Karl Marx's formulas were taught with "talmudic rote." As a boy, Clement Greenberg (who would serve as *Commentary* managing editor) believed Judaism and socialism were synonyms. The sacred canon of Marx and Friedrich Engels offered another eschatology, one that assigned the working class—the Family included—a progressive, even messianic role in history and guaranteed the triumph of that class. Family members could believe they were the persecuted, the chosen by History. ("What's a Communist?" asks a character in a Harold Brodkey story. "A man trying to act like a Jew without getting mixed up with God.") Marxism seemed to bear the same structure as Jewish belief—a yearning for harmony regained.

THE YEARNING would go unfulfilled. Some in the family had broken with the Communist Party before World War II, recoiling in revulsion from the Moscow trials of 1936–1937 and from the Stalinist purges and show trials that covered the Soviet Union with a "darkness at noon" (the title of Arthur Koestler's influential 1940 anti-Communist novel). They reacted with horror to the Hitler-Stalin pact in the summer of 1939 (between the man with a little mustache and the man with a big mustache, as Yiddish writer Chaim Grade used to say), and to Soviet foreign minister Vyacheslav Molotov's announcement during a visit to Berlin the next year that fascism was a matter of taste. The execution in late 1942 of the leaders of the Jewish Bund in Poland by Stalin's secret police caused Family members great distress. For others, the "disintoxication" took slightly longer. The Stalinization of Eastern Europe, the suppression of writers, the dissidents sent to the KGB's Lubyanka prison, the millions sent to rot in the gulag's forced labor camps as "enemies of the people," the brutality, the fear, the poverty—all these made it rather harder to look to the Soviet Union as a shining emblem of progress.

By the end of the war, the Family's anti-Stalinist socialists had become hard anti-Communists. ("There's not a man in this room who's hard enough for me!" Diana Trilling—Lionel's wife and an unforgiving literary critic in her own right—declared of the political convictions of her fellow guests at an after-dinner party.) Their hatred for Stalinism remained, now amplified by a newfound appreciation of America as a bulwark against the totalitarian horrors still freshly imprinted in memory. Their radicalism was behind them, but the *experience* of it remained. Daniel Bell remarked that radicals of the 1930s bore, "as on invisible frontlets, the stamp of those years on their foreheads." "Joining a radical movement when one is young," his friend Irving Kristol added, "is very much like falling in love when one is young. The girl may turn out to be rotten, but the experience of love is so valuable it can never be entirely undone by the ultimate disenchantment." Radicalism—and the way they wrested themselves from its grip—had left a deep mark as much on the way they thought about their place in America as on their thinking about America's place in the world.

Certain youthful notions now seemed utterly refuted. *Commentary* would come to life in 1945 amid widespread predictions that mass unemployment would resume as soon as war production ebbed. But it wouldn't take long after the war to see that the dire prophecies had failed. It became clear that Western democracy was far from finished; American power seemed limitless. Capitalism had not only weathered the Depression; it also had ushered in a postwar economic boom, granting Americans higher standards of living than ever. (The country's gross national product quadrupled in the fifteen years after the war.) Anxiety dissolved into buoyant confidence. Depression discontent and wartime belt-tightening relaxed into postwar prosperity. White-collar suburbia spread into what economist

John Kenneth Galbraith would call "the affluent society." In the face of President Franklin Roosevelt's New Deal reforms, American socialism had lost momentum even before the war. (Socialist leader Norman Thomas received 885,000 votes in his 1932 run for the presidency, but only 187,500 in 1936.) After the war, however, socialism finally shattered against the reef of the postwar boom. The unprecedented wave of prosperity swept from the Family's mind any lingering dreams of radical reform. Its members could no longer, as during the 1930s, regard the country as economically oppressive. They could not help but notice that the working class had remained indifferent to socialism; that Marx, worshipper of History itself, had turned out to be another false prophet; that Marxism had been revealed to be a great fantasy. The old Marxist talk of "the exploited masses" or "the decay of capitalism" now left them cold; the very word "revolution" rang hollow in their ears. What Trotsky had called "the death agony of capitalism" appeared in postwar light as the pangs of rebirth.

In short, Hitler and Stalin had made it abundantly clear to the Family that would soon form around *Commentary* that there were more immediate threats than middle-class philistinism and capitalist exploitation. Flirtations with radicalism had ended; the Communist god had failed. The Great Experiment of socialism had turned into a mockery of its own promises of a society in which man would no longer exploit man. Having lost their pink tint, Family members left the precincts of radical politics and alienation for what historian Arthur Schlesinger Jr. called—in his classic liberal anti-Communist book of that name—the vital center.[6] They now saw the disingenuous 1930s, as W. H. Auden had, as a "low dishonest decade." Their political childhood had come to an abrupt end. "God died in the nineteenth century," Irving Howe said, "utopia in the twentieth."

PRESIDING GENIUS

Though an ex-radical and son of immigrants, the man fated to create *Commentary* did not share the City College pedigree. Elliot E. Cohen was raised in the first years of the century in Mobile, Alabama. His father, a dry-goods shopkeeper, back in the old country had studied at the fabled yeshiva in Volozhin (in today's Belarus). The oldest child was named after George Eliot, author of *Daniel Deronda* (1876), a novel that gave a sympathetic and astonishingly early treatment of Jewish national rebirth in Palestine.[7] "There was only one thing important in my family," Elliot Cohen said. "Books." Cohen could read newspaper headlines by age three. He was admitted to

Yale at fourteen. The youngest member of the class of 1917, he won the John Addison Porter Prize, one the university's highest, awarded for excellent written work of general scholarship.[8]

Beginning in his Yale days, Elliot Cohen nursed an ambition to change the world by founding his own magazine. "Why else start a magazine?" he said. He dreamed of editing an American Jewish entry into the great tradition of American magazines of the previous century—the *Dial*, edited by Margaret Fuller and Ralph Waldo Emerson, or the *Democratic Review*, conjured into being by Nathaniel Hawthorne, Walt Whitman, and Herman Melville. Cohen aspired to create not a general-interest magazine like *Harper's* or the *Atlantic*, but something more akin to those venerable American magazines of opinion, *The Nation* and the *New Republic*, which in an era before television news had a point of view, offered a forum for serious arguments about politics and culture. Among illustrious Jewish journals, Cohen envied the cultural influence of Ahad Haam's *Hashiloach*, founded in 1896, which brought forth the revival of Hebrew literature from Odessa, and Martin Buber's *Der Jude*, launched in Berlin during World War I, which printed the leading lights of German-speaking Jewry.[9]

But of all these luminous models, it was the *Menorah Journal* in New York that shone for Cohen most brightly. Edited by Henry Hurwitz—a former student at Harvard of philosophers William James and George Santayana—the *Menorah Journal* had been breathed into life in 1915 by the founders of the Menorah Society, a circle at Harvard dedicated to promoting a Jewish humanism. Among the society's founders were Horace Kallen (the son of an immigrant rabbi and later a philosopher at the New School for Social Research), Harry Wolfson (associate editor of the *Menorah Journal* and later first chair of the Jewish Studies Department at Harvard), and Hurwitz. In its heyday in the late 1920s, when it hosted the finest American Jewish writing in the country, the *Menorah Journal* owed its vitality to its precocious managing editor, one Elliot Cohen, former president of the Yale branch of the society, who had joined the editorial staff in 1924. Under Cohen's watch, the *Menorah Journal* ran essays by Jewish historians Salo Baron and Simon Dubnow; polemics by Mordecai Kaplan (another City College alum, who first called for a "reconstruction" of Judaism, his lifelong theme, in its pages); stories by acclaimed Odessa-born writer Isaac Babel and by Tess Slesinger, a satirist of the New York intellectual Left; and poems by Brooklyn-born Jewish poet Charles Reznikoff.[10]

At the *Menorah Journal* Cohen mastered a kind of literary ventriloquism, a talent for employing others' words rather than speaking in his own.

In his column for the magazine, "Notes for a Modern History of the Jews," Cohen juxtaposed quotations to satiric effect without adding a word of his own. Take, for example, this piece of irreverence on the subject of Jewish response to anti-Semitism from 1924: "'We Jews are happy in America and contented with conditions. We don't care for [Henry] Ford and Klu Kluxes. We don't notice them.'—Louis Marshall. 'Louis Marshall devoted a large part of his annual report as president of the American Jewish Committee [AJC] to a spirited attack on the Klu Klux Klan.'—*The American Israelite*."

Already in the 1920s Cohen had grown exasperated with the sterility of organized Jewish life. Religious and lay leaders alike seemed to him shallow and pompous, their currency devalued by what he considered "spurious intellectual coin." He dismissed purveyors of Orthodox Judaism, which seemed to him "foreign to modern American conditions." Nor could the managing editor summon much respect for what then passed for a Jewish press, mostly consisting of local papers such as Philadelphia's *Jewish Exponent* (founded in 1887). "By a logic of which only editors of Jewish weeklies are capable," he wrote in the *Menorah Journal*, "they advance Judaism and promote Jewish-Gentile understanding by printing accounts of how Jacob Dupkin, who once owned only one cart of junk, now owns practically all the junk there is."[11] American Jewish leaders between the world wars—the heads of national bodies such as B'nai B'rith (founded in 1843), the American Jewish Committee (1905), Hadassah (1912), the Anti-Defamation League (1913), and the American Jewish Congress (1928)—appeared to Cohen's eyes parochial, indifferent to ideas, too tolerant of hackneyed catchphrases and third-rate cultural products. He complained in the October 1925 *Menorah Journal* that he lived in "an age that substitutes rhetoric for knowledge, bold assertions for learning, vainglorious pretensions for soundly-based convictions, bluster for strength, and braggadocio for an inwardly felt security." With no small touch of frustration, he condemned the species of mediocrity that "is so busy hunting out heretics who will not bend the knee to the phrase 'Jewish content' that it has little energy for giving 'Jewish content' any content."

> For the amazing fact is that Jewish books in English are incredibly few. It is unbelievable, for instance, until one tests it himself, how pitifully small the number of volumes the entire Reform movement in America has to its credit. This is the group in American Jewry which not only has been the most powerful and, on their own admission, the most cultured, but has had English the longest. Other groups, of course, contributed even less. . . .

The fact is there are not available the smallest fraction of texts of Jewish history, religion, philosophy and culture we shall need in our program to substitute specific knowledge of the actual concrete sources of the Jewish spirit for the hollow nonsense of theological and political abstractions. Scholarship will have to be encouraged. . . . Professorships will have to be endowed at the leading American universities. . . . Periodicals devoted to the advancement of Jewish learning and encouragement of Jewish criticism, art, and literature will have to be supported.

Though Elliot Cohen forecast that Jews' political and economic status in America was assured, the young managing editor feared that their intellectual self-respect was not. "Judaism cannot survive if intelligent Jews come to despise it," he said in that same piece. Down with defensiveness, then. "American Jewry must be made to see that a life of apology is a shameful apology for a life."

To address the problem, Cohen called for a "thoroughgoing reconstruction of Jewish intellectual values," and resolving to rescue the intellectual dignity of Judaism, he honed a talent for discovering young Jewish writers who might help him undertake the task. Felix Morrow, for instance (who would later lead a faction of the Socialist Workers Party and edit its paper, the *Militant*), came by the *Menorah Journal* offices near Union Square Park one day to take Cohen's secretary to lunch. He got more than he bargained for. "When [Cohen] fixed his eye on me, I insisted I had no interest in a Jewish magazine or in Jewish life. All right, then, would I review books by (Jewish) authors on non-Jewish subjects? What about writing the story of Brownsville, where I grew up? . . . I wrote all these and more, while still protesting my lack of interest . . . then woke up one day to realize that I owed to Elliot Cohen my professional training as writer and editor."

Another of the writers Cohen lured in this way into an investigation of his Jewishness was a mannered, fastidious Columbia undergrad from Queens named Lionel Trilling, direct descendent of a pious rabbi in Bialystok, Poland. "It seems to me," Trilling wrote in 1929,

that the whole purpose of practical Jewish endeavor is to create a community that can read the *Menorah Journal*. More exactly, of course, what I mean is that this purpose is to construct a society that can consider its own life from a calm, intelligent, dignified point of view; take delight in its own arts, its own thoughts, the vagaries of its own being. . . . The Jew is written about carefully, fearlessly, without easy 'sympathy' nowhere save in the *Journal*, nowhere else as a human being and not as a problem.

Before Trilling came across the *Menorah Journal*, he said, "I had never seen a modern Jewish publication that was not shoddy and disgusting. Here I found no touch of clumsiness or vulgarity. . . . This was perhaps the first public Jewish manifestation of which I could say that." Under Cohen's guidance, Trilling, who had thought of himself as a Marxist for a very short time, published his first story in the *Menorah Journal* in 1925, when he was twenty. (It earned him $35.) Its publication, Trilling recalled four years later, marked an important turn in his life: "With the publication of my story I was caught. I could not escape thinking about Jews. I was not obsessed with Jewishness. I did not get religion. . . . But I accepted the fact of Jewishness as an important thing. I accepted it as part of my individuality and it functioned like a personal characteristic—I could talk of it as 'mine' as one talks of a person's honesty, weakness, strength, selfishness. I wasn't very sure what it was, but it helped direct my life."

To Trilling, only six years younger, Cohen cut a Socratic figure, a man of immense personal force, the greatest teacher he had ever known: "He conversed endlessly, his talk being a sort of enormously enlightening gossip—about persons, books, baseball players and football plays, manners, morals, comedians." Apparently, nothing was trivial in Cohen's mind. Before long, Trilling was affectionately signing his letters to Cohen "Li." Cohen set about instilling in his protégé an abiding belief in the communicability of complex ideas in clear language. Between 1925 and 1931, Trilling would write two dozen pieces for the journal: book reviews, essays, and four short stories. Decades later, as a professor of English at Columbia, Trilling acknowledged the debt his own urbane prose owed to Cohen. "No man in our country in our time had a greater respect for the virtues of English prose," disciple said of mentor. "He was a man of genius."

Over time, Cohen, still managing editor, came to feel that under Henry Hurwitz the *Menorah Journal*'s proud irreverence had eroded. His boss disagreed. "I am afraid you and I have been growing apart in our conceptions of what the *Journal* should be," Hurwitz wrote to Cohen in 1931. In the last line of his resignation letter, Cohen tendered a prediction: "The *Journal* will settle down to be the tabby-cat on the hearthstone of the official Jewish community, and purr for a living." The journal came out as a bimonthly, then as a quarterly, until even the purring quieted after Hurwitz's death three decades later.

Cohen was at that time something of a Communist fellow traveler, and so after he left the *Menorah Journal*, it came as no surprise to his colleagues that he found work as executive secretary of a Communist-front organization called the National Committee for the Defense of Political Prisoners and served as a board member of the Communist League of America.

After he, like many others in the Family, broke with the party in the 1930s, Cohen spent a mind-numbing decade as public relations director of the Federation of Jewish Philanthropies.[12] Sensing that his talents were wasted and his aspirations dormant, every minute of it was a nightmare for him. He began to suffer from manic depression—lifting him high in winter, casting him low in the summer. Time's unkind pen furrowed his face, melancholy tugged at his eyes, and the hair fringing his large head silvered over with gray.

AND THEN, AS THOUGH from nowhere, an offer, and elations of a dream fulfilled. In 1945, on the basis of the reputation he had amassed at the *Menorah Journal*, the venerable American Jewish Committee—the president of which he had earlier ridiculed in his column—invited Elliot Cohen, age forty-six, to edit its new monthly, *Commentary*.

In 1906, after the Kishinev pogroms of 1903–1905 in czarist Russia, New York's patrician, uptown German Jews—grand dukes such as Jacob Schiff, Felix Warburg, Mayer Sulzberger, Cyrus Adler, Oscar Straus, and Louis Marshall—had founded the AJC "to prevent the infraction of the civil and religious rights of Jews, in any part of the world." (Some of the same men, not incidentally, had funded the *Menorah Journal*.) Among its other initiatives, before World War I the AJC had opposed immigration restrictions and lobbied against literacy tests for immigrants to America. During that war, it had organized relief for Jewish victims.

And it had since 1938 put out a bimonthly digest, the *Contemporary Jewish Record*. A soft-spoken Spinoza expert named Adolph Oko, who had served as associate editor under Elliot Cohen at the *Menorah Journal*, became editor in 1944.[13] "Polemics have been discouraged," the editors of the *Record* declared. Although the editors gave occasional space to writers who would later contribute to *Commentary*—Hannah Arendt on stateless people, New York University philosopher Sidney Hook on "Hitlerism," and George Orwell on British anti-Semitism—they took it as their main mission to publish documents of historical significance: the Nuremberg decrees, the White Paper on Palestine, letters from Chaim Weizmann to the High Commissioner on Palestine, appeals of the Jewish Agency in Palestine.[14]

The most startling thing ever to appear in the *Record* came in 1944, near the end of its life. "Under Forty: A Symposium on American Literature and the Younger Generation of American Jews" revealed the depth of the reservations young Jewish intellectuals harbored about their own heritage. "I have never seen much of what I admire in American Jewish culture, or among Jewish writers in America generally," literary critic Alfred Kazin (City College 1935) said in his contribution to the symposium. "As the Jewish community now exists," Lionel Trilling somewhat harshly remarked, "it can give no sustenance to the American artist or intellectual who is born a Jew. . . . I know of no writer in English who has added a micromillimeter to his stature by 'realizing his Jewishness,' although I know of some who have curtailed their promise by trying to heighten their Jewish consciousness." Clement Greenberg, soon to become *Commentary*'s managing editor, used the occasion to assail the smug and dreary middle-class attitudes of American Jews: "No people on earth are more correct, more staid, more provincial, more commonplace, more inexperienced." "Jews are, everywhere, a minority group," Chicago-born writer and future *Commentary* contributor Isaac Rosenfeld ventured, "and it is a particular misfortune these days to be a minority group in the United States."

After Oko died in 1944, the *Contemporary Jewish Record* limped on for four issues with about 4,200 subscribers, but had clearly lost any gusto it once enjoyed. To replace it, the AJC dukes envisioned a less stuffy magazine of higher ambitions and wider influence; they cited "the need for a journal of significant thought and opinion on Jewish affairs and contemporary issues," a publication that would explore the creative possibilities of Jewish culture in America. Even before the magazine had a name, the heads of the AJC announced its mandate: "Free from partisanship and hospitable to divergent views, the new monthly will aim to provide the reader with informed discussion on the basic issues of our time especially as they bear on the position and future of Jews in our country and in the world scene. It will also aid in the struggle against bigotry." The magazine would address itself not just to Jews, but also to the American public at large. With the unanimous support of senior staff, John Slawson, the AJC's executive vice president, chose Elliot Cohen as the man for the job.[15]

IN THE ANTICIPATORY RUSH before the first issue of *Commentary* was due out, Cohen felt his black mood lifting; his considerable gifts would once more be harnessed. A hopefulness surged through him. "It is our hope that the new magazine will be a meeting ground for our finest minds and talents," he said. "We pride ourselves on Jewish creativeness in so many fields in the modern world. We need that creativeness of thought and expression in Jewish life, too. We shall have it, we sincerely believe, if we can offer it hospitality and freedom. To do this is a primary aim of this magazine, as it is of its publishers, the AJC." It was here that Cohen's *Commentary* would depart from the highbrow import racket at *Partisan Review* (to take the closest competition), a journal, founded in 1934, that joined modernism and Marxism. Though the two little magazines shared many writers, *Commentary* would be less avant-garde than *Partisan Review*; less enamored of Ezra Pound, T. S. Eliot, James Joyce, and Gertrude Stein; less European in orientation; and, not least, more open about its own Jewishness. *Partisan Review* in its heyday ran almost nothing on Jewish issues. "The main difference between *Partisan Review* and *Commentary*," Cohen said, "is that we admit to being a Jewish magazine and they don't."

Cohen had been waiting all his life for this chance—the culmination of his deepest aspirations—and he resolved to seize it with great energy. The role of the presiding genius—a demanding, intimidating, sometimes overbearing parental figure—came naturally to him. Vis-à-vis his readers, Cohen practiced editing as pedagogy. "We think of ourselves as trying to be the best possible teacher talking to the best possible student," he said. "Education is slow, but what is faster?" Vis-à-vis his stable of writers at the new magazine, Cohen imagined himself looking on from the edge of a baseball field. "I think an editor belongs back in the shadow of the dugout," he said. "He's a talent scout. He finds new writers. He's a coach who has the sense to leave 'em alone when they're good and tell 'em what's wrong when they're bad." In practice, though, Cohen seldom left contributors alone. He edited his authors exactingly, sometimes intrusively, even if they happened to be Thomas Mann or John Dewey. (After Bernard Malamud submitted a short story to *Commentary*, young literary critic Irving Howe wrote to him, "The thought of Cohen's heavy hand on your fantasy gives me the chills.")

As a writer, Cohen, whose thoughts tended to fold in on themselves like origami, was badly blocked. "For all his wit, knowledge of literature, and skill as an editor amounting to genius," his friend Louis Berg said, "composition was agony for him. His thesis might be, and usually was, bold, original, and sound, but it became in the writing so overloaded with parenthetical thoughts and superfluous argument as to vitiate its force." To illustrate the point, Berg, a newspaperman, recalled the time he had against his better judgment allowed himself to be cajoled into coauthoring an article with Cohen. The subject was May Day. He sent Cohen a first draft. Weeks passed before he was finally called in. "His study floor," Berg said, "was lined with neat piles of paper marked Version A, Version B, and so on, literally through the alphabet, and all bearing the mark of paste and shears. It was frightening."

Rather than write, Cohen preferred to make surrogates of his writers. He would take a writer to Major's Cabin Grill across the street from the *Commentary* offices on West 33rd Street, its entrance guarded by a solid ebony statue of Buddha, and methodically lay out what he wanted. More often than not, by the time the bill came, the writer would feel that the piece was mostly written; all that was left to do was a bit of transcription work. "Working with Cohen," Lionel Trilling admitted, "put the author in danger of fulfilling Cohen's intentions, instead of the author's." Alfred Kazin, who started to write for Cohen in 1945, vented a similar frustration in his journal: "He hides his insecurities badly—simply can't let any piece alone after he has bought it. 'I wouldn't be the editor I am,' he confided in a fatherly tone, 'if I didn't show you how to make your piece even better than it already is.'" Kazin managed to hold him off, but other writers became exasperated. "Listen," Harold Rosenberg said, "Elliot, if you want to write, write under your own name!"

YOUNG MEN FROM THE BOROUGHS

Fortunately for the magazine's writers, Cohen, though a dominating presence, did not labor alone at *Commentary*'s gaunt office loft with a grime-tinted skylight on the top floor of a building across from the Empire State Building. He inherited Clement Greenberg, managing editor of the AJC's *Contemporary Jewish Record*, an assertive, bald-domed, extremely intelligent man who would become dean of American art critics, champion of Jackson Pollock and the abstract expressionists, great foe of middlebrow tastes. Before joining Cohen's staff, Greenberg had served as clerk at the Customs Service on Varick Street—Department of Wines and Liquors—then as an editor at *Partisan Review*. At Cohen's magazine, Greenberg declined to work terribly hard. He wrote more for *Partisan Review* than for *Commentary*. He treated the *Commentary* job as something of a sinecure, preferring to prepare his book on Catalan painter Joan Miró, or to pass the afternoon with his friend Delmore Schwartz (who published eleven of his poems in *Commentary*) in one of the wooden booths under the pressed-tin ceiling at the San Remo Bar in Greenwich Village. Not that this prevented Greenberg from putting on imperious airs, especially with his boss, with whom he often clashed. During their fights, Cohen would appeal to his secretary for backup. "Clem is the rudest man in New York, wouldn't you say?"

Greenberg did little to dispel the charge. One day, for instance, he accosted a *Commentary* summer intern named Alison Lurie, a twenty-year-old Radcliffe girl (who almost four decades later would win a Pulitzer). "I hope you don't turn into one of those clever bitchy woman writers I know so many of," he said. Clem's younger brother, Martin—similarly lacking in social graces—joined him on staff in 1953. (When someone asked Saul Bellow what he thought of the Greenberg brothers, the image of Confederate outlaws came to mind. "You mean Frank and Jesse?" Bellow said.)

For managing editor, Cohen chose Robert Warshow, a slim, pale, twenty-eight-year-old with steel-rim glasses. Warshow, the son of Russian immigrants, an atheist, had worked for three years for his father as a paper salesman, served as a code breaker in the U.S. Army Signal Corps during the war, and broke into journalism at the *New Leader*, a weekly newspaper of the anti-Communist Left.[16] Warshow's mind recoiled from sentimentality, and the force of that recoil propelled his brilliant, pioneering essays on popular culture—from Westerns and gangster movies to comic strips. Warshow prided himself on his restless irritation with feel-goodism. Every so often he would sniff at the *New Yorker*, at the magazine's slouching haute bourgeois casualness, the effortful effortlessness of the "caviar sophisticates." The *New Yorker*, Warshow wrote in *Commentary*, "has always dealt with experience not by trying to understand it but by prescribing the attitude to be adopted to it." It was precisely his own efforts to come to grips with immediate experience that gave Warshow such a marvelous feeling for English prose and would make him a mentor to younger men. One of his writers, James Baldwin, would credit Warshow with having taught him one of the more invaluable lessons a writer can learn: "You had to force from your experience the last drop, sweet or bitter, it could possibly give." Aspiring literary critic Norman Podhoretz thought of Warshow as everything he wanted to be.

Warshow sat back-to-back in a cramped cubicle in the editorial offices with Nathan Glazer, a twenty-one-year-old just out of City College. Before Cohen drafted him to *Commentary* from the *Contemporary Jewish Record*,

Glazer had apprenticed to émigré social theorist Max Horkheimer, who was researching anti-Semitism in an office at the AJC just across the hall from the *Contemporary Jewish Record*.[17]

Glazer's friend Irving Kristol joined in 1947, when he was twenty-seven, at the suggestion of his brother-in-law Milton Himmelfarb, another researcher at the AJC. Like Glazer, Kristol made $3,600 a year at *Commentary*. Besides enjoying the gifts of good-natured wit and kindly charm, Kristol seemed even then a born editor, a man of great deftness and patience.[18] He was also more pragmatically minded. Kristol distinguished himself at the magazine, Glazer recalled, by his "interest in politics, real politics, electoral politics, and not just the politics of left-wing anti-Stalinists, mulling over what was living and what was dead in Marxism, the fate of socialism, the future of capitalism, Communist influence in the intellectual world— no mean issues, but hardly ones to affect who won and who lost an election." Kristol was already married to Gertrude (Bea) Himmelfarb, to whom he had been introduced at a Trotskyist meeting in Bensonhurst, Brooklyn. "We met courtesy of a dating service with the high-sounding name of the Young People's Socialist League–Fourth International," he liked to say.

Despite atrocious typing skills, Midge Decter, twenty-three, was hired on Nathan Glazer's recommendation in 1950 as an assistant to Robert Warshow. She left after about a year to have a baby with her first husband, Moshe Decter, and came back in 1953, this time as Elliot Cohen's secretary.[19] Three years and another daughter later, she married Norman Podhoretz. Unlike her colleagues, she had spared herself the usual flirtation with Marxism. "The only grand posturing of my teens," she later recalled, "had been a declared intention to die on the barricades in Palestine. . . . Being a Zionist had protected me from the kind of radical shenanigans that characterized virtually all of the New York intellectuals in the prewar years."

Finally, Sherry Abel, a tall, bohemian, a motherly figure at the magazine, arrived as an editorial assistant in 1950 and right away leavened the office with her wit. Overhearing Cohen and Clem Greenberg locking horns one day, she peeked into the corner office and suggested that they ought to leave it to their shrinks to duel it out.

BY DESIGN, THERE WAS nothing slick about Elliot Cohen's magazine; its austere, sober columns were not interrupted by illustrations.[20] Yet by some mysterious alchemy, Cohen transfigured a freewheeling verbal tournament into type, with the result that his magazine's pages, crackling with what

Diana Trilling called "the life of significant contention," took on a distinct collective character. The Family's acid-tongued, fast-talking controversialists, besotted with words, shared a taste for arguing brilliantly, for challenging conventions, for convincing others they were right. The Family's old Marxism, after all, had tempted its adherents to think they had everything worked out. With a relish for verbal pugilism, they went at each other full tilt, trading salvos and fusillades, behaving in the heat of argument—as the old phrase had it—like Cossacks in a *succah* (the booth used in the Jewish festival of Succot). In relying on his carefully groomed stable of writers (almost all pieces were commissioned), Cohen managed somehow to capture the Family's tempestuous gale of argument, its rough-and-tumble literary commotion. This conferred on the magazine's pages a sureness of touch and a rhetorical dexterity. The style was learned, deft, discursive, commanding, self-assured. The best *Commentary* pieces depended for their effect on threading together a medley of bold formulations and unexpected juxtapositions.

If Cohen's writers specialized at all, they specialized in themselves. "The Jewish writer is forced to write, if he is serious, the way the pelican feeds its young," Clem Greenberg said, "striking his own breast to draw the blood of his theme." Daniel Bell, who started writing for *Commentary* in 1946 after he left his post as managing editor of the *New Leader*, once said that the intellectual, unlike the scholar, "begins with *his* experience, *his* individual perceptions of the world, *his* privileges and deprivations, and judges the world by these sensibilities." And so no matter how serious the subject, the resulting free-swinging *Commentary* style departed as far as can be from the solemnities of academic stuffiness. (With rare exception, the magazine declined to clutter its pages with footnotes.)[21] Under Cohen's steady hand, *Commentary* treated politics with a literary sensibility. It balanced treatments of Jewish and general subjects, journalistic topicality with large-bore analysis. Neither pretentious nor patronizing, it joined the rigorous with the personal, passion with intelligence, brainy heft with fluency. It clamored to go beyond the immediate subject to larger questions of culture. It brought religious intensity to secular expression. It was writing con brio. A couple of other magazines—*Partisan Review* in New York and later *Encounter* in London—shared something of this quality (and many of the same writers), but only *Commentary* was self-consciously Jewish: a transposition of Jewish periodical culture into an Anglo milieu.

The intellectuals over whom Elliot Cohen presided presented a special case of the dilemmas of integration. Before World War II, outside the intellectual arena, Jews enjoyed the first heady satisfactions of the hunger for American success. These were the years in which sons of Jewish immigrants were rewriting American music: Benny Goodman, the King of Swing, brought jazz to Carnegie Hall; George Gershwin (originally Gershowitz) composed his "folk opera," *Porgy and Bess*; Jerome Kern wrote "The Way You Look Tonight"; and Irving Berlin (born Israel Baline) gave the country "God Bless America." Alfred Stieglitz changed American photography. Mark Rothko, from an Orthodox family, and Barnett Newman, from a Zionist one, transformed American painting. In 1945, Bess Myerson from the Bronx was crowned Miss America in Atlantic City.

Sometimes, American success involved renunciation. In the 1934 pennant race, Hank Greenberg, all-star first baseman for the Detroit Tigers, refused to play ball on Yom Kippur, much as the Jewish title character in America's first "talkie," *The Jazz Singer* (1927), gave up his Broadway premier to recite the Kol Nidre. At other times, integration meant concealment or self-erasure. Gerard Swope, president of General Electric from 1922 to 1940, carefully concealed his Jewishness. Comedian Nathan Birnbaum changed his name to George Burns; Benjamin Kubelsky became Jack Benny; Betty Persky turned herself into Lauren Bacall. (The genius of Superman, invented in 1934 by two Jewish kids as an immigrant with a strange name from another planet, resided in an inversion: The schlemiel disguised an all-American hero rather than vice versa.) In the 1930s and 1940s, Jewish Hollywood moguls—Louis B. Mayer, Samuel Goldwyn, David O. Selznick, the Warner brothers—victims of their own hypersensitivity and "discretion," banished visibly Jewish characters and names from the big screen. "The greatest single Jewish phenomenon in our country in the last twenty years," screenwriter Ben Hecht wrote in 1944, "has been the almost complete disappearance of the Jew from American fiction, stage, radio, and movies."[22]

As Cohen all too keenly perceived, the Family still nursed a sense of apartness from America; its young members could not feel they belonged to it—or it to them. What bound the Family's writers together was, above all, a sense of estrangement, a holdover from the era before *Commentary*. In the years after the war, many still felt they were in America, but not of it. In one of the handful of pieces he would write for *Commentary*, Cohen observed that the American Jewish intellectual of the late 1940s thought of himself as "wary, unhopeful, isolated, and alienated."

The alienation that so preoccupied *Commentary*'s editor came in double dose. Many of his writers felt alienated from America as Jews. "Psychologically, many American Jews are uncomfortable here," Cohen complained, "though they cannot define the causes or the implications of their discomfort."[23] What is more, some valued alienation in itself, made a charm of it, as if to intensify their sense of exclusion. "The fact of being a Jew," poet-critic Delmore Schwartz said, "became available to me as a central symbol of alienation." Others acted as if to incorporate the alienation gene into the very DNA of Jewishness. "To use a language and not to own it, to live with a literature and not to possess it—this is only to say that I am a Jew," associate editor Martin Greenberg wrote in one of his early *Commentary* essays. As pariahs themselves, such writers *glorified* the pariah, as if the mere fact of being excluded in and of itself conferred a nobility, as if the truest Jew were estrangement incarnate, as if Jewish alienation were the modern condition writ small.[24] "There is nothing in the American way of life or climate of opinion, ideas, and ideals that encourages the prospect of a Jewish civilization," *Commentary*'s first issue announced.

Not all the apartness from America was self-induced. Jews at the time were routinely kept not only from hotels that declined "Hebrew patronage," but also from the higher reaches of American intellectual life. Consider, most obviously, the universities. By seeking "geographic balance," and by emphasizing qualities such as "character" over considerations of academic merit (the very word "meritocracy" did not come into circulation until the late 1950s), Ivy League admissions gatekeepers devised ways to keep out the "undesirables," the gifted but uncouth children of immigrants who in great numbers swept in and threatened to transform WASP culture beyond recognition. A. Lawrence Lowell, Harvard's president from 1909 to 1933 and a former vice president of the Immigration Restriction League, refused to allow the "Jewish problem" to spoil his school as it had, in his eyes, already ruined Columbia. By 1914, the dean of Columbia, Frederick Keppel, admitted that the large numbers of Jewish students there had made the school "socially uninviting to students who come from homes of refinement." Worried by such a prospect overtaking Harvard, Lowell worked assiduously beginning in 1922 to limit Jewish enrollment. At Yale, Robert Corwin, admissions director from 1920 to 1933, took similar steps, though more discreetly. He considered Jewish students "alien in morals and manners," and by 1924 he had reduced their numbers to no more than 10 percent of the freshman class, though even his was too high for Corwin's tastes. Referring to a published list of Jews from Connecticut admitted to Yale's class of 1933, Corwin said: "The list as published reads like some of the 'begat' portions of the Old Testament, and might easily be mistaken for a recent roll call at the Wailing Wall."[25] (A little more than twenty years later, one of the students listed, a future *Commentary* contributor named Eugene Rostow, would be appointed dean of Yale Law.)[26]

Despite an academic record of high distinction, Elliot Cohen himself had been dismissed after five years of graduate study without a doctorate by one of the eminences of Yale's English Department: "Mr. Cohen," he recalled being told, "you are a very competent young man, but it is hard for me to imagine a Hebrew teaching the Protestant tradition to young men at Yale."[27] Other Family members suffered similar fates. Unstoppably eloquent art historian Meyer Schapiro believed his application for graduate study at Princeton had been rejected because he was a Jew.[28] The head of the English Department at the newly founded Brandeis University, Ludwig Lewisohn, who would write for *Commentary* in 1950 on the future of American Zionism, was turned away from Columbia's English Department without a doctorate; the prejudices against hiring Jews, he was told, were insurmountable. Though he would regain his post, Lionel Trilling had been dismissed as an instructor at Columbia in 1936 on the grounds, he was told, that "as a Freudian, a Marxist, and a Jew" he might be "more comfortable" elsewhere. A decade later, Columbia dropped the "religion" question from its application forms only after Rabbi Stephen S. Wise appealed to the New York City Council to withdraw the university's tax exemption due to its discrimination against Jewish applicants.

Others in the Family, however, had alienated themselves from America not only as Jews, but also as intellectuals. Cohen's friend, novelist and screenwriter Tess Slesinger, called them the "unpossessed." "The intellectual," a character in her novel of that name suggests, "belongs on the sidelines—where he was born." The unpossessed thought of themselves as unencumbered, critical nonconformists, as permanent strangers, self-exiled outsiders, disturbers of the intellectual peace. It was to them axiomatic that the intellectual was better in attack than in affirmation, and that it was better to secede from the status quo than to endorse it. Eyeing middle-class values with suspicion, they blended disaffection and a mistrust of success. Not least, they stood aloof from national feeling. Love of country was not an appropriate emotion. Patriotism—hadn't Samuel Johnson called it "the scoundrel's last refuge"?—was unseemly.

But the Family's writers bore a burden even heavier than a sense of exclusion from full participation in American life. As intellectuals, they also had become estranged from Judaism. Exiles from their own tradition, they did not feel themselves heirs to a religious tradition that exerted hardly any pull on their imaginations. Before World War II, Irving Howe remarked, "We did not think well or deeply on the matter of Jewishness—you might say we avoided thinking about it." Jewishness was something onerous. This was not just a matter of changing the family name, as they or their parents had done before the war: from Horenstein to Howe, Bolotsky to Bell, Dubinsky to Draper, Abelson to Abel, Litvinsky to Phillips. More to the point, it was that Judaism played no significant role in their thinking; its teachings did not furnish their minds; its fate did not implicate them.

Cohen lamented that he presided over a group of Jews "who were only too eager to bury their Judaism if this meant admission to the literary salons of Manhattan." This was true even of his brightest protégé. "I cannot discover anything in my professional intellectual life which I can significantly trace back to my Jewish birth and rearing," Lionel Trilling said in the 1944 *Contemporary Jewish Record* symposium mentioned earlier. Although he would contribute to *Commentary*—on George Orwell, on Odessa-born Jewish writer Isaac Babel, on "Wordsworth and the Rabbis," and on being young in the 1930s—Trilling resented his mentor's offer to join its staff. "Elliot's invitation to join the contributing board of editors of his Jewish magazine—not made in good faith—impulse to 'degrade' me by involving me in a Jewish venture," Trilling jotted in his journal.[29] An association with a Jewish magazine, he later explained, would have seemed nothing more than "a posture and a falsehood."

So it was with Cohen's staff, none of whom bothered to belong to a synagogue. Irving Kristol was back then interested in religion—"theotropic," was how he put it—and in Christian theologians such as Reinhold Niebuhr and Jacques Maritain. But Kristol described himself then as an "unsynagogued Jew." "I felt no passionate attachment to Judaism," he later admitted, "or to Zionism, or even to the Jewish people." Despite the Jewish tradition of scholarship—and largely in ignorance of it—the very intellectuals on whom Cohen pinned his hopes thought of "intellectual" and "religious" as mutually exclusive states of being. Few self-respecting intellectuals then would even admit an interest in religion. "We could see no connection," Glazer said, "between the Judaism and the Jewish life we knew—none of us came from educated Jewish homes—and the culture, politics, and civilization to which we aspired."[30]

If any writer embodied the Family's alienation, it was a round-faced, sandy-haired wunderkind from Chicago's West Side, Isaac Rosenfeld, who, according to his old friend Saul Bellow, "discovered Dada and surrealism as his voice was changing." Once in New York, he served as an assistant editor at *Commentary*'s predecessor, the *Contemporary Jewish Record*. Where rootlessness was concerned, Rosenfeld, not unlike other intellectual buccaneers of his generation, made a virtue of necessity. In 1946, the Golden Boy, as Irving Howe called him, declared in *Commentary* his eternal rejection of the bourgeois, a social temptation that he said "dangles the eternal carrot of belonging before our noses with a 'Bravo, old donkey, and an end to alienation!'" Rosenfeld suggested that a society's health might be gauged by its ability "to learn from the rootless intellectual, who, precisely because he is rootless, is free to move among values in search of the best." He thought of the Jewish writer as "a specialist in alienation (the one international banking system the Jews actually control)."

In his poignant autobiographical novel, *Passage from Home* (1946), Rosenfeld elaborated the theme. The teenage hero, "as sensitive as a burn," escapes the suffocations of his father's home, only to find he doesn't know where to turn. "For as a Jew . . . I had come to know a certain homelessness in the world, and took it for granted as a part of nature. . . . We had accepted it unconsciously and without self-pity, as one might accept a sentence that had been passed generations ago, whose terms were still binding though its occasion had long been forgotten. The world is not entirely yours; and our reply is: very well then, not entirely."

The novel—Daniel Bell preferred to call it "a parable of alienation"—was a big hit in the Family.[31] Reviewing it for *Commentary*, Howe said the book made an "overwhelming impression." (This was Howe's first of thirty-five pieces for the magazine, and it launched him as a literary critic. The reviewer was himself not immune to the vanities of marginality. In his memoir, Howe recalls that when he took the review in to Clem Greenberg at the *Commentary* offices, he felt compelled to explain that he wanted to publish the review because he needed the money: "It was a stupid and aggressive thing to say, and Greenberg, who was far from stupid though not exactly deficient in aggression, was quick to understand me. If I felt ashamed about appearing in a 'bourgeois' journal, he wasn't going to assuage that feeling. 'I don't care *why* you want to print it,' he growled. 'All I care is whether it's any good.'") But the Golden Boy never came to terms with the American dream. To live that dream was to trade the lonely risks of independence for "the ecstasy of belonging," an ecstasy Rosenfeld was far from alone in declining.

IT SEEMED FITTING, then, that in 1949 Rosenfeld—now living in a shabby apartment on Barrow Street in the Village—cast himself in the lead role of a scandal that brought the wrath of the Jewish establishment down upon the young *Commentary* and strained almost to the breaking point the independence granted to *Commentary* by its publisher. The elasticity of that independence was remarkable in itself. After a decade of boredom at the Jewish Federation, Elliot Cohen refused to countenance his magazine becoming a house organ of the American Jewish Committee or a tame expression of "official" Jewish opinion. The magazine's sponsor agreed, in part because the heads of the AJC were pleased with Cohen from the start. At the first meeting after *Commentary*'s launch, Ralph Samuel, chairman of the AJC's *Commentary* committee, cited the high volume of correspondence and newsstand sales generated by the first issue and pronounced the magazine "off to an excellent start."[32] So the AJC granted Cohen full editorial autonomy; it never reviewed articles before they appeared. Two years into his tenure, Cohen saw in this unique arrangement a glimmer of hope for American Jewish life: "Can we escape the blight of institutional thinking, constitutionally addicted to precedent, more skilled in the avoidance of risks, real or imagined, than in intellectual adventuring? Permit me one act of pure, irrational Jewish faith. I think we can—and I find a bit of confirming evidence in the very existence of *Commentary* and the intellectual scope and freedom it enjoys in the very heart of Jewish institutional life."

Not that Cohen was exempt from the occasional tangle. In 1947, AJC executive vice president John Slawson raised a worry with the executive committee:

> In *Commentary* there has appeared an article called "Back to 86th Street," which describes accurately a drab spiritual life among Jews living not necessarily on that street, but belonging to a certain middle-class category.[33] There has been an article in *Commentary* on Jewish anti-Semitism, which is a self-analysis of an attitude by Jews to the fact of being Jewish. Well, these are penetrating analytical treatments, but the question arises, what

happens when unfriendly groups—anti-Semites and others—get hold of this material? The material, being in English, can be read by anyone and everyone.

Earlier that year, Ralph Samuel suggested either taking the phrase "published by the American Jewish Committee" off the cover or moving the disclaimer—to the effect that the views expressed in *Commentary* did not represent those of its publisher—from small print on the masthead to large print on its own page. The latter course was chosen.

On another occasion, Cohen published an attack by his friend Louis Berg on Adolph Ochs, which accused the revered publisher of the *New York Times* of being a cautious "court Jew."[34] This infuriated Joseph Proskauer, president of the AJC, who informed Cohen that he "deeply deplored" the essay's caricature of a man who "brought glory to the Jewish people." "The authority of the editor must not be trammeled by ukase of the publisher. You carry every month the legend: 'The opinions and views expressed by *Commentary*'s contributors and editors are their own and do not necessarily express the Committee's viewpoint or position.' Yet there are certain limitations which I think the editor should impose upon himself consistent with the fundamentals of free discussion."

But the Rosenfeld affair was something else. His sin: an essay in the magazine called "Adam and Eve on Delancey Street" (October 1949), a satiric comparison of kosher taboos with Jewish sex taboos—food as ersatz sexuality. Rosenfeld observed that Adam and Eve, by violating the Lord's injunction not to eat the forbidden fruit, gained knowledge of sex, and from that day to this Jewish food taboos have functioned as sex taboos. The *treif*, or nonkosher, Rosenfeld said, was associated with licentiousness, with the unrestrained sexuality of the goyim. *Milchigs*—milk products—are feminine; *fleishigs*—meat—masculine. "Their junction in one meal, or within one vessel, is forbidden, for their union is the sexual act."[35]

Rosenfeld's satire touched a nerve in the more staid precincts of the Jewish community. "The article bears the strongest possible resemblance to samples of the writings of Streicher I have seen," the dean of Yeshiva University said, referring to the Nazi propagandist and publisher of *Der Stürmer*. "It is not only smut," columnist Carl Alpert added, "but actually anti-Semitism worthy of the best efforts of Streicher and Goebbels." Rabbi Milton Steinberg of the Park Avenue Synagogue, whose own books had not been kindly reviewed in the magazine,[36] launched a campaign to strangle

Commentary in its cradle. In a sermon at his venerable shul on East 87th Street, he denounced the magazine and its editors for promoting "a dejudaized American Jewry, bereft of its God and Torah." Proskauer's successor as AJC president, Jacob Blaustein, decided that Rosenfeld's little exercise in *épater les Juifs*, "besides offending the religious sensibilities of a large number of our co-religionists, violated every canon of good taste." More to the point, Blaustein told Cohen, it amounted to "an abuse of the editorial freedom accorded you." He asked Cohen to repudiate it.

Isaac Rosenfeld himself was shocked by such reactions. "After all," he said, "Freud and hundreds of others had said the same thing for years, even if they didn't apply it directly to Jewish life. But why must Jewish life be the exception?" "And perhaps my article was right," he told Cohen. "Doesn't the irrational response to it demonstrate that many deep taboos are present in our religion?"

The episode revealed a yawning gap between the Family and the Jewish community at large. Brooklyn-born art critic and frequent *Commentary* contributor Harold Rosenberg (a student at City College 1923–1924)— who coined the phrase "the herd of independent minds" in *Commentary*— thought the controversy useful. "The cleavage among thoughtful Jews which Rosenfeld's piece surprisingly exposed," Rosenberg said, "seems to me one of the most significant facts of Jewish life in America. If the publication of the article was a mistake, it was one of those mistakes which open a shaft into the darkness, and of which the intelligence should always stand ready to profit." Nevertheless, Cohen was forced into abject apology and a chastened admission of "a lapse in editorial watchfulness." From now on, caught between an alienated Family of intellectuals and the Jewish establishment, the presiding genius would be warier, even as he would prove able to exert deep influence on both.[37]

❈ 2 ❈

Independence

Our intellectual marines,
Landing in little magazines,
Capture a trend.
      —W. H. AUDEN, "UNDER WHICH LYRE"

"WHEN THE MORNING WAS WAKING OVER THE WAR"

During World War II, with the Nazi ovens at full blaze, some American Jewish leaders beseeched, lobbied, rallied, sent telegrams, and set up emergency councils. But attempts to rescue Jews in Europe were on the whole feeble. The more cautious leaders and writers, blinded by a horror of special pleading and minority self-pity, downplayed "specifically Jewish" concerns.[1]

Much earlier than the American Jewish community as a whole, Elliot Cohen used *Commentary* to confront the catastrophe. In the inaugural issue of the magazine in 1945, the editor wrote: "As Jews we live with this fact: 4,750,000 of 6,000,000 Jews of Europe have been murdered. Not killed in battle, not massacred in hot blood, but slaughtered like cattle, subjected to every physical indignity—*processed.*" Cohen intended to use his magazine not to justify the ways of God to man, but at least to look squarely at the destruction and its aftermath. In those days, Holocaust commemorations in America were few and courses on the subject still fewer. At a time when many survivors felt no audience wished to hear about the horrors, the magazine's early issues were filled with descriptions of the devastation to Jewish life in Romania, Hungary, Greece, and Yugoslavia. Cecil Roth wrote on "The Last Days of Jewish Salonica." Simone Weil wrote on Hitler and the culture of false greatness. Martin Greenberg gave an account of "The Common Man of the Nazis." These were followed by reports on German reeducation and de-Nazification. Fritz Stern reported on postwar Germany.

Hannah Arendt explained why the Holocaust should be understood as "an object lesson for the consequences of totalitarianism." "It is imperative to know everything about the Holocaust," historian Solomon Bloom concluded in a 1949 *Commentary* piece.

"The Messiah has not come," assistant editor Irving Kristol wrote in another *Commentary* essay that year, "while the gas chambers have." After having served with the Twelfth Armored Division in Europe during the war, Kristol was stationed in Marseilles and had a close-up view of the DP (displaced persons) camps. Two months after his discharge from the army, he wrote a short story based on a seventeen-year-old survivor of Auschwitz he had met in one such camp. "Adam and I," as the story was called (November 1946), was in fact the first of some forty pieces Kristol would write for *Commentary*.[2]

Cohen gave *Commentary* readers a number of other firsts: the earliest firsthand account of the Warsaw Ghetto uprising of 1943; a selection of Emmanuel Ringelblum's *Notes from the Warsaw Ghetto* (1958), which had survived the war buried in a milk can; a riveting profile of Mordechai Chaim Rumkowski, "the dictator of the Lodz ghetto"; one of the first reports on the Jewish resistance to the Nazi occupation in France; and the "Journal of Kibbutz Buchenwald," an unbearably moving collective diary written by the first concentration camp survivors to emigrate to Palestine as a group.[3]

Commentary's pages also filled with accounts of survivors. The youngest contributor in the magazine's history was Ephraim Shtenkler, age ten, who recounted the story of surviving the war hidden for five years in a cupboard in a Pole's house in Zvirdje.[4] Austrian-born psychologist Bruno Bettelheim described his return to Dachau, where he had been imprisoned in 1938. Later, before becoming widely known, Elie Wiesel recorded his first trip to Germany since leaving Buchenwald seventeen years earlier and his pilgrimage to his hometown, Sighet. Pioneering historian Lucy Dawidowicz wrote about the Bergen-Belsen concentration camp, survivors of which she had aided in 1947 on behalf of the Joint Distribution Committee. (Starting in 1951, Dawidowicz would contribute more than forty pieces to *Commentary*, many of them about the Holocaust and Yiddish culture—part of her larger project of placing the murder of Europe's Jews squarely within World War II historiography.)[5] A number of these essays caused a stir and were widely reprinted.

Cohen regarded with special contempt the Germans' inability to confront the enormity of their sins. In 1950, he delivered a speech in West Berlin deploring the Germans for their "silence, as of a grave." "Where are the words of fellow sympathy, anguish and introspection," the editor asked, "of diagnosis and healing, of regeneration and wisdom, that some of us expected from your men of religious thought and spiritual leadership, from your scholars, from your historians and poets and novelists on this colossal historic tragedy?"

Most sensational of all, however, was the chronicle of a witty German-born Jewish girl sent from her hiding place in Amsterdam to Auschwitz and then to Bergen-Belsen, where she perished. In 1952, *The Diary of Anne Frank*, which would sell more than 24 million copies worldwide, first appeared in America in two installments in *Commentary* in a version condensed by assistant editor Sherry Abel. (The book had come out in Dutch five years earlier.) Robert Warshow heard about the diary, and after it was passed over by larger magazines, he persuaded Cohen to buy serial rights from Doubleday for $250.[6]

The bruising effect of this onslaught of reports and literary remains, the spirit of tragedy that emanated from them, and the recognition that European Jewry had been effaced (only half a million Jews remained on the Continent) jolted the Family to a new independence. Unlike Italian immigrants, for example, who never felt they bore the fate of Italian culture on their shoulders, American Jews had no "home" left to which they could return. "American Jewry more and more must now stand wholly on its own feet," Salo Baron, one of the great Jewish historians of the twentieth century, declared in the first issue of *Commentary*. At the very moment America was emerging from World War II as the unrivaled leader of the West—Europe's past, John Peale Bishop said during the war, was now confided to America, which alone could "prolong it into the future"—America's Jews were given unprecedented responsibility for Jews the world over. An editor's note observed that American Jewry "has a power over the fate of world Jewry such as no single Jewish community has had in a thousand years." America's Jews, the new custodians, could make that fate or mar it.

IS AMERICA EXILE?

The birth of the Jewish state very soon challenged that judgment. Zionism in America began as a rather feeble, diffuse affair, as might be expected among immigrants who had preferred to take their chances in the streets of America rather than the fields of Palestine. Of the two hundred delegates at the First Zionist Congress, chaired by Zionist visionary Theodor Herzl in Basel in 1897, only one was American.

Indeed, the anti-Zionists—and there were many stripes—enjoyed greater numbers than their opposites. Orthodox Jews expressed misgivings about ending the exile by means of human, rather than divine, agency. Socialists directed suspicion on nationalism as such. Reform leaders had turned away from particularism and peoplehood and had cast out the messianic elements from Judaism. Besides rejecting any notion of "the ingathering of exiles," Reform leaders considered Zionism a rather un-American affair. Isaac Meyer Wise, for instance, in the 1890s denounced political Zionism—he called it "Ziomania"—as "the momentary inebriation of morbid minds." The Reform movement's Union of American Hebrew Congregations declared in 1898: "We are unalterably opposed to political Zionism. The Jews are not a nation, but a religious community. . . . America is our Zion. Here in the home of religious liberty, we have aided in founding this new Zion." Liberal anti-Zionists, meanwhile, stressed the incompatibilities between Zionism and liberalism. "A national Jewish Palestine must necessarily mean a state founded on a peculiar race, a tribal religion, and a mystic belief in a peculiar soil," Morris R. Cohen of City College wrote in the *New Republic* in 1919, "whereas liberal America stands for separation of church and state, the free mixing of races, and the fact that men can change their habitation and language and still advance the process of civilization." In the same spirit, two years later Henry Morgenthau, Woodrow Wilson's ambassador to Turkey, insisted that "Zionism is the most stupendous fallacy in Jewish history." Finally, there were the non-Zionists centered on the American Jewish Committee. The AJC's Jacob Schiff, for instance, a prominent Frankfurt-born Wall Street banker, feared the separatism that Zionism demanded of American Jews. "It is quite evident," he forecast in 1916, "that there is a serious break coming between those who wish for the formation of a distinct Hebraic element in the United States, as distinct from those of us who desire to be American in attachment, thought, and action, and Jews because of our religion as well as the cultural attainments of our people."

On the Zionist side of the ledger, a similarly wide range prevailed, from the Marxist Poalei Zion (Workers of Zion), which established itself in America in 1905, to the religious Mizrahi movement, founded in Vilna in 1902 under the motto "The land of Israel for the people of Israel according to the Torah of Israel" and imported to America some dozen years later. These were joined by the Federation of American Zionists (later renamed the Zionist Organization of America, or ZOA), which was led from 1904 to 1911 by Judah Magnes (brother-in-law of the AJC's Louis Marshall). With the help of Henrietta Szold, its sister group, Hadassah, spun off in 1912. Scholars

Solomon Schechter (for whom Zionism was a "great bulwark against assimilation") and Israel Friedlander at the Jewish Theological Seminary made Zionism an essential part of Conservative Judaism. A few dissenting Reform leaders, meanwhile, such as Stephen S. Wise, lent a hand to the Zionists. This many-striped coalition picked up steam during World War I, boosted by the Americanized Zionism and "cultural pluralism" of Horace Kallen and Louis D. Brandeis. Before becoming the first Jew appointed to the Supreme Court, Brandeis headed the ZOA from 1914 to 1916. (The German Jewish establishment, including Jacob Schiff and Louis Marshall, privately opposed his nomination to the Court.) Brandeis took it upon himself to refute the charges that Zionists were un-American. "Loyalty to America demands . . . that each American Jew become a Zionist," he argued in 1915. "For only through the ennobling effect of its strivings can we develop the best that is in us and give to this country the full benefit of our great inheritance."

Between the world wars—the years of the British Mandate—things quieted down for Zion's American allies. The Arab riots of 1929 acted as a catalyst for some; Zionist writers—Mordecai Kaplan, Horace Kallen, Maurice Samuel, Hayim Greenberg—kept up the polemical pressure; and leaders from Palestine came to drum up support. But American Zionism had turned lethargic. "There is a complete lull in things Zionistic in America," Stephen Wise complained in 1930. When David Ben-Gurion visited America in February 1939, he expressed his disappointment that he failed to find a Zionist movement "organized, united, and capable of action."

During World War II, although the ZOA came under the more assertive leadership of Abba Hillel Silver, many American Jewish leaders worried that calling too publicly for a Jewish homeland would raise the specter of dual loyalty and harm the American effort to defeat the Nazis. Wealthy German Jews such as Jacob Schiff, Louis Marshall, and Nathan Straus sent funds to Palestine's pioneers, and the American Jewish Committee protested the draconian British restrictions on Jewish immigration to Palestine. But the AJC remained ambivalent about Zionists' demands for full Jewish independence in Palestine. One of the AJC patricians, Cyrus Adler, had written to Felix Warburg (another important supporter of the AJC and son-in-law of Jacob Schiff) in 1937 to express his doubts about just what the Zionists intended: "As a non-Zionist, I do not at all deplore . . . the establishment of a Jewish commonwealth. However, the term 'national home' does now and always has seemed to me a little ridiculous. It sounded like a big orphan asylum." The AJC refused to endorse the

Biltmore Program of 1942, in which representatives of American Zionist bodies, remarking on the forces gathering to "menace the Jewish National Home," for the first time explicitly called for the creation of a "Jewish Commonwealth integrated in the structure of the new democratic world." In fact, the AJC's president, Joseph Proskauer, remained adamantly opposed to the establishment of a Jewish state. By 1943, the most he would allow was an international trusteeship over Palestine. "There can be no political identification of Jews outside Palestine," he wrote that year, "with whatever government may there be instituted." And although some of the Reform opposition to Zionism had loosened in the late 1930s, even now the main planks of its anti-Zionism remained intact. Reform leaders continued to understand Judaism as an American creed, not as a national religion. "The average Reform layman," Solomon Freehof, president of Reform's Central Conference of American Rabbis, said in 1944, "dislikes the word 'national' in connection with the word 'Jewish' because it instantly implies to him that he is asked to have some national allegiance other than the one which he so proudly holds in his heart and mind for America." And yet for a growing number of Jews in America, by the war's close Hitler's murderous campaign had urgently underscored the need for a haven for Jews—Europe's, not America's.[7]

LIKE THE AJC, *Commentary* took a cool view of the Zionists.[8] None of Elliot Cohen's staff spoke Hebrew; none had visited Palestine (Cohen never would), and the editors chose to publish the leading dovish intellectuals from Palestine (as later from Israel)—Robert Weltsch and Moshe Smelansky of Ihud, Ernst Simon of the Brit Shalom peace group, and Uri Avnery, the maverick peace activist who would later found the Gush Shalom peace movement. In the March 1946 issue, for example, veteran colonist Smelansky called on the United Nations "never to permit the establishment in Palestine of an independent state, whether Jewish or Arab. . . . For a small state is valueless, precisely because it is small, because it is an artificial creation with no right to existence." Smelansky predicted that such a state "would be unable to maintain itself politically and economically by its own sole efforts." "It would be surrounded by enemies on all three of its land frontiers; and enemies would also dwell within it. . . . Despite all the heroism animating our sons, we would not be able to maintain ourselves without aid against all our internal and external foes. Consequently, we would be constrained to sell our political 'independence' to some military power that consented to spread its wing over us." In any case, Smelansky concluded, "political independence is not indispensable to people's existence and development."

The Family's chilly uncordiality to Zionism derived, for starters, from its old socialist habits of mind. "None of us were Zionists," Sidney Hook recalled in his memoirs, *Out of Step* (1987). "We were sensitive to the national aspirations of all other persecuted people, were positively empathetic with them. Yet when it came to our kinsfolk, we lapsed into a proud universalism." ("Before the charge of 'nationalism,'" Irving Howe said, "courageous men quailed, as their grandfathers might have quailed before charges of heresy.") Trotsky himself had called the attempt to solve the Jewish question by bringing Jews to Palestine "a tragic mockery of the Jewish people." In the newborn *Commentary*, Zionism appeared as a typical dreary nationalism: reactionary, bourgeois, derivative, and unworthy of the highest Jewish impulses. It was, at best, an idolatry, an ersatz Judaism. The lead article in the August 1946 issue bore the title "Nationalism Is the Enemy: Has Zionism Taken the Wrong Road?"[9] How unfortunate, Ernest Munz remarked in the piece, "to find Zionism—at a moment when the very preservation of civilization seems to depend on humanity's ability to rise above nationalistic ideologies—fostering a worldwide movement of the most intensely nationalistic character. . . . No group in the world has been so obviously chosen to be the protagonist in the fight against nationalism as have the Jews, whom nationalism itself singled out for destruction."[10]

The same year, to mark the fiftieth anniversary of Theodor Herzl's *The Jewish State*, the classic book that had anticipated the Zionist movement, *Commentary* asked Hannah Arendt to assess the Zionist visionary's legacy. The still-obscure forty-year-old philosopher had arrived in New York five years earlier—a "Weimar Republic flapper," Delmore Schwartz called her, transplanted to the Upper West Side. Martin Heidegger's former student and lover, Arendt had fled to France in 1933 and had been interned in Gurs in 1940. On her arrival in America, she had started to publish in English—in *Menorah Journal* and the *Contemporary Jewish Record*, among other magazines. At *Commentary*, it fell to Clement Greenberg to edit the grande dame. ("This young man," Arendt said of the associate editor, "has some sense of manliness and honor.") In her *Commentary* piece, her fourth contribution to the magazine, Arendt painted Herzl as a false messiah guilty of three errors: He sought to bring a people without a country to a country without a people, though no such country existed; he believed that establishing a Jewish state would end anti-Semitism when all who had eyes to see knew that it would accomplish no such thing; and he could not have foreseen that the Zionism he inspired asked for a state at a time "when the whole concept of national sovereignty had become a mockery."[11]

Others in the Family feared what the Jewish state might become: a regression to tribalism, a militaristic Sparta, a collective aggressive egoism, a dependent vassal. If anything, *Commentary*, like the *Menorah Journal* before it, favored a binational state. "To turn the whole of Palestine into a national state," the magazine argued in 1946, "whether Arab or Jewish, would be grossly unjust, nor is it now a possible course." The next year, Alvin Johnson (a former editor of the *New Republic*) suggested in *Commentary* that territorial partition would be fatal to Palestine.

Above all, the prospect of a Jewish state forced the Family to insist that the Diaspora was far from doomed. A glimmer of the hope that the Family was just starting to place in America could be seen in a 1946 *Commentary* essay by Israel Knox (City College class of 1932) called "Is America Exile or Home?":

> The United States is neither Galut [Exile] nor *hutz la-aretz* [Diaspora]. It is the home of five million Jews. And it is, in the final consideration, our freest home. . . . Granted, there are forces at work in America for the curtailment of that freedom; but there are forces at work for its expansion, too. And we ourselves can help tip the scale, we too are involved in the "destiny" of America. . . . By committing ourselves intimately to the democratic destiny of America, by aligning ourselves with the forces for its preservation and its deepening, we not only build firm foundations for our own survival—we act out the spirit and the implications of the Jewish ethos. . . . We—and our children and our children's children—are here to stay. . . . *This* is our home!

"What may come in Palestine is not likely to be of any real meaning to general civilization," the March 1947 *Commentary* gloomily forecast, "and it therefore will hardly be in the great tradition of Jewish cultures that have made Judaism a thing of value in the world's history."

RETURN TO ZION

The birth of Israel weakened—though not yet fatally—the Family's aloofness from Zionism. The transformation, although far from total, arrived abruptly. In September 1947, the United Nations Special Committee on

Palestine unanimously recommended that Palestine, then under the British Mandate, be granted independence. Shortly thereafter, on November 29, the General Assembly passed a resolution calling for the partition of Palestine into a Jewish state and an Arab state. The February 1948 *Commentary* greeted the decisions with ringing endorsement:

> A world of dreams has come true against the background of twenty centuries of martyrdom and a tenacious struggle for survival—this was the first, the emotional reaction to the United Nations decision on Palestine. More than a state and a haven of refuge were created in that fateful hour. The ethnic identity and continuity of Jewish national existence was reasserted. An epoch of national renascence was inaugurated. . . . The recognition of the Jewish people as a distinct ethnic entity and, by virtue of its ethnic distinction, a national entity, is one of the most important political features of the developments at the UN. The Ad Hoc Committee of the UN admitted Jews on an equal footing to the community of nations.[12]

In May 1948, Israel declared its independence. "Palestine and the rebuilding of a Jewish homeland," even Hannah Arendt now conceded in the May 1948 *Commentary*, "constitute today the great hope and the great pride of Jews all over the world." But she had two reservations. First, she was persistently skeptical about Israel's ability to extinguish the embers of anti-Semitism. In late 1948, in a letter to Elliot Cohen, she expressed the conviction that "world political developments may well again crystallize around hostility to the Jews." Second, Arendt insisted on the distinction between a Jewish homeland and what she called the "pseudo-sovereignty of a Jewish state," especially if achieving it meant war. For even were the Jews to win such a war, she wrote,

> the land that would come into being would be something quite other than the dream of world Jewry, Zionist and non-Zionist. The "victorious" Jews would live surrounded by an entirely hostile Arab population, secluded inside ever-threatened borders, absorbed with physical self-defense to a degree that would submerge all other interests and activities. The growth of a Jewish culture would cease to be the concern of the whole people; social experiments would have to be discarded as impractical luxuries; political thought would center around military strategy. . . . Palestine Jewry would eventually separate itself from the larger body of world Jewry.[13]

THE BIRTH OF ISRAEL served the Family as a source of inspiration, but it also animated a new resentment, for the new state threatened to rob American Jews of a sense of full participation—even of kinship—with the Jews laboring in Israel's fields and securing its borders. Had Israel rendered Diaspora Zionism obsolete?

With no small condescension, Israeli leaders, dedicated to realizing the Zionist dream of the "ingathering of the exiles," hastened to make clear that they would tolerate no meddling from Diaspora Jews; in their eyes Israel now occupied the center and the Diaspora the periphery. Echoing the early cultural Zionist Ahad Ha'am's description of Jewish life in the West as "slavery in the guise of freedom," Prime Minister Ben-Gurion went so far as to chide Diaspora Jews for their faith in a future outside of Israel. The strapped homeland might still depend financially on the Diaspora (hence his own fund-raising trips to the United States), but at a Hadassah convention Ben-Gurion warned that American Jews were "in danger of gentle extinction." He liked to cite a line from the Talmud: "Whosoever lives outside the land of Israel is considered as if he had no god."[14] And the prime minister dismissed that most sensitive of American Jewish dilemmas. "Dear Yaakov," he counseled AJC president Jacob Blaustein. "Don't be afraid of dual loyalty. Every human being must have many loyalties."

Finally, all this became too much to bear, and at a meeting in the summer of 1950 at the King David Hotel in Jerusalem, Blaustein cajoled Ben-Gurion to sign an agreement affirming:

1. That Jews of the United States, as a community and as individuals, have only one political attachment, namely, to the United States of America;
2. That the Government and people of Israel respect the integrity of Jewish life in the democratic countries and the right of the Jewish communities to develop their indigenous social, economic, and cultural aspirations, in accordance with their own needs and institutions; and
3. That Israel fully accepts the fact that the Jews in the United States do not live "in exile," and that America is home for them.

Ben-Gurion, however, was not long restrained. "A Zionist is a person who settles in Israel," he announced with characteristic bluntness at a 1951 banquet at the Waldorf-Astoria. In a letter to *Commentary* a couple of years later, Ben-Gurion—whose back issues of the magazine rest on the shelves of his former study in Tel Aviv to this day—reiterated the point: "I know with certainty that the only complete security for the existence of the people of Israel is its existence in Israel."[15]

Elliot Cohen resented such pronouncements almost as acutely as Blaustein did and declined to entertain the view that Jews in America were less authentic than Jews in Israel. The prime minister's pleas offended the editor's sense of American exceptionalism; surely, America did not conform to the Herzlian rule that anti-Semitism would afflict Jews wherever they were in the minority.[16] *Commentary* described Ben-Gurion as "the chief exponent of an Israeli attitude that springs from an unqualified ignorance of the character of American Jewry." Cohen commissioned a piece by Yehezkel Kaufman called "Anti-Semitic Stereotypes in Zionism," which upbraided Zionists who imagined Diaspora Jews as sunk in parasitic, distorted, degraded lives. Although it might have been true that the Jews of the Diaspora needed a spiritual center in Israel, Cohen suspected that Jews in Israel could pick up a thing or two from American Jews—the value of religious liberty, for starters, not to mention cultural pluralism and the separation of synagogue and state.

NEW YORK OF THE EAST

Even after the birth of Israel, then, some of the Family retained the pre-1948 coolness to Zionism—an ideology now embodied in a state. In 1950, Robert Weltsch (who before the war had edited the *Juedische Rundschau*, the official organ of the Zionist Organization in Germany) told *Commentary* readers that their own influence might be needed to keep the fledgling state from straying from the Jewish ethical tradition: "It will be a miracle if the young Israelis now growing up in an atmosphere of permanent watchfulness and semi-military preparedness do not fall prey to nationalist narrow-mindedness which inclines to underestimate, even scorn, universal and supra-national human values. A determined lead to preserve the Jewish humanist approach can be taken only by American Jewry."[17] In another *Commentary* essay that year, "Self-Hatred and Jewish Chauvinism," Clem Greenberg bemoaned what he called "the rise of militant, aggressive Jewish nationalism" and compared it with the German variety:

> Like the German, Jewish nationalism was born of a history of humiliation and defeat, and required a sharp blow or succession of blows in order to be awakened to action: the pogroms of czarist Russia and the growth of

secular and doctrinaire anti-Semitism were for us what subjection to Napoleon was to the Germans. The decisive shock, without which Jewish nationalism might still have remained the province largely of East European intellectuals, was Hitler's destruction of six million of us, which has been the equivalent (and much, much more) of what the 1918 defeat was for the Germans. . . . If we can survive only by all of us becoming nationalists, then we Jews have lost all justification for persisting as a group.

Whatever force Judaism carried, added Ernst Simon (chairman of the Department of Education at the Hebrew University in Jerusalem), had gathered from Jews saying no to history's false promises of redemption: Christianity, Islam, Communism—and now Zionism. "To attribute a Messianic character to the State of Israel," Simon cautioned in the April 1953 issue, "is equivalent to losing the criteria of true Redemption."

Cohen did not hesitate to use *Commentary* to point up the many ironies besetting the new state, starting with the fact that Israeli independence, rather than end Jewish dependence on the outside world, merely shifted that dependence from the political to the economic realm.[18] He worried that, although their new country offered a remarkable instance of the past made present, young Israelis seemed to have lost a sense of historical continuity; they saw the Diaspora not as history, but as a suspension of history.[19]

The Family's wariness of Zionism could after all now draw not just from speculation and skepticism, but also from concrete disappointment. A case in point: Twenty-one-year-old Norman Podhoretz, fated to become *Commentary*'s editor less than a decade hence, wrote a letter to his teacher Lionel Trilling about his first visit to Israel over six weeks in 1951: "I finally went away . . . with a slightly bitter taste in my mouth and a sense of having been strangely dispossessed. I felt more at home in Athens! . . . They are, despite their really extraordinary accomplishments, a very unattractive people, the Israelis. They're gratuitously surly and boorish. . . . They are too arrogant and too anxious to become a real honest-to-goodness New York of the East." Trilling passed a copy of the letter to Elliot Cohen, who had Irving Kristol invite Podhoretz to try his hand writing for *Commentary*—the beginning of a lifelong association.

In its cold-warm-cold ambivalence toward Zionism, the Family acknowledged the threat that Israel posed to its nascent sense of at-homeness in America, the real Promised Land. Just as America was becoming in the Family's eyes a new Zion, a new object of longing, two shocks—the death of European Jewry and the birth of Israel—jolted the Family from alienation to affirmation, into a dramatically different view of America and Jewishness alike.

Discovery

You will awaken with the dignity
Of beauty still upon you, and go forth
Like one who has not long since worshipped.
—ALLEN GROSSMAN, "THE LAW"

JEWISHNESS IS TWENTIETH-CENTURY AMERICANISM

Beginning in the late 1940s, Elliot Cohen and his brood looked upon America and saw that it was good. "Intellectuals for the first time in a hundred years discovered something to celebrate in America," assistant editor Nathan Glazer said. They began to reconcile themselves to the country.[1] Over *Commentary*'s first decade, discovery followed fast upon shock. Much to their own wonderment, the Family intellectuals began to feel closer to their country, to overcome the addiction to what Saul Bellow's character Herzog (in the 1964 novel *Herzog*) called "the cheap mental stimulants of Alienation." *Commentary*'s writers began to see themselves *sub specie Americani*. They no longer assumed that a sense of belonging endangered the free exercise of critical intelligence. They no longer associated the dread conformity with dull conventionality. "It has come to seem more reasonable," Harold Rosenberg said in the May 1951 issue, "to get to the top floor by taking an elevator than by blowing up the building." "Conformity," Irving Kristol insisted in *Partisan Review* (July–August 1952), "if we mean by that profound consensus on moral and political first principles, is the condition for a decent society." Frequent *Commentary* contributor Leslie Fiedler, an ex-radical from Newark, reported a new gratitude. "What a lot of us said in the depths of our hearts was, 'If the system has been this good to us, it can't be as bad as we thought it was.'"

What was it about America that allowed for this? The paterfamilias, and the Family with him, flung open the gates of America to discover a country both protean and malleable—not yet fully formed. They marveled at the fluidity of American life. "For America is always new," Delmore Schwartz wrote in *Commentary*, "and always full of the unknown and undiscovered." So in equal measure were they unfinished. "We are no mere outsiders trying to break into an already achieved perfection," Cohen exulted, "but partners in a still half-finished enterprise that needs us, too."

In part, simple economics equipped the transformation. Jews on the whole rode higher on the wave of postwar prosperity than did any other ethnic group in the country. Social mobility and geographic mobility went hand in hand as Jews migrated from tenements to suburbs (a move chronicled in a much-cited *Commentary* article by Herbert Gans about a community outside of Chicago).[2] By 1957, the proportion of Jews in white-collar jobs had reached 55 percent, from only 10 percent in 1940. The Jewish professional and managerial class supplanted the Jewish working class, further eroding the class distinctions between German Jews and the more recently arrived Eastern Europeans.[3]

Other equipment was supplied by an America just beginning to place a new premium on ethnicity—a word the *Oxford English Dictionary* informs us was first used by Jewish sociologist David Riesman in 1953. The country seemed just then to be entering a new mood of cultural pluralism. In the November 1947 *Commentary*, Hannah Arendt could hardly restrain her wonder: "In America one does not have to pretend that Judaism is nothing but a denomination and resort to all those desperate and crippling disguises that were common among the rich and educated Jews of Europe." A couple of years later, another article in the magazine questioned "whether America asks of her minority groups to do something for America; rather she seems to expect them to do things for themselves, and thereby for all Americans." Like American Jews in general, it now struck the Family with the force of epiphany that religion could be a means of American belonging, that in their adopted country Jewishness need bear no taint of foreignness, that religion had become a medium through which a great many Americans identified themselves. Family members discovered ethnic assertion as a sign of Americanization—that here they could draw sustenance from distinctiveness. Rare glimmers of this idea had been glimpsed before. As early as World War I, Louis Brandeis had affirmed that "there is no inconsistency between loyalty to America and loyalty to Jewry. The Jewish spirit, the product of our religion and our experiences, is essentially modern and essentially American." But

Commentary now gave full articulation and wide dissemination to the idea that Jews did not have to lose their Jewishness to become full-fledged participants in American life; that Jewish self-consciousness could liberate, rather than handicap, them for American life; that they no longer had to cast timorous glances over their shoulders at the goyim. Through the magazine, the Family was figuring out that a closeness to America need not entail a distance from Judaism. On the contrary, America held out the promise of a belonging *enhanced* by a sharp sense of one's own tradition.

Still more discoveries followed. The Family ascertained that ethnicity was not a form of primitivism, that it could turn the "parochial" into literature, exclusion into distinction. It's no coincidence that *Commentary* hosted the rising stars of a brilliant new generation of sociologists: Daniel Bell, Harlem-born Seymour Martin Lipset (City College 1943), and Earl Raab (City College 1940) on social mobility; David Riesman on the new middle class; and Nathan Glazer and Daniel Patrick Moynihan in *Beyond the Melting Pot* (1963) (two main sections of which appeared in the magazine). These writers, keen observers of a society they wished ardently to join, became the eyes with which America saw itself.[4]

The Family also discovered, as the subtitle of a 1948 *Commentary* essay put it, "The Sense of Alienation Is Not Exclusively Jewish." Cohen had brought into the magazine weighty pieces on anti-Semitism by philosopher Jean-Paul Sartre (articles that would be published as *Anti-Semite and Jew* [1948]).[5] At the same time, Cohen believed that the Family need not be defined by anti-Semitism. "Here in America," *Commentary* averred in 1949, "where Jews are not the only 'foreigners,' nor the only target of racialism, it should be clear that being singled out by an enemy is not the cause of our difference from others, is not what makes us Jews."

For all these reasons, the unprecedented possibilities of American Jewish flourishing fired Cohen's mind. "We may well see the Jewish intellectual-religious tradition flower in ways that will stand comparison with Spain, Germany, Eastern Europe, and elsewhere," he said. In the magazine's first issue, the editor expressed the hope that such a flowering would "harmonize heritage and country." To permit Jewishness to speak in harmonious American accents, Cohen encouraged Jews to shed their defensiveness and to gain thereby a new self-respect. His own staff began to discover a usable past, a lost inheritance, a Jewish culture worth studying, a culture with relevance, with its own pleasures, but no less a part of what Matthew Arnold, the subject of Lionel Trilling's first book, called "the best that has been thought and known in the world" than any other. Trilling remarked that managing editor

Robert Warshow now "acknowledged, and with pleasure, the effect that a Jewish rearing had had upon his temperament and mind, and he was aware of, and perhaps surprised by, his sense of connection with Jews everywhere." "*Commentary* magazine," Nathan Glazer later said, "gave me an unrivaled opportunity to study, informally but continuously, the life of American Jews." On Irving Kristol's suggestion, a group including Glazer, Kristol, Milton Himmelfarb, and Daniel Bell—led on occasion by the eccentric Vienna-born philosopher of religion Jacob Taubes—began to meet on Sunday nights to study the writings of Moses Maimonides.[6]

To celebrate America, Cohen felt, was not necessarily to insist upon an identity with it. To discover a common idiom and to accept a double inheritance need not obscure distinctions. "Indeed," historian Daniel J. Boorstin wrote in *Commentary*, "those who would equate 'Judaism' with 'Americanism,' by the very terms of their argument may well prevent the discovery of any fruitful relation between cultures."[7] Instead, what was urgently needed, David Riesman urged in the magazine, was a reinterpretation of Jewish tradition that would, in turn, "foster a Jewish self-image independent of the majority ethics."

Cohen believed that if only he could promote such a rethinking, if he could ground the magazine in a Jewishness it felt no need to apologize for, *Commentary* would host the country's first sustained conversation of the parallels between Jewishness and America. Consider by way of example this *Commentary* piece from 1949:

> It is Jewish—but also a mode of thought most congenial to the American climate—to accept no permanent separation of the theoretical and the practical, of the dream and the reality. . . . And it is Jewish—but at the heart of the American democratic vision, too—to think of the congregation and the society as not being divided into the elite and the masses, the priest and the laity, the cadre and the rank-and-file, the master and the man; but to think of each person as being his own master and his own man. And it is Jewish—and very American, in the best sense—to have very strong and intense commitment to one's self and one's own kind, and at the same time to have the deepest ties and bonds with man universal.

"Maybe *here*," Cohen concluded in 1952, "right on our own doorstep, is the long-yearned-for political alternative, after all." Following his lead, the Family was in the postwar years already well along in replacing its early flirtation with Marxist utopia with an abiding love of America.

As Elliot Cohen predicted, the Family's fresh look at itself brought into focus a new ease, a *heimisch* (homey) tone, an appreciation of "ordinary" Jewish life, an erosion of ambivalence about Jewishness, a new vogue of *Yiddishkeit*. Before *Commentary*, almost no sociology or history was being written about American Jews. Cohen, a man fond of James Thurber's motto "It is better to know some of the questions than all of the answers," convened a Family meeting of thirty experts around a conference table at the Warwick Hotel on the corner of Sixth Avenue and West 54th Street in 1948 to address the problem.[8] One participant, Hyman Grinstein of Yeshiva University, proposed that one deterrent to writing about the Jews in America "is the fact that one never knows what an anti-Semite will do with your material. If, for example, we were to prove that the Jews developed capitalism in the United States, of course, that would be something that a Jew would even hesitate to publish."[9]

"Not *Commentary*," Cohen joked. But the presiding genius felt the question was a serious one, and he opened the meeting on a serious note:

> *Commentary* is a young magazine, a mere infant not yet three years old. But the aspiration behind it is, I daresay, some decades old now. For at least that long there has been an ambition afloat among Jews—so-called "intellectuals" and so-called "laymen" alike—to have a review on matters of concern to American Jews, a review which would not be narrow, or parochial or sectarian, but which would represent the full interplay of Jewish social and cultural interests with the broad intellectual currents of our country and of Western culture in general. Obviously—as we pondered our new magazine venture—a major, if not central, part of the enterprise would be to encourage and make available writing on the experience and history of Jews in America. We cannot pretend that we were innocents in the matter—we knew some of the problems; we knew it would not be easy. At the same time, we did not expect to have to report at this time that—whatever modest progress we can claim in other directions—our achievement in this field is certainly meager.
>
> Our editorial conscience troubles us; our friends and readers begin to plague us. The few examples we have offered of writing on the Jewish past in America have met with enormous responsiveness, beyond almost anything we have printed. In a word, there is a need and a demand. But why don't we get more?

To get more, Cohen inaugurated a monthly department, "From the American Scene," which sketched Jewish life in America without drawing on the palettes of folksy kitsch or anxious defensiveness. The sketches were filled with what *Commentary* contributor Isaac Rosenfeld termed "the genre of *delicious* writing." One essay described the Jewish delicatessen (the sign advertising "A Nickel a Schtickel").[10] Another, "By the Waters of the Grand Concourse," cast a glance toward Jewish life in the West Bronx, a community "as dense, traditional, and possessive as William Faulkner's Yoknapatawpha County." The department offered portraits of the *Aufbau*-reading German Jewish émigrés of Washington Heights, aka the "Fourth Reich"; the *landsmanshaften*, the Jewish immigrant societies; and the *batlan*, the flaneur who turned idle talk into an art and whose languid life was "a continuous Sabbath afternoon." Irving Howe reported on the Americanization of Jews in an overwhelmingly Protestant New England town. Another piece took an impressionistic look at East Broadway:

> *East Broadway, East Broadway, vu di liebe brent,*
> *Vu yeder Sadie iz a lady un yeder Sam a gent.*
> *(East Broadway, East Broadway, where love is heaven-sent,*
> *Where every Sadie is a lady, and every Sam a gent.)*

Cohen himself considered the lighthearted section "nearest of all to the heart of the magazine's purpose," and in 1953 he decided to collect some twenty of these vignettes into a volume called *"Commentary" on the American Scene*. In the book's introduction, sociologist David Riesman observed that the luxury of reminiscing downward is given to those who have risen a little. "If the writers and prospective readers were not themselves reasonably secure in their Americanization, they could hardly profess such an interest in the humble incunabula of Jewish communal life," he wrote.

BORN AGAIN

Another branch of the Family felt secure enough in its Americanization to express its burgeoning Jewishness not merely as ethnic reminiscence but also as religious faith. In the years just after World War II, American universities offered not a single Jewish studies program. Starting in the 1920s, Salo Baron had taught Jewish history at Columbia (his appointment required special intervention of the university's president, Nicholas Murray Butler), Harry Wolfson had served as professor of Jewish philosophy at Harvard, and that had been about it. (Wolfson was appointed to the Near East Languages and Civilizations Department; the Philosophy Department was not yet prepared to hire a Jew.)[11] Before *Commentary*, meanwhile, almost no original Jewish theology worthy of the name was being published in America, and European Jewish theology remained largely inaccessible to Americans. In the May 1949 *Commentary*, ex-Marxist turned theologian Will Herberg registered his astonishment that "the largest Jewish community in the world . . . does not possess one single significant journal of Jewish theology."[12] Four issues later, German-born theologian Emil Fackenheim, whom Irving Kristol had recruited to *Commentary*, put the matter in even starker terms: "That the scarcity and meagerness of Jewish theological thinking is a disgrace to American Judaism is a point which need not be argued."[13]

With a few bold strokes, Elliot Cohen worked to remedy this, and to lend Judaism greater intellectual respectability. A 1946 editor's note announced that one of the magazine's main interests was to serve "the need for rethinking basic religious issues in modern terms." Although on occasion the presiding genius opened *Commentary*'s pages to non-Jewish theologians,[14] he aimed his best effort at hosting the most sophisticated Jewish thought of the day. Incredibly enough, he succeeded: Mordecai Kaplan wrote for the magazine on Judaism as civilization; Emanuel Rackman on leading Orthodox thinker Joseph B. Soloveitchik;[15] and Leo Baeck on Maimonides. Emil Fackenheim addressed the fundamentals of Jewish belief.[16] A department called "Cedars of Lebanon," inherited from the *Contemporary Jewish Record*, translated essays by the big-hitters of twentieth-century Jewish thought, such as Franz Rosenzweig and Martin Buber.[17]

Almost at once, *Commentary*'s theological sophistication made a deep imprint on its readers. "*Commentary* is already, and I think will remain, one of the finest reviews I have ever come to know," Leo Baeck wrote in 1946. "To my mind it might well become one of the centers and focuses for a revival of Jewish learning and a renaissance of Jewish thought." "The magazine affected my growing sense of self as both an American and as a Jew," a subscriber named Sam Bluefarb said. "I was 'born again,' so to speak, not so much out of a sudden, rediscovered Judaic tradition—although that cannot be discounted—as by an emotional and intellectual change. I had begun to reconcile those earlier socialist ideals with newer (actually older) spiritual values."[18]

In the early 1950s, *Commentary* presciently grasped the significance of two of the century's outstanding Jewish thinkers: Martin Buber and Abraham Joshua Heschel. Buber had left Germany in 1938 to become professor of social philosophy at the Hebrew University of Jerusalem, where he inadvertently laid much of the groundwork for the Jewish spiritual explosions of the 1960s. *Commentary* published Buber himself and some trenchant commentaries on Buber by Emil Fackenheim, Will Herberg, Leslie Fiedler, and Norman Mailer.[19] Later, Gershom Scholem criticized Buber's selective interpretation of Hasidism, and Buber fired back a full-length defense, treating *Commentary* readers to the spectacle of two heavyweight German-born theologians living in Jerusalem slugging it out in a New York magazine.

Having earned rabbinic ordination in Warsaw and a doctorate in the philosophy of religion at the University of Berlin, Heschel had arrived in America from Germany in 1940 and would teach at the Jewish Theological Seminary for a quarter century. In *Commentary*, Irving Kristol, Will Herberg, and Marvin Fox took turns assessing Heschel's attempts, by means of a distinctive poetic prose, to translate the Jewish religious experience—from the biblical prophets to the Hasidic pietists—into an American idiom. Heschel let loose his first critique of the mediocrity of American Jewish thought in *Commentary* and gave the magazine a chapter of his book *The Sabbath* (1951).[20]

NONE OF *COMMENTARY*'S WRITERS blazed a trail from leftist atheism to religion more publicly than Will Herberg. Born in 1901 in a shtetl near Minsk, Herberg came to America with his parents three years later. A committed Marxist, he worked as an organizer and director of "agitprop" at the Young Workers League and at the International Ladies' Garment Workers' Union. In the 1920s, he joined the Young Communist League, apprenticed himself to American Communist Jay Lovestone, contributed to the *Daily Worker* and *Revolutionary Age*, and became managing editor of the Communist newspapers *Workers Monthly* and the *Communist*. Like any good Marxist, Herberg considered religion an illusion of the oppressed.

By the late 1930s, however, like the rest of the Family, Herberg had wearied of Marxism, in particular of its moral relativism, the notion, as he put it, that whatever "was in the interest of the proletariat was good." In his influential January 1947 *Commentary* essay, "From Marxism to Judaism," Herberg explained that he had come to see the Marxist faith as a bankrupt illusion, an idolatry, an "amoral cult of power," a "delusive utopianism." Like fascism, he realized, Marxism drowned individual freedom in the chilling bath of collectivism. When Marxism confronted Nazism, he wrote, "it could not meet the challenge of totalitarianism because it was itself infected with the same disease. By the logic of its own development, the ideal of unlimited freedom had become the reality of unlimited despotism." Herberg was no less committed than before to the ideals of freedom and social justice, but he now felt that Judaism better squared with those ideals and offered "a more secure spiritual groundwork for a mature and effective social radicalism."

And so the more his hold on Marxism weakened, the stronger Herberg's attachment to the faith of his fathers became. He began to feel that embracing Judaism might make him in some paradoxical sense a better Marxist. "For the great contributions of Marxism were, it seemed to me, in the fields of economic understanding, social thought, and political action. And these could best be conserved, I now saw, within the framework not of a shallow materialism, but of a profound religion that would give full recognition to the transcendent aspects of man's nature and destiny." He found in Jewish tradition not only powerful teachings of the dignity of man (created, as Genesis has it, "in the image of God") but also a "keen sense of the perils of power"—the notion that men can ultimately subject themselves only to God, not to human rulers. "From Marxism to Judaism" explained how Herberg came to see Judaism as

> the sworn foe of the totalitarian state in its claim to absolute control over the individual and all his activities. Unconditional obedience to a universal and transcendent God precludes the possibility of total and absolute subjection to any earthly power. Earthly powers making such claims are usurpers and pretenders to the prerogatives of Deity. They are to be resisted to the bitter end. "For unto Me are the children of Israel slaves," says the Talmud; "they are not slaves unto slaves." . . . It is most vital to emphasize, as Judaism does, that faith cannot be placed, finally and unreservedly, in any person, institution, or order of this world.[21]

Of necessity, Herberg taught himself. In 1947, after visiting Hebrew Union College, Herberg said, "They take theology seriously at H.U.C., but unfortunately their theology is not very serious." So he soaked his mind in the writings of Franz Rosenzweig (about whom he would write in *Commentary*), Martin Buber (a collection of whose essays he would edit), and Solomon Schechter.

By the late 1950s, Herberg's conversion spun him out of *Commentary's* orbit and into the sphere of a new conservative magazine, *National Review*, where he served as the first religion editor.[22] But not before he had called attention—in his best-seller *Protestant, Catholic, Jew* (1955) and in his two dozen pieces on religion for *Commentary*—to the new pervasiveness of religious self-identification in America, "the triple melting pot."[23] Belonging meant affiliation with a religious community—and here Herberg elevated Judaism to parity with the Christian denominations; all were denominations of what he liked to call "the American religion." This meant, as he put it in a sharply worded *Commentary* piece from November 1952, that Jews had to abandon their "crippling minority-group defensiveness"—a sentiment upon which Elliot Cohen could hardly improve.

IMAGINING THE JEWS

If the best fiction, as Norman Mailer once wrote in the magazine, attempts to "clarify a nation's vision of itself," *Commentary's* fiction acted not only as a record of the Family's evolution, but also as a midrash—an exegetical narrative—on the American Jewish experience itself. Before World War II, although the Jew-as-entertainer was a familiar figure on the American stage—Al Jolson, Fannie Brice, the Marx Brothers—the Jew-as-novelist hardly appeared. There were accomplished Jewish writers before the war: Abraham Cahan, Paul Rosenfeld, Anzia Yezierska, and Ludwig Lewisohn in the 1920s, and a crop of social realists in the 1930s, including Henry Roth, Michael Gold, Daniel Fuchs, Clifford Odets, and Meyer Levin. But these were isolated figures, and there seemed something contrived in the ways they strained to make Jewish experience relevant to America. Because fiction was in those days expected to concern itself with the general, the universal, some writers masked the Jewishness of their characters or wrote in what Norman Podhoretz would later call a "facsimile-WASP style." "As a struggling young writer," novelist Meyer Levin remembered in *Commentary*, "I told readers I had early discovered that the big-paying magazines were not interested in stories about Jews. . . . So I wrote a novel about 'American' youngsters by giving non-Jewish names to the characters I knew in my heart were Jewish kids."

The Jew-as-character-of-fiction had fared not much better. American Jewish writing before the war was a fiction of mawkish quaintness, what Irving Howe called Second Avenue tearjerkers, stuffed with sentimentalized stereotypes: the suffering schlemiel; the Lower East Side immigrant who peddles his way from rags to riches; the wise, pious patriarch struggling to accept the Americanized son; the son desperate to escape the old world, "too foreign in school and too American at home," as Will Herberg put it.[24] Even worse were Jewish characters imagined by non-Jewish writers. The Jew appeared as the annoying stranger (Robert Cohn in Ernest

Hemingway's *The Sun Also Rises* [1926]); as rebellious young radical (Ben Compton in John Dos Passos's *U.S.A.* [1938]); or as unscrupulous businessman (Harry Bogen in Jerome Weidman's *I Can Get It for You Wholesale* [1937]). Abe Jones, in Thomas Wolfe's *Of Time and the River* (1935), Howe complained in *Commentary*, was "dreary, tortured, melancholy, dully intellectual, and joylessly poetic, his spirit gloomily engulfed in a great cloud of Yiddish murk."

This state of affairs carried over into the 1940s. The Family writers found nourishment in Herman Melville or Ralph Waldo Emerson, in English poets or Russian novelists—but not in Jewish texts. The motives of Jewish writers, managing editor Robert Warshow complained in 1946, "are almost never pure: they must dignify the Jews, or plead for them, or take revenge upon them, and the picture they create is correspondingly distorted by romanticism or sentimentality or vulgarity." One *Commentary* writer, straining in 1948 to find promising Jewish contributions to contemporary American literature, could point to only three minor talents: Harriet Lane Levy, William Manners, and Charles Angoff. American Jewish writing, *Commentary* reported the next year, lay fallow, "steeped in apologetics and in false provincial pride."

ELLIOT COHEN GRASPED that the Family's discoveries of America could have literary reverberations, could release among the Family a great literary efflorescence that had only yesterday seemed an impossibility. By taking Jewish writing seriously, by refusing to disdain it as a parochialism, Cohen's magazine planted the seeds of a generous literary fertility. Cohen had always demanded that Jewish writing of any kind conform to the highest standards. The future American Jewish culture "cannot be purely imitative," he insisted. "As to Jewish culture," he said, "the first question we should ask is not whether it is Jewish, but whether it is good. And 'good' means on a par with the best in the culture of society in general." In literature as in all else, Cohen recoiled from apologetics, defensiveness, sectarianism, sentimentality, and self-congratulation. What lay fallow would grow in the 1950s into a jungled abundance that surprised even the presiding genius.

Several seasons passed before the new literary fruit showed itself. The first *Commentary* fiction—like "The Girl Who Loved Seders," by well-known translator Ralph Manheim (March 1949)—was perfectly parochial. But very soon new Jewish writers, to borrow a phrase Philip Roth used in *Commentary*, launched "an imaginative assault upon the American experience." Writing became for them a priestly calling, an instrument of upward mobility, a gateway for fighting their way into the great American beyond. It seemed to Cohen as though he were watching before his very eyes the passing of dominance from the southern school of William Faulkner to the urban Jewish school of Saul Bellow. A new kind of fiction, not intended to flatter the Jewish ego, was coaxed forth from the novelist branch of the Family, language-obsessed writers seeking, in Irving Howe's phrase, to shower the country with words. And what words! These scribes brought with them to the great culture rush the tones of Jewish speech and verbal performance: a street brashness and detached irony, an ability to career between different registers and inflections, from high to low, from wide-ranging erudition to urban idiom.

AMONG THE FIRST FRUITS *Commentary* reaped was Bernard Malamud's "The Prison," a 1950 story that beautifully dilated upon the theme of Jewishness as confinement. The magazine would run eight more of Malamud's stories (at $30 a page), including "Idiot's First," and five of the thirteen stories in *The Magic Barrel* (1958), the collection that would earn Malamud (City College 1936) a National Book Award.[25] "*Commentary* gave him the perfect audience," his friend Philip Roth said. In fact, young critic Norman Podhoretz made his *Commentary* debut in 1953 with a review of Malamud's first novel, *The Natural*. "Well, you seem to know something about novels," Cohen had told Podhoretz; "you know something about symbolism, you know something about Jews, and you know something about baseball. Here's a symbolic novel by a Jewish writer about a baseball player. I guess you're qualified to review it."

What begins in Malamud's flat cadences becomes visionary in Saul Bellow's exuberance. In a review of Bellow's second novel, *The Victim* (1947), *Commentary* recognized with more than a little prescience what Bellow had done. That novel, Martin Greenberg (then an editor at Schocken Books) announced in the January 1948 issue, was "the first attempt in American literature to consider Jewishness not in its singularity, not as constitutive of a special world of experience, but as a quality that informs all of modern life." Bellow animated the book's hero, Asa Leventhal, with a feeling of somehow not belonging, a loneliness Greenberg recognized as "the malaise of the megalopolis." In a similar vein, Alfred Kazin hailed *The Adventures of Augie March* (1953) as Bellow's "attempt to break down all possible fences between the Jew and this larger country."[26] The book's famous first line, announcing a turn from alienation to affirmation, made this obvious enough: "I am an American, Chicago born—Chicago, that somber city—and go at things as I have taught myself, free style, and will make the record in my own way: first to knock, first admitted; sometimes an innocent knock, sometimes a not so innocent." Forging a passage from marginality to American literature writ large, Bellow's own pieces for *Commentary* reprised the theme. In the February 1951 issue (a month before Cohen ran Bellow's story "Looking for Mr. Green"), Bellow condemned the self-doubt that cramped older Jewish writers, a timidity about writing in a language their immigrant parents did not speak. "As long as American Jewish writers continue to write in this way," Bellow said, "we will have to go elsewhere for superior being and beauty, and will thus continue to be foreigners."

Philip Roth, to complete the triumvirate, made his *Commentary* debut in 1957, at age twenty-four, with a charming piece that Norman Podhoretz, then assistant editor and only three years older than the writer from Newark, had rescued from the slush pile. "You Can't Tell a Man by the Song He Sings," included two years later in *Goodbye, Columbus*, was Roth's first published story. The magazine also ran "Eli, the Fanatic," Roth's brilliant story about the confrontation between assimilated Jews and ultra-Orthodox Holocaust refugees intent on setting up a yeshiva in their suburb.[27] Roth had first come across Cohen's magazine as an undergrad in the periodical room in the Bucknell University library in the early 1950s. "I was stunned," he recalled. "So *this* is what it's like to be Jewish." By offering a sophisticated Jewishness, free of parochialism and apologetics, *Commentary* did for Roth what the *Menorah Journal* had done for Lionel Trilling three decades before. "*Commentary* furnished a whole education," Roth said, "a way of being Jewish and intelligent and American—all at once."

By now *Commentary* fiction was consistently first rate.[28] Cohen ran two parables by Henry Roth, the author's first publications since *Call It Sleep* in 1935, as well as stories by Delmore Schwartz, Nelson Algren, and Alison Lurie (the intern so beloved of Clem Greenberg), who published her earliest story in *Commentary* when she was all of twenty. Cohen fertilized all of this with translations of Yiddish literature: stories by I. J. Singer, Zalman Shneour, Y. L. Peretz, and David Bergelson, as well as Chaim Grade's first published story, "My Quarrel with Hersh Rasseyner," a powerful meditation on faith after the Holocaust.[29] Most spectacularly, *Commentary* published Isaac Bashevis Singer, whose "Yentl the Yeshiva Boy" (translated by Marion Magid and Delmore Schwartz's ex-wife, Elizabeth Pollet), first appeared there in English in September 1962, as did some of the vignettes that would make up *In My Father's Court* (1966). "*Commentary* is one of the rare magazines in

America which takes seriously both the writer and the reader," the future Nobel laureate Singer said. "I also have a personal feeling about *Commentary*: it was the first magazine which published me in English."[30]

Jewish writers, ex-alienated men, were suddenly in vogue. Norman Podhoretz used to joke about the Jewish writer who took the name Nathanael West that had he arrived in the 1950s rather than the 1930s, he would have changed his name back to Nathan Weinstein. After the American Jewish literary profusion had peaked, Edward Hoagland, the essayist married to Marion Magid, grumbled (in *Commentary* itself) that the Family's writers had all but forged a new establishment, making it difficult for a WASP like him, who "could field no ancestor who had hawked tin pots in a Polish *shtetl*."[31]

In later years, some of these plaints would turn uglier. Gore Vidal complained that Jewish writers like Bellow, Roth, and Malamud "comprise a new, not quite American class, more closely connected with ideological, argumentative Europe (and talmudic studies) than with those of us whose ancestors killed Indians." Truman Capote bitched in a *Playboy* interview (March 1968) about a Jewish literary cabal: "a clique of New York-oriented writers and critics who control much of the literary scene through the influence of the quarterlies and intellectual magazines. All these publications are Jewish-dominated and this particular coterie employs them to make or break writers by advancing or withholding attention. . . . Bernard Malamud and Saul Bellow and Philip Roth and Isaac Bashevis Singer and Norman Mailer are all fine writers, but they're not the *only* writers in the country, as the Jewish mafia would have us believe." (Perhaps Capote's line would have been softer had the *Commentary* review of his bestselling *In Cold Blood* [by William Phillips, May 1966] not dissented so vigorously from the notion that the "competently though too mechanically told" book represented some kind of literary breakthrough.) But as boosters and detractors could agree, America's new Jewish writers had come into their own.

THE AGE OF CRITICISM

Even as Cohen's magazine helped forge a new literary temper, *Commentary* acted as a greenhouse for a new style of literary criticism, too, incubating the first generation of critics to emerge from America's working class. Before World War II, the upper reaches of American life had as a matter of course excluded Jews as much from the study of literature as from the creation of it. No matter how assiduously the Family's critics may have schooled themselves in classics like Walt Whitman's *Democratic Vistas*

(1871) or Van Wyck Brooks's *America's Coming of Age* (1915), they were disqualified by heredity from the Republic of Letters. "Jews, it was often suggested, could not register the finer shadings of the Anglo-Saxon spirit as it shone through the poetry of Chaucer, Shakespeare, and Milton," literary critic Irving Howe recalled. "I wouldn't recommend that you study English," the head of Northwestern's English Department had told Saul Bellow. "You weren't born to it."[32] The Family could not help but notice that currents of anti-Semitism ran deep within the Anglo-American literary tradition itself—from William Shakespeare's Shylock, to Charles Dickens's Fagin, to F. Scott Fitzgerald's Meyer Wolfsheim. "We reexamine our literary heritage as Jewish writers and readers of English—and we wince!" Leslie Fiedler wrote in *Commentary*. "We enter into our supposed inheritance, only to find we are specifically excluded."

The attraction to fascism exhibited by poets W. B. Yeats, Ezra Pound, and T. S. Eliot didn't help matters. The Library of Congress's decision in 1948 to award the Bollingen Prize to Pound's *The Pisan Cantos* vaulted Elliot Cohen into high indignation, and he dedicated *Commentary*'s first symposium to the question of literary anti-Semitism.[33] The responses he received bespoke a newfound literary self-confidence. Many advocated a separation of wheat from chaff. Alfred Kazin replied, "If we were to read only those who love us, even among ourselves, our intellectual diet would be thin indeed." Lionel Trilling commented, "Anti-Semitism is, as Nietzsche said, a vulgarity; it is indeed remarkable how often notable minds of our day can support their quanta of vulgarity; but it would be foolish not to take from them what they have to give." Saul Bellow suggested that the direction of judgment had reversed: "Modern reality, with the gases of Auschwitz still circulating in the air of Europe, gives us an excellent opportunity to judge whether they [modern Jew-despising writers] are right or wrong." So long to inferiority.

In the beginning, *Commentary* literary critics aimed their attentions at Jewish writers. Irving Howe, born and bred in the Bronx, would write for the magazine on, say, Daniel Fuchs, who had authored several novels about Jews in Williamsburg. Tellingly, the magazine's first critical essay on a goyish writer was called "F. Scott Fitzgerald and Literary Anti-Semitism." When the magazine examined Pearl Buck—as in a 1948 review of *Peony*—it was for her description of Judaism. But the more Family critics assimilated—and assimilated into—American literature, the more confidently did they put Jewish writers in the highest fraternity of Gentile company. Both outside the magazine and inside its pages, Jews began to write about American fiction under the assumption that it was their inheritance, too.[34] And they wrote not just about fiction. The magazine's poetry criticism included John Berryman on W. H. Auden and a consideration of Sylvia Plath, who had studied with Alfred Kazin at Smith.

Commentary critics, never afraid to contradict the prevailing estimate of a reputation, shared a contempt for middlebrow mushiness. James Gould Cozzens, Arthur Miller, Leon Uris, Herman Wouk—these were almost too gauche to bother with.[35] The result was an urgent style that combined scholarly rigor with journalistic flair. The urgency came from the way the Family's strenuous strivers took literature as a matter of high gravity, as a secular scripture, as if it should yield to moral, and not just aesthetic, judgments. Writing, as vocation and avocation both, became in their hands a kind of emancipation, a gesture of self-fashioning; it was everything. The Family's rhapsodists of American literature met America through its writers, the highest manifestations of national feeling.

Alfred Kazin, who would write some twenty pieces for *Commentary*, offers a case in point. Born in Brownsville, Brooklyn, a son of immigrants, Kazin came to City College at age sixteen. In 1942, at twenty-seven, he published *On Native Grounds*, a tellingly titled history of American prose from the 1890s through the 1930s. Like Philip Roth, Kazin acknowledged the extent to which his view of the possibilities of Jewish writing was indebted to *Commentary*:

> I remember that as the first issues began to appear at the end of that pivotal year of 1945, I was vaguely surprised that it dealt with so many general issues in so subtly critical and detached a fashion, regularly gave a forum to non-Jewish writers as well as to Jewish ones. Like many Jewish intellectuals of my time and place, brought up to revere the universalism of the socialist ideal and of modern culture, I had equated "Jewish" magazines with a certain insularity of tone, subject matter, writers' names—with mediocrity. To be a "Jewish" writer . . . was somehow to regress, to strike attitudes, to thwart the natural complexities of truth. . . . "Jewish" magazines were not where literature could be found, and certainly not the great world. "Jewish" magazines worried over the writer's "negative" attitude toward his "Jewishness," nagged you like an old immigrant uncle who did not know how much resentment lay behind his "Jewishness." But *Commentary*, to the grief of many intellectual guardians of the "Jewish" world, marked an end to that.

For Kazin, literary criticism was "the great American lay philosophy." He and the other Family generalists who came to command the literary heights—Trilling, Rosenfeld, Howe—wrote not to advance an academic point, not to advise the author, guide the book buyer, or impress the professional specialist, but to assess the larger meaning of a work. (The adjective "academic" was for them always a pejorative, a synonym of "pedantic" and antonym of intellectual audacity.) They considered criticism a branch of literature itself, a rival form of imagination. Unlike the New Critics who treated literature as something hermetically self-contained, the Family critics believed that writing was a political act; they read a work with an eye for what it said about its cultural environment. They practiced literary criticism as social criticism. These inebriates of literature wrote in a way, Kazin said, "that pure logic would never approve and pure scholarship would never understand."[36]

Before too long, by pursuing things unattempted yet in the precincts of American Jewish writing, Elliot Cohen was beginning to feel that his magazine was changing the world. Before *Commentary* (to paraphrase Leon Trotsky on Russian writer Nikolay Gogol), American Jewish literature in English, stuck in imitation, merely tried to exist. After *Commentary*, it existed.

≪ 4 ≫

Anti-Communists

More substance in our enmities
Than in our love.
　　　　　　　—W. B. YEATS

RED JEWS

The Jew-as-Communist canard had threaded its risible way through American life—from Henry Ford to Father Charles Coughlin of Michigan to Representative John Rankin of Mississippi—ever since *The Protocols of the Elders of Zion* gained wide circulation in the 1920s. The insinuation was of disloyalty among the "Judeo-Bolsheviks." In a 1923 book called *The Jews in America*, to take one of innumerable examples, Pulitzer Prize–winning journalist Burton Hendrick referred to Jews' "enthusiasm for the doctrines of Karl Marx, in preference to the doctrines of Washington and Jefferson and Franklin and Lincoln and Roosevelt." In his 1951 book *The Iron Curtain over America*, John O. Beaty, professor of English at Southern Methodist University in Dallas, claimed that Khazars (i.e., Jews), having already driven the United States into an "unnecessary war" with Germany ("the historic bulwark of Christian Europe"), sought to propagate Communism in America as triumphantly as they had in Russia. Reverend Gerald L. K. Smith called Beaty's book "the greatest . . . of its kind ever to appear in print."

The more common the notion of Communism-as-Jewish conspiracy became, the more fervently organizations such as the American Jewish Committee (AJC) worked to dissociate Jews from Communism. Starting in 1938, the American Jewish Federation to Combat Communism and Fascism pledged to "controvert the false propaganda that 'all Jews are Communists'" and to "give continued unanswerable proof of the loyalty and patriotism of American Jews and their love of flag and country." Pledging "to be watchful of any and all attempts . . . falsely and viciously to identify Jews and Communists," the AJC commissioned Will Herberg to write a study on why Judaism and Communism were incompatible. The organization also fought to excommunicate Communist-controlled organizations—such as the Jewish Peoples Fraternal Order, part of the International Workers Union, and the Social Service Employees Union—from the Jewish fold. It even sent a letter to the House Un-American Activities Committee affirming that "Judaism and Communism are utterly incompatible." Even J. Edgar Hoover remarked on the problem: "One of the most malicious myths that has developed in the United States," the FBI director said, "is that persons of the Jewish faith and Communists have something in common."

Yet the stereotype had been made only more vivid thanks to Julius (City College 1939) and Ethel Rosenberg, New York Jews who had been charged with giving A-bomb secrets to the Soviets and who with their electrocution at Sing-Sing in 1953 would become the first civilians in American history executed for espionage. The Rosenbergs themselves lent credence to those who blamed their Jewishness for the couple's treason. "Our upbringing," Julius wrote to Ethel, "the full meaning of our lives, based on a true amalgamation our American and Jewish Heritage, which to us means freedom, culture and character, has made us the people we are." (The Rosenbergs' defense lawyers, as well as the judge, were also Jews.)

The Rosenberg case—and those who exploited it as a Jewish issue—put many American Jewish leaders into a defensive crouch. Anxious lest the case offer Americans an excuse to "impute to the Jews as a group treasonable motives and activities," the AJC opposed clemency for the Rosenbergs and advocated the death penalty. Rabbi S. Andhil Fineberg of the AJC accused the Rosenberg Committee, which defended the couple, of acting as a Communist front aiming to lure Jews into a sympathy with the Rosenbergs, about whose guilt he had no doubts.[1] In the pages of *Commentary*, Robert Warshow eviscerated Julius and Ethel Rosenberg for their clichéd Popular Front Communism as much as for their disingenuous Jewishness. (Julius's sister, also named Ethel, had contributed several pieces to *Commentary*.) American Communists sought to exploit the case to show that anti-Communism led inexorably to anti-Semitism. The National Committee to Secure Justice in the Rosenberg Case claimed in 1952 that "the suspicion of anti-Semitism taints the whole trial." Historian Lucy Dawidowicz vehemently denied this. "It is obvious," she wrote in the July 1952 issue, "that the Communists, by such propaganda, aim to enlist Jews in defense of Communists and their interests. . . . Because a spy or a Communist is a Jew, the Communists proclaim that all Jews are collectively involved. More—the Communists take it upon themselves to make this involvement a reality, so far as their powers permit."[2]

On the other hand, many American Jews, concerned with civil liberties, associated the demagogic, bigoted anti-Communism of Joseph McCarthy with anti-Semitism and fascism. They wished to be hard on Communism, but not too hard.

ENEMIES ABROAD: UNCLE JOE

After the war, Communism was on the march—in Eastern Europe, in the blockade of Berlin, in China, and in Korea. After the Soviet-backed North Koreans invaded South Korea in 1950, President Harry Truman called for massive rearmament. Liberal anti-Communism, the animating principle of the Truman Doctrine, committed the United States to containing Soviet aggression and coming to the aid of countries threatened by expanding Communist influence.

The Family regarded the struggle against Communism—seen not merely as military menace but also as grave ideological threat—as (to use Diana Trilling's words) "the great moral imperative of our time." Having spent formative years on the Left, these ex-radicals knew the face of the enemy better than anyone. They knew on their own pulses that Communism wasn't a legitimate part of the progressive social order, a species of liberalism, or a necessary prelude to a bright, classless utopia, but the darkest of despotisms. Their brushes with Communism had inoculated them, had made them acutely aware of how political enthusiasms can lead to self-deception and how ideology can falsify experience. Lionel Trilling, writing in the March 1952 *Commentary*, mourned the Family's past blindness to Soviet totalitarianism. "Communism's record of the use of unregenerate force was perfectly clear years ago," he said, "but many of us found it impossible to admit this because Communism spoke boldly to our love of ideas and ideals." No longer could the Family tell itself that Joseph Stalin had perverted Communism, as if Communism were something other than what was practiced in the Soviet Union.

Karl Marx had declared that, among its other virtues, Communism would abolish "human self-alienation." The Family overcame alienation not through Communism but through a firm opposition to Communism. And so it was that the *Commentary* cognoscenti joined the liberal anti-Communist cold war consensus, with its style of political pragmatism and moderation, its stress on incremental reform.

Even before creating *Commentary*, Elliot Cohen had been a confirmed anti-Communist, and by the time of the magazine's birth, almost no one was anti-Communist enough for him. William Phillips once said that the paterfamilias "inhaled Communism and exhaled anti-Communism." If anything, Cohen's anti-Communism, like Pharaoh's heart, hardened over time, with the result that by the time Cohen invented *Commentary*, the Communist utopia had long since appeared to him as another authoritarianism—a travesty of his hopes.

This was why Cohen's was not an anti-Communism of the Right— whether of Senator Joseph McCarthy and J. Edgar Hoover's brand of domestic red-hunting, Father Coughlin's anti-Semitic variety, or John Foster Dulles's Christian kind. Cohen did not credit the notion that Communism was the culmination of liberalism or that there was an essential continuity between the two. Even William F. Buckley's more palatable flavor of anti-Communism Cohen found distasteful. He greeted the birth of *National Review* in 1955 by commissioning a withering attack called "Scrambled Eggheads on the Right" from the pen of Dwight Macdonald, who thought the new magazine dull, amateurish, full of "soufflés that collapse into soggy facetiousness." Bill Buckley, wrote Macdonald, "would be an excellent journalist if he had a little more humor, common sense, and intellectual curiosity; and also if he knew how to write."[3]

More often than not, on the subject of Communism Cohen turned to his indefatigable Marxist theoretician, Sidney Hook, who would write frequently for *Commentary* beginning in 1946. In 1933, after he had started lecturing on philosophy at New York University—the first identifiable Jew to teach at the Washington Square campus—Hook had broken with the Communist Party, another former fellow traveler who had become the staunchest of anti-Communists. In the late 1930s, Hook had organized the American defense committee for Leon Trotsky (then exiled in Mexico) chaired by philosopher John Dewey. In Hook's first *Commentary* pieces, he drew a stark distinction between democracy, however flawed, and Soviet totalitarianism. One had to choose, Hook felt, "between endorsing a system of total terror [the Soviet Union] and *critically* supporting our own imperfect democratic culture with all its promises and dangers." Though it was necessary to remedy injustices at home, Hook wrote, "this would no more be sufficient to stop Stalin than social reforms in England and France were sufficient to stop Hitler."

Ironically enough, the other writer Cohen used to supply the theoretical foundation for hard anti-Communism was Hook's nemesis, Hannah

Arendt, who had not yet joined the ranks of the so-called anti-anti-Communists. After some early hesitation, *Commentary* laid out the case that the totalitarianism of the Left (Communism) was as dangerous as the totalitarianism of the Right (Nazism).[4] Among the distinguished Jewish refugees from Germany adopted into the Family—including Walter Laqueur, George Lichtheim, and Hans Morgenthau—none gave this idea more forceful expression than Arendt, whose book *The Origins of Totalitarianism* (1951) taught the Family that, despite outward differences, Hitler's Germany and Stalin's Soviet Union were in essence two forms of coercive statism, two sides of the totalitarian coin.[5]

With fascism defeated, Communism loomed in Elliot Cohen's mind as the new enemy, and he resolved now to use the magazine to wage a "struggle for hearts and minds," to define the cold war as a struggle between freedom and totalitarianism, and to explain that struggle in moral terms. Cohen concluded that America should not only fight Communism on the diplomatic playing field, but also wage an ideological war and export American values abroad. In fact, the editor placed a great deal of faith in the American people to wage that war. Cohen felt that even secular Americans held in their heart a version of "Thou shalt have no other gods before Me." There was no "ism" to which Americans granted divinity; they rejected, Cohen said, "all proposed faiths and ideologies that would give any political thing supra-human and transcendental value." Unlike *Partisansky Review*, as Edmund Wilson used to call it, which held fast to a vague Marxism, Cohen's magazine had from the beginning considered the Soviet Union not a worker's paradise but a grave threat to democracy. Norman Podhoretz recalled of those days, "All articles were carefully inspected for traces of softness on Communism: a crime of the mind and character which might even give itself away in a single word." (Cohen even rejected Robert Warshow's groundbreaking essay on Charlie Chaplin.[6] "No fellow-traveler of Stalin," Podhoretz said, "genius or not, was going to be praised in *his* magazine.")

Under Cohen, *Commentary*'s reportage emphasized Soviet crimes. He published an early firsthand description of a Soviet slave-labor camp, reports on the liquidation of kulaks, and accounts of the brutal suppressions of the 1956 revolts in Poland, East Germany, and Hungary. Cohen elicited a piece from Mel Lasky, the editor of *Der Monat*, on "Why the Kremlin Extorts Confessions." He regularly featured ex-Communist historian Franz Borkenau, a great student of Kremlin intrigue.[7] Soviet crimes were also the frequent subject of "This Month in History," a department written by Sidney

Hertzberg (a *New York Times* foreign correspondent who had been the AJC's first choice as *Commentary*'s managing editor).

On this score, too, Cohen's politics was deeply informed by his Jewishness. At first, even the most hostile critics believed the Soviet Union had put an end to Jew hatred. ("Our fraternal feeling towards the Jewish people," Joseph Stalin's deputy Vyacheslav Molotov had said in late 1936, "is determined by the fact that it gave birth to the genius who created the ideas of the Communist liberation of mankind, Karl Marx, . . . that it gave many heroes to the revolutionary struggle against the oppressors of the working people.") *Commentary*'s first issue in 1945 offered a sanguine prediction: "Certainly in the Soviet Union the Jews will continue to enjoy the minority safeguards which the Lenin government had enacted in the early stages of the Revolution."

By 1949, when *Commentary* published a report on "The New Anti-Semitism of the Soviet Union," none could deny that anti-Semitic feeling— suspicion of "rootless cosmopolitans"—pervaded Russian officialdom and that Jews had been purged from the political apparatus. "It appears likely," the report concluded, "that so long as the Soviet Union remains a closed society, paranoiacally suspicious of the outside world and preventing any renewal or revitalization of the bureaucratic apparatus by free elections or free discussion, anti-Semitism will be an inevitable component of its new order."[8] Cohen made sure the magazine looked at cases of Soviet state anti-Semitism.[9] These included the Moscow "doctor's plot," in which a predominantly Jewish group of doctors was accused of conspiring to poison Soviet leaders, and the execution of Yiddish writers such as Solomon Mikhoels (in 1948), Perez Markish, and Itzik Fefer (both in 1952). Cohen even printed the proceedings of the Slansky show trials in Prague in 1952, in which fourteen leading Czech Communists were charged with participating in a "Jewish nationalist-Zionist-imperialist" conspiracy. (Eleven were executed.)

After Stalin's death in 1953, Cohen refused to be lulled by the Kremlin's new conciliatory talk of détente and summits. As a number of *Commentary* essays charged, such talk masked Soviet attempts to "win by means other than overt aggression" (Sidney Hertzberg) and to hasten the "dismantling of the Western defensive alliance" (Paul Kecskemeti). If the Soviets harbored imperialist ambitions, Cohen reasoned, if Communism represented an even greater threat to the survival of democracy than Nazism had, it followed that a détente with the Soviets would risk throwing the whole game away. Nor did Nikita Khrushchev's denunciation three years later of the cult of personality that had grown up around Stalin calm Cohen's fears that America was lowering its guard and relinquishing its resistance to the Soviet threat. For all the talk of renouncing Stalin's brutality—and despite Western hopes that the Stalinist orthodoxy was cracking—the Soviets still crushed uprisings in Hungary and Poland. This, in the editor's view, was "Stalinism without Stalin." The Great Thaw turned out to be no thaw at all, and Cohen's anti-Communist vigilance remained as tenacious as ever.

THANKS IN LARGE PART to the magazine's articulate anti-Communism, the young *Commentary* was widely hailed. In the magazine's first five years, circulation grew to 20,000 from less than 5,000. By 1949, the Voice of America had broadcast twenty *Commentary* essays in occupied Germany. The mayor of West Berlin wrote to Cohen to sing the magazine's praises. The magazine was read in samizdat in Eastern Europe and printed in translation by an underground press in Poland. President Truman's press secretary read *Commentary* every month. Philosopher and liberal anti-Communist John Dewey, who contributed several pieces for *Commentary* in the late 1940s, told his protégé Sidney Hook that it was the best magazine in the country. "What distinguishes it to my mind," Dewey said in 1948, "is its breadth and the kind of balance that comes only from views free from clichés, *partis pris*, and the declamatory writing that organs of all stripes seem to favor today."[10] The same year, Supreme Court justice Felix Frankfurter (City College 1902) said that he found *Commentary* "by long odds one of the most stimulating and truth-seeking publications that comes my way, and a good many of them do." Five years after *Commentary*'s founding, *Time* named it one of the nation's finest magazines. There were problems: paper shortages, a dearth of advertising. But Elliot Cohen's dream had become reality. "It was much greater than he had ever hoped," his wife, Sylvia, said. "It was a bombshell."

These were but the first glimmers of influence that accompanied the magazine's comportment with the larger political mood. As the cold war got chillier with the outbreak of the Korean War in 1950, the Family discovered that its critique of Communism became more relevant to American foreign policy than ever.

ENEMIES AT HOME: JUMPING JOE

Elliot Cohen may have cared somewhat less about the peril of internal subversion than about the threat of Communism abroad, but he sensed that there was a war to be waged at home, too. Writing in *Commentary*, Harold Rosenberg defined a Communist in stark terms: "Since all truth has been automatically bestowed upon him by his adherence to the party, he is an intellectual who need not think." This domestic front of the cold war—against American Communists and fellow travelers who defended the Soviet Union—took form in reaction to the pro-Communist "peace conference" held over a weekend at the Waldorf-Astoria in March 1949, attended by 3,000 delegates. Cohen commissioned a report on the conference from William Barrett (another City College boy), associate editor of *Partisan Review* and close friend of Sidney Hook. Barrett despaired of the conference as a "propaganda spectacle." Alarmed by the spreading intellectual influence of Communism, the Family mobilized an ad hoc disruption of the conference—a resistance that coalesced into the American Committee for Cultural Freedom, an affiliate of the Congress for Cultural Freedom.[11]

But Communists were capable of far worse than thoughtless propaganda. Contrary to the Communist Party of the USA slogan "Communism Is Twentieth-Century Americanism," Cohen regarded American Communism, far from an indigenous radical movement, as a disloyal, subversive allegiance to a foreign power, financed by "Moscow Gold." As Irving Kristol put it in one of his early *Commentary* pieces, Communism was not just a political party; it was also "a conspiracy to subvert every social and political order it does not dominate." If Communists were not dissenters, not merely "liberals in a hurry," but conspiracists, he felt, there could be neither dialogue nor accommodation with them. Not to be outdone, Sidney Hook went so far as to describe American Communists in *Commentary* as "agents of a foreign power," "tools of the Soviet regime," a "paramilitary fifth column" that was "absolutely controlled by a declared enemy." On the one hand, Hook passionately defended free expression. "*Before* impugning an opponent's motives, even when they legitimately may be impugned, answer his arguments." On the other, the philosopher distinguished between "heresy" and "conspiracy": Whereas heresy ought to be tolerated, he thought, by participating in a conspiracy, a member of the Communist Party rendered himself unfit to teach in American universities.

Though the Family wished otherwise, it wasn't alone in its worries about Communist conspiracy. From 1950 to 1954, the Family had to worry about a browbeating senator who called Communism "a conspiracy on a scale so immense as to dwarf any previous such venture in the history of man." At first, the Family didn't take Joseph McCarthy or the House Un-American Activities Committee (HUAC) seriously. (HUAC had been originally established in 1938 to investigate American anti-Semitic fascists, before its hearings addressed Communist infiltration of the labor movement.) *Commentary*'s first mention of him, in a report on the 1950 midterm elections, claimed the Republican senator's importance had been exaggerated.[12] "It is a shame and an outrage that Senator McCarthy should remain in the Senate," Nathan Glazer wrote a couple of years later, "yet I cannot see that it is an imminent danger to personal liberty in the United States." But unlike *National Review*, *Commentary* never defended "Jumping Joe"; on the contrary, it resented him for so badly damaging the anti-Communist cause.[13] Cohen refused to let the wild-eyed countersubversive conspiracy hunters on the Right run away with the anti-Communist banner; he wished to uphold a responsible anti-Communism. In keeping with the sentiment of an overwhelming majority of American Jews, the editor considered the Irish Catholic swashbuckler from Wisconsin a thug, a Red-hunting rabble-rouser, a "second-string blowhard."[14] In the March 1953 *Commentary*, Nathan Glazer classed McCarthy "with those out-and-out demagogues who appeal to passions which they themselves do not hold, or do not take seriously." In the January 1955 issue, James Rorty—formerly an editor at the *New Masses*—portrayed McCarthy as a bullyboy automaton, "a kind of monstrous political robot unequipped with steering mechanism or reverse gear."

At the same time, the Family also sensed a danger from the Left. Irving Kristol, in a much-cited 1952 *Commentary* piece, his first political essay, suspected that liberals who worried about the civil liberties of American Communists were often driven by an ideological sympathy for their "fellow progressives." He urged them to think of Communism not as a form of leftism but as "a movement guided by conspiracy and aiming for totalitarianism." Kristol attributed McCarthy's rise to liberals' failure to have appropriated a sane anti-Communism themselves. "Did not the major segment of American liberalism, as a result of joining hands with the Communists in a popular front, go on record as denying the existence of Soviet concentration camps? Did it not give its blessings to the 'liquidation' of the kulaks? Did it not apologize for the mass purges of 1936–38, and did it not solemnly approve the grotesque trials of the old Bolsheviks?" Although it was obvious to Kristol that McCarthy was a "vulgar demagogue," the support the senator enjoyed was perfectly understandable: "For there is one thing that the American people know about Senator McCarthy; he, like them, is unequivocally anti-Communist. About the spokesmen for American liberalism, they feel they know no such thing, and with some justification."

In the subsequent backlash against McCarthyism and anti-Communists, some thought the magazine had been soft on McCarthy. Irving Howe called Kristol's article "a back-handed apology for McCarthy" and pronounced *Commentary*'s record on the question "shabby." "On the issue of civil liberties," Howe wrote, the magazine "has squirmed, evaded, and played possum." "The country may have worried about McCarthy," he added, "but *Commentary* worried about those who profited from the struggle against McCarthy." Left-wing playwright Lillian Hellman accused the magazine of failing to rise to the defense of McCarthy's victims. "*Commentary* didn't do anything," she wrote in her memoir *Scoundrel Time* (1976), and offered an explanation for the alleged reluctance to rock the boat: "The children of timid immigrants are often remarkable people: energetic, intelligent, hardworking; and often they make it so good that they are determined to keep it at any cost."

The charge that ideology masks interests is an old Marxist move, a habit of judging ideas not by their content but by their function. But this did not prevent critics like Howe and Hellman from feeling appalled by the sight of upwardly mobile Jews who only yesterday had endorsed socialist revolution now rationalizing the American anti-Communist capitalist bourgeois society to which they had gingerly reconciled themselves.

Irving Howe had led the charge. Beginning in the 1950s, he felt that the magazine had started to use anti-Communism as an ideological mask that blinded the Family to the need for radical social change. "My complaint against *Commentary*, for example," he wrote in *Partisan Review* in 1954, "was not that it ceased to be socialist; it never had been that; but rather that it has become an apologist for middle-class values, middle-class culture, and the status quo." Its writers were becoming, in Howe's phrase, "partisans of bourgeois society"; hardly anything worse could be imagined. When intellectuals "become absorbed into the accredited institutions of society," Howe wrote in *A World More Attractive* (1963), "they not only lose their traditional rebelliousness but to one extent or another they cease to function as intellectuals." In celebrating America, Howe felt, the magazine had capitulated to an inegalitarian social order. It had domesticated itself. It had succumbed to what Howe called "the politics of acquiescence."

Some of this sort of complaint appeared in *Commentary* itself. When modern capitalism broke through the ghetto walls, David Riesman had remarked in the November 1948 issue, many Jews discarded their own values and "surrendered their inherited ethical system in return for a chance to participate in the wider world." ("Were not intellectuals of more use to this country when they had less use for it?" Riesman asked.) Irving Howe had already worried—in 1951!—that within a decade or two the Family's writers would discover to their dismay that "the new zeal, the intolerance, the fatal inability to make distinctions and discriminations, and the huffy impatience which characterized so much of our home-bred Marxism in the 1930s has carried over entire to the anti-Marxism of the 1950s." Three years later, he complained in *Commentary* that in its pages "liberalism is most skillfully and systematically advanced as a strategy for adapting to the American status quo."

In 1954, moved by such outrage, Howe founded his own socialist magazine, a nonconformist anti-*Commentary* dedicated to condemning America as a "mass society." ("When intellectuals can do nothing else they start a magazine," he said.) An editorial statement announced that the new journal aimed "to dissent from the support of the status quo now so noticeable on the part of many former radicals and socialists," and so Howe called his journal *Dissent*. (He thereby paved the way for Woody Allen's crack in *Annie Hall*: "I heard that *Commentary* and *Dissent* had merged and formed *Dysentery*.") Naturally, *Commentary* resisted *Dissent*'s attempt to outflank it from the Left. Nathan Glazer greeted *Dissent*'s first issue with a scathing review in *Commentary*, calling Howe's magazine "an unmitigated disaster." "If this is socialism," Glazer wrote, "no further explanations are required for its failure to catch on in America." He concluded with the observation that the new journal's editors seemed to share Marx's need for a ritual scapegoat: "Marx had his 'nigger Jew [Ferdinand] Lasalle.' . . . The editors of *Dissent* have their 'Sidney Hook and other writers for *Commentary*.'"[15]

Although in the country at large the backlash against McCarthyism muffled expressions of anti-Communism during the Eisenhower years, *Commentary*'s anti-Communism would march on, unabated and undeterred.[16]

THE END OF THE BEGINNING

Even before the magazine's tenth anniversary in 1955, *Commentary*'s morale began to sag as Elliot Cohen grew increasingly ravaged by depression and his behavior became ever more erratic. Sometimes he kept manuscripts in a limbo of indecision for months; at other times he made lunch appointments with three writers on the same afternoon. He would send Sidney Hook telegrams in the middle of the night: "YOU WERE RIGHT! I WAS WRONG!" When Trilling sent his student Steven Marcus down from Columbia to see the presiding genius, Cohen could only drone on about baseball.

Even under better circumstances, Cohen had not been an easy companion. "Like most dedicated people," his friend Louis Berg said, "he could be ice-cold to those who seemed to stand in the way of his goals." But now he clashed more often even with his own staff. He appeared to Martin Greenberg as "a bully who dressed up his personal ideas as though they were a holy mission." The offices filled with what his secretary Midge Decter remembered as "the heavy air of irritable discontent."

As the pall descended, Irving Kristol found it increasingly frustrating to work at the magazine. Cohen "would commission an article," Kristol said, "it would come in, I would edit it, he would edit it, the author would approve the editing, and then at the last minute, before going to the printer, Elliot Cohen would decide he wanted to rewrite the whole thing himself, making quite a different point." Sensing that his boss's "editorial interventions had become ever more capricious and arbitrary," Kristol left in 1952 to serve as executive secretary of the American Committee for Cultural Freedom and ten months later, on Sidney Hook's recommendation, to coedit the journal *Encounter* in London.[17] When he returned five years later to the United States, Kristol would spend a decade at Basic Books, where he would become executive vice president, and then in 1965 would found (with Daniel Bell) *Public Interest*. Kristol would continue to write for *Commentary* up through the 1990s.

Much to Cohen's dismay, Nathan Glazer, for whom the editor felt a fatherly regard, left in 1954 for Anchor Books, at Doubleday, where he helped Jason Epstein foment the paperback revolution in American publishing. Glazer left with a sense of gratitude; he felt that he got more of an education at the magazine than in graduate school, and he, too, would write often and brilliantly for the magazine (contributing ninety times over the years). Robert Warshow died of a heart attack, at age thirty-seven, in 1955, and although Cohen had at times disliked his managing editor intensely, he was hit hard by the sudden death and found it tough to run things without him. Warshow was replaced by Harvey Shapiro, an ex-B-17 gunner who stayed less than a year before William Shawn poached him as a fiction editor for the *New Yorker*. A penniless eighteen-year-old from the East Bronx named Al Pacino sorted mail for a little while, but he, too, went on to greater things. Isaac Rosenfeld, the alienated man, died in 1956 at age thirty-eight.[18]

Emotionally paralyzed, tormented by pangs of irrational remorse for the attacks he had directed at Communists, Cohen, fifty-seven, could finally bear no more. He checked into the Payne Whitney Clinic on the Upper East Side in 1956, leaving Martin Greenberg temporarily to run the show, with occasional assists from his brother, Clem, and Sherry Abel. Just before, Cohen had promised a job to Norman Podhoretz, twenty-six, who had started as an assistant editor in December 1955, days after his discharge from the army. Clem and Marty Greenberg, neither of whom abounded in social graces, treated Podhoretz coldly and resented the young man's unconcealed ambitions. Podhoretz "has no content," Clem Greenberg said; "he has never believed in anything." The brothers cut his salary to $5,700 a year, ignored his editorial comments, and conferred about manuscripts in his absence. They banned writers he liked. Podhoretz commissioned a piece from Robert Graves; they rejected it. Self-doubt began to leave its residue on Podhoretz's confidence. What clinched his resolve to resign was the Greenbergs' reluctance to run an essay he had helped commission from Hannah Arendt on integration of blacks into the schools of Little Rock, Arkansas, a piece Marty Greenberg feared "would set the AJC on fire." Podhoretz thought "it would be a dereliction of our intellectual duty" not to run it. In the end, Arendt gave the essay to Irving Howe at *Dissent*, and Podhoretz quit, as he would later put it, "in a voluptuous emission of obscene expletives shouted . . . in the highest register my cigarette-roughened vocal chords could attain." Podhoretz's first stop was the head of the AJC's personnel department, where he denounced the Greenbergs for betraying Cohen's magazine. Rather than accept Podhoretz's resignation, the AJC fired Clem Greenberg and persuaded Podhoretz to stay on with an increased salary ($7,500 a year) and a promotion, though he and Marty Greenberg were no longer on speaking terms. A year later, Podhoretz left—quietly this time.

In 1958, Cohen returned to *Commentary* shaken and diminished. It's true that his magazine still earned a great deal of praise. In June 1959, Senator John F. Kennedy called it "one of the most stimulating and well-edited periodicals that has come to my attention." Douglas MacArthur wrote from the U.S. Embassy in Tokyo that year to say, "*Commentary* arrives regularly at my office and it is always a very welcome caller." The magazine still published enormously influential pieces. The new associate editor, a thirty-one-year-old recruit from the *New Leader* named Anatole Shub (another City College boy), scored a minor coup by commissioning Michael Harrington's landmark *Commentary* article "Our Fifty Million Poor" (July 1959), which showed that nearly a third of Americans lived "below those standards which we have been taught to regard as the decent minimums for food, housing, clothing and health." The essay became the basis for Harrington's best-seller *The Other America* (1962), which in turn helped jumpstart Lyndon Johnson's war on poverty.

But henceforth things would not be the same. The editor happened to see his friend Felix Morrow on the street one day. "Do you know somebody who needs an office boy?"

"Why?" Morrow asked. "Does your boy want some additional work or something?"

"No, I mean me!"

Addled by anxiety, the presiding genius finally could not break free of the troubled thoughts that besieged his mind, and he submitted to their bidding. In May 1959, at age sixty, Elliot Cohen sat down in the kitchen of his apartment on West 85th Street and Central Park West, pulled a plastic dry-cleaning bag over his large head, and tied the bag tight with a string. His wife, Sylvia, found the body. At the funeral, his voice quivering with emotion, Lionel Trilling eulogized his friend as "the *only* great teacher I have ever had."

PART II

Between No and Yes

$\ll 5 \gg$

The Devil's Decade

Is not every able editor a Ruler of the World,
being a persuader of it?
—Thomas Carlyle

GODHEAD

Seven years after Elliot Cohen's suicide, during the time of tumult that goes by the name of the 1960s—amid the commotions of counterculture, sexual revolution, and antiwar New Left—Norman Podhoretz, *Commentary*'s second editor, was feeling beleaguered, beset by inquietude. He wished to register his refusal to be swept up with the hopped-up hippies and Yippies and communards and Dionysians—the "narcotized, beflowered" kids, as Saul Bellow's hero Sammler called them. A stocky, pugnacious, hard-charging man in his thirties with unflagging energy and a marvelous baritone voice, Podhoretz had already published a book of literary essays, *Doings and Undoings: The Fifties and After in American Writing* (1964). But now in a gesture of self-disclosure, he was setting down his memoirs, a kind of midpassage report of his journey from lower-middle-class Brooklyn to uptown Manhattan, in which he would confess his own lust for success, his aching ambition. He set out to refute the notion that the pursuit of success somehow corrupted.[1] There was nothing to be ashamed of, he would insist, in worshipping what William James had famously called the bitch-goddess success, and he hoped he might even achieve it through this very book. He thought of the memoir as a "Mailer-like bid for literary distinction, fame, and money all in one package." (Seven years earlier, his friend Norman Mailer had published his self-revelatory and self-promoting collection of miscellany, *Advertisements for Myself.* "Mailer's ambition for greatness . . . ," Podhoretz later wrote, "was one of the main sources of my attraction to him.")

Doting on his memories, Podhoretz decided to start the tale at P.S. 28 in Brownsville, where as a bookish boy he was assigned to a remedial-speech class to correct the Yiddish accent he'd picked up from his immigrant parents. At home he was the favored child, the precocious only son. "The adult world," he would boast, "and especially the female part of it, was one vast congregation of worshipers at the shrine of my diminutive godhead." But not at school. He would tell how his favorite high school teacher regularly called him "a filthy little slum child."

Podhoretz, burning to impress, resolved to take his hunger for success as the theme of his story. "I could not bear the idea of not being great," he would write. He would use the memoir to tell how, ridding himself of his Yiddish-inflected curbstone English, he worked a transformation on himself, a conversion to culture that took flight in the late 1940s, when a full-tuition Pulitzer scholarship allowed him to enroll at Columbia. He would tell of commuting to Morningside Heights with a brown paper bag lunch to sit at the feet of Lionel Trilling, who came to think of him as "perhaps the very best student I have ever had." Podhoretz would praise his urbane teacher, his guide to the elusive meanings of literature, as "the most intelligent man I have ever known." He would recount his pride at earning an A+ in Trilling's course on the English Romantics. When *The Liberal Imagination* came out in 1950, Trilling inscribed a copy to his student: "in great admiration and high expectation." The accolade, Podhoretz now wrote, "made me positively giddy."

Podhoretz thought the memoir should add that while at Columbia, at the urging of his father, he had spent two nights a week and Sunday afternoons in class at the Jewish Theological Seminary. It was here that he first met Midge Rosenthal, about to marry her first husband, Moshe Decter (soon to be managing editor of the *New Leader*). Norman and Midge would marry in October 1956. But Podhoretz reflected that he might also use the episode to contrast the lessons at the seminary—"the endless pep talks disguised as scholarship, the endless harping on the sufferings of the Jews"—with the exhilarating seminars at Columbia. "Western Culture," he would say, "made what the Seminary had to offer look narrow, constricted, provincial, and finally less relevant to me personally than the heritage of what was, after all, a Christian civilization." The memoirist would then tell how Kellett and Fulbright scholarships sent him overseas for three years to Cambridge, where he was assigned a manservant and studied with the eminent literary critic F. R. Leavis. He would tell of how he served in the army for a couple of years; how when he got back, he joined *Commentary* as an assistant editor; and how, in 1960, he seized the editor's reins at the age of thirty.

But Podhoretz decided he would linger most of all—and with the greatest candor he could summon—on his undisguised hunger to be regarded as the Family's up-and-coming literary star. He was on the make, after all. His desire for fame, he would admit, "was self-acknowledged, unashamed, and altogether uninhibited." The desire was at first for literary fame. "What I wanted," he would confess, "was to see my name in print, to be praised, and above all to attract attention." While still in his twenties, he had reviewed for *Commentary*, *Partisan Review*, and the *New Yorker*. Publishers took him to lunch. He was invited to fancy parties on Sutton Place. But he would insist that the desire he so unabashedly husbanded was not his alone. "Ambition," Podhoretz would write, "seems to be replacing erotic lust as the prime dirty little secret of the well-educated American soul." As he would be the first to acknowledge, Podhoretz's avidity was as much social as intellectual. Only later, the milkman's son would recall in the memoir, did he become aware of "how inextricably my 'noblest' ambitions were tied to the vulgar desire to rise above the class into which I was born." As the new editor, Podhoretz relished the invitations to dinner parties at William Phillips's place, at Philip Rahv's country home, at Mary McCarthy's in the East Nineties, or at Richard Clurman's place on East 72nd, where he could hobnob with the likes of Henry Luce, Abba Eban, William F. Buckley, and Edward Albee. (Clurman, *Time*'s chief of correspondents, had worked briefly as an editorial assistant at Elliot Cohen's *Commentary* in the late 1940s.)

The memoir would divulge that these Family parties weren't necessarily fun. They often seemed like little more than an occasion to indulge in biting gossip. "It was almost considered bad form," Podhoretz would write, "or a mark of low intelligence, to say anything kind in conversation about any other member of the group." But the gatherings had another function. "Parties were sometimes fun and sometimes not," Podhoretz would say, "but fun was beside the point: for me they always served as a barometer of the progress of my career. . . . Every morning a stock-market report on reputations comes out in New York. It is invisible, but those who have eyes to see can read it. Did so-and-so have dinner at Jacqueline Kennedy's apartment last night? Up five points. . . . Did so-and-so's book get nominated for the National Book Award? Up two and five eighth's."

Podhoretz had come to feel that his own stock was rising, but when the manuscript was at last finished—and here's the more personal edge of the sense of besiegement he felt—*Making It*, as Podhoretz called his memoir-polemic, did not exactly go over well. Roger Straus of Farrar, Straus and Giroux, who had advanced Podhoretz $25,000, declined to publish the book. Some friends advised the author not to publish it at all. Daniel Bell thought it lacked irony, Lionel Trilling considered it a lamentable piece of work, and Diana Trilling deemed it humorless and "crudely boastful." "If I were God, I'd drown it in the river," Jason Epstein said (though his firm, Random House, did in the end bring it out into the harsh light of day).

Podhoretz was no naïf; he had expected a rough handling. "For taking my career as seriously as I do in this book," he predicted, "I will no doubt be accused of self-inflation and therefore of tastelessness." But when it came out in late 1967, *Making It* fared even worse than he had anticipated. English-born writer Wilfrid Sheed, then a critic at *Esquire*, wrote that the book "was pockmarked by clichés and little mock modesties." Edgar Z. Friedenberg wrote that Podhoretz's "lifeless" book "tells us very little about anything that has happened in his life except as it affects his self-esteem or concerns his quest for class, status, and power. . . . Podhoretz amid his growing collection of trophies is so impersonal that there are times when it seems that *Making It* might better have been called *Manhole in the Promised Land*." "From the reviews," Diana Trilling said, "one might have supposed that he had written *Mein Kampf*." "It was with all the fury of a military betrayal that the Establishment turned on Podhoretz," Mailer said. They whispered against the book, he said, "in thin quivering late-night hisses." But Mailer turned out to be one of the whisperers; in the pages of *Partisan Review*, the self-assertive author of *Advertisements for Myself* called *Making It* a "blunder of self-assertion, self-exposure, and self-denigration."[2] One of Podhoretz's friends went so far as to advise Midge Decter to have her husband committed.[3]

IT WAS NEITHER the first time nor the last that Podhoretz would ignore the counsel of close friends. In 1960, when Podhoretz was thirty, just after *Commentary* had moved into its new digs in the blue and silver American Jewish Committee (AJC) building on East 56th, the AJC invited him to succeed Elliot Cohen. Irving Kristol, who himself had turned down the offer, advised his friend to do the same. "No, Norman, you don't want to be the editor of *Commentary*. The magazine is okay, it's a good magazine, but it's not going anywhere, and you're on your way to being a very distinguished cultural and literary critic. Stick with it, you'll end up replacing Edmund Wilson in our pantheon." Publisher Jason Epstein, who had given his friend Podhoretz a part-time job at Anchor Books and then worked with him on a line of children's books at Random House, warned Podhoretz that the magazine was "finished, played out, through." The Trillings, too, thought Podhoretz would be making a dreadful mistake that would likely ruin him as a critic.

Podhoretz in those days smoked four packs a day. He could belt back thirteen martinis over a chat with Willie Morris, the precocious editor of *Harper's*. He wasn't going to be deterred by a smattering of cautious advice. "This doesn't mean that I'm not scared stiff," he told English novelist and physicist C. P. Snow. "I've never been so nervous and frightened before. But I'm also exhilarated by the possibilities that may now open up for me, and by the power (which is something you can understand as my high-minded friends can't), and by the money (my income will be more than doubled)."

And so it was that Trilling's spirited student Podhoretz succeeded Trilling's teacher Cohen. Bernard Malamud sent a note of congratulations: "I remember your saying once that you 'were meant for' *Commentary*. Fate listened."

Some features of *Commentary's* physiognomy would remain intact. Podhoretz kept the magazine's sedate, austere look. He was proud of its decorum, its unadorned cascades of type. "No 'journal of opinion,'" he said, "ever came before the world with so chaste a presentation, chaste even in format and typography—the stately Fairfield columns, the severe rectangular proportions." The magazine's restrained design contributed to its rhetorical force. "When you looked at the cover of an issue of *Commentary*, you saw a quiet pattern of type that suggested homage to the classic virtues—order, harmony, balance, the whole taking precedence over the individual parts. . . . The subject of each piece was always stressed above the name of its author, even when the author was a figure like Thomas Mann or John Dewey or Jean-Paul Sartre."

But the new editor, flexing his new power, changed much else. Though not unmindful of his predecessor, rather than deferentially perpetuate the ancien régime, Podhoretz intended to stamp his personality on the magazine, to make it his. And so with Podhoretz's arrival, the sound of the magazine changed, as though transposed into a new key; the velocity of its sentences grew brisker. Podhoretz himself had a taste for pugnacity. He liked to goad, to lacerate, to flout received opinion. So it is no surprise that he lent the magazine a somewhat more adversarial, abrasive, all-guns-blazing style than before.

To match the new tone, Podhoretz designed an expanded letters to the editor section, longer and more disputatious than any other American magazine's. His *Commentary* was not meant to be passively received. Over several rounds of correspondence, rebuttals, rejoinders, and exchanges—as between Lionel Abel and Noam Chomsky, say—were barbed with acrimony, and the author always got last right of reply. Sometimes that reply would consist of a single line, like Gershom Scholem's simple declaration: "I find Mr. Greenspan's comments on my essay despicable."[4]

Before Podhoretz, *Commentary* was not always thought of as a general-interest magazine. Dan Wakefield, a self-proclaimed WASP, had his first piece in the magazine in 1958, when he was a staff writer at *The Nation*. His parents proudly mentioned the fact to a Jewish neighbor in his hometown, Indianapolis. The response was incredulity. "Oh, Dan couldn't have an article in there; it's a Jewish magazine."

This, too, was about to change. True, Podhoretz's father encouraged in him some religious feeling, and Podhoretz had grudgingly attended those classes at the Jewish Theological Seminary, but at this stage, to hear former managing editor Clem Greenberg tell it, Podhoretz "didn't give a shit about the Jews." Podhoretz accepted the job, he reported, "only on the understanding that I had a mandate to change it from a Jewish magazine that carried a certain amount of general material to a general magazine that carried a certain amount of Jewish material." Podhoretz regarded this as a matter of natural growth. "My own policies as editor of *Commentary* simply pushed the logic of Cohen's strategy further than he himself had done: the 'new *Commentary*' bespoke, and reflected, a more advanced stage of acculturation than the old, and was accordingly more general than Jewish in emphasis, but it remained explicitly Jewish in part of its contents and identifiably Jewish in the intellectual style (that of the Family) with which it treated even subjects of wholly general nature." Six years into his tenure, Podhoretz would pause to consider the differences between his magazine and his predecessor's: "*Commentary* today is less concerned than it used to be with the sociology of the American Jewish community, with the social sciences in general, with the character of the American middle class. It does, however, remain as interested as ever in the meaning of the Holocaust, the role of the U.S. in international affairs, the importance of ethnicity and religion in American life, the quality of contemporary culture, the problems of education, the elusive nature of Jewishness."

The unwritten law that mandated a "Jewish article" in every issue still stood, but Podhoretz cut the "From the American Scene" department so dear to Elliot Cohen. The new editor thought the section had been "rarely free of a distressingly vulgar coziness." Jacob Neusner, a prolific scholar of rabbinic Judaism (two years younger than Podhoretz) who wrote several times for the magazine in the mid-1950s, remarked that Podhoretz "made it his policy to remove 'all the mezuzahs from the doors.'"[5] Podhoretz also cut poetry (his insistence that he would edit poetry as rigorously as prose hadn't gone over well with poets) and gave up the practice of printing a short story every month.

IN THE FIRST YEARS of the new regime, Podhoretz also overhauled the staff. His friend Robert Silvers, then an editor at *Harper's*, declined Podhoretz's job offer. Joseph Epstein, then working at the *New Leader*, tried out for a position, but he was a bit intimidated by Podhoretz's aggressiveness at the interview, which Podhoretz opened with the words "I consider that anything good in the *New Leader* is there by accident."

Marion Magid, a wry Barnard grad from a family of Labor Zionists, a lover of the Yiddish language, came aboard as assistant editor in 1963 and would stay for thirty years (as associate editor from 1966 through 1968 and as managing editor starting in late 1968). She impressed her colleagues as a femme savante, a joyful, lustrous-haired wit, a delight to be around. Once she accompanied Podhoretz to a meeting of radicals in Union Square. She surveyed the scene and whispered, "Do you realize that every young person in this room is a tragedy to some family or other?" Blocked as a writer, she championed the magazine's fiction and was much adored by her writers.[6]

Before Magid, Podhoretz hired Ted Solotaroff (named after Theodor Herzl), a lanky thirty-two-year-old from Elizabeth, New Jersey. Solotaroff idolized Isaac Rosenfeld. He took deep interest in the new crop of American Jewish writers. He said they "resuscitated, activated, and educated the Jew in me who had been languishing in an empty back room of my mind, sent there, in part, by my literary education and ambition." A piece Solotaroff published in the *Times Literary Supplement* in November 1959 called "A Vocal Group: The Jewish Part in American Letters" had caught Podhoretz's eye, and soon the editor lured Solotaroff away from his dissertation on Henry James. "It was a bit like working in a mom-and-pop deli," Solotaroff said, "with Marion the wisecracking daughter who sat above the fray at the cash register and I the helper who potched around." Solotaroff's usual companion for a lunch of hamburgers and bowls of sliced onion at Prexy's was assistant editor Harris Dienstfrey, a coolheaded twenty-six-year-old who lasted only a couple of years. "Norman takes up too much of the oxygen," Dienstfrey said.[7]

In 1964, to augment his supporting cast, Podhoretz hired Werner Dannhauser, a brilliant rake who had come to the country in 1939 as a nine-year-old refugee from Germany and had discipled himself to German-Jewish émigré philosopher Leo Strauss at the University of Chicago.[8] As a contributing editor, Podhoretz brought on George Lichtheim, a friend of Dannhauser's and a sharp student of Marxism who would write more than six dozen pieces for *Commentary*.

Podhoretz retained only one member of Cohen's staff: Sherry Abel. Now managing editor, she took Solotaroff under her wing. "*Commentary* editors, my dear Ted, are very presumptuous," she told him by way of induction. "It's part of our role. It's how we've managed to publish so many sociologists and rabbis." Solotaroff was struck by the soft voice Abel had "and a way of saying your name that must have produced many erections in its time."

With the help of a running account at Le Moal downstairs on Third Avenue, an air of informal conviviality and family feeling pervaded the staff. The Podhoretzes threw great parties. At one of the parties Norman and Midge hosted in 1964 at their roomy place on West End Avenue and West 105th Street, the guest of honor was Jackie Kennedy, whom Philip Roth kept referring to as "the shiksa." But *Commentary* remained in its essence a one-man magazine. Podhoretz would send around manuscripts, and his staff would add comment-sheets—barnacles, as they used to call them—but in the end he made all the decisions. "He was *Commentary*, and *Commentary* was him," Solotaroff recalled.

Not that the supporting cast much minded. They rather admired Podhoretz's deftness as intellectual impresario, his mastery of the art of pairing author and subject, and the way he "aimed" younger writers. They envied, too, his preternatural ability to make even the most clotted prose flow. He seemed to possess a natural gift for untangling syntax, for encouraging writers to realize their own intentions more fully. Podhoretz could put a wooden piece of writing through his typewriter and turn it into something supple. Editing with him, Solotaroff said, "was like learning to be a coach under Vince Lombardi." Indeed, so seamless was Podhoretz's editing that writers couldn't understand why their prose elsewhere fell flat. One day, Midge Decter walked into the offices of the Zionist magazine *Midstream* to find the editor, Shlomo Katz, with his head in his hands. "The good stuff they give to *Commentary*, and to me they give the shit!" What Katz didn't fathom, as Decter did, was that these were the very same writers—and submissions.

The new editor also demonstrated considerable skill at cajoling and flattering a writer to get the desired piece. Political scientist James Q. Wilson, who started writing for the magazine in 1966, used to say that in the course of badgering writers, Podhoretz had invented a new grammatical construction: the passive imperative. Podhoretz called Wilson one day in 1965, for example, and said, "It is necessary that you write an article for this magazine about Adam Clayton Powell." And so was it done.

COMMENTARY'S NEW COMPLEXION overlaid a much deeper shift, however. On the one hand, beginning in 1960 the magazine returned to the spirit of dissent. On the heels of what was perceived to be the anti-intellectual mood of the Eisenhower White House, the Kennedy era saw intellectuals—"the best and the brightest"—connected to government in unprecedented ways: men such as Arthur Schlesinger Jr., Richard Goodwin, John Kenneth Galbraith, McGeorge Bundy, Patrick Moynihan. The Camelot cabinet even included two Jews: Arthur Goldberg and Abraham Ribicoff. Yet *Commentary* did not yet partake of the reconciliation. Almost as soon as he became editor, Podhoretz, with his customary independence of mind, put an end to the magazine's celebrations of American virtue. "The major change since I took over," the editor told a reporter from *Newsweek* four years into his reign, "is that we're more critical—more critical of American society, of certain assumptions about the cold war." He later remembered that he hoped to "take a fresh look at all the weary ideas and attitudes whose constant reiteration in the *Commentary* of the recent past . . . had made it so predictable."

On the other hand, neither Podhoretz nor any of the *Commentary* cognoscenti embraced the new Left as warmly as did their friends over at the *New York Review of Books*—"the chief theoretical organ of Radical Chic," as Tom Wolfe called it.[9] Founded during the New York newspaper strike of 1963 under the editorship of Robert Silvers and Barbara Epstein, the *New York Review* married fashionable New Left politics with Upper East Side literary sophistication. Unlike Silvers, Podhoretz never published radicals such as Stokely Carmichael, Jerry Rubin, or Tom Hayden,[10] nor was he inclined to tape a psychedelic poster of Che Guevara to his door.

Unlike the older generation of the Family, Podhoretz had never been a socialist or Trotskyist, but he had grown up on the immigrant Left. His father worked as a milkman for Sheffield Farms; after Podhoretz had become a successful writer and editor, he remembered, his mother "would gaze wistfully at this strange creature, her son, and murmur, 'I should have made him for a dentist.'" He said he "never even laid eyes on a Republican until I reached high school, where I was amazed to discover that one of my English teachers was actually a member of that exotic species." Yet as he took over the magazine, something of the previous generation's sense of alienation clung to Podhoretz: "the feeling that this was not *my* country; I was not really a part of it; I was a citizen, and a highly interested one, of a small community in New York which lived by its own laws and had as little commerce as it could manage with a hostile surrounding environment. As an intellectual I was as ghettoized as my ancestors in Eastern Europe had been as Jews." Once more—as a 1961 *Commentary* symposium called "Jewishness and the Younger Intellectuals" confirmed—alienation from country and from Jewish tradition existed in intimate proximity.[11]

Podhoretz, now at the height of what he thought of as his "radical exuberance," his "infection of utopianism," began his tenure by jostling *Commentary* off the beaten liberal path. His first issues serialized *Growing Up Absurd* (1960) by counterculture hero Paul Goodman (City College 1932), a pacifist-anarchist enfant terrible whose reputation Podhoretz now aimed to rehabilitate.[12] The book would become a bible of the New Left. Goodman's manuscript, Podhoretz said, "was everything I wanted for the new *Commentary*, and more." "I can recall reading those *Commentary* pages in a sweat of approbation," Jason Epstein said. "Yes; yes; yes; exactly; yes; yes; yes; perfect!" More than a decade earlier, Irving Howe, writing in the old *Commentary*, had called Goodman "exuberantly reckless and irresponsible" and had deplored his "cute rebelliousness." Now, joining in the rebelliousness, the new *Commentary* hailed Goodman—in a paean by no less a mandarin than George Steiner—as a kind of prophet.[13]

In step with the times, Podhoretz brought into his pages many other fashionable left-wing Dionysians who were hostile to the liberal status quo. He published his friend Norman Mailer, whom he had first met in the late 1950s at Lillian Hellman's opulent Upper East Side apartment. ("The other Norman" playfully called Podhoretz a "bastard bureaucrat.") The new editor ran German-Jewish radical theorist Herbert Marcuse's critique of the classicist and philosopher Norman O. Brown (aka Nobby), he of polymorphous perversity, and then Nobby on Marcuse.[14] Other new names appeared. Political theorist George Kateb, introduced to Podhoretz by poet John Hollander, contributed essays on subjects from Kennedy to Marcuse.[15] Susan Sontag, who had briefly joined the *Commentary* staff in 1959, wrote on science-fiction films.[16] Podhoretz commissioned a book review from media theorist Marshall McLuhan and a learned piece from Hannah Arendt that aimed, as she put it, "to rehabilitate the word 'revolution.'" In the July 1966 issue, he gave a platform to Tom Kahn, executive director of the League for Industrial Democracy, to argue that "a militant and democratic New Left is needed in America." Kahn criticized the New Left, but did so, he averred, "out of a hope growing nearly desperate that this outburst of radical discontent will stick, that it will sink deep roots, that it will energize a new political movement, and transform national institutions." Meanwhile, as if to cement its leftist credentials, *Commentary* fired another salvo at William F. Buckley's conservative magazine, *National Review*. Echoing Dwight Macdonald's earlier attack, in 1965 the magazine—in a piece called "The Conservative Mindlessness"—averred that from "rightist intellectuals" like Buckley and James Burnham, there had been heard "almost nothing but insults to the intelligence."

From about 20,000 in 1960, paid circulation rose past 40,000 in 1965 and to 64,000 in 1968. Annual advertising revenue rose from about $10,000 in 1960 to more than $100,000 six years later. "Norman was publishing the most interesting magazine in America," Victor Navasky of *The Nation* said. "*Commentary*," Irving Howe exulted in 1963, "once the center of the more embittered, sophisticated anti-radicalism, is these days a new magazine."

OUR NEGRO PROBLEM

Impatient with the status quo, riled by the conviction that politics could achieve far more than the New Deal dreamed of, the new editor began the decade by reappraising American success and prosperity. In 1953, sociologist William Peterson had taken to *Commentary* to extol the strength of the American economy. Almost seven years later, in his inaugural editorial, Podhoretz raised the possibility that "the prosperity of the Eisenhower Age [was] a deceptive sign of vigor and health." While Dwight Eisenhower drifted, Podhoretz said, American affluence faded.

Podhoretz also used the magazine to lead the charge for reform in poverty, education, housing—and, especially, civil rights. This last issue had for years acted as a mainstay of the magazine. As far back as 1949, Charles Abrams, later chair of the New York State Commission Against Discrimination, noted that "*Commentary* has really become the center around which sound thinking on racial questions revolves." The same year, James Baldwin, whose earliest stories appeared in *Commentary* (including his first published short story when he was twenty-four), suggested in the magazine that "the full story of white and black in this country is more vast and shattering than we would like to believe."[17] Elliot Cohen, in 1950, commissioned a hefty essay from Anatole Broyard called "Portrait of an Inauthentic Negro."[18] Cohen ran James Rorty's reports on desegregation and a twenty-two-year-old David Halberstam's report on the White Citizens Councils which fought racial integration in the South. Unlike *National Review, Commentary* endorsed the 1954 *Brown v. Board of Education* school desegregation decision.[19]

But in the 1960s, as the civil rights struggle migrated from South to North, from voting and education rights to equality in jobs, income, and housing, as race riots broke out in Watts, Newark, and Detroit, Podhoretz's magazine devoted more attention to race than almost any other nonblack American publication.[20] Driven by the conviction that racial inequality denied the purpose for which America was created, Podhoretz convened and moderated a roundtable discussion at Town Hall in 1964 on "Liberalism and the Negro." To his left sat Sidney Hook and black writer James Baldwin; to his right, Nathan Glazer and Swedish economist and sociologist Gunnar Myrdal, author of the monumental book *An American Dilemma: The Negro Problem and Modern Democracy* (1944). The invited audience included Joseph Epstein, Lionel Abel, and William Phillips. (In the heat of discussion, Baldwin, as always a brilliant performer, turned to Hook. "I'm quite sure you know nothing about the black experience apart from your maid." Hook was incensed. "We don't have a maid!" he yelled. Whereupon a woman's voice rose from the audience: "Sidney, let him talk, Sidney. Let him talk." It was Mrs. Hook.)

Nearly every month now, another major *Commentary* piece on the subject thumped down: "Negro Militants, Jewish Liberals, and the Unions" (Tom Brooks); "Integration and the Negro Mood" (Harold Isaacs); "The Negro and the Democratic Coalition" (Samuel Lubell); "The Negro and the New York Schools" (Midge Decter); "Negroes and Jews: The New Challenge to Pluralism" (Nathan Glazer); "The President and the Negro" (Pat Moynihan). In 1965, Podhoretz commissioned his friend Bayard Rustin, organizer of the 1963 March on Washington and mentor to Martin Luther King Jr., to describe the civil rights movement's evolution. Rustin wrote that the movement was no longer about sit-ins and freedom rides; it was "concerned not merely with removing the barriers to full *opportunity* but with achieving the fact of *equality*." The civil rights movement, Rustin announced in the widely discussed piece, now aimed to revolutionize life for whites no less than for blacks.[21] Black writer Julian Mayfield argued in *Commentary* that traditional leaders such as Reverend King were losing their claim to speak for blacks and might soon be replaced by new leaders "who have concluded that the only way to win a revolution is to be a revolutionary." And Norman Mailer once more attacked liberals from the Left. "The liberal premise—that Negroes and Jews are like everybody else once they are given the same rights—can only obscure the complexity, the intensity, and the psychotic brilliance of a minority's inner life," Mailer charged in the October 1963 issue.

As the decade approached its climax, the magazine struck ever-more radical notes. In its pages eminent southern writer Robert Penn Warren interviewed two activists from the Student Non-Violent Coordinating Committee: Robert Moses and Stokely Carmichael. Journalist Jervis Anderson (then a graduate student at New York University, later a staff writer for the *New Yorker*) introduced *Commentary* readers to Eldridge Cleaver, "minister of information" for the Black Panther Party in Oakland, California, praising Cleaver as "the essential stylist of the new black generation" and "an immensely talented essayist" (though also perhaps "lacking in certain fundamental moral qualities").

Indeed except for short editor's notes, the first piece Podhoretz wrote for the magazine since ascending to the editor's throne was a shockingly candid confession called "My Negro Problem—and Ours" (February 1963). Slicing through the hypocrisy with which the subject of race had been swaddled, Podhoretz recalled growing up "in an 'integrated' slum neighborhood where it was the Negroes who persecuted the whites and not the other way around." He remembered Brownsville street brawls with "enviably tough" black kids: "There is a fight, they win and we retreat, half whimpering, half with bravado. My first nauseating experience with cowardice, and my first appalled realization that there are people in the world who do not seem to be afraid of anything, who act as though they have nothing to lose." He concluded with the radical suggestion that the problem of integration could be solved only by means of miscegenation—"the wholesale merging of the two races."

Jewish leaders were mortified by the essay's admission that if his own daughters were to marry black men, Podhoretz would give his blessing. Take, for example, Arthur Hertzberg, rabbi of Temple Emanu-El in Englewood, New Jersey, who had officiated at Norman and Midge's wedding and had written on American Jewish affairs for the magazine in the 1950s and 1960s. "This assertion," Hertzberg recalled, "was denounced from almost every synagogue pulpit in America. How dare a Jewish editor advocate intermarrying and the dissolution of the Jewish people?" (When Ted Solotaroff urged his boss to reconsider his conclusion, the editor rejected the suggestion out of hand: "I don't ever want to hear you tell me again what's good or bad for *Commentary*. Ever!") Much to Podhoretz's delight, almost before the piece came out, it was notorious, a succès de scandale. "I was prouder of it than anything I had ever done as a writer," he said.

LA GUERRE EST FINIE

Podhoretz's most sweeping change involved dismissing hard anti-Communism, the old *Commentary*'s axiom of faith, just as in the country at large the coalition of liberal anti-Communists was breaking apart. By the early 1960s, in Senator McCarthy's wake, anti-Communism, which until then had enjoyed a bipartisan consensus as a guide to American foreign policy, had become a disreputable faith. Just how disreputable would be made clear by Barry Goldwater's resounding defeat in the 1964 presidential election.

In this sense, the new magazine shared something of the New Left's skepticism toward anti-Communism. The Port Huron Statement of the Students for a Democratic Society had condemned the fact that in America's

> status quo politics, where most if not all government activity is rationalized in Cold War anti-Communist terms, it is somewhat natural that discontented, super-patriotic groups would emerge through political channels and explain their ultra-conservatism as the best means of Victory over Communism. . . . Thus much of the American anti-Communism takes on the characteristics of paranoia. Not only does it lead to the perversion of democracy and to the political stagnation of a warfare society, but it also has the unintended consequence of preventing an honest and effective approach to the issues.

Podhoretz now began to suspect that hard anti-Communists like Elliot Cohen had exaggerated the danger; that world Communism was by then no longer unified, as the split between the USSR and China made obvious; and that it no longer threatened America with internal revolutionary subversion. Podhoretz coaxed a controversial piece from New Left spokesman and militant labor activist Staughton Lynd that made the case that the cold war arose not from a struggle of good against evil, but "from a tangled situation to which both sides contributed"—a tangle caused in part by American diplomatic chauvinism. (Shortly thereafter, Ted Solotaroff found himself awkwardly defending Lynd's article at a Family party at the Kristols. "If you weren't so naïve, every word out of your mouth would be shameful," Diana Trilling answered him. "Norman doesn't have that excuse.")

Podhoretz was far from alone in his conversion. In the pages of the new *Commentary*, many writers now reexamined the anti-Communist creed they themselves had once so ardently upheld. In the June 1960 issue, David Riesman and Michael Maccoby called cold warriors "imperialistic" and attacked as simplistic the notion that the Soviet Union was unappeasably expansionist.[22] (Diana Trilling, once more speaking for the older generation, called the piece "a hodge-podge of non-thinking." "It's an appalling piece," she told Podhoretz. "It rather shocks me that you printed it.") In one of his bimonthly foreign affairs columns for *Commentary*, Hans Morgenthau submitted that making anti-Communism the chief priority of foreign policy would only aggravate American impotence.[23] "Communism today," historian Arthur Schlesinger Jr. wrote in *Commentary*'s symposium in the September 1967 issue, "is a boring, squalid creed, tired, fragmented and, save in very exceptional places and circumstances, wholly uninspiring. *La guerre est finie.*" In his contribution to the symposium, William Phillips wrote that to be an anti-Communist in those days, "one had to be pathologically single-minded, allergic to change, and in love with existing institutions." His coeditor at *Partisan Review*, Philip Rahv, added that cold war anti-Communists "have turned into sophists and sycophants of the American ruling elite." Irving Howe challenged "the ideological racketeers who made anti-Communism into a kind of spray gun with which to attack every liberal or radical opinion." "Anti-Communism," he warned, "can form a protective mask for detestable politics." Sociologist Robert Nisbet, who had started writing for *Commentary* in 1960, questioned anti-Communists who risked investing "every strategic goal with limitless moral intensity." Finally, Paul Goodman averred that "one of the chief bad effects of anti-Communism on the climate of opinion" was the way "it lulled the American self-delusion of righteousness."

Podhoretz's anti-Communist fervor much cooled, the new *Commentary*—in the persons of Harold Rosenberg, Staughton Lynd, and Robert Nisbet—urged an end to the strategy of attempting to check the spread of Communism, or "containment," the centerpiece of American cold war policy. Elliot Cohen's *Commentary* had hinted that containment, which had its origins in a 1947 *Foreign Affairs* article by the State Department Soviet expert George Kennan, did not go far enough in countering the Communist threat.[24] The new *Commentary* argued instead that the policy went too far; that containment "involved and still involves an identification of the United States with governments whose only qualification for our friendship is their anti-Communism," as Lynd wrote.[25] Other *Commentary* writers went so far as to urge an end to the arms race by means of unilateral American disarmament. H. Stuart Hughes of the National Committee for a Sane Nuclear Policy, who would write twenty-five pieces for *Commentary*, demanded "the renunciation of thermonuclear deterrence as an instrument of national policy." Another contributor criticized Republican senator Barry Goldwater's presidential campaign for the 1964 election as "nuclear buccaneering to defend a vague, Arizonan conception of 'freedom.'" As these kinds of declarations now heard in *Commentary* made abundantly clear, some of the Family, at least, had turned decisively against anti-Communism.

HOT DAMN, VIETNAM

Until now, the Family had tended to see American intervention abroad as a mark of benevolence; but for the *Commentary* of the 1960s—with the America of the Marshall Plan rapidly becoming the America of Vietnam— intervention began to signify something less noble.

Ever since President John F. Kennedy had sent his chief military adviser, General Maxwell Taylor, on a seven-day fact-finding mission to Vietnam in late 1961, Podhoretz had opposed American military involvement in Southeast Asia. He considered it "an illegitimate and unintelligent expansion of the policy of containment." *Commentary* accordingly launched an early and trenchant critique of the Vietnam War. In a remarkable 1962 essay, Hans Morgenthau of the University of Chicago (who had visited Vietnam in 1955 and met with President Ngo Dinh Diem) warned in the magazine of extending American support "to regimes whose political weakness compels us in the end to commit ourselves militarily beyond what our national interest would require." "Such a war," Morgenthau wrote, "cannot be won quickly, if it can be won at all, and may well last . . . five or ten years, perhaps only to end again in a stalemate." David Halberstam of the *New York Times* reported for *Commentary* in 1965 on the pressures on reporters in Saigon to file optimistic stories: "Many of us came to love Vietnam," he wrote; "we saw our friends dying all around us, and we would have liked nothing better than to believe that the war was going well and that it would eventually be won. But it was impossible for us to believe those things without denying the evidence of our senses."[26] (In those years only one *Commentary* writer—Oscar Gass, who had served as economic adviser to governments in the Far East—defended a limited American war against the Vietcong. "The take-over by Ho Chi-Minh's men in Saigon would probably make the Nazi occupation of Vienna and Prague look like a picnic," Gass wrote at the end of 1965.[27])

Even during the height of his 1960s exuberance, however, Podhoretz permitted the magazine only so much leash. He insisted that the war was an unwise or imprudent mistake, not an immoral crime that somehow laid bare an irredeemable rot in American society. He refused to believe that the country was, to use Diana Trilling's vivid phrase, "feeding dead Vietnamese babies into the slot machine of its imperial gamble." The war, Podhoretz said then, was mistaken, wasteful, imprudent, and tragically ill conceived, but not criminal.[28] He had little patience for those like Noam Chomsky who compared American "butchery in Vietnam" with Hitler's Final Solution, or for reports from Hanoi in the *New York Review* by Mary McCarthy and Susan Sontag (whom Podhoretz dubbed "the dark lady of American letters") that cast the North Vietnamese in a glowing light.[29] Here, for instance, is Nathan Glazer writing in *Commentary* in 1968: "I cannot accept the idea that the fundamental character of American society, its political or economic life, is the prime cause of the horrors of Vietnam. In the end, I cannot help believing, the Vietnam war must be understood as the result of monumental errors."

Yet as the decade wore on, Podhoretz's own opposition to the war grew in vehemence. Summing up *Commentary*'s 1967 symposium on liberal anti-Communism, Podhoretz observed that nearly all the respondents agreed "that the American effort to contain Communism by military means cannot be justified either politically or morally." One of the contributors to that symposium, Paul Goodman, declared, "I do not think that the Vietnamese adventure has ever seriously been about 'Communism'; it is, rather, an incident of American expansion that happens to have gotten out of hand." Brooklyn-born ex-Communist historian Theodore Draper, who started writing for the magazine in 1961, called the war "a political debacle, a military folly, and a moral disgrace." In the June 1967 issue, Paul Theroux, a twenty-six-year-old writer living in Uganda, explained why he had refused to enroll in the Reserve Officers' Training Corps at the University of Massachusetts— "the thought of wearing a uniform appalled me"—and why he left for Africa rather than face the draft.[30] Marion Magid's husband, Ted Hoagland, boasted in *Commentary* of sending his torn draft card to LBJ.[31] In 1968, the year of the Vietcong's Tet Offensive, Podhoretz ran Mailer's "The Battle of the Pentagon," a 23,000-word excerpt from *Armies of the Night*, a "nonfiction novel" about the previous year's antiwar March on the Pentagon.[32] ("Something close to Tolstoyan," Diana Trilling gushed in *Commentary*, "an essential text of contemporary left-wing politics.") Mailer's piece concluded on dark note: "Brood on that country who expresses our will. She is America, once a beauty of magnificence unparalleled, now a beauty with a leprous skin. She is heavy with child—no one knows if legitimate. . . . She will probably give birth, and to what?—the most fearsome totalitarianism the world has ever known?" Finally, in the lead piece in the May 1971 issue, Nathan Glazer called for full and immediate American withdrawal from Vietnam. "As one who has never believed anything good would ever come for us or for the world from an unambiguous American defeat," Podhoretz wrote in the editor's introduction to that issue, "I now find myself . . . moving to the side of those who would prefer just such a defeat to the 'Vietnamization' of the war which calls for the indefinite and unlimited bombardment by American pilots in American planes of every country in that already devastated region."

Norman Podhoretz had turned against the bland liberal consensus of the 1950s—the liberalism of Elliot Cohen, Lionel Trilling, and Sidney Hook. He had bid farewell both to hard anti-Communism and the celebration of America, criticized the flexing of U.S. military muscle in Southeast Asia, and steered the magazine sharply leftward into a decade of antiestablishment iconoclasm. But that was just the first turn of the screw.

❡ 6 ❡

Mugged by Reality

"And what will Commentary *make of this confession?
I can't imagine it's good for the Jews."*
—Peter Tarnopol in Philip Roth's *My Life as a Man*

COUNTERCULTURE CARNIVAL

As the 1960s grew frenetic, more students born into the affluent, professional, liberal middle class began to turn on the aspirations and conformities of that class. "We are people of this generation," declared the preamble to the campus radicals' manifesto, the 1962 Port Huron Statement, "bred in at least modest comfort, housed now in universities, looking uncomfortably to the world we inherit." Anyone over thirty, warned the leader of the Free Speech Movement at Berkeley, was not to be trusted. The devotees of non-conformity rejected liberal bromides and middle-class hypocrisies and the cult of success. The personal had become political. Students for a Democratic Society (SDS), haters of the "system," bewailed the corruption of American society, the power of the state, and the brainwashing at the hands of the mass media. Antiwar protestors, enraged by the escalations in Vietnam, borrowed direct-action techniques from the civil rights movement. And then came the inexorable slide of the hip counterculture toward Haight Ashbury. As he was going to trial for inciting violence at the 1968 Democratic National Convention, Abbie Hoffman published his book *Woodstock Nation* (1969), in which the Yippie leader summed up the anarchic style of radicalism he had come to personify:

> When I appear in the Chicago courtroom, I want to be tried not because I
> support the National Liberation Front of Vietnam—which I do—but
> because I have long hair. Not because I support the Black Liberation

Movement, but because I smoke dope. Not because I am against the capitalist system, but because I think property eats shit. Not because I believe in student power, but that the schools should be destroyed. Not because I'm against corporate liberalism, but because I think people should do whatever the fuck they want, and not because I'm trying to organize the working class, but because I think kids should kill their parents.

As the decade deepened, Norman Podhoretz and the *Commentary* Family grew to resent the new generation of alienated youth. Although the magazine had anticipated their arrival,[1] Podhoretz, now in his late thirties, began to disdain the student radicals for what he regarded as their infantile ideas and hipster boorishness, their fantasies of revolution, and their self-indulgence. He did not admire the Age of Aquarius. Ambition for success was one thing, the author of *Making It* felt. Something very different was a culture that, as he said, "treated the pursuit of individual fulfillment as an absolute . . . and which is very nearly incapable of conceiving anything worth fighting, let alone dying, for."

In the late 1960s, this man in a respectable marriage objected to what appeared to his eyes as an emphasis on self-fulfillment and spontaneous personal expression among the new peddlers of Nirvana, a preoccupation with sexual perversity, a rejection of bourgeois conventions and restraint—everything his teacher Lionel Trilling had identified as the "adversary culture." "The refusal to be bound by rules, any rules," Podhoretz's wife, Midge Decter, said, "turned children against their elders, impelled them to don rags and roam the country simulating poverty, destroy their brains with drugs, burn books, and rage against the very idea of responsibility, social, intellectual, or personal."

Podhoretz's fury was not altogether new. A decade earlier, in *Partisan Review*, he had rehearsed for the full-dress battle to come with a scathing attack on Jack Kerouac and Allen Ginsberg and the howling Beat poets who had appropriated the theme of alienation. The brash young critic was already then known to pull out all the stops. Joseph Epstein said that Podhoretz practiced an "emperor has no scrotum" style of criticism. It wasn't enough to reveal why the Beats were literarily misguided, for example; Podhoretz chose to denounce them as "hostile to civilization." The "Know-Nothing Bohemians," as Podhoretz dubbed them, were "spiritually underprivileged"; they were "young men who can't think straight and so hate anyone who can." Their worship of instinct and spontaneity acted as "a cover for hostility to intelligence." There was something ridiculous, Podhoretz felt, in these "young men who can't get outside the morass of self."[2]

Podhoretz's by-now ex-friend Allen Ginsberg (they had both studied under Trilling at Columbia in the 1940s) took the attack hard. A little more than a year afterward, at a party at Norman Mailer's place on West 94th, Ginsberg's anger burst its dam. "You big dumb fuckhead!" the self-described "Buddhist Jewish pantheist" screamed at Podhoretz. "You idiot! You don't know anything about anything!" "I realized early," Ginsberg said years later to an interviewer, "that if they were going to do that to us who were relatively innocent—just a bunch of poets—if they were going to make us out to be monsters, then they must have been making the whole universe out to be a monster all along, like from the Communists to the radicals to the anarchists to the Human Being in America." And yet Ginsberg still thought of Podhoretz as "a sort of sacred presence in my life." "If he weren't there like a wall I can butt my head against, I wouldn't have anybody to hate."

The encounter made a lasting impression on Podhoretz, too. "In that period of my life," he would write in his second memoir, *Breaking Ranks* (1979), "there was nothing that appealed to me less than the idea of refusing to grow up and settle down—which . . . was what Kerouac and Ginsberg and their friends stood for—and nothing that I wanted more than to take my rightful place as an adult among other adults." Nor, for Podhoretz, was Ginsberg's style of homosexuality a mark in his favor. "Ginsberg was also fulsomely praised as a pioneer of the gay-rights movement, which indeed he was," Podhoretz later recollected in *Ex-Friends* (1999). "Yet so far as I have been able to determine, no one thought to draw a connection between the emergence of AIDS and the rampant homosexual promiscuity promoted by Ginsberg (with buggery as an especially 'joyful' feature that is described in loving detail in poem after pornographic—yes, pornographic—poem)."[3]

A decade after these events, Podhoretz was struck with fresh horror by the dissipations of the New Left, which appeared in his eyes as a frivolous rebellion without a cause. Unlike the old leftists of the 1930s, members of the New Left of the 1960s, who had little connection with the working class, did not invest much faith in the working class as an agent of social change. The labor movement was now thought to be, as the Port Huron Statement put it, "too acquiescent." And the New Left, though united in antagonism to "the Establishment" and "the military-industrial complex," lacked the coherence the old Left had enjoyed by dint of its allegiance to the Communist Party. Podhoretz deplored what he felt were the growing authoritarianism and clenched anger of the student *enragés*, their unearned self-regard, their shrillness and obscenity. He looked with exasperation at the New Left, in which he saw a hunger for simplicity, a crude opposition to the system, a puerile glorification of violence as a creative act, a romanticization of Third World authoritarians—Gamal Abdel Nasser and Fidel Castro, Chairman Mao Zedong and Uncle Ho Chi Minh.[4] In 1969 *Commentary* announced that the Movement, as the decade's amalgamation of radicals was then called, "missed the opportunity to become a powerful agent of regeneration." "The Movement has no future within politics," the magazine concluded the following year.

The new radicals' strong-arm tactics, moreover—invading classrooms, shouting down speakers—smacked to the Family of 1930s-style Stalinism. By 1970, the magazine was calling the Black Panthers "totalitarian." In Nathan Glazer's classic *Commentary* essay from that year, "On Being Deradicalized" (the Family took to calling it "The Confessions of Nat Glazer"), the former assistant editor and now professor in the Graduate School of Education at Harvard attributed his move from mild radicalism to mild conservatism to the discovery that the radicalism of the late 1960s belonged "squarely in the succession to the simple-minded, grotesque, freedom-denying radicalism of the Leninists and Stalinists of the 1930s." In Glazer's view, the new irrationalists had merely replaced capitalism, the enemy of the 1930s, with imperialism, and the working class with the Third World.

In 1967, Neal Kozodoy, the newest member of *Commentary*'s staff, gave a talk on youth culture to a meeting of the National Conference of Jewish Communal Service in Atlantic City. A year earlier, Podhoretz had persuaded Kozodoy, twenty-four, to leave his graduate studies at Columbia, where in his master's paper he had trained his eye on the love poetry of medieval Hebrew poet Moshe Ibn Ezra, and to replace Ted Solotaroff as assistant editor. (Solotaroff left to edit *Book Week*, the Sunday book supplement of the *New York Herald Tribune*, and then to start the *New American Review*.)[5] Kozodoy had grown up in Chestnut Hill, Massachusetts, a western suburb of Boston, where his father was head of the math department at Boston Latin, one of the finest prep schools in the country. Neal, like his father, was a graduate of the school. When Kozodoy stumbled upon *Commentary* at age seventeen or eighteen, he was stunned by its rigorous writing about the full sweep of Jewish experience. "I couldn't believe my eyes," he recalled. At Harvard, Kozodoy coedited (with Josiah Lee Auspitz) a Jewish journal called *Mosaic*. This came to the attention of Norman Podhoretz, who called it "the most brilliant undergraduate publication I'd ever seen" and promptly hired Kozodoy. That decision, Podhoretz said in retrospect, "was the most consequential thing I had ever done or ever would do in my entire professional life." (Kozodoy joined as assistant editor, became associate editor in late 1967, and rose to executive editor late the next year.)

On that day in Atlantic City, *Commentary*'s new assistant editor was hardly impressed by his peers: "I am not at all sure that young people, in the long run, will have been rendered a service by being pandered to so lavishly, by being asked at every turn to speak up, say what they think, tell how they react, put forward their own suggestions," Kozodoy said. "They are not all of them serious, certainly not all of them charitable, and when they find their elders so eager to capitulate, it is little wonder that they in turn do not always act responsibly."[6]

Nor could *Commentary* countenance the assault of the late 1960s on universities as instruments of the ruling class. Many of the new radicals had come to see the very idea of intellectual standards as an instrument of repression. They regarded the very act of interpretation as reactionary; they denounced it, in Susan Sontag's phrase, as "the revenge of the intellect upon art." (It's no coincidence, as they used to say, that unlike the 1930s, the 1960s did not produce much in the way of a body of radical literature.) The Family veterans of the 1950s age of criticism, naturally, could not look with favor on the new distrust of the critical intellect. They could not but grow contemptuous of what Midge Decter called "both the heedless and mindless leftist politics, and intellectual and artistic nihilism of fashionable literary-intellectual society." Refusing to be swept aside by the new radicals and wishing to conserve standards (aesthetic, moral, and cultural), ex-radicals bemoaned the Movement's contempt for the past, for authority, and for the Western tradition itself.

In the midst of this revolt against authority, the Family awakened to the realization that it had institutions such as universities to protect. Diana Trilling sent Podhoretz a 28,000-word report on the student takeover of Columbia in 1968. In it she cited a letter SDS leader Mark Rudd had sent to the university's president: "We will destroy your world, your corporation, your University." Trilling and the rest of the *Commentary* crowd felt stunned by what they regarded as the craven liberal capitulation on the part of liberal professors and other "apologists" who ingratiated themselves with the students.[7] They were shocked, that is, by the unwillingness of liberals to defend liberal values.

If at first the Family rushed to the defense of universities, its magazine soon came to defend America itself. In essay after essay, *Commentary* greeted with boos and hisses the prevalent notion that America had gone mad. The *Commentary* crowd, with its alienated days behind it, could not abide what it regarded as the New Left's bitter anti-Americanism, the New Left's feeling that what used to be the land of opportunity was now irredeemably racist and imperialist and fundamentally sick, the Movement's habit of blaming all ills on what some campus radicals had contemptuously taken to calling "Amerikan" society.

THE PAROCHIALISM OF UNIVERSALISM

Podhoretz's revulsion against anti-Americanism—within the Woodstock Nation and elsewhere—came first. But he also reacted to the radical Left as a Jew who wished to persuade his fellow intellectuals and fellow Jews alike "that radicalism was their enemy, and not their friend." He harbored a dual fear, in other words, of the illiberal fits of the counterculture. He identified a threat from the Movement not only to intellectual and democratic principles, but also to Jewish interests.

Along with many others, Podhoretz's Jewish awareness had been stoked at the beginning of the decade by the trial in Jerusalem of Adolf Eichmann, the SS lieutenant colonel who, as chief of the Gestapo's Jewish Office, had helped implement the Final Solution. *Commentary* in 1961 ran superb reports by Elie Wiesel and Harold Rosenberg on the trial.[8] But these were overshadowed by another account. In *Eichmann in Jerusalem* (1963), based on a five-part series for the *New Yorker*, Hannah Arendt, calling the proceedings a "show trial," scorned the Israeli prosecutor, Gideon Hausner, and portrayed the former high-level Nazi in the dock not as a rabid anti-Semite but as a thoughtless, banal bureaucrat—a mediocrity.

It wasn't Arendt's views on the "banality of evil" that ruffled feathers. *Commentary* had itself reported years earlier that Auschwitz commandant Rudolf Höss's appearance at the Nuremberg trials was that of "an unimaginative technocrat of genocide." No, what offended was Arendt's claim that "to a truly extraordinary degree," the Nazis had received Jewish cooperation in carrying out their genocidal plans. "Wherever Jews lived," Arendt noted, "there were recognized Jewish leaders, and this leadership, almost without exception, cooperated in one way or another for one reason or another with the Nazis." Without such cooperation, she claimed, there would have been much misery, but the number of Jewish victims would hardly have been as high as it was.[9]

"The idea of making the century's great crime look dull is not banal," Saul Bellow's character Sammler, a Holocaust survivor, says (*Mr. Sammler's Planet*, 1970), and Norman Podhoretz was inclined to agree. He had considered Arendt a friend and teacher. (Although in a letter to Mary

McCarthy, Arendt rather condescendingly referred to Podhoretz as "one of those bright youngsters with bright hopes for a nice career.") He had been invited to her roomy flat on Riverside Drive for her famous New Year's parties. In his early twenties, he had been moved by her volume *The Origins of Totalitarianism* (1951). "Reading it threw me into so fevered a condition of intellectual exhilaration that I had to keep putting it down every few pages in order to regain the composure to go on," he said. When her theoretical treatise *The Human Condition* came out in 1958, he sent Arendt a mash note: "I can hardly contain my excitement over it. The book is superb, fully equal to the astonishing daring of what it undertakes, a major work in every respect."

But now, in a particularly impassioned essay in *Commentary* (September 1963), Podhoretz took Arendt—a writer "bent on generating dazzle," he said—as an example of "the perversity of brilliance." "[In] place of the monstrous Nazi, she gives us the 'banal' Nazi; in place of the Jew as virtuous martyr, she gives us the Jew as accomplice in evil; and in place of the confrontation between guilt and innocence, she gives us the 'collaboration' of criminal and victim." Podhoretz went on to accuse his soon-to-be-ex-friend of judging the Jews by a higher standard than other victims of totalitarian murder: "The Nazis destroyed a third of the Jewish people. In the name of all that is humane, will the remnant never let up on itself?"[10]

This was a bold stroke, and in response Arendt invited Podhoretz up to her apartment. For several hours, with his *Commentary* essay in hand, the philosopher challenged him point by point. But before showing him out, she could not help expressing her suspicions about his motives. "Let me ask you a question before you go," she said. "Why did you do it?"

Podhoretz replied that he had written his article "reluctantly, out of a sense of duty."

"You're lying, of course," Arendt said, "but it was foolish of me to expect that you would be man enough to tell me the truth." She suspected he had been only too pleased to score rhetorical points at her expense.

As Arendt knew, however, Podhoretz's essay was far from alone in its outrage. In the magazine's next issue, Irving Howe—who in his memoir *A Margin of Hope* (1982) remembered how he had recoiled from "the surging contempt with which she treated almost everyone and everything associated with the trial"—worried aloud that Arendt's reports "reached a mass audience almost certainly unequipped to judge them critically." Werner Dannhauser, just about to join the *Commentary* staff, thought that like nearly all of Arendt's work, the Eichmann book was characterized by "a will to overstatement." Alfred Kazin called its thesis "appalling German intellectual swank." Jerusalem sage Gershom Scholem accused Arendt of heartlessness, of insufficient "love of the Jewish people." Philip Rahv of *Partisan Review* told Podhoretz, "I think the *goyim* will be delighted to discover that the millions of Jews the Nazis murdered are at least partly responsible for their own deaths."

Whatever else the Arendt controversy accomplished, however, within some breasts it tapped hitherto uncharted reservoirs of Jewish feeling. "Unwittingly," Howe said, "it served a great purpose. The book was like a therapeutic session where you discover that, welling up within you, there is a great mass of feeling that you had not known."

NOT THAT PODHORETZ'S *Commentary* had neglected Jewish affairs during the tumultuous decade. He ran, for example, Norman Mailer's six-part series on Martin Buber's interpretations of Hasidic folklore, in preparation for which Mailer had Podhoretz take him to a Yom Kippur service at the Lubavitch shul at 770 Eastern Parkway in Crown Heights, Brooklyn. In the December 1962 issue, Mailer introduced his freestyle commentary on Buber's classic book *Tales of the Hasidim* (1948) on a characteristically personal note:

> Seven years ago, riding the electric rail of long nights on marijuana, I used to dip into *The Early Masters* and *The Later Masters* [the two volumes of *Tales of the Hasidim*] and find some peculiar consolation—these pieces were the first bits of Jewish devotional prose I read which were not deadening to me. . . . I had, of course, grown up in Brooklyn, my parents were modestly Orthodox, then Conservative. I went to a Hebrew School. The *melamed* [teacher] had yellow skin, yellow as atabrine. I passed through the existential rite of a Bar Mitzvah. I was a Jew out of loyalty to the underdog. I would never say I was not a Jew, but I looked to take no strength from the fact. What Hebrew I learned was set out to atrophy. I left what part of me belonged to Brooklyn and the Jews on the streets of Crown Heights. In college, it came over me like a poor man's rich fever that I had less connection to the past than anyone I knew. . . . But I have a debt to Buber. I have a fondness for the Hasidim. There was a recognition those seven or eight years ago that if I had nothing else in my mind or desire which belonged to Jewish culture, that if I were some sort of dispossessed American, dispossessed even of category, still I had, I had at least, a rudimentary sense of clan across the centuries . . . like an orphan discovering that in fact he has a beautiful mother.

Podhoretz meanwhile covered Jewish thought in more conventional ways too. In 1966, with the doctrinal reforms of Vatican II still fresh, he put together a groundbreaking *Commentary* symposium on "The State of Jewish Belief," designed to address not Jewishness, but Judaism per se. Thirty-eight rabbis and theologians responded—Orthodox (including Eliezer Berkovits, Norman Lamm, Aharon Lichtenstein, and Emanuel Rackman), Conservative (Arthur Hertzberg), Reform (Emil Fackenheim and Eugene Borowitz), Reconstructionist (Mordecai M. Kaplan), and neo-Hasidic (Zalman Schachter).[11] The editor's questions, which touched on divine revelation, chosenness, and the political dimensions of Jewish belief, left two matters conspicuously absent: They did not give even passing mention to the Holocaust, nor, less than a year before the Six-Day War, did they inquire about the religious significance of Israel.[12]

Then there was a series of *Commentary* essays in which Robert (Uri) Alter broke through the rigid barrier that had until then separated biblical from literary criticism.[13] "I never imagined I was launching a school or trend," Alter said, but that is precisely what he set about doing. A Bronx-born son of Romanian Jewish immigrants, Alter had studied with Lionel Trilling, who had introduced him to Podhoretz in 1957. Alter began contributing to *Commentary* when he was twenty-six with a piece, his first in English, singing the praises of S. Y. Agnon. (This was in 1961, when almost nothing had been written in English on the Israeli writer who five years later would be awarded the Nobel Prize. In the first six years of Podhoretz's editorship, six of Agnon's stories appeared for the first time in English in *Commentary*'s pages.)[14] But what touched Alter most vitally and animated his breakthrough *Commentary* essays was the attempt to forge an American Jewish way of reading the Bible. If other critics regarded the novel as a bible, Alter wished to read the Bible as a novel—to attend to its narrative art, character, motive, and imaginative subtlety. If the biblical authors, as he contended, "were among the pioneers of prose fiction in the Western tradition," then we should read the biblical narratives not as sacred history but as prose fiction, as products of a literary artistry that employed wordplay, reiteration, intricate patternings, modulations, and shifts of perspective. To come into contact with the religious power of scripture, a force that expressed itself by means of poetry and parable, we would profit from heeding the literary instruments of the text's address rather than questions of authorship or historical and philological background.

Writing for *Commentary*, Alter later said, was "an education for me as a writer." It gave him his ideal audience. So much did he feel in tune—at least for a while—with the magazine's editorial line that he was made a contributing editor.[15] One of his early *Commentary* essays, "Teaching Jewish Teachers" (July 1968), in fact, shed light on how the Family clarified its identity in the present by confronting the Jewish past:

> An intellectual would hardly think of talking about political theory without ever having read a word of Machiavelli, Hobbes, Burke, or Marx. . . . If a Jewish intellectual insists on the Jewish component of his intellectual identity (of course he is free not to), he at least ought to feel a suspicion of incongruity in the fact that has never read a word of Maimonides, that he wouldn't know a *sugia* in the Talmud from a *sura* in the Koran, that Akiba and Rashi, Judah Halevi and Bialik, are no more than names in an encyclopedia to him. . . . If one knows almost nothing about the Jewish past, one is at liberty to invoke it in mawkish adulation—the "soaring universalism of the prophets," the "touching piety of the *shtetl*"—or in arrogant hostility— the "obscurantist fanaticism of the Talmud."

With his help, the magazine would from now on delight in exposing what Alter called "the parochialism of Jewish universalism."

For a second contributing editor, Podhoretz recruited Milton Himmelfarb (City College 1938), Irving Kristol's brother-in-law, a researcher at the American Jewish Committee, and a man with such a matchless understanding of American Jews that in short order he became, as Werner Dannhauser said, the conscience of *Commentary*. Himmelfarb's subtle *Commentary* essays on Jews and Judaism—he would in time contribute more than eighty—ranged from an analysis of intermarriage to a brilliant introduction to political philosopher Leo Strauss to an impassioned argument that without Adolf Hitler, German anti-Semitism alone could not have resulted in the Final Solution.[16] His pieces were distinguished by the graceful way they carried his learning and their pithy witticisms. Noting the discrepancy between Jewish politics and Jewish pocketbooks, for example, Himmelfarb commented in the March 1969 *Commentary* that American Jews earned like Episcopalians and voted like Puerto Ricans.[17] Like Alter, Himmelfarb's polemical instincts were most strongly engaged when he got to talking about the Jews' xenophilia, the tendency to become so busy serving others' causes that they neglected their own. "Jewish students will occupy a university building," he remarked about the campus unrest in the late 1960s, "or approve its occupation, to support the demands of blacks, but not to prevent or abolish quotas that will hurt Jews." One fact by now obvious to

Himmelfarb, as to the rest of the Family, was that the country deserved the admiration of the Jews. In America, he wrote, "Jews may decide for themselves how Jewish they want to be, and when; and that is why they respond with gratitude and devotion."

AUNTIE SEMITISM

The young radicals of the 1960s, keenly aware of the ways politics was bound up with social class, were nothing if not antitraditional and anti–middle class; and American Jews—teachers, lawyers, doctors, social workers—were by the 1960s nothing if not traditional and middle class. "All the roles that Jews play are roles that the New Left disapproves of," Nathan Glazer remarked in *Commentary*. The radicals, moreover, were lacking in piety toward the past. The New Left, said Irving Howe, "cares nothing for the haunted memories of old Jews. . . . It is bored with the past: for the past is a fink."

The first signal that postwar taboos on anti-Semitism on the Left had ebbed was sent by African Americans. *Commentary*'s clear-eyed attention to black-Jewish relations began two decades earlier with an arresting piece by James Baldwin in February 1948. "Jews in Harlem are small tradesmen, rent collectors, real estate agents, and pawnbrokers," Baldwin wrote.

> They operate in accordance with the American business tradition of exploiting Negroes, and they are therefore identified with oppression and are hated for it. I remember no Negro in the years of my growing up, in my family or out of it, who would really ever trust a Jew, and few who did not, indeed, exhibit for them the blackest contempt. On the other hand, this did not prevent their working for Jews, being utterly civil and pleasant to them, and, in most cases, contriving to delude their employers into believing that, far from harboring any dislike for Jews, they would rather work for a Jew than for anyone else. . . . But just as society must have a scapegoat, so hatred must have a symbol. Georgia has the Negro and Harlem has the Jew.

Nathan Glazer had reported in the December 1964 issue ("Negroes and Jews: The New Challenge to Pluralism") on the ways the common black-Jewish efforts on fairness in employment, housing, and education were descending into a "well of ill-feeling." By challenging merit-based college admissions, he said, blacks defied the very system that had enabled Jews to succeed. But in the latter half of the 1960s—as blacks increasingly believed that neither judicial victories like the 1954 school desegregation decision nor legislative victories that mandated legal equality (the Civil Rights Act of 1964, the Voting Right Act of 1965) were enough to bring about real equality—Norman Podhoretz noticed with dismay a darkening tone. In a March 1967 piece for *Harper's*, Ralph Ellison, author of *Invisible Man* (1952) (who had three years earlier written an essay for *Commentary* called "On Becoming a Writer"), charged "some of the *Commentary* writers" with serving as "apologists for segregation." Podhoretz was appalled: "I think you owe both the magazine and its contributors an apology for this irresponsible and false accusation," he wrote in a letter to Ellison. Other blacks began to talk of the "Jewish establishment" keeping down black students. The fifty-seven-day New York City teachers' strike of 1968, extensively covered in *Commentary*, pitted the black demand for decentralized "community control" against the largely Jewish teachers union. In the uproar that followed, a black activist at the African-American Teachers Forum charged that Jewish teachers had "educationally castrated" black students.

So closely had Jews been associated with the civil rights achievements of the 1950s that angry white southerners had not infrequently vented their frustrations as much on Jews as on blacks. Less than a month after the Supreme Court struck down segregation in public schools in May 1954, for example, a white publication called the *American Nationalist* ran the headline "South Indignant as Jew-Led NAACP Wins School Segregation Case." In Mississippi, Rabbi Arthur Lelyveld had been beaten in Hattiesburg for organizing voter registration drives, and civil rights activist Rabbi Perry Nussbaum had his synagogue and his house bombed in Jackson.

But starting a decade later, it no longer seemed to matter much to a new generation of black leaders—Stokely Carmichael, Malcolm X, Eldridge Cleaver, and LeRoi Jones—that Jewish pursuers of justice had helped found the National Association for the Advancement of Colored People and the National Urban League; that they had thickened the ranks of civil rights attorneys and freedom riders; that Jewish activists Andrew Goodman and Michael Schwerner had been murdered in 1964 together with their black Freedom Summer coworker; that Rabbi Joachim Prinz, formerly a rabbi in Nazi-era Berlin, had spoken movingly at the 1963 March on Washington he helped organize; or that Abraham Joshua Heschel had linked arms with Martin Luther King in the 1965 march through Selma, Alabama.[18] Now, in *The Autobiography of Malcolm X* (1965), the activist formerly known as

Malcolm Little relayed his realization "that so many Jews actually were hypocrites in their claim to be friends of the American black man."

The Jewish backlash against such hurtful developments was expected, widespread, and sometimes criticized as excessive. As the January 31, 1969, *Time* magazine cover story put it, "In light of Judaism's centuries-long experience of persecution, it is not surprising that some of the reactions to anti-Jewish statements made by black leaders have verged on hysteria." Some American Jews urged patience. "It will not hurt us Jews to swallow a few insults from overwrought blacks," left-wing journalist I. F. Stone said. But with increasing pace after the murder of Martin Luther King Jr. in April 1968, the Family was forced into the recognition that what had been a common American march for justice and civil rights was fast becoming a struggle for black power, and that the struggle for integration was fast becoming an insistence on separatism.[19] "Many Jews suffered traumatic shock," sociologist Earl Raab observed in *Commentary* in 1969, "when the Negroes detached themselves from the marching army and said, 'Wait a minute, we've got a different interest here, a different drummer and a different pace.'"

VILIFICATIONS AND SCHLEMIELS

The second signal of the potential for a resurgent anti-Semitism was broadcast loud and clear in the form of a new virulence toward Israel after the Six-Day War in the summer of 1967. In mid-May 1967, Egypt's president Gamal Abdel Nasser expelled the United Nations peacekeeping force from the Sinai, amassed his troops on the Israeli border (eighty thousand soldiers and nine hundred tanks), choked off the Straits of Tiran, and threatened to drive Israel's Jews into the sea. "Our basic aim is the destruction of Israel," Nasser declared on May 26. Cairo Radio announced, "The battle has come in which we shall destroy Israel." Syrian artillery on the Golan Heights shelled kibbutzim, and Jordan's King Hussein put his army, reinforced by Iraqi troops, at the disposal of the Egyptian command.

The most immediate effect of the anxiety this caused to American Jews—when it seemed that Israel might very well be overwhelmed by the Soviet-equipped Arab armies—proved to be an intense outpouring of feeling and new depths of Jewish solidarity. American Jews made unprecedented contributions of both money and manpower. Some 10,000 applications came in by the first day of the war from young American Jews volunteering to go to Israel. The Israel Emergency Fund of the United

Jewish Appeal raised $100 million in three weeks. Israel Bonds raised $190 million in 1967, up from $76 million the year before.

In the event, Israel's stunning victory over four armies left the Sinai, the West Bank, the Golan Heights, and all of Jerusalem—including the Old City and the Western Wall—in Israeli hands. Anxiety turned into ebullient pride. The American percentage of annual immigration to Israel rose from about 1 percent in the years between 1948 and 1967 to almost 20 percent in 1971 (or about 10,000 immigrants a year). Jewish tourism and United Jewish Appeal "missions" from North America boomed—a new pilgrimage. American Jews worshipped the charismatic Moshe Dayan, commander during Israel's War of Independence in 1948, chief of staff of the Israel Defense Forces during the Sinai campaign in 1956, and minister of defense during the Six-Day War. American Jewish anti-Zionism, which had been deteriorating since 1948, was dead.

Like most American Jews, the Family relished Israel's triumph. This was a regeneration, and the Family, too, shared in the sense of solidarity. The prospect of another annihilation of Jews brought home the value of a state. "We relearned the old truth that you can depend only on yourself," Milton Himmelfarb said. Alfred Kazin reported in his journal that when he thought of "the touching faith of the Jews in redemption, their only redemption, through Israel, I feel an inexpressible pride in our ability to live, to fight it through, to *live*." "Jews all over the world walk with greater pride upon the face of the earth because of the state of Israel," associate editor Werner Dannhauser said just after the war. "The Israelis have simply showed us all that Jews need not always be powerless before the murderous intentions of their enemies," Podhoretz wrote to Erich Fromm, "and it is this rather than any stirring of militarist or chauvinist fervor, that has moved so many Jews outside Israel."

At the same time, black anger found in Israel a convenient target. An ad for the International Committee to Support Eldridge Cleaver—signed, among others, by Allen Ginsberg, Norman Mailer, Susan Sontag, and Noam Chomsky—happened to appear in the same issue of the *Black Panther* that praised Palestinian Fatah militants for knowing "only the gun as the sole means to achieve victory." "Palestine Guerrillas versus Israeli Pigs" read a headline in that paper. ("Muslim Arabs are systematically murdering black people in Sudan," Milton Himmelfarb said, "and Israel is supposed to be the enemy of blacks.") The Black Caucus voted to condemn "the imperialistic Zionist war." Israel came to be seen as a new apartheid regime—or worse.

Black militants held no monopoly on such rhetoric. To many in the New Left, the Six-Day War came to appear not as a war of self-defense, but as a clash between white men and dark men, between the tool of a superpower and its innocent, Third World victims.[20] Tom Hayden of SDS spoke of Jewish fascists. A Student Non-Violent Coordinating Committee newsletter compared the Gaza Strip with Dachau and charged that "Zionists lined up Arab victims and shot them in the back in cold blood." Many in the Movement began to see Israel as a beachhead of Western imperialism, an outpost of bellicosity and chauvinism, an intransigent American protectorate embodying all the sins imputed to the West. The Soviets had demonized Israel in similar terms, but this was the first time such charges sprouted from American soil.

The moral burden had shifted, as had the scales of sympathy. The country that had been regarded as an exemplary laboratory for socialism, a refuge for Holocaust survivors, was losing what luster it had enjoyed on the Left. What had been deemed a brave Eden was now seen as tainted with racism and militarism. Zionists who had revolted against an occupying British colonial power now stood accused themselves of colonialist occupation. In the eyes of the Movement, the kibbutznik now became the colonizer, the victim became the villain, David became Goliath, the Palestinian—at the mercy of the merciless Israeli soldier—became the new Jew. Palestinian nationalism good, Israeli nationalism bad. Before 1967, Palestinians had lived in the shadows of Arab states. After the war, it no longer seemed a question of twenty Arab states bent on Israel's annihilation, but of a Palestinian minority fighting a powerful oppressor for a national homeland. The liberal conscience had found a new cause.

This troubled Podhoretz and his cohorts. It wasn't that they were averse to criticisms of the Jewish state. Before the Six-Day War, *Commentary*'s pages still occasionally echoed with some of the old discomfort with Zionism. In a 1961 symposium, *Village Voice* columnist Nat Hentoff had referred to "the proliferation in microcosm in Israel of the chronic, aggressive insecurities of all nation-states."[21] Jason Epstein had compared Israel with Disneyland, "too much a creature of will and not enough the result of long, slow, organic history." George Steiner took to *Commentary* in 1965 to pronounce the nation-state "alien to some of the most radical, most humane elements in the Jewish spirit."[22]

The Family retained worries about the Jewish state after the war, too. In the late 1960s, *Commentary*'s writers in Israel, leftist intellectuals such as

Amos Elon and Shlomo Avineri, reported critically on Israel's occupation of the West Bank.[23] In the August 1967 issue, German-born historian Walter Laqueur, who would write seventy pieces for *Commentary*, fretted that Israel had planned better for war than for peace. Laqueur wondered whether the conquered territories were worth holding, given that administering them would be "bound to create nightmarish problems." The next year, Israeli historian Jacob Talmon told *Commentary* readers that victory might be harder to bear than defeat: "For an Israel which lost its old bearings—Jewish, liberal, and idealistic—would become repulsively similar to the arch persecutors of the Jews. It would alienate diaspora Jews . . . and it would forfeit the sympathetic attention and anxious good will of that part of world public opinion which has been a source of strength to the state." At a time when almost no one else did so, Israeli political scientist Shlomo Avineri called in the June 1970 issue for Israeli peace talks with Palestinians—even with Yasser Arafat—about the creation of a Palestinian state on the West Bank and in Gaza. Five years later, historian Ted Draper urged compliance with UN Resolution 242's demands that the West Bank be returned to the Arabs: "Jews should not rule over land inhabited so massively by Arabs," he wrote. "It is bad for the Jews and bad for the Arabs."[24]

But not long after the Six-Day War, the Family grew less able to abide the political anorexia from which some Jews suffered, the will to cease to exist as a body. The Family's response to the war boosted a new comfort with particularism; on the whole, the wisps of early coolness toward Zionism gave way to a heated defense of it as a movement of self-liberation. In the October 1967 issue, Robert Alter wondered at Jews eager to perform a "self-abasing mental backbend" to take up the Arab side. (Frequent *Commentary* contributor Ruth Wisse, who had written a dissertation on the schlemiel as modern hero, later called this defeatist posture "the schlemiel inheritance.") A year after the war, theologian Emil Fackenheim, a survivor of the Sachsenhausen concentration camp, formulated in *Commentary* what would become his best-known idea: that the simplest, most fundamental lesson of the Holocaust was survival. The Torah had decreed 613 commandments, and now a "commanding Voice," he said, had issued a 614th: "*Jews are forbidden to grant posthumous victories to Hitler.* They are commanded to survive as Jews, lest the Jewish people perish. . . . They are forbidden to despair of the God of Israel, lest Judaism perish."

After the 1967 war, no longer believing that all enemies of the Jews attacked from the Right, Podhoretz began fiercely to defend Israel against those on the Left who accused Israel of tribalism, of less than noble exercises of Jewish power, and of imperiling of Jewish spirituality. Now that his enemies began to connect anti-Zionism with anti-Semitism, the editor began to wonder at double standards. He questioned how those on the Left who remained so blasé when it came to brutalities in the Communist countries could demand from Israel something approaching moral perfection. He wondered why Israel's exercise of self-determination and self-defense alone invited charges of imperialism and aggression. "Of all the millions of square miles of territory conquered through aggression by various nations since 1945 alone," Podhoretz wrote, "only those taken by Israel in a war of self-defense were expected to be returned."

By now, the *Commentary* crowd's patience had worn thin for those universalists who avoided allegiance to any nation-state. To those who claimed that Israel endangered Jewish lives, *Commentary* pointed out that more Jews perished at the hands of the Nazis in a single day at Babi Yar—the ravine near Kiev where 33,771 Jews were machine-gunned to death in September 1941—than during all the Arab-Israeli wars and Palestinian terrorist attacks combined. To those who complained that Israel was an artificial state, the Family's members questioned whether those who leveled this charge about a country whose people had a distinctive consciousness thousands of years old would be inclined to say the same of Algeria, even though Algerian consciousness was about as new as the borders drawn by French colonialists. And to those who thought the prospects for Mideast peace rested primarily on Israeli shoulders, Robert Alter countered in the magazine that the Arab position on Israel "has been blind, fanatic, self-deceptive, self-destructive, harshly inflexible, and in many respects morally obscene."

The great nineteenth-century Lithuanian rabbi and moralist Israel Salanter once said, "My neighbor's material needs are my spiritual needs." So it was that the material security of Israel—as the locus of Jewish survival—came to play a central role in American Jewishness. As for the *Commentary* clan, the turn toward Israel coincided with the first taste of rejection at the hands of those regarded until now as allies.

A CLASS FOR ITSELF

By the end of the 1960s, Norman Podhoretz came to believe that the attacks on Israel and the Jews from the Left had punctured the illusion that anti-Semitism, tainted for two decades by association with Hitler's atrocities, had been permanently weeded out of American soil. "The anti-Semitism of the Left has moved in recent years out of the foul-smelling catacombs of the radical tradition and into the common light of day," he said in 1972. "On the radical Left—despite the fact but also of course because of the fact that so many of its members are Jews—the hostility to Israel often spills over in to a hostility to Jews, just as the hatred of middle-class values often spills over into the hatred of Jews."

Jews had traditionally identified the Left—which in Europe had favored Jewish emancipation, enfranchisement, and religious tolerance—with forces of enlightenment, and the Right with forces of bigotry. American Jews' close association with liberalism, after all, had not come from nowhere. Podhoretz, however, had begun to suspect that political utopianism had become more characteristic of the Left than of the Right. Now he saw that hostility to Israel and the Jews could be far more virulent on the far Left than on the ideological Right. His former comrades on the Left thought themselves aligned with human progress; Podhoretz saw them instead as in league with the worst forces of reaction.

The dual attack—from anti-Zionists and from militant blacks— signaled to the Family the collapse of the liberal coalition. Until now, that coalition had held firm to the principle that public policy ought to recognize not group interests but individual rights. "There are no minorities in the United States," Woodrow Wilson had insisted. "The whole concept and basis of the United States excludes them." "You cannot become true Americans," Dorothy Thompson had admonished *Commentary* readers in 1950, "if you think of yourselves in groups."

The vocabulary of status groups dated back to the 1950s, to Richard Hofstadter and Daniel Bell. Indeed, the identification of politics and interest represented a recovery of an old theme, an elaboration of the idea of politics Podhoretz had held since he was young. He could never suffer someone who was reluctant to admit he had interests from which his politics derived. "The very existence of politics," he had opined as a twenty-seven-year-old assistant editor, "depends on a willingness to acknowledge the legitimacy and indeed the necessity of selfish interests in society. . . . What act could be less in need of justification than defending and preserving oneself?"[25]

But only in the late 1960s and early 1970s, in the age of "identity politics," did the *Commentary* crowd acquire—and begin explicitly to defend— the politics of interest. In a February 1972 *Commentary* piece called "Is It Good for the Jews?" Podhoretz explained why Jews ought to look "at proposals and policies from the point of view of the Jewish interest." Those who remembered their Karl Marx might have recalled the distinction between a "class *in* itself," which merely exists, and a "class *for* itself," which self-consciously fights for its own interests. The Family now chose to cast the Jews as a class *for* itself, to see both the American majority and minorities in terms of competing groups. The very term "WASP," Podhoretz said, showed that "white Americans of Anglo-Saxon Protestant background are an ethnic group like any other." The magazine's new tone involved a renewed defense of Jewish particularism. "Any Jew who achieves some sense of solidarity with the Jewish people as a whole," Robert Alter wrote in the February 1969 *Commentary*, "has begun an exercise in the moral imagination of humanity by first identifying with this particular part of it."

This was the moment that *Commentary* introduced what would be a not-so-fugitive theme, a leitmotif of the decades to come: What is bad for the Jews is bad for America and the West itself. The Jewish position in America, Podhoretz wrote in his introduction to the August 1971 issue, "is threatened by the same forces which have mounted so abandoned an assault on the values and institutions of the liberal democratic order in recent years."

THE FAMILY'S RECOIL from the counterculture—as Jews and as politically engaged intellectuals—earned it both praise and scorn. "When the combination of *zeitgeist*, media coverage, and the exploitation of the bad world situation made these movements appear overwhelmingly persuasive and almost irresistible," modern Orthodox rabbi Irving "Yitz" Greenberg said, "*Commentary* offered an independent, often devastating judgment. I am persuaded that this saved us from the triumph of trends and tendencies which were bad for Israel and the Jews specifically, and for culture and values generally."

Other Jewish leaders felt somewhat less pleased by the magazine's turn. "It is too bad that *Commentary* chooses to run with, rather than buck the tide of, Jewish withdrawal from larger society," Rabbi Balfour Brickner, of the Union of American Hebrew Congregations, wrote in 1971. "*Commentary* has always been a bellwether for the thinking of the Jewish Establishment," Jewish radical Sol Stern said, and the magazine now reflected the views of "American Jews who have made it here and don't want anyone rocking the boat."

But the tide had turned, and Podhoretz's position on the counterculture had set; he regarded the Movement as "more complacent, more arrogant, and if not actually more philistine then at least more insidiously so than any the world has ever seen before." "I was one of the people," the editor recalled, "who participated rather actively in the movement of those days to revive the dormant spirit of radical social criticism within the American intellectual community, both through my own writing and through the kind of writing which, as the newly appointed editor of *Commentary*, I was able to encourage others to do. Yet by the end of the decade I found myself almost entirely out of sympathy with the political workings of the radical ethos." Podhoretz had broken ranks yet again, declared full-scale war on the Left, and turned toward a decisive affirmation of America.

Sensing that the increasingly militant spirit of students, blacks, and the "blame America first" crowd had overflowed into excess, *Commentary* writers fought the New Left—in which Jews were, of course, as heavily overrepresented as they were in the old Left—as doggedly as they had once battled the Stalinists.[26] As the 1960s waned, the magazine's radicalism dissipated, and *Commentary* countered the counterculture. Suddenly, Richard Nixon's vice president, Spiro Agnew, was approvingly citing the magazine *against* the radicals.[27]

Some magazines—especially those that have veered sharply away from their own basic assumptions—find occasion to critique themselves. The *New Statesman*, for instance, a British weekly, ran a devastating piece in the 1960s by Irish diplomat and man of letters Conor Cruise O'Brien on the *New Statesman* of the 1930s. Not so *Commentary*, which neither now nor later paused to take full measure of its gyrations or to reckon with its reversals, perhaps because its editors regarded them as continuities. But as the 1970s came into view, it became as clear as day that the Family had come to regard bourgeois America as the best bulwark against Communism, just as it had once been against Nazism. "The defense of middle-class values," Norman Podhoretz said, "seemed necessary to the preservation of liberty, democracy, and even civilization itself." The new-new *Commentary* would from now on affirm that politics was rooted in self-interest and freedom was grounded in law; that liberty was not license; that liberalism was not "liberation"; that patriotism was a virtue; that America was a noble, if imperfect, society; and that to improve American society, one first had to preserve it.

≪ 7 ≫

Come Home, Democrats

Correcting course in a storm is a way of staying the course.
—Daniel Patrick Moynihan

NAME-CALLING

Depending on one's point of view, by the early 1970s either Norman Pod-horetz had betrayed the Left, or the Left had betrayed him. Podhoretz thought of himself as faithful to cold war liberalism even as most liberals had failed its principles—at home, by yielding to the student revolutionaries and the new attacks on Israel and the Jews, and abroad, by seeking to appease the Soviet empire through détente and by rationalizing American weakness. Much as the Trotskyists had regarded themselves as the true heirs of a Communism that the Stalinists had betrayed, *Commentary's* editor—as a voice of moderation on the Left and then as a member of the disillusioned Left—now saw himself not as a betrayer of liberalism, but as among its true heirs.

The ideological nomenclature—a far more important matter to the Family than mere party affiliation—was itself in flux. Was the *Commentary* Family a group of paleoliberals? Did they occupy a place on the right wing of the Left or on the left wing of the Right? Were they perhaps conservatives who wished to conserve liberal values? The names muddied. Nineteenth-century liberalism, with its emphasis on free markets, was now called conservatism; nineteenth-century paternalistic conservatism was now labeled liberalism. (Woodrow Wilson had identified liberalism with restraining the growth of government.) "Yesterday's liberalism is today's conservatism," said distinguished historian and frequent *Commentary* contributor Gertrude Himmelfarb.

By then, most people were calling Podhoretz and the rest of the Family "neoconservatives," but as the term was coined as an insult, much as the word "capitalism" was invented by a French socialist, it didn't exactly "take" right away.[1] In December 1970, after Robert Bartley ran a piece about him in the *Wall Street Journal*, Podhoretz said he would have been happier had Bartley resisted the temptation to call him a conservative. One White House aide called it instead "the red-white-and-bluing of Norman Podhoretz." Other members of the Family chose the pace of change each for himself. With a sense of relief and even liberation, Irving Kristol accepted the neoconservative label earliest. "I no longer had to pretend to believe—what in my heart I could no longer believe—that liberals were wrong because they subscribe to this or that erroneous opinion on this or that topic," Kristol wrote of his conversion. "No—liberals were wrong, liberals are wrong, because they are liberals." Nathan Glazer had in 1970 copped to being a "mild conservative," but he harbored an ambivalence about the new label. "The term neoconservatism was hijacked," he recalled much later.

> In its early application, in the 1970s, it referred to the growing caution and skepticism among a group of liberals about the effects of social programs. It was later applied to a vigorous and expansionist democracy-promoting military and foreign policy, especially in the wake of the dissolution of the Soviet Union. There was some reason to the hijacking—after all, a second generation of "neoconservatives," some of it literally second-generation, was promoting this policy. But some of us who were labeled early as neoconservatives, a characterization not of our choosing, such as Daniel P. Moynihan, Daniel Bell, and myself, found it astonishing and unsettling.

THE NAME OF DESIRE

Whatever the name of the apostasy, the 1972 election, in which the dovish Democratic nominee George McGovern lost forty-nine states to Richard Nixon, marked the turning point. Podhoretz came to see McGovern's presidential campaign—built on a platform calling for withdrawal from Vietnam and steep cuts in defense spending—as embodying countercultural attitudes; the party the senator from South Dakota had captured seemed less representative than ever. The McGovernites, Podhoretz said, had proven "hostile to the feelings and beliefs of the majority of the American people." As a nonprofit, unlike the *New Republic* or *National Review*, *Commentary* couldn't endorse political candidates, but in 1972 several members of its staff—

including Podhoretz—voted Republican for the first time in their lives. (Just how atypical this was may be gauged by the fact that Jews voted for McGovern in higher percentages—65 percent—than any other white group.)

Following McGovern's landslide loss, 520 electoral votes to 17, Podhoretz pinned his last hopes on two Democratic politicians of the old school of New Deal liberal anti-Communists: Senator Henry "Scoop" Jackson of Washington and Senator Daniel Patrick Moynihan of New York (whom *Harper's* referred to in 1976 as "the candidate from *Commentary*"[2]). The Family's New Deal Democrats still clung to the hope of somehow redeeming the Democratic Party from its descent into McGovernism—aka the New Politics—and returning it to the internationalist tradition of Harry Truman. The Family wished, in other words, to recall Democrats to their senses. In late 1972, "Scoop" Jackson Democrats, including Midge Decter, Norman Podhoretz, Jeane Kirkpatrick, Penn Kemble, Max Kampelman (a former chief of staff for Senator Hubert Humphrey), and Ben Wattenberg (a former aide to President Lyndon Johnson), founded the Coalition for a Democratic Majority, cochaired by Senators Jackson and Moynihan, for just this purpose. (Its manifesto was drafted by Podhoretz and Decter.)

In the meantime, to clarify matters somewhat, Podhoretz ran a symposium of sixty-four writers in the September 1976 issue under the title "What Is a Liberal—Who Is a Conservative?" In her reply, Midge Decter clung to the right to call herself a liberal: "For people like me to relinquish 'liberal' . . . for us to hand the term over without a fight to the enemies and would-be usurpers of our revolution, is to risk not only acquiescing in the betrayal of that revolution but losing the sense of who we really are as well. . . . How, then, can I settle—as I sometimes long, for the sake of peace and quiet to do—for the title of conservative? . . . Consequently there is no way I can be relieved of my obligation to do battle with those who are seeking to undo my revolution and abscond with its good name."

But with Scoop Jackson's defeat to Jimmy Carter in the 1976 Democratic presidential primaries, and Moynihan's decision three years later not to challenge Jimmy Carter's nomination as a candidate for a second term, Podhoretz finally threw up his hands. Podhoretz voted for Carter in the election of 1976, though later regarded this as "the worst political mistake of my life." As the Carter administration took over from Gerald Ford's caretaker administration, the peanut farmer from Georgia froze out the anti-McGovernites. Of the sixty names submitted to Carter by the Coalition for a Democratic Majority for possible appointments, only one got a position. (Peter Rosenblatt was appointed special representative to Micronesia, "Not

Indonesia, not Polynesia, not Macronesia, but Micronesia!" Elliot Abrams exclaimed.) In Podhoretz's view, the new president hewed to a McGovernite line in the whole tone of his administration. Carter's foreign policy appointments—such as Secretary of State Cyrus Vance, whom Podhoretz called "Lillian Hellman in pinstripes," and top arms reduction negotiator Paul Warnke—far from confronting Soviet aggression seemed rather to accept a reduction of American power. The editor was confirmed in this view by Carter's 1977 speech at Notre Dame, in which the president dismissed the "inordinate fear of Communism." The new president conducted foreign policy, Pat Moynihan wrote in *Commentary*, "under the pretense that we have no enemies in the world."

For another thing, Podhoretz distrusted Carter's instincts on the Middle East. *Commentary* welcomed the Camp David Peace Accord signed in September 1978 by Israeli prime minister Menachem Begin and Egyptian president Anwar Sadat, but not Carter's role in bringing it about. Robert Tucker argued in the November 1978 issue that "the Carter administration's disapproval of the strategy of a separate peace and its continued obsession with the goal of a comprehensive settlement" had delayed an agreement that could have been reached much earlier. A couple of years later, Alan Dowty similarly criticized the administration's "dogged devotion to total salvation rather than limited but practical achievements" and suggested that Sadat "saved U.S. diplomacy 'in spite of itself' by interposing his own dramatic peace initiative."[3]

Podhoretz himself was troubled by the Carter administration's moves to sell F-15s and Sidewinder missiles and $5.1 billion worth in other arms to Saudi Arabia; he lamented the president's veto of the sale of Israeli Kfir jets to Ecuador. He shook his head in disbelief when Carter called Syria's dictator Hafez al-Assad "a strong supporter in the search for peace." He bewailed the ways the president bungled the hostage debacle in Iran and failed to secure the release of the fifty-two Americans seized at the U.S. Embassy in Tehran. Podhoretz furthermore felt nothing but scorn for Carter's ambassador to the United Nations, Andrew Young, who met secretly with a representative of the Palestine Liberation Organization; he was appalled when Young's successor, Donald McHenry, voted in 1980 in favor of a Security Council resolution that deplored Israeli settlements in the West Bank; and he was made queasy by references made by the president's brother, Billy, to "the Jewish media."[4]

The upshot was that much to his surprise, Podhoretz, waking up to the conservative implications of his own line of thinking, no longer felt at home in the Democratic Party. And so he deserted the party that had deserted him. What had started as a defense of traditional liberalism was dragging Podhoretz, and his magazine with him, to the Right. Having failed to halt the leftward slide of the Democrats, Podhoretz arrived at the conclusion that "one ought to join the side one was now on instead of engaging in a futile attempt to change the side one used to be on." And he was hardly alone in the sentiment.

ANGRY SAXONS

Not that the Family jumped into conservative waters. For one thing, those waters seemed shallow. The first discussion of conservatism in *Commentary* had been conducted by Gertrude Himmelfarb in 1950, and it wasn't warm. Contemporary conservatives, she wrote then, "attest to conservatism's distrust of intelligence and free inquiry. . . . The conservative suspects that the truth, which gives life and dignity—and power—to an aristocracy or elite, might bring catastrophe if allowed to permeate the lower layers of society."

As far as the Family was concerned, America lacked an intellectually deep conservative tradition, though if one cared to listen, one could hear faint stirrings of a conservative movement.[5] There were traditionalists like Russell Kirk who stressed religion, authority, and virtue as bulwarks against relativism, urged a recovery of the moral foundations of democracy, and lamented the dissolution of the West. There were ex-radical anti-Communists such as Whittaker Chambers and James Burnham. There were conservative economists who popularized the ideas of a pair of Austrian capitalist intellectuals, Friedrich Hayek and his mentor Ludwig von Mises. Influential conservative books began to appear: Richard Weaver's *Ideas Have Consequences* (1948), Eric Voegelin's *The New Science of Politics* (1952). William F. Buckley complained about the death of the ideas of free enterprise and limited government at Yale in *God and Man at Yale* (1951) and founded *National Review* in 1955. The late 1940s and early 1950s saw attempts to locate an indigenous American conservative tradition—such as Peter Viereck's *Conservatism Revisited* (1949), Russell Kirk's *The Conservative Mind* (1953), and Clinton Rossiter's *Conservatism in America* (1955).[6]

Lionel Trilling famously expressed skepticism about such attempts in the introduction to his book *The Liberal Imagination* (1950):

In the United States at this time liberalism is not only the dominant but even the sole intellectual tradition. For it is the plain fact that nowadays there are no conservative or reactionary ideas in general circulation. This does not mean, of course, that there is no impulse to conservatism or to reaction. Such impulses are certainly very strong, perhaps even stronger than most of us know. But the conservative impulse and the reactionary impulse do not, with some isolated and some ecclesiastical exceptions, express themselves in ideas but only in action or in irritable mental gestures which seek to resemble ideas.[7]

As late as 1971, Nathan Glazer could write in *Commentary*, "There now exists no powerful force within the intellectual world to challenge the intellectuals on the Left." The American intelligentsia had until then taken shape almost entirely on the Left, and the Family had considered conservatism sour, stagnant, even vulgar. It was an anomaly, a forlorn, "forbidden faith" (as political scientist Raymond English called it in 1952); conservatism was deemed, as Clinton Rossiter called it a decade later, "the thankless persuasion." It stood on the margins of respectability.

It did not help that conservatism was a traditionally Jew-free province of American life. The Family had instinctively regarded the old Right as a brackish cesspool home to anti-Semites, anti-immigration nativists, reactionaries, chauvinists, protectionists, and isolationists. In the old country, the Right included the anti-Dreyfusards and the monarchists in France, for example, and the Nazis in Germany. In postwar America, the Family had associated conservatives with xenophobes, Dixiecrats, or John Birchers; southern agrarians full of nostalgia for the antebellum South and a mildewed distaste for modern industry; rich "Rockefeller Republicans"; or Catholic Ivy League *National Review* types.

Whether the Jews' attachment to liberalism amounted, as Irving Howe said, to "a watered-down residue of the socialism that East European Jews brought to this country," it was plain that the Jews' attraction to the Democratic Party, the party of immigrants and minorities, ran as strong and deep as their antipathy to the Republican Party, the party of big business and rural America. American Jews had given unswerving loyalty to the Democrats since the days of Franklin D. Roosevelt, who died the year *Commentary* was born. In 1932, FDR won 83 percent of the Jewish vote; in 1936, 85 percent; and in 1940, 90 percent. In 1936, even the socialist Yiddish paper the *Forward* endorsed his bid for reelection. "In the Jewish world," its editorial announced, "the feeling for Roosevelt burns and blazes." It didn't hurt that he surrounded himself with Jewish advisers (so much so that some called him President Rosenfeld) such as Henry Morgenthau Jr., secretary of the treasury Benjamin V. Cohen, Samuel Rosenman, and Felix Frankfurter. The day Roosevelt died, Norman Podhoretz—all of fifteen—wrote a poem for his high school paper comparing the president with Moses—two great leaders who perished on the very cusp of the Promised Land. The adult Podhoretz liked to repeat a Yiddish quip of Jonah J. Goldstein, who ran for New York City mayor in 1945. For the Jews, said Goldstein, there existed only three *velt'n* (worlds): *die velt* (this world), *yenner velt* (the next world), and *Roosevelt.*

Since World War II, the Jews' faith in the Democrats had waned hardly at all. In 1948, 75 percent of them voted for Harry Truman, although only half of the electorate as a whole did so. Four years later, the Republican candidate, Dwight D. Eisenhower, earned more than 55 percent of the general vote, but only 36 percent of the Jewish vote. In 1960, 82 percent of Jewish voters cast a ballot for John F. Kennedy, who barely beat out Richard Nixon. In the next election, an astounding 90 percent of Jewish voters preferred Lyndon B. Johnson, who received 61 percent of the general vote, over Republican Barry Goldwater. In 1968, Hubert Humphrey—LBJ's vice president—got 81 percent of the Jewish vote in his loss to Nixon. And on and on the trend predictably continued.

When the Family left the liberal fold, some conservatives extended a welcome mat even as some liberals said, in effect, "Good riddance." In 1971, a *National Review* editorial held out a hand to the new *Commentary*—"C'mon in, the Water's Fine" was the headline—and the next year its editor, Bill Buckley, wrote to Podhoretz to congratulate him on a "superb job." Robert Bartley of the *Wall Street Journal* assured *Commentary* that "the term conservative is nothing to fear."

But most traditionalist conservatives and "paleoconservatives" feared the Family seemed keener on winning arguments than on winning elections. Far from giving the Family a warm reception, they distrusted its ideological impulses and accused it of carrying the old liberal attraction to grand-sounding abstractions. As Russell Kirk used incessantly to repeat, "Conservatism is the negation of ideology."[8] Patrick Buchanan said that the neoconservatives' tactics "left many conservatives wondering if we hadn't made a terrible mistake when we brought these ideological vagrants in off the street and gave them a warm place by the fire."

About one thing the paleocons had the Family pegged: Its members could summon no real sympathy for the Grand Old Party. They simply regarded the Republican Party as a useful vehicle. "Republicanism—capital R—has never been the name of conservative desire," Midge Decter said. "It is just that for those who still pin at least some hopes on the outcomes of elections, the GOP is all there is." "The Republican party," Elliott Abrams conceded in a *Commentary* symposium on "Liberalism and the Jews," "has over the years shown itself no bastion of support for many things Jews hold dear, such as the struggle for civil rights and civil liberties, and (in no small part through the labor movement) for social justice." This state of affairs, Abrams wrote, "leaves us floating, with the attachment to Democratic-party liberalism broken but not replaced by any real sympathy for the Republicans." "We are, for the moment, homeless," Gertrude Himmelfarb said.

RETREATING TO THE TRIBE

Despite Podhoretz's sharp break with the milieu that had nurtured him, his job was secure, his career by no means shattered. But in certain quarters, he had become politically non grata. He and Midge used to have dinner with Jason Epstein, cofounder of the *New York Review of Books*, at least once a week. No longer. The *New York Times Book Review* no longer asked Podhoretz to contribute. Recognizing his knack for personalizing political quarrels and for making new enemies of old friends, he liked to say that if he wanted to drop names, he needed only list his ex-friends.

Between the years 1965 and 1980, by which time *Commentary*'s neoconservative about-face would be complete, a number of writers were expelled—or expelled themselves—from the stable of contributors. As *Commentary* tore itself away from the adversary culture of the Left, it hemorrhaged writers. Some admirers of the old *Commentary* lamented what Podhoretz had done with it. Irving Howe, who had written thirty-five pieces for the magazine since his review of Isaac Rosenfeld's novel in 1946 and had known Podhoretz since the mid-1950s, ceased speaking to Podhoretz or writing for his magazine after 1974. "I find it troubling that the most influential and respected American Jewish journal in the U.S. should in the last few years have veered so sharply to the Right in its politics," Howe said in 1975. "I contributed to *Commentary* when it was the natural voice of liberal Jewish debate," George Steiner recalled. "Almost overnight it was decided that I was no longer welcome and that my work was neither to be reviewed nor even mentioned," he said. "I assume that this boycott (to this day) arose from both my doubts about Vietnam and my deepening fear about the development of Israel's policies and society."

Edward Hoagland, who had written several essays for the magazine in the late 1960s and had been married to managing editor Marion Magid, felt that the new *Commentary* was "banging the drum for the Cold War and fisting the Arabs." In the summer of 1970, he wrote to Podhoretz about his distress. "*Commentary* forsakes the ethnic glory of its past for an ethnic provincialism . . . losing influence and significance at a great rate all the while." Podhoretz wrote back, calling the letter smug and shallow. "I have strong fans and mild fans," Hoagland replied, "but no one, so far as I know, who thinks [my books] shallow and smug. You would be better off if you could say the same. . . . Since so far as I know you never 'make up' quarrels, I'm sure I am now a past contributor." He was.

Urban sociologist Herbert Gans had his last of a dozen contributions in 1969. "Like many others I had a big fight with Norman (maybe about blacks or anti-war radicals) after which I got an extremely nasty letter from him which as I recall said basically that I couldn't write, and he couldn't now understand why he ever published me, and that was it. Maybe it was a form letter." William Pfaff last wrote for Podhoretz in 1970, though their real falling out came a dozen years later. "I was eventually attacked by him as an anti-Semite because of my criticism (in an *International Herald Tribune* column) of Israeli policy in Lebanon. He had developed what we might call a little racket by then, in which he published denunciations of writers under pretentious titles ("J'Accuse!" etc.). The writer was then invited to write a groveling letter to Norman, and he would then report their confession and pronounce absolution. . . . I wrote a non-groveling letter which he refused to publish. I have since considered him an intellectual fraud, and dishonest to boot." Dennis Wrong's final essay (of about thirty) also came in 1970. "*Commentary*'s unflagging zeal to expose 'the Left,'" the sociologist complained, "dominates even its movie reviews." Literary critic Alfred Kazin, whose last of twenty-four contributions appeared in 1979, complained of a groupthink that brooked little disagreement: "The solidarity they display on every question of opinion! The last time I wrote for *Commentary* an assistant keeper of the flame struggled for an hour on the long-distance line to Notre Dame, where I was then teaching, to persuade me to take out a derisive description of Richard Nixon." The offending reference was cut out, as was the writer. Others departed more quietly. Daniel Bell's final article came in 1971, Ted Draper contributed his last piece in 1979 ("I broke with Podhoretz when he changed the political line of *Commentary*," he said), and Daniel Patrick Moynihan's last of fifteen pieces appeared in 1981.[9]

Others of the old comrades-in-arms died: Theodore Frankel, editor and contributor, in 1971; Paul Goodman in 1972; Alexander Bickel in 1974; Hannah Arendt and Lionel Trilling in 1975; Will Herberg in 1977.[10] George Lichtheim took his life in 1973, at age sixty-one.

An infusion of new writers, who would become stalwarts of the neoconservative *Commentary*, replaced the lost blood. Chicago essayist Joseph Epstein started writing for the magazine in the mid-1960s. In the 1970s, for his new stable of contributors Podhoretz recruited Jeane Kirkpatrick, a political scientist teaching at Georgetown who in her college days had joined the Young People's Socialist League (YPSL) in Columbia, Missouri; Joshua Muravchik, a young neoconservative writer and former national chairman of YPSL; Edward Luttwak, a Romanian-born military strategist associated with the Center for Strategic and International Studies in Washington; Yiddish scholar Ruth Wisse; Michael Ledeen, then executive editor of a new quarterly, the *Washington Review of Strategic and International Studies*; and Richard Pipes, a Russian specialist at Harvard who chaired "Team B," the group appointed in 1976 by the President's Foreign Intelligence Advisory Board to prepare an alternative estimate of Soviet strategic objectives to the one issued by the CIA. In 1974, Podhoretz recruited William J. Bennett, then teaching law and philosophy at Boston University. (For a *Newsweek* column in 1978, by which time he had published ten pieces in the magazine, Bennett used as his tagline "William Bennett is a regular contributor to *Commentary*." Almost as soon as *Newsweek* hit the stands, a call came from Podhoretz: "Who the hell do you think you are?" The two men became lifelong friends, and Bennett later said that Podhoretz's "struggles to move American Jewry to the Right, and to remind countless Americans how right is their country" made him "a political Moses of our age.") On Nathan Glazer's recommendation, Podhoretz also brought aboard Elliott Abrams, a Harvard Law student and Podhoretz's future son-in-law. Abrams's first *Commentary* piece, in 1972, made him "a minor celebrity," he told Podhoretz.[11] Abrams would soon go to Washington, where he would work as special counsel for Senator Henry Jackson and then as chief of staff for Senator Moynihan.

By the time *Commentary*'s twenty-fifth anniversary arrived in 1970, the magazine was as widely read as ever (paid circulation that year reached 62,000). "*Commentary*, still under thirty and thus to be trusted," pronounced Gilbert Harrison, owner and editor of the *New Republic*, "is and always has been a model of civilized discourse, a triumph of editorial intelligence, taste, and independent judgment." Throughout the transition, a begrudging acknowledgment of the magazine's power persisted. Writing in the late 1970s, for example, Catholic journalist Peter Steinfels said that "*Commentary*'s main battle pieces are often spectacular—frontal assaults, verbal rocketry, a matchless sense of the adversary's weakest points."

But the magazine's swing to the neoconservative direction cost it some readers, too. Arthur Waskow of the Jewish Renewal movement compared *Commentary*'s "bully-boy devotion to the American Empire" with that of "the worst Hellenizers to Antiochus." In late 1969, JoAnne Medalie, wife of antiwar Columbia professor Seymour Melman, wrote in to explain why she was letting her longtime subscription lapse:

> Born in 1930, I discovered *Commentary* during my college years in the early '50s. For me it had great value in my evolving identity as a third-generation American Jewish intellectual. . . . *Commentary* took a decided turn for the worse when it changed its editorship to Mr. Podhoretz. It shifted from its mission as a fresh, occasionally daring, and usually intelligent journal . . . to a vehicle for its editor to "make it" with what he conceived of as the New York literary establishment. The quality and number of articles related to Jewish matters declined. . . . In the early years of the Podhoretz editorship, however, there was a sufficient number of lively and fresh articles . . . such as the pieces by Paul Goodman and Oscar Gass, in addition to the occasional story by I. B. Singer, to make *Commentary* worth keeping. . . .
>
> In the past several years, however, *Commentary* has ceased to contain material that has any life. It has become an extremely dull, politically right-wing, constricted magazine catering to a smug, middle-brow audience identified with the established values of a bygone era. . . . Like almost everyone I know, I have turned increasingly to the *New York Review of Books* for some of the kinds of intellectual pleasures that *Commentary* once offered me.

Feminist writer Vivian Gornick, a subscriber who had been Irving Kristol's secretary at *Public Interest* in the late 1960s, denounced Podhoretz's magazine in similar terms in 1970: "Every time *Commentary* sets out to observe any of the numerous and, God knows, legitimate social-protest movements that are tearing our lives apart, it ends up sounding like a Jewish mother, arms folded across fat breasts, mouth compressed into fat face, saying: 'After everything I've done for you, *this* is what I get back!' For, in the view of fat and self-satisfied *Commentary*, what is behind all the social stirrings, all the churning and screaming and profound injustice thousands of people feel characterize their daily existences, is merely the dissatisfactions of a handful of ungrateful and maladjusted middle-class children."[12]

Some readers complained that Podhoretz's magazine had become too insularly Jewish. Morris Dickstein, who had written an essay for the January 1970 issue on Allen Ginsberg, canceled his subscription in 1975, after fifteen years: "I resented being deprived of a magazine that bridged my literary-political interests and my Jewish interests, one that wasn't in any way parochial." Some Jewish intellectuals, Jamaican-born Harvard sociologist Orlando Patterson added, "have given in to the demands of the conservatives and the chauvinists, have returned in sentiment, if not religion, to the Jewish fold, and blindly support the Zionist cause. This group is best represented by the intellectuals centered on *Commentary* magazine, the journal of the AJC, which for years was the bastion of all that was finest in Jewish and American liberalism but which, during recent years, has, sadly, retreated to the tribe."

What some considered a retreat, Norman Podhoretz thought of as an advance that had just begun.

PART III

Insiders

⪻ 8 ⪼

If I Am Not For Myself

I am my beloved's, and my beloved is mine.
                              —Song of Songs 6:3

KEEPERS OF THE JEWISH CONSCIENCE

By 1980, the last of *Commentary*'s liberal inhibitions had disappeared. Norman Podhoretz and the *Commentary* insurrectionists against the Left threw their support behind Ronald Reagan, himself an anti-Communist who was fond of explaining why he had switched parties in the early 1960s with the words "I didn't leave the Democratic Party; it left me." Podhoretz, Midge Decter, and Nathan Glazer—who had met Republican candidate Ronald Reagan in a private dining room at the Union League Club at 37th Street and Park Avenue in 1978—now gave him their votes, and they were not the only Jews to throw in their lots with the Gipper. In 1980, Reagan received the highest proportion of the Jewish vote—39 percent—of any Republican presidential candidate since 1928. Many Jews had apparently learned, as contributing editor Milton Himmelfarb said, that "the right hand need not wither if it strays from the Democratic lever." ("The first time I pulled a lever for someone not on a socialist line," Irving Howe said, "I felt sick.")

Commentary entered the 1980s by reconsidering the Jews' traditional commitment to liberalism. For the January 1980 issue, the editors asked fifty-two writers whether the time had come to challenge the notion that Judaism and liberalism were inherently congruent—whether the elective affinities between the two had dissolved. Many replied that liberalism had changed. If the old liberalism endorsed equality of opportunity, the minimal state, individuality, pluralism, and anti-Communism, post-1960s liberalism ran instead under the banners of egalitarianism, environmental-ism, isolationism, and the kind of self-flagellation refined almost into an art form by those who believed America had lost moral credibility. The old liberalism, many contributors to the symposium said, served Jewish inter-ests; but the new liberalism had emerged from the 1960s with some emi-nently antiliberal ideas. "We may begin to suspect," Gertrude Himmelfarb wrote, "that the liberalism that brought us into modernity, that gave us our freedom as individuals and tolerated us as Jews, has been replaced by a new liberalism that is inhospitable to us both as individuals and as Jews."

In his reply, executive editor Neal Kozodoy, who had served as Pod-horetz's right-hand man since 1966, preferred to gauge liberalism by Jewish standards rather than to judge Judaism by liberal ones. The question of a Jewish detachment from liberalism, he wrote in the symposium, arrived both too late and too early. It came too late because the liberal calls for social justice merely echoed the oldest and most powerful principles of Jewish charity and communal obligation. "As a social doctrine liberalism has noth-ing further to teach the Jews," he said. But in another sense, Kozodoy felt the question premature. He had in his mind the recent bewildering Andrew Young affair, in which Jimmy Carter's ambassador to the United Nations resigned after meeting with an official of the Palestine Liberation Organiza-tion in violation of what was then American policy. After tendering his res-ignation, Young had bitterly denounced Israel for engaging in "terroristic" raids and for "constant bombing" in Lebanon. More surprising, as a *Com-mentary* article about the incident reported, was the way "the black Ameri-can leaders who rallied to Young's side portrayed him as the victim of a concerted Jewish campaign to oust him." "No episode in contemporary American history," the article argued, "has been marked by a greater out-pouring of animosity against Jews." Jesse Jackson, who not five years later would infamously call New York "Hymietown," blamed the resignation on "capitulation" to pressure exerted by "our former allies, the American Jewish community." The Black United Front deplored "Zionist racist pressure." Yet as the president himself belatedly admitted, there had been no such pres-sure. "Any claims or allegations that American Jewish leaders or anyone else urged me to ask Andy for his resignation," Carter finally acknowledged almost six weeks after the resignation, "are absolutely and totally false." *Commentary* concluded that "though the Young affair appeared to be about black-Jewish relations, it was actually about democracy and its enemies" and about "the determination to render America incapable of defending Israel or any other ally, or even itself."[1]

Kozodoy, for his part, felt the American Jewish response to these accusations was on the whole beset by a characteristic spinelessness:

> For the blunt and crippling truth is that the Jews of this country, especially those Jews who speak for the interests of their fellow Jews and who are the appointed keepers of the Jewish conscience, have not yet fully developed the habits and attitudes appropriate to free men. As the aftermath of the Andrew Young affair made clear, some Jews seem particularly adept at dodging what a more self-respecting political culture would define as their duty, and what a liberal order guarantees as their right: the duty and the right to stand up and defend oneself when attacked. At a time when American Jews as a group were being subjected to a shameless effort of delegitimation, and when even their right to look to their own, peaceable interests was being insolently proposed as a matter for open debate, the keepers of the Jewish conscience responded to the abuses directed at their community and its record with talismanic invocations of their credentials as the fellow victims of historic persecution . . . and with impassioned reiterations of the Jewish commitment to defend the rights of *others*. That the accommodating message was duly received and duly registered may be easily inferred from the fact that no black leader, either during the carnival of vilification or since, has felt called upon to offer an apology for the public lies that were told, in the name of American blacks, about American Jews. . . . Two hundred years after the Bill of Rights, one hundred years after the inception of their own glorious movement of political and spiritual regeneration, thirty years after the realization of their national dreams, the keepers of the Jewish conscience still find it more in their nature to slither than to stand. One can "understand" this disposition in a hundred forgiving ways; one can even acknowledge its appeal, the exemption it offers from the dilemmas of political action. But it is a debility which, so long as it remains in place, will continue to render the Jews peculiarly open and vulnerable to the depredations of their enemies, and in times of crisis an intolerable burden to their friends. A disposition fatal to Jewish pride has become a menace to Jewish survival.[2]

"If I am not for myself," asked the sage Hillel, "who will be for me?"

The theme of self-respect, self-interest, and loyalty to one's own carried the magazine into the new decade—and into the neoconservative persuasion. This note would become the "concert A" by which the *Commentary* orchestra tuned itself, a timbre to which it would ceaselessly return. Time and again, *Commentary* would condemn the Jewish Left for preferring self-castigation to self-defense. A 1982 piece, for example, praised the new generation of Jewish leaders for having unlearned that habit: "They are comfortable with the idea that there is such a thing as Jewish interest, and they have learned well the lesson that Jews need not be ashamed to fight for those interests—just as blacks, unions, and business groups fight for theirs."

"Looking about the current scene," *Commentary* had noticed in 1951, "it is hard to discern where the high purposes, challenging ideas, and crusading ardor that socialism once contributed to American politics and social thinking are to come from." Three decades later, the magazine itself supplied an answer: The purposes, ideas, and ardor now belonged to the neoconservatives, whose endurance—irony of ironies—turned out to be one of the more lasting legacies of the intramural infighting on the Left (much as American anti-Communists proved to carry the most lasting legacy of the American Communist Party that had schooled them).

A neoconservative was in the first instance a disabused liberal—in Irving Kristol's enduring phrase, "a liberal mugged by reality." Or if not mugged, at least chastened. Naturally, one need not share that biography to share the set of attitudes derived from it. Some converted to the neoconservative persuasion and others came to it by inheritance.[3] Beyond biography, *Commentary* fashioned a powerful new hybrid political persuasion and offered the ideal window through which to see that persuasion, for it was here that the mature magazine came to rest. From here on, our story can hew less closely to chronological lines; on the fundamental questions, *Commentary*'s cast of mind was now fully formed, and would remain firmly set from the mid-1970s onward.

"OH MY AMERICA, MY NEWFOUNDLAND!"

Neoconservatism, a movement without an electoral base, was not an "ism" at all; it was less a set of doctrines than a constellation of political instincts, a mentality. As *Commentary* would with perfect consistency show, to be a neoconservative meant most of all to mount a muscular defense of one's own. This, in turn, meant that the magazine turned itself into a dual démarche—against Soviet expansionism abroad and left-wing pieties at home.

In domestic affairs, Norman Podhoretz and the *Commentary* Family became preoccupied with the country's cultural malaise, which naturally they blamed on the 1960s. The discredited ideas of that decade, as they saw it, were enjoying a pernicious afterlife. The Family sensed that the counterculture had involved not just the antiwar movement, but also a wholesale denial of American values. "The central aspect of the antiwar movement," Jeane Kirkpatrick wrote in the magazine, "was less its rejection of the Vietnam War than its rejection of the United States." Midge Decter, whom some on the Left had since taken to calling the Dragon Lady, denounced what she called "the seizure of national self-hatred that had spread like typhus from the sixties radicals into the major institutions of the culture."[4] In the Family's eyes, the rebels of that decade had come of age, the counterculture had become the culture, and the antiestablishment had become the establishment.

In the domestic cold war—the battle to wrest cultural control from the Left and to ensure a "containment" of liberals—the Family came to feel in the 1970s and after, that defending one's own meant first of all making common cause with America. In America, Podhoretz exulted, "More liberty and more prosperity abounded than human beings had ever enjoyed in any other country or any other time. I now recognized that these blessings were also more widely shared than even the most visionary utopians had ever imagined possible." Sometimes, as Jeane Kirkpatrick quipped, one must face the truth about oneself no matter how pleasant it may be. The Family came to believe that the country was a political miracle, the greatest power the world had known. "Love of country—the expression now sounds almost archaic—is an ennobling sentiment," Gertrude Himmelfarb argued in *Commentary*. "It elevates us, invests our daily life with a larger meaning, dignifies the individual even as it humanizes politics." "The self-imposed assignment of neoconservatism," her husband, Irving Kristol, added, is "to explain to the American people why they are right, and to the intellectuals why they are wrong."[5]

Podhoretz especially had no use for the intellectual who could love everything except what is his own and still less use for the kind of self-doubt that slipped into self-loathing. Legitimate self-criticism, Podhoretz concluded, must be rooted in self-respect. "Self-respect is spiritually superior to self-flagellation," he said, "in nations no less than in individuals." "The idealist finds virtue only where he is not," Diana Trilling once observed, "in the country which is not his country, in the class which is not his class." This species of idealist Podhoretz could do without.

THE PUBLIC INTEREST

As he swung into his neoconservative phase, Podhoretz came to feel that defending one's own meant distinguishing social problems that can be tackled by public policy from those that cannot. The editor liked to cite Samuel Johnson's lines:

> *How small, of all that human hearts endure,*
> *That part, which laws or kings can cause or cure!*

It is left to God, not mortals, Podhoretz believed, to realize utopian visions of perfect justice and peace. Lenin and Chairman Mao loomed in his mind as cautionary examples of men who had trespassed into eschatology with calamitous result.

On the whole, the Family favored Social Security, unemployment insurance, and some form of national health insurance. "Had we not defended the major social programs," Nathan Glazer said, "from Social Security to Medicare, there would have been no need for the 'neo' before 'conservative.'" They were less in favor of abolishing the liberal welfare state than of pointing out its limits—the ways it harmed the poor and weakened families, demeaning those it intended to help. And so, as the magazine came into neoconservative maturity, *Commentary* began to challenge paternalism and social engineering—the enduring temptations of the Left. It located what Glazer, in a classic 1971 *Commentary* essay, had called "the limits of social policy."

Podhoretz left much of the technical work of limit-seeking for the *Public Interest*, the journal founded in 1965 by Irving Kristol and Daniel Bell, which took a more empirical approach and an altogether more unruffled style. ("We don't think of ourselves as a New York magazine," Bell said. "We're really a Washington and Cambridge magazine.")[6] Yet Podhoretz's *Commentary*, too, gave searching scrutiny to the unanticipated consequences—the dependency and social decay—that liberal programs, often accompanied by a guilty urge to *do something*, brought to the people they were supposed to help. The magazine's writers showed how administrative incompetence and faulty theories in some cases meant that reforms made matters worse, even as federal social spending soared. *Commentary* employed the techniques of social science, which formerly had served the Left, to show how parts of LBJ's sweeping Great Society reforms had been as ineffectual as they were well meaning.[7] In short, the magazine declined to travel the road built by what Saul Bellow once called the Good Intentions Paving Company. "The road to the worst political hells of our time has been paved with the idealistic intentions of those who know better than the rest of us what we *truly* want and need," one *Commentary* writer wrote.[8]

Among the forms of redistribution just then coming into vogue was redistribution by race, guided by Supreme Court justice Harry Blackmun's view that "in order to get beyond racism, we must first take race into account." The Family felt that past discrimination against blacks, terrible injustice though it was, did not justify present discrimination against other groups. In its new phase, *Commentary* rejected the notion that social disadvantage resulted, as if by an immutable law, from past exploitation or prejudice. Horrified both by the looting during the New York City blackout of 1977, for example, and the bend-over-backward political correctness it unleashed, Midge Decter excoriated in the September 1977 issue what she called a "very liberal and very racist idea: that being black is a condition for special moral allowance."[9] For expressing such views the Family was roundly attacked, even by some former friends.[10]

Podhoretz and the *Commentary* cohort were no more immune to outrage concerning the blights of slavery and discrimination than anyone else. But as they now discovered, good goals—like equality for blacks—yielded bad programs, such as affirmative action, another social policy that ill served those it intended to help.[11]

Sidney Hook had argued in the magazine against affirmative action back in 1964, the year Congress passed the Civil Rights Act. But on the grounds that artificially contriving equality of reward was incompatible with liberty, *Commentary* now intensified the attack on all manner of quotas, "reverse discrimination," and racial preferences in admission and hiring.[12] In the June 1975 issue, Nathan Glazer observed that American Jews in particular were threatened by what he was already in the early 1970s calling "affirmative discrimination" and the assumption that groups that were ahead had stepped to success on the backs of groups behind. To counter the charge, he said, "Jews should appeal to those beliefs in individual freedom, effort, and merit, not simply because they are good for Jews, but because they are good in themselves, because they are good for the U.S., because they are the best principles on which a good society can be organized."[13]

This is precisely what *Commentary* set about doing. Thomas Jefferson had favored the natural aristocracy of America, based on "virtue and talents," to the artificial aristocracy of Europe, "founded on wealth and birth." In an attempt to uphold the traditional liberal ideal of a color-blind society, Podhoretz would come to argue that the new system of preferential treatment amounted to nothing more than institutionalized racism—an implicitly racist form of reverse discrimination, likely to erode standards of merit and excellence. Affirmative action had the effect, he said, "of casting suspicion on the achievements of blacks both in their own eyes and in those of others." It reinforced stereotypes and exacerbated race consciousness. It bred resentment and cynicism, not to mention mediocrity. It violated the law. With respect to employment, for instance, the Civil Rights Act had made quite clear that "nothing contained in this title should be interpreted to require any employer . . . to grant preferential treatment to any individual or to any group because of race, color, religion, sex, or national origin . . . on account of an imbalance which may exist with respect to the total number or percentage." Last, affirmative action restricted Jewish admissions to universities in the name of "diversity."[14] And so *Commentary* launched a steady barrage on affirmative action right through the 1990s,[15] abhorring all the while the spread of affirmative action categories and the sense of "entitlement" from blacks to other "underprivileged" groups.

SHOOTING HEROINES

Women provided an example of just such a group. "The Jews have suffered more than any other group in humanity," Nobel Laureate Pearl Buck had suggested in *Commentary* in 1946, "with the sole exception of women." A quarter century later, as the Family grew increasingly uncomfortable with feminist crusaders, the magazine began to launch wave after wave of assaults on the feminist style of egalitarianism, replete with *ad feminam* broadsides on the likes of Susan Brownmiller, Germaine Greer, and Camille Paglia.[16]

Midge Decter, self-appointed scourge of feminists, author of *The Liberated Woman and Other Americans* (1970) and *The New Chastity and Other Arguments Against Women's Liberation* (1972), charged that the women's movement had damaged courtship and marriage. (In a letter protesting Decter's critical review of a biography of Janis Joplin, Timothy Leary wrote, "I'd rather shoot heroin with Janis than shoot heroines with Midge.") Writing in *Commentary*, Harvard professor Harvey Mansfield called feminism "the greatest blight on our national prospect and the greatest threat to moral responsibility." Ruth Wisse, who started writing for *Commentary* in 1976, charged that women's lib "has done to the American home what Communism did to the Russian economy." Carol Iannone announced that in its fullest form feminism "was less a rational program with fixed goals than an irrational shriek of hatred against the human condition itself." Joseph Epstein dismissed "the madder kinds of academic feminism that see a phallo under every centrism." And Yale polymath David Gelernter penned a *Commentary* piece called "Why Mothers Should Stay Home."

This stance no doubt had something to do with an assertion of manliness—a virtue the Family felt that it possessed in a fuller measure than its domestic enemies did. In one of his forty *Commentary* pieces, James Nuechterlein, editor of the "theoconservative" journal *First Things*, claimed that the Left, to its lasting detriment, had "feminized" itself. By adopting a politics of compassion and sentimentality, he said, and by confusing charity with politics and society with family, the Left had absorbed a dangerously effete and effeminate set of political instincts: "an ethic of noncoercion, a preference for emotion over rational analysis and for noncompetitive modes of social interaction, a focus on being rather than doing and . . . a reluctance concerning the exercise of power."

The Podhoretzes weren't too keen on gays, either; they resented the ways homosexuals were presenting themselves as an oppressed minority and undermining "family values."[17] Norman commissioned a piece from James Q. Wilson entitled "Against Homosexual Marriage." Midge Decter let loose a fusillade called "The Boys on the Beach" (September 1980), in which she summoned memories of the summers she had spent in the early 1960s with her family on Fire Island in order to make the point that homosexuals are "by inclination highly promiscuous—promiscuity is after all the natural condition of young males undomesticated by women." In the wake of the gay liberation movement, Decter feared, the ostentations of homosexual sadomasochism had run rampant. "The once rather special preferences of a rather special tawdry corner of homosexual low-life have now moved into the mainstream," she wrote. (Gore Vidal unfavorably compared her essay to the loathsome anti-Semitic tract *The Protocols of the Elders of Zion*.)[18]

Nor did the AIDS outbreak of the 1980s do much to soften *Commentary*'s editorial line on the matter. One writer suggested that upholding laws against sodomy might limit the spread of the virus.[19] A lawyer named Michael Fumento declared that the scale of the epidemic had been overstated, that the epidemic was largely confined to gay men and intravenous-drug abusers, and that the government was spending too much on AIDS research.[20] (After his first *Commentary* article came out in 1987, Fumento was hired as an AIDS specialist for the U.S. Commission on Civil Rights. In 1990, he published a book based on a *Commentary* article called *The Myth of Heterosexual AIDS*.) "HIV-AIDS is a disease that for homosexuals has been the result of a particular habit of conduct," Midge Decter later added in the magazine. "It has also brought to their community untold death and suffering. Speaking of decency, how has it come to be a mark of compassion to display one's understanding and support for the conduct of friends and associates who are willfully killing themselves?"

Podhoretz, who regularly lamented the cultural acceptance being extended to homosexuality, weighed in to say that the AIDS epidemic confirmed that "there is a suicidal impulse at work in homosexual promiscuity." In November 1987, during a debate at Central Synagogue, just down the street from the *Commentary* offices, Harvard Law professor Alan Dershowitz expressed his distaste with something Podhoretz had written in one of his columns. "Curious," Podhoretz had remarked in the passage Dershowitz found offensive, "that in an age of ubiquitous pornography and blunt speech, it should be hard to say in plain English that AIDS is almost entirely a disease caught by men who bugger or are buggered by dozens or even hundreds of other men every year." In the face of Dershowitz's reprimand, Podhoretz stood his ground. "The sentence that Alan Dershowitz quoted from my column on AIDS, which he ridiculed by his tone, was factually correct, and I defy him or anyone else to challenge the truth of that statement. My position on gay rights has to do with my fear of the rise and spread of tendencies in this society and in this culture which undermine in a very drastic way the possibility of maintaining the family as the key institution of our society."

VIRTUCRATS

Back in the day, Marxists attuned to the ways in which moral norms served "class interests" had tended to regard the bourgeois family with contempt; Karl Marx, in *The Communist Manifesto* (1848), had called family life a form of legalized prostitution. But because defending one's own also meant conserving one's values, Podhoretz and the *Commentary* neoconservatives now defended family values with all the ardor they could muster; a new tone of middle-class social conservatism set in. Strains of cultural conservatism could already be heard in Lionel Trilling's writing of the 1950s, but propelled by the force of its reaction to the excesses of the 1960s, Podhoretz's *Commentary* now began explicitly to stress traditional values and "moral clarity." It adopted classical conservative themes; it urged that public life be brought into harmony with private virtue, that values be seen as gifts from the past, encoded in American institutions.

About the prospects of this, Podhoretz, fearing the West was demoralized and lacking in a sense of self-worth, was far from sanguine. Opening a new vein of cultural alarmism, he and the magazine's neoconservative writers worried that the "acids of modernity" were corroding the moral order. Dour reflections about the rising rates of divorce, teenage pregnancies, and illegitimacy brought these writers into a state of profound perturbation. They perceived a crisis of authority, a popular culture degraded from within, a society corrupted by an easygoing ethical relativism and a decline of civic-mindedness, a contemporary art scene defiled by obscenity and exhibitionism; all of this vexed them.

In a symposium on "The National Prospect" in the fiftieth anniversary issue, *Commentary* gave vent to this pessimism. "Much of our popular culture is vulgar, violent, mindless, and perverse," wrote Bill Bennett, secretary of education under President Ronald Reagan and "drug czar" under President George H. W. Bush. "We now live in a culture that is deeply corrupted," Hilton Kramer (the editor of the *New Criterion*) remarked, "a liberal culture that in the name of unrestricted freedom has brought us to a condition of moral insensibility."

And so the Family neoconservatives—none of them Orthodox Jews— joined the Kulturkampf on the side of tradition. Allan Bloom may have called it the Quarrel of the Canons, but *Commentary* sensed the real battle was larger—not about "the inclusion of this or that book," as historian Gertrude Himmelfarb said, "but about the very idea of greatness." More than ever before, America appeared in *Commentary*'s eyes as a great nation, favored heir to a noble civilization. Himmelfarb called in the magazine for the "remoralization of society." She praised Victorian values—a set of modest virtues within reach of ordinary people. She wished to draw a lifeline, as the subtitle of one her books put it, "from Victorian virtues to modern values."[21] George Gilder—a conservative who once called *Commentary* "my favorite publication"—contributed a piece called "In Defense of Monogamy."[22] Leon Kass, professor at the University of Chicago's Committee on Social Thought, urged "a restoration of sexual self-restraint." Wendy Shalit, a sophomore at Williams, launched a writing career that would take her from *A Return to Modesty* (1999) to *Girls Gone Mild* (2007) with *Commentary* pieces that inveighed against coed bathrooms—"an allegory of the present intellectual atmosphere in our universities, where everything is relative, nothing is 'essentially' different from anything else."[23]

GOD'S COUNTRY AND MINE

In the 1970s, *Commentary*'s promotions boasted that its writers "regularly challenge the conventional wisdom and the fashionable pieties which have been debasing discourse, perverting language, and deadening thought." In the late 1960s, Podhoretz had attacked the guardians of the academy who had succumbed to the counterculture; now he broadened the attack to include the heirs to that capitulation: Marxist indoctrinators, postmodernists, feminists, Afrocentrists, multiculturalists of every stripe, and all other members of the "tenured Left."[24] The neoconservative *Commentary* joined the fight against fashionable "deconstructionists,"[25] whom executive editor Neal Kozodoy charged with "gaily precipitating the crash of entire edifices of humanist learning." It ridiculed the Modern Language Association for hosting talks like "De-Sublimating the Male Sublime: Autoerotics, Anal Erotics, and Corporeal Violence in Melville and Burroughs." It gave plenty of space for Joseph Epstein to lament the ways "language is under attack by feminists, by proponents of Black English and bilingualism, by homosexuals, and by a general resurgence of the populist strain in our culture." It argued that by denying a common cultural heritage, the apostles of "diversity" were turning universities into what *Commentary* contributor Abigail Thernstrom called "islands of repression in a sea of freedom."

Podhoretz's newfound respect for the great collective wisdom inherent in inherited traditions extended, naturally enough, to religion. This time around, however, the magazine's interest in religion—and the virtues religion cultivates—was less in its theological dimension, as in the 1950s, than in its social utility. This meant much more than taking shots at what Adam Wolfson called in *Commentary* "the thoroughly secularized and secularizing Democratic party." It meant, from the 1970s and on, displaying an entirely new manner of friendliness toward religious values.[26]

With rare exception, the new *Commentary* remained mute on abortion.[27] But on other matters, it hewed to the agenda of the religious Right: The magazine argued that separation of church and state need not entail the elimination of religion from society.[28] It looked askance at "judicial activism," at judges who took it upon themselves to create rights not enumerated in the Constitution.[29] And later *Commentary* would come out in favor of giving public dollars to "faith-based initiatives."[30]

At a time when such sentiments were almost unheard of among American Jews, the Family suspected that secular humanism (William Kristol, son of Irving, called it "the opiate of the elite") posed a greater danger than Christian fundamentalism. The real danger, Irving Kristol wrote in *Commentary*, came not from an invigorated Christianity, "but from an upsurge of anti-biblical barbarism that will challenge Christianity, Judaism, and Western civilization altogether."[31] In the December 1953 *Commentary*,

Jacob Taubes, a scholar of "political theology," had stressed the traditional Jewish rejection of Christianity as another in a long series of Jewish heresies. Despite a suspicion of interfaith dialogue, Podhoretz's magazine now extended a hand to the Christian Right—to Jerry Falwell's Moral Majority, Pat Robertson's Christian Coalition, and the "theocons"—as allies in the culture wars.[32] Podhoretz gave space, for instance, to his old friend Richard John Neuhaus, a Lutheran pastor who had become a Roman Catholic priest, to denounce the "hysterical" alarm at the rise of the religious Right. (In 1990, Neuhaus persuaded Decter to join his Institute on Religion and Public Life; she would serve as an editor at Neuhaus's journal, *First Things*, from 1990 to 1995.)

Contrary to most American Jews, who harbored a deep distrust of Christian Zionists and their Evangelical eschatology, the Family assigned high value to Evangelical support for Israel, which had been galvanized by the Six-Day War and had grown stronger ever since. "The fact that the Moral Majority is pro-Israel for theological reasons that flow from Christian belief is hardly a reason for Jews to distance themselves from it," Irving Kristol wrote in the October 1984 *Commentary*: "It is their theology, but it is our Israel." Decades later, his son William Kristol would urge the magazine's readers to "acknowledge that Christians United for Israel may be more important for the Jewish future than the Jewish Community Relations Councils."

Battle lines sharpened when Pat Robertson provoked charges of anti-Semitism with descriptions in his book *The New World Order* (1991) of a secret society of Jewish bankers and others who conspired to rule the world. Soon after, Podhoretz took to *Commentary* to defend the founder of the Christian Coalition. "Robertson's support for Israel," the editor wrote, "trumps the anti-Semitic pedigree of his ideas about the secret history of the dream of the new world order." Not only did Christians oppose the spread of relativism, but also, as Podhoretz put it in a *New York Times* op-ed, "on Israel, the most important issue of Jewish concern, the religious Right was on the side of the angels."[33] When, in 1994, the Anti-Defamation League (ADL) came out with a 193-page censure of the Christian Right's "assault on tolerance and pluralism in America," Midge Decter defended Pat Robertson and other Evangelical conservatives in *Commentary* ("The ADL vs. the 'Religious Right,'" September 1994). She also put together a full-page *New York Times* ad with seventy-five Jews as signatories, most from the Family, that accused the ADL report of defaming conservative Christians, of ignoring their stalwart support of Israel, and, what's more, of conflating Judaism with liberalism.

According to its critics, the new *Commentary*'s concord with the religious Right and the magazine's references to upholding the Judeo-Christian notion of an objective moral order smelled of cynical opportunism. ("Where there are politics there are bedfellows," Saul Bellow wrote in another connection, "and where there are bedfellows there are likely to be fleas.") Yet by now Podhoretz genuinely saw things differently. He understood religion not as a threat to freedom, but as its underpinning. And he keenly sensed the vital role religion played in America's self-definition—and the preservation of the nation's moral character. America was chosen, favored of God. The theme culminated in an essay by David Gelernter, a Yale professor who had been injured opening a mail bomb sent by the Unabomber. Gelernter argued that not only did the Puritans regard themselves as God's chosen people, as the new Israel building Jerusalem (to steal a phrase from Blake) on America's green and pleasant land, but also that America's very essence was religious. "Americanism," Gelernter wrote in *Commentary*, "is in fact a Judeo-Christian religion; a millenarian religion; a biblical religion."[34] Of course, like other religions, Americanism aspired to universal application.[35]

COMMENTARY HAD FROM its earliest days concerned itself with the social effects of science.[36] But Podhoretz's neoconservative mood of moral seriousness now extended indirectly to the ways the magazine joined the debates between scientific materialists and religious believers. He invited Leon Kass, the Family's most prominent critic of the biotechnological avant-garde, to lead *Commentary*'s charge. The man whom the *New York Times* once called "the religious right's favorite intellectual" explained how the common assumption that scientific evidence proved doctrines of materialism and determinism threatened to erode man's godlike dignity. And so Kass argued for limiting the unfettered pursuit of scientific progress (something akin perhaps to limits on social policy). He called for restrictions on embryonic stem cell research and warned of the dehumanizing dangers of genetic engineering and other "excesses of human willfulness."[37] He laid out the case in the pages of *Commentary* that "scientism"—the notion that a purely scientific view can give adequate account of our humanity—threatens to overturn our "traditional self-understanding as special creatures with freedom and dignity." Kass also sought ways to harmonize evolutionary theory with biblical claims about creation and with what he called "the biblical account of our humanity."[38]

Before its neoconservative years, *Commentary* gave only sporadic attention to capitalism; when it did, the attention was negative. In the magazine's first symposium, in 1945, Protestant theologian Reinhold Niebuhr had recommended the "socialization of some forms of property" in order to avoid economic collapse.[39] In the 1960s, the magazine had opened its pages to Michael Harrington and Paul Goodman, who explained why capitalism bred dehumanization, promoted crass materialism, and undermined a sense of community.

But now Podhoretz sensed that defending one's own meant defending the free market and a strong private sector. This was part of loving America, the capitalist country par excellence. At a time when American capitalism had slumped—"Can Capitalism Survive?" a *Time* magazine cover story wondered in 1975—Family writers argued that capitalism created wealth for more people better than socialism did and vastly improved material well-being. They defended the conservative preference for cutting tax rates to stimulate economic growth.

Podhoretz's magazine also took on critics of growth.[40] It showed that rates of real income, life expectancy, and literacy were soaring, that economies got cleaner as they grew richer,[41] and that, as P. T. Bauer put it, "so far from the West having caused the poverty of the Third World, contact with the West has been the principal agent of material progress there." Because he felt as little sympathy for income redistribution abroad as at home, Bauer and other economists set forth the case in *Commentary* that foreign aid to poor countries, by rewarding the policies that caused impoverishment, actually retarded Third World development.[42]

But generally speaking, Podhoretz and the neoconservatives preferred to fold economics into politics. The conflict between free enterprise and collectivism seemed to them secondary to the clash between political democracy and totalitarianism. Podhoretz now published Catholic intellectual Michael Novak, author of *The Spirit of Democratic Capitalism* (1982), who offered moral justifications of democratic capitalism as superior to socialism in both theory and practice.[43] He also published George Gilder, author of the best-selling capitalist manifesto *Wealth and Poverty* (1981) (edited by Midge Decter). Podhoretz said that he felt proud that the neoconservatives were defiantly demonstrating that capitalism "was not only good in itself, being a form of freedom, but that it was also a great bulwark against totalitarianism." Not content with purely economic arguments, then, the magazine now extolled capitalism as a form of freedom.[44] It linked liberty in politics with liberty in economics (and, on the flip side of the coin, socialism with the totalitarian temptation). And to explain why liberal democracy required a market economy, Irving Kristol and Milton Friedman each argued in *Commentary* that capitalism was a necessary but not sufficient condition for political freedom.[45]

Soon enough, however, *Commentary*'s love of America and the Family's "defense of its own" occasioned changes in ways other than political.

LITERARY LEGIONNAIRES

Only in America, some members of the Family felt, can one make a good living loathing one's country. As its neoconservative tendency became more pronounced, the Family grew tired of writers who in its view remained trapped in their old radical litanies and were still consigning bourgeois America to eternal damnation. "The contemporary literary scene is rife with writers whose chief stock in the trade of ideas is a crude anti-Americanism," said Joseph Epstein.

Podhoretz, for his part, began to wonder at Americans who let themselves be educated by writers who were the enemies of all things American. "This is the only ruling class in history," he complained, "that has been unable to co-opt the 'poets,' that has not been celebrated by its artists, that has come to subsidize a class of artists who are not only hostile to it but evidently hostile to the death." And so the editor came down hard on novels that portrayed ambition and middle-class success as unseemly. In consequence, Podhoretz started to turn against writers he himself had earlier boosted. In the 1960s, he had opened *Commentary* both to Norman Mailer and to extravagant praise of Mailer. ("He is a seer trying to jar complacent men into an awareness of the despair that lies beneath their conventions.")[46] Now Podhoretz ran a piece by Joseph Epstein called "Mailer Hits Bottom." *Commentary* had published James Baldwin's earliest work. Now Podhoretz felt Baldwin's writing had been addled by radical politics; he wrote in the magazine of Baldwin's "conversion to a species of black nationalism" and of "the hectoring and self-pitying tone of the books written under its spell."

A bloodier example of waning enthusiasm arrived with *Commentary*'s roughing up of Philip Roth. In the early 1960s, the magazine had aired the loudest defenses of Roth from charges that his pitiless portrayals of suburban Jewish life added fuel to anti-Semitic fires and distorted the image of American Jews—in short, that his stories indulged in *shmutz*, that they were a *shande*. Saul Bellow set out the first such defense. In his *Commentary* review of *Goodbye, Columbus* (1959), Roth's debut book, Bellow wrote: "Here and there one meets people who feel that the business of a Jewish writer in America is to write public relations releases, to publicize everything that is nice in the Jewish community and to suppress the rest, loyally. This is not at all the business of Jewish writers, or writers of any kind." Several years later, Roth gave a talk along similar lines at Yeshiva University up in Washington Heights, but the students, unappeased, pronounced his stories *treif.* They wished to know whether he would dare write about Jews as unsparingly if he were living in pre-Nazi Germany. Afterward, Roth told his friend Ted Solotaroff that he was "surprised by the colossal brutality of the argument from the other side, and finally overwhelmed." So blindsided did he feel by the attacks that Roth vowed never again to address a Jewish audience. Nevertheless, in a *Commentary* essay called "Writing About Jews" (December 1963), which originated with the Yeshiva experience, Roth showed he was perfectly capable of defending himself. "If there are Jews who have begun to find the stories the novelists tell more provocative and pertinent than the sermons of some of the rabbis," he wrote, "perhaps it is because there are regions of feeling and consciousness in them which cannot be reached by the oratory of self-congratulation and self-pity."

But as Podhoretz removed himself ever further from his early 1960s exuberance, *Commentary* examined Roth's satires of the American Jewish bourgeoisie, and rejections of the claims of Jewish loyalty, with a harsher eye. In 1969, Peter Shaw, an associate editor, charged *Portnoy's Complaint* (1969) with "fanaticism in the hatred of things Jewish." Three years later, Irving Howe took to *Commentary* to launch a full-scale attack on the "unfocused hostility" that Howe detected as "the ground-note of Roth's sensibility," most of all in *Goodbye, Columbus* and *Portnoy's Complaint*. He called the latter, Roth's novel-as-monologue, "a vulgar book . . . full of contempt for Jewish life." ("Do me a favor, my suffering people," Alexander Portnoy raves, "and stick your suffering heritage up your suffering ass.") "The cruelest thing anyone can do with *Portnoy's Complaint,*" Howe said, "is to read it twice." In the same issue, Podhoretz joined the fray, charging Roth with incessantly returning to the same point: that Americans are disgusting, boorish people. Roth's popularity, Podhoretz said, could be explained by the rise of a new class that shared the sentiment. The next year, *Commentary* charged Roth with "evasions of artistic responsibility" and "literary onanism."[47]

Such stabs cut Portnoy's creator to the quick. Joseph Epstein said that Howe's *Commentary* essay "left Philip Roth in the spiritual equivalent of intensive care." Almost fifteen years later, in *The Anatomy Lesson* (1983), Roth satirized Howe as the literary critic Milton Appel, a "sententious bastard" who had published a harsh reconsideration of Nathan Zuckerman's work in a Jewish monthly. "You pervert my intentions, then call me perverse!" Zuckerman screams at Appel. "You lay hold of my comedy with your ten-ton gravity and turn it into a travesty."

Saul Bellow's relationship to the magazine had also grown testy, as the following exchange shows. Podhoretz had asked to see a talk Bellow had delivered in Miami.

8 March 1976

Dear Norman:

I did give a talk in Miami but I intend to make it part of a longer piece. And now tell me this: If you were described in someone's magazine as a "burnt out case" would you be at all inclined to contribute articles to that magazine? [48]

Sincerely yours,

Saul Bellow

———————

March 11, 1976

Dear Saul:

You ask whether I would be inclined to contribute articles to a magazine in which I had been described as a "burnt-out case." The answer to your question is Yes. In fact, I have contributed pieces to magazines which printed far worse things about me. Besides, if I thought you were a "burnt-out case," would I be eager to publish you? And believe me, I am.

Yours,

Norman Podhoretz

IN LATER YEARS, *Commentary*'s swing distanced it away from its own star literary critics, too—at least those who remained on the Left. Midge Decter leveled an attack on Irving Howe, who in the eyes of the Family had held onto sound literary instincts even as his political ones went awry—he was literarily kosher but politically *treif*.[49] Conservative literary critic Kenneth

Lynn scolded Alfred Kazin for his "lack of professional self-discipline" (July 1984). In another *Commentary* piece, Lynn wrote that Leslie Fiedler, who had written more than twenty pieces for the magazine, "has done his best to impoverish the study of literature by breaking down standards and transforming academic study into a theater of the self" (January 1983).

One sometimes heard it said of the *New Statesman*, the left-wing British weekly edited for thirty years by Kingsley Martin, that the "back of the book" repudiated everything in the front. Literary editors such as Margaret Marshall at *The Nation* and Leon Wieseltier at the *New Republic* ran their own ships; book reviews were not subject to the general editorial line. (Incidentally, Wieseltier, another student of Lionel Trilling, published his first piece in *Commentary* as a Columbia senior in 1973.)[50] None of *Commentary*'s editors, by contrast, tolerated an independent literary editor. Some of its writers grew less comfortable with the magazine's style of reviewing. In the late 1970s, for example, just after graduating from Barnard, Daphne Merkin, later a staff writer for the *New Yorker*, published several book reviews in *Commentary*. (Her first appearance in print, in fact, was an attack in the magazine on what she called Chaim Potok's "sentimentalized version of Orthodox Judaism.") Soon, however, she said she "became disenchanted by the editors' insistence on putting politics into every frail vessel of a book or a film that came along."

Starting in the 1980s, the magazine replaced its regular fiction reviewer, Pearl K. Bell (Alfred Kazin's younger sister and Daniel Bell's wife), with conservative writer Carol Iannone, who could be trusted to wage the literary fight. In various *Commentary* pieces, Iannone charged, for example, that Grace Paley's imagination was "formed and finally trapped by ideology," that William Gaddis's novels were weighed down by "their quotient of counter-culture faddism," and that the Pulitzer and the National Book Award prizes bestowed on African American author Alice Walker's *The Color Purple* (1982) "seemed less a recognition of literary achievement than some official act of reparation."

In his book *My Love Affair with America* (2001), Podhoretz would denounce "critics of the Left to whom art was a 'weapon,' and who praised or damned novels and poems and plays entirely for the political or ideological positions they took, and not for how well or badly the writer's intentions— whatever they might be—were realized." On another occasion, he would record dismay that his old Cambridge mentor F. R. Leavis, in his writing on D. H. Lawrence, "sins against the disinterestedness in whose absence literary criticism becomes a species of covert ideologizing." Yet it became clear as day that Podhoretz's own literary judgments—and by extension, the magazine's—had become ever more "ideological."[51] The magazine's literary criticism in its neoconservative phase had become a form of ideological gate-keeping, a way of establishing the true canon. More than ever, Podhoretz and the Family began to see every product of the mind as something that reflected a political allegiance. They increasingly put literature through a political grinder. Those who had come to politics via literature—whose politics took on some of the suppleness of literature—now saw literature through the prism of politics (or of their own political predilections), as the pursuit of politics by other means.

ART AND ARDOR: AMERICAN JEWISH WRITING, TAKE TWO

So Podhoretz found new writers. Of these, Cynthia Ozick, two years his senior, came close to his ideal, as much for her political inclinations as for the lilt and cadences of her beautiful sentences. A daughter of Russian immigrants, Ozick had grown up in the Pelham Bay corner of the Bronx and studied at New York University and Ohio State, where she had devoted her MA thesis to Henry James. She, too, had attended Lionel Trilling's graduate seminar at Columbia, though without much enjoyment. Her first publication in *Commentary* was a poem accepted by Susan Sontag ("Apocalypse," September 1959). Ozick's first *Commentary* piece, in July 1964, was not a short story but a brilliant dissection of John Cheever, "the Chekhov of the suburbs" as he was known, and his phony view of America: "Look, he seems to cry, observe our golden beginnings—how far we have fallen from them!" In the course of working through several drafts of the review with Ted Solotaroff, Ozick could not restrain herself from praising the magazine. "As a reader," she told Solotaroff, "there is no magazine, and no editorial board, I respect more than *Commentary* and its writer-editors; as a writer, there is no periodical I should feel more at home in, intellectually and morally. . . . Access to print in *Commentary* is access not merely to the leading serious journal, but to that small group of minds which, indisputably, governs much of the important political and literary thinking in this country." Ozick looked to Podhoretz—"the gadfly of fools and the rebuker of knaves," she called him—with special admiration.

Ozick's first story in *Commentary*, "Envy; or, Yiddish in America," a novella really, follows an embittered Yiddish writer named Edelshtein.[52] Doomed to oblivion, literally and figuratively childless, Edelshtein rails against the ignorance of American Jewish writers: "What do they know, I mean of knowledge . . . Yiddish! One word here, one word there. *Shickseh* on one page, *putz* on the other, and that's the whole vocabulary. . . . They know ten words for, excuse me, penis, and when it comes to a word for learning, they're impotent." Never content passively to send a manuscript to the printer, Podhoretz's practice was to edit the magazine's fiction as intensively as its essays. On his advice, Ozick drastically revised the story, and when it came out in 1969, "Envy" met with instant success. Intensely grateful for Podhoretz's guidance, she called him deus ex machina and *ba'al hanifla'ot*— "wonder-worker." "In the last five months," she told Podhoretz, "thanks to the miracle you wrought—I've had more attention, pleasant and unpleasant, than ever in my whole life before."[53]

Philip Roth provided some of the pleasant attention: "*Envy* is a marvelous story," he told her, "and it makes me envious. . . . You've written the story that I have been waiting for years to see." Yet Ozick and Roth were very different kinds of animals, and the differences between the two shed a great deal of light on *Commentary*'s new sensibility. "I am not a Jewish writer," Roth insisted; "I am a writer who is a Jew." Ozick, in contrast, felt herself to be elaborating a Jewish literature in English, a writing that drew deeply on the wellsprings of Jewish history and languages and literatures past. She espoused a kind of literary version of *Commentary*'s exaltation of particular Jewish identity: "Literature does not spring from the urge to Esperanto, but from the tribe," she wrote. "If we blow into the narrow end of the *shofar*," she suggested in an essay called "Toward a New Yiddish," "we will be heard far. But if we choose to be Mankind rather than Jewish, we will not be heard at all." To choose to be Jewish, however, did not entail living in opposition to the larger culture. Alienation, she wrote in her essay "Highbrow Blues," remained "the philistinism of the intellectual." In a letter to Podhoretz (February 8, 1971), Ozick elaborated on her literary credo:

> Since I mean to write out of a purely Jewish vision, not an accommodating one, I will write *as if* I were an actual member of a majority culture; I will write out of the heart of a Jewish civilization, *as if* it were really there: temporal, crowded, palpable. Looking at Chartres (or at any book I'm to review), I will judge it not for its significance to Gentiles but for its significance to me. Isn't that only natural? Isn't it pretense for a Jew to see otherwise? If you find it offensive that I look at Europe, or at books, solely out of Jewish history and Jewish metaphor, which is to say Jewish eyes, or if you find this extreme, then I have to charge you with artifice, by which I mean accommodation to the force of the majority. I never want to accommodate at all.[54]

As usual, Ozick put things a little starkly, but such was *Commentary*'s postulate too; it had learned to assess the movements of politics and literature by their significance to *us*—*our* interests, *our* vision.

Occasional flashes of brilliance would still brighten the magazine's fiction pages over the next decades: Allegra Goodman's first published story at age seventeen, the first of ten that would appear in *Commentary*; vivid fiction by Norma Rosen and Johanna Kaplan (both of whose first published short stories appeared there), Fernanda Eberstadt and Tova Reich.[55] But in general, an imaginative impoverishment seemed to set in. The newer fiction lacked a sense of urgency, as if beside the point, for the themes of Jewish marginality and alienation had exhausted themselves. The Bellow-Roth-Malamud trifecta had long since mined the vein of postimmigrant Jewish ethnic experience. Those three, as Cynthia Ozick said, "had taken the post-immigration experience as far as it could go. Anyone who hoped to push forward in that same direction of portraiture and sensibility was bound to end up as an imitator. For new work, the aftermath of the immigration was played out and offered nothing but repetition and desiccation—or something worse: ventriloquism, fakery, nostalgia, sentimentalism, cardboard romanticism." The storm of conflicting emotions subsided, self-consciousness dissipated, and a literary moment had passed. With Jewish assimilation into the country's culture more or less complete, the strain of duality—the tension between Jews and America—slackened, and the bow of the imagination, to borrow Edmund Wilson's phrase, could seldom be drawn as tight as before.

≪ 9 ≫

Zealpolitik

*When I tell any truth, it is not for the sake of convincing
those who do not know it, but for the sake of defending
those that do.*

—WILLIAM BLAKE

A LIGHT UNTO THE NATIONS

Starting in the early 1970s, the new *Commentary* would articulate with special urgency the inextricable links between the threats to freedom at home and those abroad. For the next four decades, the magazine would resolutely interpret the mandate to defend one's own to include promoting democracy and freedom abroad. Ever since Thomas Jefferson proclaimed America an "empire for liberty," this notion had enjoyed a long pedigree as one strain of American foreign policy.[1] But as the neoconservative currents billowed its sails, the magazine affirmed with special forcefulness the superiority of freedom, the fate of which devolved on America.

This affirmation went in two directions. In one sense, the world depended on America. To use former Hubert Humphrey speechwriter Ben Wattenberg's term, the writers and editors at the magazine regarded American dominance as an "imperium of values." The danger, they thought, came precisely from an American abdication of power. Harvard political scientist Samuel P. Huntington argued in *Commentary* that greater American power—political, economic, and military—"can only have positive effects on the state of liberty and democracy throughout the world."[2] They saw America—and its military might—as a force for good. For example, in a 1975 issue Robert Tucker, then professor of international relations at Johns Hopkins, explored the prospects for American military intervention to break the oil embargo and solve the oil crisis of 1973–1974, and thereby to protect a vital national interest. In deploring "the absence of the meaningful threat of force" to resolve a crisis that had quadrupled oil prices, Tucker's piece aroused a storm of controversy.[3] But the vitriol poured on the article only confirmed, as military strategist and frequent *Commentary* contributor Edward Luttwak said, that "the country's opinion-making elite no longer view the protection of American and/or Western interests as legitimate."

For his part, Norman Podhoretz lamented the paralysis of America's power to act in the world and the nation's shattered self-confidence. He began to talk about "the retreat of American power" and a "new national mood of self-doubt and self-disgust." He warned against succumbing to the loss of clarity and confidence that followed Vietnam. Should the new isolationism triumph, he wrote just before the nation's bicentennial, "the United States will celebrate its two-hundredth birthday by betraying the heritage of liberty which has earned it the wonder and envy of the world from the moment of its founding to this, and by helping to make that world safe for the most determined and ferocious and barbarous enemies of liberty ever to have appeared on the earth."[4]

In another sense, however, the neoconservatives came to believe that America depended on the world, that disorder abroad threatened equilibrium at home. "Neoconservatism believes that American democracy is not likely to survive for long in a world that is overwhelmingly hostile to American values," Irving Kristol said. What set neoconservatives apart from isolationists was the insistence that no *cordon sanitaire* protected the United States from global threats. At a time when democracies were under totalitarian assault across the globe, American freedoms could not survive, as Walter Laqueur said, "once the lights go out in the rest of the world." Anything less than pursuing a foreign policy dedicated to the expansion of liberty, Patrick Moynihan wrote in the May 1974 *Commentary*, "risks the contraction of liberty: our own included." Because the magazine's writers believed the spread of democracy offered the best shot at encouraging a peaceful and prosperous world,[5] they lauded American efforts to promote democracy in places such as El Salvador, Chile, the Philippines, South Korea, and Warsaw Pact countries.

To the *Commentary* neoconservatives, then, defending one's own meant opposing American self-abasement vis-à-vis the Third World, a new version of the "white man's burden." In March 1975, Moynihan published a hefty *Commentary* piece called "The United States in Opposition," which urged the country's representatives to acknowledge that they now stood as an opposition minority in relation to Third World despotisms and to stop apologizing for an imperfect democracy. "It is time," he wrote, "that the American spokesman came to be feared in international forums for the truths he might tell." Moynihan had started to write for Podhoretz in 1961, when he was a thirty-four-year-old former aide to New York governor Averell Harriman, with a report on the New York Democrats. But "The United States in Opposition" represented a breakthrough. As to why he gave it to Podhoretz, "it was clear that only he could edit it," Moynihan said, "and, such was the time, that only he would publish it." In the early 1970s, the future New York senator called his friend Podhoretz "very simply the finest literary-intellectual editor of this age—and he has, of course, paid for it."

Podhoretz knew he had a bombshell on his hands, a piece that could set the terms of the whole foreign policy debate, and so for the first time in the magazine's history, he called a press conference to launch an article. As the reactions testified, Podhoretz's judgment was not far off. Ernest Lefever, a founder of the Ethics and Public Policy Center, called Moynihan's piece "the most significant analysis of U.S. foreign policy I have seen in a decade." Secretary of State Henry Kissinger read it through at one sitting and found it "staggeringly good."[6] A month later, Kissinger asked Moynihan to serve as ambassador to the United Nations. Moynihan accepted with haste and served, with obvious relish, for eight months. His fiery speech against the UN "Zionism is racism" resolution was largely written by Podhoretz.[7]

UNREALISTS

Commentary's activist defense of democracy and its stress on the follies of American inaction abroad would earn it the scorn of two sets of rivals. Paleoconservatives—some of them isolationist disciples of Senator Robert Taft, who had opposed the Marshall Plan to rehabilitate Europe—had long opposed what George Washington called "foreign entanglements" except where American interests were under direct threat. These traditional conservatives argued that intervention was to foreign policy what welfare was to domestic policy.

Then there were the pragmatic-minded foreign policy "realists," who argued that narrowly construed national interests, not values, ought to guide America's foreign commitments. Realists, who regularly scolded *Commentary* for practicing *moralpolitik* rather than *realpolitik,* advocated pruning American objectives for the sake of preserving a balance of power between nations.

Commentary had voiced reservations about George Kennan's brand of *realpolitik* as far back as 1952. But with think pieces such as Nathan Glazer's "American Values and American Foreign Policy" (July 1976), the magazine, in a bid to end the realists' dominance, began to take a more expansive view of the country's national interest. That interest, *Commentary* now argued time and again, extended not only to tangible assets like economic benefits, but also to American values. The magazine's writers explained that a value-free foreign policy that prized stability above all else amounted to an unacceptable relativism. They came to see that realists—such as Henry Kissinger, the national security adviser and secretary of state to Richard Nixon, and former *Commentary* contributor Hans Morgenthau—blinded themselves to the internal character of regimes; to the power of ideas; to the role of culture, ideology, and religion; and to the moral considerations of statecraft. "The 'realistic' foreign policy that pursues 'national interest' without regard to morality," Jeane Kirkpatrick (then a professor of political science at Georgetown) wrote in the February 1980 *Commentary*, "ultimately founders on its lack of realism about the irreducible human concern with morality."

In the neoconservative view, realism ill suited a nation whose very founding rested on the assertion of universal moral principles. The Family preferred to put the cold war on moral footing, to join strategic thinking with moral purpose. Robert Kagan, who started writing for *Commentary* at age twenty-two in 1981, said that neoconservatism "combines an idealist's moralism, and even messianism, with a realist's belief in the importance of power." This was an ideology that comported well with the notion that America possessed a special destiny, that it was a light unto the nations.

A FLOCK OF HAWKS

McCarthyism and then the Vietnam War meanwhile had put hard anti-Communists into disrepute. They were blamed—by the southern Democrat senator J. William Fulbright most prominently—for leading the country into a disastrous military adventure. Revelations in 1966 and 1967 that the CIA had been covertly funding anti-Communist groups such as the Congress for Cultural Freedom and the magazine *Encounter* (coedited by Irving Kristol) hadn't helped matters. In a September 1967 symposium called "Liberal Anti-Communism Revisited," *Commentary* had itself featured some of the *mea culpas*.[8] The result was that by the early 1970s the very term "Communism" had faded out of the American conversation about the cold war. Liberals were defecting from cold war anti-Communist resolve; the political elite no longer shared the conviction that the society it led was good or even that the cold war could be won. After the withdrawal from Vietnam in 1975, America seemed to the neoconservatives to be in a state of retreat from its own power. Drawing on the principled anti-Communism of Elliot Cohen's *Commentary*, however, Norman Podhoretz intended to resurrect anti-Communism for the post-Vietnam era.

The Family's hegira to the Right involved a recalibration of its views of the Vietnam War, which Podhoretz now understood to have been an altruistic effort to free the Vietnamese from Communism. In *Commentary* and in his 1982 book *Why We Were in Vietnam*, Podhoretz offered moral justifications for a war that had devoured some 58,000 American lives.[9] The American intervention, he wrote, was "an act of imprudent idealism whose moral soundness has been . . . overwhelmingly vindicated by the hideous consequences of our defeat." One had but to look at the boat people and the murderous campaign of Pol Pot's Khmer Rouge, he said, to see that far from putting an end to the suffering of the people of Vietnam, Cambodia, and Laos, the end of the war only exacerbated it.[10]

But Podhoretz seemed more exercised by the antiwar movement than by the war itself. "The antiwar movement," he now said, "bears a certain measure of responsibility for the horrors that have overtaken the people of Vietnam." Ever since entering its neoconservative phase, *Commentary* repeatedly expressed dismay at the ways liberals had been chastened by Vietnam. It wished to exorcise what as late at the July 1995 issue Robert Kagan was calling "the Vietnam-era demons still coursing through the Democratic soul." As Podhoretz saw it, those demons bore treacherous gifts: a loss of political will; a failure of nerve; an enervation, demoralization, and defeatism; and a retreat from internationalism into isolationism.

Podhoretz scoffed at the faint of heart who held the United States primarily responsible for the cold war. During the 1970s (and even more so after the Soviet invasion of Afghanistan in December 1979), he became preoccupied with Soviet expansionism. He warned that the military balance had shifted in favor of the Soviet Union, which, far from remaining a status-quo power, still seethed with aggression and still held great confidence in its armed forces. In 1970, *Commentary* was still attacking the Nixon administration from the Left as too bellicose. The magazine had charged it with not pursuing SALT (the Strategic Arms Limitation Talks) assiduously enough. By the Carter administration, however, the magazine presented the SALT II disarmament treaty not as an achievement of diplomacy but, in the words of Eugene Rostow (under secretary of state for political affairs under LBJ and director of the Arms Control and Disarmament Agency under Ronald Reagan), as "an expression of American acquiescence in the Soviet drive for overwhelming military superiority."

Podhoretz regarded the Soviet Union as a revolutionary state. "Like Nazi Germany," he said, "the Soviet Union aims to overthrow the present international system and to replace it with one in which its own power is dominant." To get at the nature of Soviet barbarism, he commissioned think pieces on totalitarianism by the likes of dissident Polish philosopher (and ex-Communist) Leszek Kolakowski ("Totalitarianism and the Lie," May 1983) and memoirs about Soviet life, such as Vladimir Bukovsky's "The Soul of Man Under Socialism" (January 1979).[11]

The American pursuit of détente, a policy into which appeasement appeared inherently built, seemed to Podhoretz merely a form of beating a strategic retreat; he was impatient with it. One of the architects of détente, Henry Kissinger, was in turn impatient with him. "Nixon and his heir, Gerald Ford, sought to carefully wear the Soviets down," Kissinger wrote, "but the neocons yearned to vanquish Communism with a burst of ideological élan." Podhoretz could no more contemplate bringing the conflict with the Soviet Union to diplomatic resolution than he could imagine negotiating a peaceful settlement with Adolf Hitler. "Fear begets pacifist illusions which then beget appeasement," Podhoretz said. He and the magazine made frequent appeals to the "Munich" analogy to show that the spirit of appeasement was alive and well.[12] The stench of appeasement, Podhoretz wrote in 1983, "now pervades the American political atmosphere."

But not all barbarisms are equal. Podhoretz urged greater support for Central American anti-Communists because he preferred right-wing dictatorships to left-wing ones: They were less pervasively repressive, he felt, less permanent, and more susceptible to American influence. "Even authoritarian regimes at their worst," Podhoretz wrote, "generally allow more freedom—economic, cultural, religious—than the mildest of Communist states." Jeane Kirkpatrick, in her 1979 *Commentary* essay "Dictatorships and Double Standards," defended American support for authoritarian regimes facing Communist insurgencies. She argued that totalitarian regimes posed a greater threat than run-of-the-mill autocrats, who "do not disturb the habitual rhythms of work and leisure, habitual places of residence, habitual patterns of family and personal relations." "Right-wing autocracies," she added, "do sometimes evolve into democracies." Communist dictatorships, however, cannot be expected to do so. "The history of this century provides no grounds for expecting that radical totalitarian regimes will transform themselves," she wrote. In Kirkpatrick's view, Carter's foreign policy—more tolerant toward the repressions of Communist enemies than of authoritarian friends—amounted to "a posture of continuous self-abasement and apology."

Resolved to show that he was made of sterner stuff, Podhoretz argued that appeasement would culminate in "Finlandization," by which he meant a kind of gradual accommodation that led a country to acquiesce in Soviet wishes to the point of blurring its own sovereignty. In a long 1980 *Commentary* call to arms entitled "The Present Danger," based on a talk to the Council on Foreign Relations in Washington and timed to boost Ronald Reagan in his presidential contest with Jimmy Carter, Podhoretz reaffirmed his view of the cold war as a struggle "for freedom and against Communism, for democracy and against totalitarianism." He alluded to the possibility of a "final collapse of an American resolve to resist the forward surge of Soviet imperialism." This, Podhoretz said, would entail nothing less than "the Finlandization of America." "Politicians and pundits would appear to celebrate the happy arrival of a new era of 'peace' and 'friendship' and 'cooperation' between the Soviet Union and U.S.," he predicted. "Dissenters from this cheerful view would be castigated as warmongers."

It was precisely at this point that the Family's thinking about the unanticipated consequences of social policies such as affirmative action intersected with its views on the unintended—and much more threatening—consequences of Soviet socialism. Whether at home or abroad, Family members believed, centralized state planning endangered individual liberty.

As the house foreign affairs style became more alarmist during the 1980s, however, *Commentary* carved out one large exception to its mistrust of the state. In articles such as "Why an American Arms Build-Up Is Morally Necessary" (February 1984), the magazine advocated more defense spending, which measured in real terms had fallen during the 1970s. Throughout the 1980s, the magazine made the case against arms control on the grounds that it could weaken American superiority and allow the Soviets to translate nuclear superiority into political advantage.[13] Although Podhoretz applauded the ways Ronald Reagan worked to restore confidence "in the utility of military force as an instrument of worthy political purposes," he grumbled against the administration's negotiating a reduction in intermediate-range nuclear missiles. "Arms negotiations with the Soviet Union is a lie and a fraud and a deceit to the nation," Podhoretz declared in January 1983. *Commentary* hailed the Strategic Defense Initiative (SDI), a space-based antimissile defense system known as "Star Wars" when Reagan announced it in 1983.[14] The magazine defended the Pentagon against charges of waste, fraud, and mismanagement. Eliot A. Cohen—then writing his dissertation on military manpower, later professor at the Paul H. Nitze School of Advanced International Studies and Counselor of the State Department—argued in a 1982 *Commentary* essay that the all-volunteer army had failed and that it was time for a reserve draft.

So it was that the Family came to conclude that defending one's own meant defending America from the Soviet menace, and this in turn brought the magazine into a hard anti-Communism that once again, after the 1960s lapse, became *Commentary*'s driving force. Midge Decter recounted in her memoir that the magazine's "true animating passion was a deep hatred for Communism in any and all of its manifestations, whether . . . the liberal fellow travelers of the Communists or even the liberals whose mind-set had unknowingly been influenced by the Communists." The Family's earlier anti-Communism was a movement of the Left, rooted in the anti-Stalinism of the 1930s. It acquired its urgency, Irving Howe said, "from a wish to achieve a profoundly democratic and egalitarian society." As neoconservative anti-Communists, by contrast, the Family now attacked from the Right flank and opposed socialism in any form. The conflict between the United States and the Soviet Union, *Commentary* now argued, could be reduced neither to a power struggle, as realists had it, nor, as traditional conservatives had it, to a collision between the faithful and the godless. Rather, the cold war was at its heart what Podhoretz called "a clash between civilization and barbarism"—a fight for democratic freedom against tyranny.

FROM STRENGTH TO STRENGTH

By resurrecting anti-Communism, a once marginal group of renegade leftists, who had felt themselves handicapped for American life, now found that their ideas had become extraordinarily relevant to their country during the great age of American power; their quarrels had foreshadowed larger political shifts. The squabbles of the *Commentary* clan had become the politics of governments. Its preoccupations had become the country's, and its scale of ambition widened accordingly.

The stars over Reagan's skies favored the magazine, which now enjoyed an audience in Washington as never before. Its neoconservative persuasion now firmly in place, *Commentary* wielded a political influence out of all proportion to its size.[15] It had gained the ear of many who moved in the upper echelons of Reagan's administration. More members of the Family began to enjoy the perquisites of power. They were honored and consulted; they were makers and shakers. Podhoretz was invited to lunch in the cabinet room with Reagan and his aides. He had made it.

This isn't to imply that all had been smooth with Reagan. In 1981, a *Commentary* essay by Robert Tucker called "Carterism Without Carter" reprimanded Reagan for failing to support Israel's bombing of the Iraqi nuclear reactor and for deferring to Saudi Arabia. Tucker expressed the hope "that the Reagan administration would provide the occasion for the United States to assume once again a leadership role commensurate with its power." In 1982, Podhoretz disclosed his distress in a *New York Times Magazine* piece called "The Neoconservative Anguish over Reagan's Foreign Policy," which faulted the president with not following through on his ideas about how to confront the Soviet menace.[16] Podhoretz was dismayed by Reagan's approval of the sale of American AWACS planes to Saudi Arabia, by his expressions of disapproval of Israel's 1982 incursion into Lebanon to flush out the Palestine Liberation Organization (PLO), and by his withdrawal of U.S. troops from Lebanon after an Islamic suicide bomber killed 241 American troops in the U.S. Marine barracks in Beirut in 1983.

On the other hand, Reagan appointed Family members to senior positions (though not in economic or welfare policy). After reading "Dictatorships and Double Standards" (the president's chief foreign policy adviser Richard Allen had passed it along), Reagan made Jeane Kirkpatrick ambassador to the United Nations (the first woman to serve in that post), where some delegates nicknamed her "the ambassador from *Commentary*." Still liberal on domestic issues, she began jokingly calling herself a "welfare-state conservative"; by then she too had grown exasperated with the Democrats. "We had acted like good Democrats for a long time," Kirkpatrick said in the spring of 1980. "Meanwhile the Republican Party keeps telling us they like what we say. They call me. They write to me. They say, 'What a marvelous article.' We are really treated quite badly by the Democratic Party and meanwhile we are bombarded with friendly messages from Republicans." *Commentary* contributor (and former Young People's Socialist League chairman) Carl Gershman served as Kirkpatrick's chief counselor and then headed the National Endowment for Democracy. Elliott Abrams was appointed in 1981, at age thirty-three, the youngest assistant secretary of state in the twentieth century. Bill Bennett was appointed secretary of education, where William Kristol served as an aide. Gertrude Himmelfarb held a presidential appointment on the Council of the National Endowment for the Humanities. Robert Kagan served in the State Department during Reagan's second term. Richard Pipes served on Reagan's National Security Council.

In 1965, in an article about the *New Republic*, Podhoretz had written, "A sense of alienation from political power may be good, even necessary, for the health of magazines based in New York."[17] Fifteen years later, newly in step with the *Zeitgeist*, Podhoretz no longer felt that way. He got himself appointed to the board of the U.S. Information Agency. He attended White House dinners. President Reagan blurbed his book *The Present Danger* (1980). ("I urge all Americans to read this critically important book.") No wonder Podhoretz sensed that the election of Reagan in 1980 was a mark of the neoconservatives' "spreading influence." At a Family conference held by the Committee for the Free World at the Plaza Hotel in 1983, Podhoretz exulted (according to Alfred Kazin, who was in attendance): "We are the dominant faction within the world of ideas—the most influential—the most powerful. . . . People like us made Reagan's victory, which had been considered unthinkable."

Many outside the Family, of course, looked with skepticism on such boasts. Irishman Conor Cruise O'Brien, for instance, commented in 1986: "Of course you can imagine—if you are a neoconservative—the esoteric influence of *Commentary*, etc., as spreading out at secondhand, through the media, and so filtering down to the plebs who, when they pressed those levers, were indirectly under the spell of Mr. Podhoretz and his friends without ever having heard of them. But it all seems a mite fanciful to me."[18]

Fanciful or not, now that Podhoretz felt the touch of officialdom, he could not help enjoying the magazine's new influence. "Only those of the *Commentary*-Georgetown-neoconservative team are in the inner circle," former diplomat Seymour Finger said. "Elliot Cohen both feared much and hoped for much," Patrick Moynihan observed in the magazine's fortieth anniversary issue in 1985. "But I doubt that even he could have hoped for the influence *Commentary* has had on democratic thought these four long decades."

Neoconservatives were in ascendancy. "It was the first time in our lives that we felt truly welcomed," Midge Decter said, "and truly close to the political action." Podhoretz's wife got closer to the action by founding, in 1980, the Committee for the Free World (heir to the Committee on the Present Danger). The new committee brought together Family intellectuals dedicated to the fight against totalitarianism. It aimed to "conduct a battle of ideas in defense of Western values and institutions." (Neal Kozodoy, *Commentary*'s executive editor, served as secretary.) Decter called it "my very own battle station" and edited its lively eight-page monthly newsletter, *Contentions*.

For all its newfound influence, however, the *Commentary* crowd would sometimes huddle within—take a comfort in, even—a sense of embattled vulnerability. Back in 1973, Ernst Pawel, a biographer of Franz Kafka, Heinrich Heine, and Theodor Herzl who had written several pieces for the magazine in the late 1960s (he was a friend of managing editor Marion Magid), was already lamenting the "wholly unwarranted sense of isolation haunting the pages of the new *Commentary*." This was a couple of years after Moynihan complained in the magazine that the American press had been becoming "more and more influenced by attitudes genuinely hostile to American society and the American government."[19] Decades later, members of the Family, having reached undreamed-of influence, would in their own estimations remain the beleaguered outsiders, the underdogs, the dissidents, a saving remnant, as if they alone held the line. They would still feel that theirs was a dissonant voice in an American culture dominated by the Left. As late as 1993—during the Bill Clinton "interregnum" in Republican dominance, Bill Kristol, Irving's son and editor of the *Weekly Standard*, described this sense in *Commentary*: "Liberals have reclaimed control of the executive branch, and will soon once again take over the federal judiciary. Liberals continue to dominate Congress and most state and local governments; they rule virtually unchallenged over our educational institutions and our cultural and philanthropic organizations; they shape most of the products of the mass media, journalism, book publishing, and Hollywood."

"Embattled intellectuals," James Q. Wilson once wrote, "are dogmatic intellectuals."

WHO KILLED COMMUNISM?

Some foresaw that very soon, *Commentary*'s great foe, and America's, would vanish into the dustbin of history. In a speech at Notre Dame in 1981, President Reagan declared that Communism was "a sad, bizarre chapter in human history whose last pages are even now being written." "Soviet political and economic institutions are in serious trouble," Richard Pipes granted in *Commentary* in 1984.

But the magazine was not all prescience. Many *Commentary* writers, like almost everyone else, dismissed as fantasy the notion of Soviet collapse until the very moment of collapse. For one thing, they considered political reform impossible under the Soviet system. After Mikhail Gorbachev, protégé of hard-liner Yuri Andropov, assumed power as general secretary in 1985, *Commentary* disregarded his gestures toward *perestroika* (restructuring) and *glasnost* (openness) and suspected that any relaxation attested only to a renewed Soviet confidence. The magazine cautioned against underestimating the ruthless coercive power of the party apparatus. At issue, Nick Eberstadt wrote in the May 1987 *Commentary*, "is not whether the party under Gorbachev will 'democratize' or whether the economy will 'reform.' These hardy perennials of hopeful discussion in the West have survived sixty-five winters with the Soviet state, and will no doubt last a good many more." In July 1988, Walter Laqueur advised that "no substantial further advances should be expected for years to come."

Also that year, Podhoretz coaxed pieces from former Soviet *refusenik* Natan Sharansky and from French expert on Russia Alain Besançon that called into question the notion that Gorbachev's reforms would lead to genuine democratization. In December 1988, Gorbachev told the United Nations that he would unilaterally reduce the Soviet army by 500,000 soldiers and withdraw 10,000 Soviet tanks from Eastern Europe. The next month, ex-socialist French philosopher Jean-Francois Revel argued in *Commentary* that *glasnost* might be genuinely new, but it was at the end of the day merely an instrument through which Gorbachev could consolidate his power. "Gorbachev aims to achieve by seduction what Brezhnev and Gromyko almost succeeded in achieving by threats," Revel said.

Most Family experts felt certain, then, that reports of the death of Soviet totalitarianism had been much exaggerated, and their magazine warned of the Soviet threat to the last. As late as 1987, *Commentary* talked up the Soviet will to expansion. "The Soviet Union will not soon collapse from its internal problems, change its view of the world, or abandon its ambitions," historian of ancient Greece Donald Kagan wrote that year, "although there is much to be said for trying to assist the disintegration of the Soviet empire when good opportunities arise." "The momentum of [the Soviet Union's] drive to seek further conquests shows no sign of abatement," Hilton Kramer wrote, also that year. Angelo Codevilla, a fellow of the Hoover Institution, insisted in the November 1988 issue that the Soviet Union presented as much of a threat to the United States as ever; Moscow's "offensive capability has never been higher," he said.[20]

Shortly thereafter, the *annus mirabilis* 1989 saw the serial collapse of Communist rule. Poles brought Solidarity to power. Hungary legalized non-Communist parties. The Berlin Wall crashed down in November. East

Germany threw open its borders, disbanded the Stasi, and took the first steps toward reunification. The Czechs, born aloft by the Velvet Revolution, elected playwright and poet Václav Havel as president. Romanians executed Communist dictator Nicolae Ceausescu. The Evil Empire toppled, and Eastern European liberated itself.

All of this came as a shock. "The Communist regimes . . . haven't surrendered power voluntarily—they've been forced by all kinds of pressure," Podhoretz told *Newsweek* in December 1989. "But I did not anticipate they would give way without a bigger compulsion or armed rebellion or war." The anti–cold war brigades and the anti-anti-Communists in American life, who had all along regarded the Soviet Union as immune to outside pressure, insisted that Communism had collapsed on account of its own internal weaknesses.[21] But it seemed to those around *Commentary* quite obvious that the cold war policies they had supported—ideological pressure combined with arms buildup and SDI—had at the very least hastened the demise of the enemy and had contributed to the victory of the American idea over the Communist idea.[22] "If I were someone who had been preaching unilateral disarmament," Midge Decter said in late 1989, "I'd be ashamed." The Family took the view that it was precisely the application of American power—much as George Kennan had predicted in his fabled 1947 *Foreign Affairs* essay—that in the end promoted the breakup of the Soviet empire. Anyone who believed otherwise, James Nuechterlein averred in the September 1990 *Commentary*, "might as readily believe in the ministrations of the tooth fairy."

In the summer of 1991, an even bigger surprise: After Boris Yeltsin thwarted an attempted coup in Moscow, the Baltic states, Ukraine, Belarus, and Moldova declared independence. Gorbachev resigned that December, and the Communist regime in Mother Russia was no longer.

As the Family entered the 1990s, it felt confirmed that its hostility to Communist subversion at home and expansionism abroad had been justified. The more Soviet material came to light, the more could Americans see that Communism was exactly as horrific as the Family had all along said it was.[23] "The decisive final battle of the cold war," one *Commentary* piece suggested in 1995, "was waged not with tanks and missiles but with typewriters and ideas." Podhoretz said that former dissidents had told him as much "with tears in their eyes when they describe how much *Commentary* meant to them in their darkest days." As the Family began writing the postscript to the West's victory, it felt that it had been proven right on the century's most significant political question.

As dawn dispels night, the question of Communism, which had dominated American foreign policy for so long, faded from view. The great confrontation of good and evil was replaced by smaller, less intellectually engaging, if still horrific conflicts: Bosnia, Haiti, Rwanda. Relations with Asia would assume greater significance, and Arthur Waldron, Aaron Friedberg, and Francis Fukuyama each wrote learned articles for *Commentary* on that part of the world. But having insisted that the conflict between the United States and the USSR was "the central issue of our time," as Norman Podhoretz put it, the magazine he captained now lost something of its *raison d'être* and coherence. "Are we a gang of friends, a family?" asked Midge Decter at a meeting of the Committee for the Free World in Washington in April 1990. "Or are we a long, sour marriage held together for the kids and now facing an empty nest?" By 1990, *Commentary* had about 29,000 paid subscribers, half of the numbers it had enjoyed in the early 1970s.

The Family neoconservatives still regarded it as America's inescapable mission to spread democracy, especially in the Middle East. As bearers of the legacy of anti-Communism—and its moral vocabulary—they held ever more tightly to their faith that American dominance served the causes of peace and human rights. The end of the cold war, they felt, by no means ended the necessity for a vigilant defense. They supported the expansion of the North Atlantic Treaty Organization and continued to lament cutbacks in military spending.[24] And one lesson they drew from the war in the Balkans was that military force, not UN diplomacy, got the job done.

But after enjoying unprecedented access to the higher echelons during the Reagan years, the neoconservatives were largely frozen out by the administrations of George H. W. Bush and Bill Clinton.[25] These were the lean years. The Family was made deeply unhappy by Bush's team of realists, led by James Baker and Brent Scowcroft. They disapproved of the new tone Bush took in relations with Israel—such as his attempt to withhold loan guarantees unless Prime Minister Yitzchak Shamir agreed to a settlement freeze—as much as of his tepid response to China's brutal suppression of prodemocracy protesters in Tiananmen Square. "The Reagan Doctrine," George Weigel of the Ethics and Public Policy Center wrote in the January 1992 *Commentary*, "which was about the struggle between ideas and values as much as it was about the clash of interests, seems as dead in the Bush administration as it would have been under Michael Dukakis."

In one respect, however, Bush earned the Family's gratitude: He pardoned Elliott Abrams, who had been convicted in 1991 on two misdemeanor counts of unlawfully withholding information from Congress during its investigations of the Iran-Contra affair, in which members of the National Security Council illegally diverted funds received for weapons sold to Iran to U.S.-backed rebels in Nicaragua. Podhoretz commissioned a defense of Abrams from his old friend Robert Bork.[26] The former circuit judge for the U.S. court of appeals wrote in *Commentary* that the charges against Abrams "were based on prosecutorial hair-splitting." Bork claimed that Judge Lawrence Walsh (the independent counsel appointed to investigate the affair) and his staff "went after Abrams because they badly needed trophies." Bork concluded that Abrams "remains an example of integrity and courage under great pressure. Few things in his presidency became George Bush as well as the pardons he extended to Abrams and others."[27]

In 1992, Bush's bid for reelection garnered a mere 11 percent of the Jewish vote. As for the victor Bill Clinton—for whom 80 percent of Jewish voters cast a ballot—the Family felt at first encouraged: by his strong foreign policy declarations during the campaign, by his emphasis on spreading democracy, and by his appointment of James Woolsey as director of the CIA. Joshua Muravchik, for one, a scholar at the American Enterprise Institute and a frequent *Commentary* contributor since 1972, actively supported Clinton's campaign. (He was angling to be appointed assistant secretary of state for human rights.) The Family thought much less highly, however, of Clinton's choice of Warren Christopher as secretary of state; of his nomination of Lani Guinier, the "quota queen," to head the civil rights division of the Department of Justice; of the way he shut neoconservatives out of his administration.

"IN ITS PROSPERITY YOU SHALL PROSPER"

In a far different corner of the foreign policy edifice, the further the Family swung into its neoconservative phase, the more ardently it believed that defending one's own entailed a strong defense of Israel. The 1973 Yom Kippur War, which saw Israel subject to simultaneous surprise attacks from Egypt and Syria, had revealed Israel's vulnerability and renewed apprehensions about Israel's precariousness.[28] The war had also laid bare Israel's dependence on America, and not everyone felt sanguine about that dependence.[29] Into the 1970s, some voices in *Commentary* could still be heard to dismiss talk of a confluence of Israeli and American interests. "It is to indulge in nothing less than sheer delusion to speak of a congruence of interests between the two states," Robert Tucker wrote in a 1975 issue. "Washington's interests in the Middle East have become more diverse and complex than ever. The security of Israel is only one of these interests that must be balanced against others which may at any time be seen as threatened by the manner in which an Israeli government interprets its essential security requirements."

But the more resolute Podhoretz's neoconservative sensibility became, the more firmly he insisted on what he now took to calling "the inextricable connection between the survival of Israel and American military strength." He worried that an American retreat into a post-Vietnam isolationism, or a significant cut to the American defense budget, would threaten the security of Israel, too. A strong Israel, as he never tired of repeating, remained vital to American national interest in Mideast stability. Eugene Rostow (who had founded the Committee on the Present Danger the previous year) warned in the April 1977 *Commentary* that the destruction of Israel "could spell the end not only of the Atlantic alliance, but of liberal civilization as we know it."[30]

For saying this aloud, *Commentary* was once more reviled. Anthony Lewis of the *New York Times*, for example, lamented in 1976 a new alignment that "includes strong supporters of Israel who since the Yom Kippur War have become a significant factor in the growing support for larger U.S. defense budgets. The magazine *Commentary* is at the heart of this element."

But by 1980, *Commentary* gave full voice to the idea that what was bad for Israel—the soft underbelly of the West, as the Family thought of it—was bad for America, and that what was good for America was good for Israel. "I knew very well," Podhoretz said, "that an American foreign policy dedicated to 'the survival and the success of liberty' was good for Israel." He believed that America's commitment to free, democratic nations translated into firm U.S. support of Israel. Support for Israel required a strong America, and hostility to Israel was bound up in anti-Americanism.[31] For readers and contributors such as Ruth Wisse, who was Harvard's Martin Peretz Professor of Yiddish Literature, articulating this was the magazine's noblest and most pressing mission. "*Commentary* has been for all my adult life the touchstone of sanity," Wisse said, "because it has been the chief source of hope—hope that America will stay true to its high promise and that if it does, Israel will be allowed to realize its own high promise. The fate of these two polities is more closely entwined than most people realize."

In fact, *Commentary* articulated the case that American interests converged not merely with Israel's interests, but also with Jewish interests *per se*. The security of Jews worldwide, Midge Decter wrote in the January 1980 issue, "rests with a strong, vital, prosperous, self-confident United States." As the prophet Jeremiah told the Jews exiled to Babylon: "Seek the welfare of the city to which I have exiled you, and pray to the Lord in its behalf, for in its prosperity you shall prosper" (Jeremiah 29:7).

DESIGNER KAFTANS

In the 1970s and after, *Commentary* also redoubled its efforts to repel the assault on Israel's legitimacy. Saul Bellow once said that what the Alps were to skiers, Israel had become to moral critics. As Hannah Arendt had foretold in one of the magazine's earliest issues, the state of Israel, designed to solve the problem of anti-Semitism, had become its easiest target. The Family began to loathe those critics who slaked their thirst for easy moral outrage at Israel's expense. Attacks on Israel at the United Nations—as in the General Assembly resolution equating Zionism with racism in 1975 or the Human Rights Commission finding Israel guilty of war crimes the next year—especially rankled.[32] Writing in the July 1984 *Commentary*, Irving Kristol (now professor of social thought at New York University's Graduate School of Business Administration, coeditor of *Public Interest*, and a member of the *Wall Street Journal's* board of contributors) said, "We all know—one would have to be deaf and dumb not to know—that the UN is, above all, an organization bent on delegitimizing, even eventually destroying, the state of Israel."

The growing hostility to Israel at the UN and elsewhere, the campaign to tarnish Israel's moral image, and the deterioration of Israel's international standing all caused Podhoretz great worry. Not that he especially liked *being* in Israel, although he considered himself one of its fiercest defenders. He loved the Zionist *idea* more than Israel's uncomfortably alien reality. He had consistently held to the view he expressed in 1957: "To support a movement whose essential purposes are to restore the Jews to an honorable status among the nations," *Commentary's* then-assistant editor asserted, "to repair the ravages done to the Jewish personality by two thousand years of Diaspora, to insure that Jewish lives shall not be in constant jeopardy, and to save Jewish lives that are immediately threatened, *because* one is a Jew, and for no other reason, is simply to acknowledge that no apologies are required for asserting one's right to existence—which also means to human dignity, on this earth."

All these years later, Podhoretz saw evidence of a "new anti-Semitism" among those who attacked Israel as a spearhead of American imperialism. (At a dinner party in the late 1960s hosted by the Trillings, he asked Oxford intellectual historian Isaiah Berlin to justify his contributions to the *New York Review of Books*: "Why do you lend your prestige and support to a paper that regularly publishes enemies of Israel like Noam Chomsky and I. F. Stone?" Podhoretz asked. "I see," Berlin replied. "You are accusing me of being a fellow-traveler of a fellow-traveler.") In late 1982, while American Jewish journalist Thomas Friedman was writing reports on the Sabra and Shatila massacres for the *New York Times* that would earn him a Pulitzer, Podhoretz was driven to outrage by the condemnations of Israel over its offensive in Lebanon. In September 1982, Podhoretz committed to paper an irate piece for the magazine called "J'Accuse," wherein he sought to place the outrage in its proper context. The vilifiers of Israel, Podhoretz felt, were tainted with the familiar old hatred.

> In the broadside from which I have borrowed the title of this essay, Emile Zola charged that the persecutors of Dreyfus were using anti-Semitism as a screen for their reactionary political designs. I charge here that the anti-Semitic attacks on Israel which have erupted in recent weeks are also a cover. They are a cover for a loss of American nerve. They are a cover for acquiescence in terrorism. They are a cover for the appeasement of totalitarianism. And I accuse all those who have joined in these attacks not merely of anti-Semitism but of the broader sin of faithlessness to the interests of the United States and indeed to the values of Western civilization as a whole.[33]

In 1985, a party was held in the Rainbow Room atop Rockefeller Center to celebrate Podhoretz's twenty-five years as editor, with Secretary of State George Schultz, former secretary of state Kissinger, New York mayor Ed Koch, UN ambassador Jeane Kirkpatrick, and scores of other notables in attendance. Podhoretz, now fifty-five, his ideas having reached their final order, took the occasion to sum up the magazine's faith—and his own:

> I am proud that I have been able, in and through *Commentary*, to defend my *own*—my own country, and the values and institutions for which it stands; my own people and the religious and cultural heritage by which we

have been shaped. . . . *Commentary* has defended America at a time when America has been under moral and ideological assault. *Commentary* has defended the Jewish people and the Jewish state when they, too, and for many of the same reasons, have been subjected to a relentless assault on their legitimacy and even on their very existence. For me there has been no conflict or contradiction involved in defending this dual heritage by which I have been formed.

In the years ahead, the question of anti-Semitism would never stray far from Podhoretz's mind. In 1986, writing in *The Nation*, Gore Vidal called Norman and Midge "the Lunts of the right wing (Israeli fifth column division)." (The reference was to America's theatrical duo Alfred Lunt and Lynn Fontanne.) Though he had written for *Commentary* some fifteen years before,[34] Vidal now wrote that the Podhoretzes seemed "more and more like refugees from a Woody Allen film: *The Purple Prose of West End Avenue.*" Even though he wrapped himself in "our flag," Vidal wrote, wearing it "like a designer kaftan," Norman Podhoretz's "first loyalty would always be to Israel."[35]

Infuriated by the implication that American Jews who supported Israel were essentially traitors, Podhoretz generously repaid Vidal's scorn. His blood was up, and responding in high dudgeon, he called Vidal's piece "the most blatantly anti-Semitic outburst to appear in an American periodical since World War II."[36] Podhoretz then allowed himself a heated denunciation of Vidal in *Commentary*, under the title "The Hate That Dare Not Speak Its Name" (November 1986). "It would have been hard to find better evidence than this entire episode," Podhoretz later said, "for the case I had been trying to make since 1967 that anti-Semitism had now found a comfortable and hospitable home on the Left." Replying to a letter to the editor of *The Nation* from an American Jewish Committee official, Vidal stood his ground. "The Podhoretzes are doing more to arouse the essential anti-Semitism of the American people than anyone since Father Coughlin."[37]

Criticism of a different type came from within the Jewish community itself, for even as the Family defended the Jews, its departure from American Jewish sensibilities had become too stark to ignore. Milton Himmelfarb pointed out in *Commentary* that Jews had voted for Michael Dukakis in 1988 in virtually the same percentages as unemployed voters (64 percent), just as they had for other Democratic candidates: George McGovern in 1972 (65 percent), Jimmy Carter in 1976 (71 percent), and Walter Mondale in 1984 (67 percent). In 1986, *Tikkun* magazine took advantage of the breach and launched itself as a kind of anti-*Commentary*. "It was important to define ourselves as an alternative to *Commentary*," *Tikkun* editor Michael Lerner said, "because *Commentary* was the spokesperson for the view that liberal politics were out of step and disloyal to the Jewish world." In his inaugural editorial, Lerner, a former New Left activist from Berkeley, wrote: "With boring predictability, Norman Podhoretz leads the monthly charge of Jewish intellectuals clamoring for respectability by endorsing every move the Reagan administration can dream up." The new magazine's advertisements for itself underscored the point: "The neoconservatives don't speak for the Jews. . . . Finally, a liberal alternative to *Commentary* magazine." (Such attacks led Elie Wiesel and Robert Alter to resign from the forty-eight-member *Tikkun* editorial board. "I didn't like the aggressive tone they have taken against *Commentary*," Wiesel said. "A magazine can't just be a reactive thing," Alter added.) In 1988, Ruth Wisse—who over the course of several *Commentary* pieces peeked under the cloaks of anti-Zionists and found what she regarded as anti-Semitism lurking beneath—voiced *Commentary*'s verdict on its rival:

> Jewish criticism of Israel has increased at the same rate as left-wing and anti-Zionist propaganda. The disinclination of Jews to counter the Arab denial of their national legitimacy means that they must move ever more to the defensive. Thus *Tikkun*, the first American Jewish magazine to revive the old Jewish agenda of the 1930s (as the new Jewish agenda) and to argue the Palestinian case within the Jewish community, was founded, predictably, in California, where anti-Israel propaganda is most sustained.

ASSAILING OSLO

Commentary's articles on the Israeli-Palestinian conflict, meanwhile, had been attracting wide attention. In 1975, *Commentary* published a piece by Bernard Lewis, professor of Near Eastern studies at Princeton, arguing that, although the idea of Palestine may be "an ideological figment," the Palestinians "are real people, with a real problem, the solution of which is long overdue."[38] The magazine also ran pieces by Jeane Kirkpatrick on the PLO's campaign to legitimize itself and delegitimize Israel.[39] Israeli defense minister Ariel Sharon appointed Menahem Milson, a professor of Arabic literature at the Hebrew University of Jerusalem, to be the civil administrator of the West Bank after reading his 1981 *Commentary* article, "How to

Make Peace with the Palestinians," which contended that peace depended on "freeing the population of the territories from the grip of the PLO."[40] The magazine also countered the claim that Israeli intransigence or Jewish settlements in the West Bank presented the chief obstacle to peace, and questioned the credibility of Palestinian spokesmen such as Edward Said, the Columbia University anti-Orientalist.[41] *Commentary* published a 17,000-word article—the result of a three-year investigation—that concluded that Said's account of his childhood was "a tissue of falsehoods." The article claimed, for example, that the Palestinian advocate had spent his formative years not in Jerusalem, as he'd said, but in Cairo. (Shortly thereafter, Said told the *Chronicle of Higher Education* that the *Commentary* article amounted to "reckless defamation.")

Over the course of the 1990s, *Commentary* sought to expose what it saw as the deceptions and the self-deceptions of the 1993 Oslo Accords between Israel and the PLO. This represented something of an about-face for the magazine. When the Likud Party was in power during the 1980s, Podhoretz had argued that American Jews had no moral right to weigh in on Israel's security policies. "Since those policies literally involved life and death of the state and its people," he said, "only those whose lives were actually on the line had the standing to participate in the public debate over them." "The Jews who choose to remain in the Diaspora are free to function in their own lands as they wish and as they can," Ruth Wisse wrote in 1980, "but in assisting, supporting, and caring for the survival and security of Israel, they have to follow the guidelines of the elected government of the state, which has been entrusted with the powers of rule." A *Commentary* symposium on "American Jews and Israel" in February 1988, with Likud's Yitzhak Shamir in the prime minister's office, advanced the same line. "The Law of Return," Gertrude Himmelfarb wrote then, "guarantees to every Jew a place in Israel; as Norman Podhoretz has pointed out, if we choose not to avail ourselves of that opportunity, we forfeit the moral right to pass public judgment on matters which for Israelis—but not for us—are questions of life and death."

Starting with the Oslo Accords, however, with Israeli prime minister Yitzhak Rabin poised to make unprecedented concessions and return the territory in the West Bank and Gaza Strip that Israel had gained in the Six-Day War, Podhoretz decided "to speak out against the course Israel is now taking." Coming out against the policies of an elected Israeli government, he charged that the peace process was a "trap," a delusion of wishful thinking that would lead to a major war. (Podhoretz liked to cite the prophet Jeremiah: "They have healed the brokenness of My people superficially, saying, 'Peace, peace.' But there is no peace" [Jeremiah 6:14 and 8:11].) For this change of course, Podhoretz was roundly criticized. "If a foolish consistency is the hobgoblin of a little mind (Emerson)," Richard Cohen wrote in an April 1993 *Washington Post* column, "then Norman Podhoretz has a mind as big as all outdoors." To his critics, Podhoretz replied that there is "all the difference in the world between attacking Israel as an immoral or criminal state, which is what has so often been done by American Jewish leftists, and expressing doubts and anxieties over the prudence of the policies being pursued by the Israeli government, which is what I am trying to do."

And so over the course of the decade, in contrast to the applause from most quarters, *Commentary* continued to chide Oslo, an agreement the magazine predicted would lead not to peace but to renewed conflict. It considered the plan endorsed by Yitzhak Rabin and Yasser Arafat a folly, a costly misadventure; it argued that it was a gross error to rehabilitate the PLO and to arm thousands of Palestinian policemen. Contrary to the men David Bar-Illan once castigated in the magazine as "Israel's new Pollyannas," *Commentary* opposed trading land for peace on the grounds that Israeli concessions, and offers of concessions, seemed to be met only with Palestinian violence. *Commentary* called Oslo's supporters "proponents of peace at any price." The magazine's authors, executive editor Neal Kozodoy said, saw that the agreement's "implementation could not allay but rather only inflame extremist passions among Palestinians, not enhance but worsen Israel's security, not mitigate but excite the Arab determination to achieve the eventual destruction of the Jewish state." The assassination in November 1995 of Rabin, though it was, as Podhoretz called it, "one of the great infamies of Jewish history," did not shake *Commentary* from this view.[42]

Beginning in September 2000, after the Oslo peace process collapsed into a second and ghastlier intifada, the *Commentary* crowd felt vindicated. By then the magazine's man in Israel was Hillel Halkin, who had started contributing in 1969, a year before he immigrated there. In the September 2005 issue, after the intifada subsided, Halkin reviewed the damage Oslo had wrought. "Rarely in history has a country so foolishly opened its gates to a Trojan horse," Halkin said, "as Israel did when it welcomed Yasser Arafat and his PLO brigades, handed over to them most of the West Bank, and gave them the arms to impose their rule on the local inhabitants."

"When war finally came," Podhoretz noted, "even many on the Israeli Left who had worshiped at the shrine of Oslo finally acknowledged that its viciously reviled critics had been right all along."

LEAVING IT

In the last decade or so of the century, the Family's complexion changed. Even more than at the journal the Family used to call the *New York Review of Each Others' Books*, *Commentary* had from the beginning behaved like a Family, a reticulum of consanguinity: Managing editor Sherry Abel—whose brother Albert Goldman was Leon Trotsky's lawyer and friend—was *Commentary* contributor Lionel Abel's ex-wife. Isaac Rosenfeld's wife was Alfred Kazin's secretary, and Kazin lived for a short while in Rosenfeld's flat. Daniel Bell married Kazin's sister Pearl, who reviewed fiction for the magazine and who shared an apartment with Sondra Tschacbasov, soon to be the second Mrs. Bellow. Contributing editor Walter Laqueur's sister-in-law married the son of Leo Strauss, the political philosopher who exerted great influence on Irving Kristol, who was married to historian Gertrude Himmelfarb. That made Kristol Milton Himmelfarb's brother-in-law and father of Bill Kristol, cofounder of the *Weekly Standard* with John Podhoretz, son of Midge Decter—Robert Warshow's and then Elliot Cohen's secretary—and Norman Podhoretz. Elliott Abrams, who as a law student lived in former assistant editor Nathan Glazer's house, married Decter's daughter Rachel (Pat Moynihan and Scoop Jackson signed the *ketuba,* the Jewish marriage contract). Of adulteries, tact forbids us to speak, but associate editor Werner Dannhauser had a fling with Norman and Midge's daughter Ruthie, much to her father's displeasure. Before either was married, managing editor Marion Magid and associate editor Ted Solotaroff had been lovers. Neal Kozodoy's second wife, Maud Kinnell, daughter of poet Galway Kinnell, grew up in Vermont with the daughter of Marion Magid and Edward Hoagland. Midge Decter's grandson Sam Munson would become the magazine's first online editor. Then there were multigenerational *Commentary* contributors the Kagans (Donald, the father, and Robert and Fred, the sons) and the Pipes (Richard and his son Daniel).[43]

And what of the book reviews? The magazine called Decter's *An Old Wife's Tale* (2001) "a book you would have to read no matter who wrote it. . . . Reads like a casual, anecdotal ramble through the woods that opens out regularly onto huge vistas and big truths, expressed with breathtakingly simple clarity." Roger Hertog gave money to *Commentary*, and the magazine kindly reviewed his wife, Susan Hertog's, book *Anne Morrow Lindbergh* (1999): "exhaustively researched and lovingly written. It has the texture and fineness of hand embroidery." Conrad Black, aka Lord Black of Crossharbour, donated to the magazine, and the magazine, though critical in some respects, called his book *Franklin Delano Roosevelt: Champion of Freedom* (2004) "impressive both as a labor of love and as a labor of labor."

But now entering its third generation, the Family's tight weave had loosened, as immigrant families in particular tend to do, weakened by defection, dispersal, and assimilation. Death took Sidney Hook; Clem Greenberg; Irving Howe (whose demise went unremarked in *Commentary*, except for a not particularly generous piece five years after his death by Joseph Epstein);[44] managing editor Marion Magid, who had been at the magazine since 1963 (at her funeral Neal Kozodoy called her "the darling of our hearts"); Sherry Abel; and writers Lucy Dawidowicz, Jacob Katz, William Barrett, and Peter Shaw.

Commentary's relationship with the unrepentantly liberal American Jewish Committee was also in flux. Indeed, it was a minor miracle that the marriage lasted as long as it did. During the decades the AJC sponsored the magazine, it occasionally intervened, as when Podhoretz ran a frank piece in 1964 on the female orgasm in "the era of sexology."[45] The article, which discussed the Sex Research Project directed by Dr. William H. Masters into the female physiological response to sexual stimulation, led to a member of the board resigning and a short-lived campaign to fire the editor. But to an extent unprecedented in American journalism, the AJC always upheld its commitment to the magazine's editorial autonomy, even when *Commentary* increasingly took positions at odds with those of its sponsor.[46]

In 1990, however, the AJC suffered a financial crisis, and cut sixty of its staff. *Commentary*, conceived by the AJC and nourished by it for forty-five years, was now cut loose. Podhoretz had to raise funds from right-wing outfits such as the John M. Olin Foundation, the Smith Richardson Foundation, and the Scaife Family Charitable Trust, and patrons such as Roger Hertog, Tommy Tisch, and Nina Rosenwald. (In 2006, the magazine would legally separate from the AJC entirely and form Commentary, Inc.)

After thirty-five years at the helm, the old warrior Norman Podhoretz—Paul Johnson once called him "the archetype of the New York intellectual"—felt it was at last time to rest content, "a time for satisfaction over a just war well fought," as he said. In the summer of 1995, when Elliot Cohen would have been ninety-six, Podhoretz, age sixty-five, retired. A black-tie banquet at the Pierre marked the occasion—with Ariel Sharon, Henry

Kissinger, Conrad Black, Rupert Murdoch, Bill Buckley, Robert Bork, A. M. Rosenthal, Ed Koch, Elie Wiesel, Tom Wolfe, and hundreds of others in attendance. One of those who rose to praise the guest of honor was Cynthia Ozick. "He has written some of the finest and cleanest and most persuasive prose of our time," she said.

Not that Podhoretz intended to hang up his gloves; his polemical passions were by no means exhausted. Freed from editorial duties, as "editor-at-large" he would now write even more frequently for the magazine. As it happens, one of his first *Commentary* essays after retiring was a eulogy for neoconservatism. The adjectival "neo" had lost most of its meaning, Podhoretz argued; it had become impossible to define a distinctive neoconservative point of view. Neoconservatism was a victim of its own victory.[47]

Podhoretz had very early on recognized Neal Kozodoy, his right-hand man since 1966, as an immensely capable editor. He had groomed Kozodoy and entrusted him with a great deal of power in return for the younger man's loyalty. For most of Podhoretz's tenure, Kozodoy—unheralded and with very little of the glory—had been indispensable to the running of the magazine. Now his labors received their just reward, and to no one's surprise, Podhoretz handed him the editorial reins. At Podhoretz's retirement dinner, Kozodoy—invoking a passage from the Song of Songs (8:6–7)—was moved to startling effusiveness in contemplating the pleasures of knowing his mentor's love: "It is ardent and vivifying, it is musical, it is supernally delicate; it is full of grace, and it is full of expectancy, and it is full of mirth. . . . For me it flames with the flame of that vast inspiriting force of love which, despite everything, pulses like music itself through Creation; which many waters cannot quench, nor rivers drown; which it is given most intimately to men and women to know, and to true friends to perfect, and to reciprocate."

Though Kozodoy exhibited a more circumspect style than his precursor, whose act would be hard to follow, the transition to *Commentary*'s third generation was seamless. "I expect the magazine to continue with the same point of view," Podhoretz said. He held to his promise never to step into the office after he retired—but then again, he didn't have to.

◅ 10 ▻

World War IV

Nations as well as individuals come to ruin through the over-exercise of those very qualities and faculties on which their dominion has been founded.

—WINSTON CHURCHILL

BEST IN THE BUSINESS

The brilliant editor of *Commentary*, Neal Kozodoy—looking far younger than his fifty-nine years—presided in a corner office in the blue metallic American Jewish Committee building on East 56th Street in midtown. As a remembrance of things past and as a gesture of continuity, he stowed behind his computer—which was for e-mail, not for editing—the clipboard on which five decades earlier then–managing editor Robert Warshow had scrawled his fluid essays, longhand, in pencil. Kozodoy, too, worked on manuscripts only in pencil.

On the right wall, bound into number-laden volumes, some 650 back issues of the monthly lined the shelves. On the top left rested volume 1, number 1, dated November 1945, which gathered between its covers a report by British anti-Communist writer George Orwell on Winston Churchill's stunning defeat in the British general elections that year and an essay by great historian Salo Baron on "The Spiritual Reconstruction of European Jewry." To these were added a book review by Mary McCarthy (like the magazine, she was then in her Left anti-Stalinist phase), a poetry review by Randall Jarrell, and a translation of a theological essay by German Jewish thinker Franz Rosenzweig. More than a half-century later, *Commentary*, now the flagship of the neoconservatives, still held to a formula that joined Jewish with general concerns, literature with contemporary politics, an urgency about the present moment with a sense of historical perspective.

An editor of genius, a discoverer of new talent, a first-rate intelligence, Kozodoy was gifted with an unerring ear for language—a perfect literary pitch. And for Jewish literacy he did not lack. He had translated from the Hebrew Elie Wiesel's book on Soviet Jews, *The Jews of Silence* (1966), and had helped write eminent Israeli historian Jacob Katz's classic book on the Jewish Emancipation, *Out of the Ghetto* (1973). Kozodoy had published a masterful essay on medieval Hebrew love poetry. As editor of the Library of Jewish Studies, he oversaw the publication of volumes edited by leading Jewish scholars.[1] His mind was finely thatched with ideas.

Kozodoy had joined the magazine as a young graduate student in 1966 and never left; he had devoted his life to it. But unlike his prolific mentor, Norman Podhoretz, who by the time of his retirement from the magazine had written six books of literary criticism, foreign policy, and autobiography, Kozodoy had published very little under his own name. Apart from his short contribution to *Commentary*'s symposium on liberalism and the Jews, he had written only two pieces for the magazine in his thirty-five years there: a tender admiration of the historian Lucy Dawidowicz for preserving Jewish memory (May 1992) and, a year earlier, an evisceration of Philip Roth's *Patrimony* (1991), a memoir of the novelist's father, for betraying it.[2]

But this is to give a false sense of the man's enormous self-effacing industry, for Kozodoy had with unremitting effort, month in and month out, rewritten the magazine. With faultless consideration, he labored to give his writers a greater fluidity than they had unaided. He was generous in recognizing new talent and in furthering nascent careers. In his understated way, he worked very, very hard, often until his eyes could absorb no more words.

It is true that in moments of frustration, Kozodoy seemed to feel himself a first-class mind among feeble-minded second-class talents, a thoroughbred yoked to donkeys. In those moments, one sensed in him a buried fury. He was also a fastidious perfectionist, a stickler for punctiliousness—personally supervising copyediting, paper stock, typography, and even the seating charts of the magazine's annual dinners at the Union League Club. If one of his staff fell short, the tufts over his eyes would move together, flashes of distemper would darken his brow, and a cold, lowering look would shoot out: "Why the *fuck* can't you get this right?" he'd say. Much of the office bonhomie and easy conviviality had evaporated since Podhoretz's departure six years earlier, for Kozodoy was less sociable than his predecessor, less affected by joie de vivre. Only on the rarest of occasions did the editors take lunch together or meet elsewhere than East 56th Street.

Not that the editor lacked for good humor and graciousness. Once a month, he convened his staff around a small table in the antechamber to his office to brainstorm titles for the next issue. Joining him were senior editor Gabriel Schoenfeld (who wrote his Harvard dissertation on Bolshevism and the French revolutionary tradition, had served on the staff of Senator Moynihan during his first term and edited a journal called *Post-Soviet Prospects*) and managing editor Gary Rosen (former speechwriter for New Jersey governor Thomas Kean and author of a book on James Madison). In one of these titles meetings, Rosen wanted to title a piece "How Not to Conduct Interfaith Dialogue." Schoenfeld protested: "But that would imply we think there is a *proper* way to dialogue." "We do," Kozodoy said. "'Fuck you! No, fuck you! Fuck me? Fuck you.'"

Most often Kozodoy was magnanimously content to cultivate what his friend Bill Bennett, *Commentary* contributor and former secretary of education, called a "gift for chronic anonymity." *Commentary*, as everyone knew, did not exist to showcase a writer's "voice." To keep up the magazine's high standards of seriousness and political responsibility, its exacting editors had always leaned very hard on their writers, and Kozodoy—in the interests of simple, straightforward exposition—leaned hardest of all.

Some writers responded well to Kozodoy's heavy-handed scraping and sanding of their sentences. A member of the *Wall Street Journal*'s editorial board, on sending in her first contribution, said: "I'm thrilled to be able to contribute to *Commentary*; I'd always imagined it to have been edited on Olympus." Many a young writer felt that to write for Kozodoy was to be given, over the course of many rewrites, the world's most rigorous writing tutorial.

Other writers bridled at the rough fate that awaited their precious prose, an unyielding leash-pulling Kozodoy once described as the means whereby "thoughts which might otherwise have taken refuge in ambiguity or fuzziness have been coerced into rigor and trenchancy and boldness." Bill Bennett called his editor "the butcher of 56th street" (Henry James once called editing "the butcher's trade") and quipped that if he submitted a magnum opus, Kozodoy would hack it down to a book review. "Manuscripts the size of the Titanic," Bennett said, "came back as dinghies." This was only a slight exaggeration. Bennett's first *Commentary* essay, "In Defense of Sports," came in at 12,000 words; Kozodoy pared it down and published it at 2,500. "Congressional hearings are nothing after having had your manuscripts taken apart at *Commentary*," Bennett said. Chicago essayist and longtime *Commentary* contributor Joseph Epstein, who considered Kozodoy a founding member of the "less-is-more school" of editing, once e-mailed the following note: "Dear Neal, Wrote five fine paragraphs of the Solzhenitsyn piece yesterday, four of which you should be able to remove easily." *New York Times* columnist David Brooks remarked that although he couldn't remember his first book review for *Commentary* (it ran in 1988), he remembered his third, because that was the first time a sentence of his had appeared in the magazine. John Podhoretz, son of Norman, joked: "Neal is to wordsmithery as the Nazi dentist played by Laurence Olivier in *Marathon Man* is to teeth, only without the clove oil."

To some contributors, this was a source of everlasting complaint. Every once in a while a despairing writer would inform Kozodoy: You can publish this, but only under your name. "*Commentary* is so over-edited," a young writer at the *Wall Street Journal* said, "it turns off decent writers and leaves you either with geniuses like Joseph Epstein who need no editing or third-raters who don't mind being rewritten." For the record, Epstein, who had written more than 130 pieces for the magazine since his debut in 1964, dedicated one of his books "To Neal Kozodoy, the best in the business."

Whether the butcher or the best in the business, Kozodoy had his own ruthless way of talking about submissions with his staff: "There's no movement," he would say of a manuscript, "it doesn't rise, doesn't fall—just beads on a string." About a submission: "Well, I *guess* we can do something with this." He was not a man quick to express enthusiasms.

"One fine day," a young Jewish writer and political activist remembered, "I almost fell out of my chair. Out of the blue Neal Kozodoy called to invite me to write a piece for the magazine. I had been enthralled with *Commentary* at the height of the Reagan years and it had remained a dream of mine to publish in its pages. To research and write the article I dropped everything I was doing and devoted several weeks to the project. With some trepidation as to whether my text was worthy and whether he would be disappointed I submitted it to Kozodoy. He responded to acknowledge receipt but even after several weeks offered no comments or feedback. Finally we had a telephone conversation. He dryly said that he was accepting the piece."

"Yes," the writer said in trepidation, "but what did you *think* of it?"

"What are you, needy?" came Kozodoy's reply.

Since taking over, Kozodoy had, like his mentor, published big-think symposia such as "On the Future of Conservatism" (with William F. Buckley, David Frum, Francis Fukuyama, Mark Helprin, Gertrude Himmelfarb, William Kristol, and others) and "American Power—for What?" (with twenty-one respondents, including Elliott Abrams, Robert Kagan, Jeane Kirkpatrick, Charles Krauthammer, Michael Ledeen, and Edward Luttwak). These, too, he heavily edited. David Brooks, to cite him again, once said that the typical *Commentary* symposium consisted of twenty-six entries, each written by Neal Kozodoy.

Kozodoy had meanwhile brought into the magazine a great many distinguished essays on Jewish literature and affairs: Norma Rosen on Yiddish writer Isaac Bashevis Singer, Jon Levenson on theologian Abraham Joshua Heschel, Bible scholar James Kugel on the Dead Sea Scrolls, Gabriel Schoenfeld on Holocaust reparations. And thirty years after *Commentary*'s landmark 1966 symposium on "The State of Jewish Belief," Kozodoy gathered together forty-seven prominent rabbis and thinkers in a symposium called "What Do American Jews Believe?"

In the main lineaments of its foreign policy *Commentary* floundered in the decade of disorientation that came on the heels of the Soviet collapse. It lived in a kind of caesura. But the winds of war were once more gathering, and the magazine was about to enjoy a new gust of purposefulness. The requiem-chanters for neoconservatism would soon be silenced.

NEOCONSERVATISM IN POWER

In the wake of the election in 2000 of George W. Bush (the first Republican president since the 1950s to have majorities in both houses of Congress) and the September 11, 2001, attacks, political currents shifted in the Family's favor. As Bush's job approval rating hit 90 percent, Norman Podhoretz felt in sync with the nation's spirit. "As a 'founding father' of neoconservatism who had broken ranks with the Left precisely because I was repelled by its 'negative faith in America the ugly,' [the phrase is Todd Gitlin's] I naturally welcomed this new patriotic mood with open arms," he said.

Podhoretz was in tune with the tenor of the Bush administration. Some of this feeling came suffused with personal admiration. Only 19 percent of Jewish voters had cast a ballot for Bush in 2000 during his contest with Al Gore. Equally predictably, in 2004 Democrat John Kerry would get 76 percent of the Jewish vote (though only 48 percent of the popular vote) in his failed attempt to oust Bush. Yet unlike most of his coreligionists, Podhoretz considered George W. Bush a great man and felt confident that history would judge him as such. In the meantime, Podhoretz sang hosannas to the president. "Out of the blackness of smoke and fiery death let loose by September 11," Podhoretz wrote in the September 2002 *Commentary*, "a kind of revelation, blazing with a very different fire of its own, lit up the recesses of Bush's mind and heart and soul." In 2004, Bush would return the favor and bestow the Presidential Medal of Freedom, the nation's highest civilian honor, on Podhoretz (Irving Kristol had been awarded the medal two years earlier).[3] "Podhoretz ranks among the most prominent American editors of the twentieth century," Bush said at the ceremony. "And he's doing pretty well in the twenty-first. Never a man to tailor his opinions to please others, Mr. Podhoretz has always written and spoken with directness and honesty. Sometimes speaking the truth has carried a cost. Yet, over the years, he has only gained in stature among his fellow writers and thinkers. Today we pay tribute to this fierce intellectual man and his fine writing and his great love for our country."

Midge Decter, meanwhile, spent her time after 9/11 writing a concise book about Bush's secretary of defense, Donald Rumsfeld—"Rumstud," as the president had called him. (Decter and Rumsfeld cochaired the Committee for the Free World during the Reagan administration.) *Rumsfeld: A Personal Portrait* (2003) was so full of effusions about his flinty manliness that the *New Yorker* called it "Midge's Mash Note."[4]

More to the point, the *Commentary* clan as a whole felt in sync with the Bush Doctrine—the thinking that found its clearest expression in the president's West Point address of June 2002, the National Security Strategy unveiled that September, and his second inaugural. This doctrine endorsed not only a punitive war against the sponsors of terrorist attacks, but also preemptive war, waged unilaterally if necessary, against terrorists and the regimes that harbored them. Dark mutterings to the contrary, there was no nefarious conspiracy among neoconservatives ensconced in Dick Cheney's office, the E-ring of the Pentagon, or the Defense Policy Board to overthrow traditional American foreign policy. But the Family influence on the Bush Doctrine was unmistakable; its established neoconservative members felt they had laid its intellectual groundwork. What they had long been advocating was now practiced in the upper reaches of government: a belief that American power could be used for moral purposes to promote democracy and freedom abroad; a notion that regimes could be irredeemably evil; a refusal to defer to the United Nations where America's vital security interests were concerned; and an insistence, as Bush's second inaugural phrased it, that "the survival of liberty in our land increasingly depends on the success of liberty in other lands."

This was a second ascendancy, even more exhilarating than that of the Reagan years. Members of the Family were makers of policy, shapers of opinion. "I spent the late 1990s," Bill Kristol (editor of the *Weekly Standard*) wrote in *Commentary*, "along with a few allies, advocating something more or less like the Bush Doctrine *avant la lettre*." Bush, Colin Powell, and Condoleezza Rice were no neoconservatives, but one neoconservative went so far as to say that the National Security Strategy, the watershed document that President Bush issued in September 2002, "sounds as if it could have come straight out from the pages of *Commentary* magazine, the neocon bible." Writing in *Foreign Affairs* (November–December 2003), Joshua Micah Marshall wrote, "Rarely in American history has such a cohesive and distinctive group managed to exert so decisive an influence on such a crucial issue as the neocons did on Iraq from the collapse of the twin towers through the early stages of the occupation of Baghdad almost two years later." Writing in a 2005 issue of *Commentary*, columnist Charles Krauthammer asserted that the Bush Doctrine "is, essentially, a synonym for neoconservative foreign policy" and hence "marks neoconservatism's own transition from a position of dissidence . . . to governance." The Bush administration, he said, was "neoconservatism in power."

WAGING DEMOCRACY

The magazine now steered by Neal Kozodoy hadn't always taken kindly to the idea that democracy could be "exported ready-to-run," as Elliot Cohen had once put it. "Since the essence of democracy is self-dependence," the first editor had observed in *Commentary*, "it must in every land constitute itself." In a 1956 issue, Irving Kristol had urged: "It is about time we recognized that not all the peoples and nations in the world want to be free and happy, as we in America understand those terms."

Two dozen years later, in that classic *Commentary* essay "Dictatorships and Double Standards," Jeane Kirkpatrick rejected the belief that democratization is possible "anytime, anywhere, under any circumstances."

In the relatively few places where they exist, democratic governments have come into being slowly, after extended prior experience with more limited forms of participation. . . . Decades, if not centuries, are normally required for people to acquire the necessary disciplines and habits. . . . Hurried efforts to force complex and unfamiliar political practices on societies lacking the requisite political culture, tradition, and social structures not only fail to produce desired outcomes; if they are undertaken at a time when the traditional regime is under attack, they actually facilitate the job of the insurgents.[5]

Or consider what the old *Commentary* had to say during the Vietnam War:

- American power "has now come to be regarded as the instrument of willful and irrational caprice," with the result that "the international prestige of the United States is lower than at any time within recent memory" (Maurice Goldbloom, 1965).[6]
- "Vietnam is not important to us. Nor is it a bastion of freedom. Nor is it a testing place for democracy" (J. K. Galbraith, 1966).[7]
- The Vietnamese adventure is "an incident of American expansion that happens to have gotten out of hand" (Paul Goodman, 1967).
- "Freedom is not a system, and as we are discovering in Vietnam, it cannot be introduced by system builders" (Harold Rosenberg, 1967).[8]

September 11 had turned the tables. The new *Commentary* now applied the old Marxist logic of historical necessity to the spread of democracy. The waves of democracy in the 1980s and 1990s had persuaded many neoconservatives that the Islamic Middle East would eventually go the way of Communist Eastern Europe. Hadn't Francis Fukuyama assured that liberal democracy was the final form of human government, the inexorable culmination of History?[9] Nation-building and democratization now became centerpieces of the Family faith, along with the notion that American staying power abroad amounted to a referendum on the country's own moral health. As a result, the Family would soon become defined by the war on terror as decisively as it had once been by World War II and then by the cold war.

All along, *Commentary* had tirelessly called for intervention and the use of force to defend American interests abroad and had proposed to drain the Middle East of terrorism by means of exporting democracy. This was especially true of the Family's ambitions to replace Mideast despotisms with democracies. Here, in the words of neoconservative analyst Robert Kagan—former member of the Policy Planning Staff and the Bureau of Inter-American Affairs at the State Department—is the *Commentary* credo four years before September 11, 2001: "We could and should be holding authoritarian regimes in the Middle East to higher standards of democracy, and encouraging democratic voices within those societies, even if it means risking some instability in some places. . . . For the day we adopt a neutral attitude toward the fate of democracy in the world is the day we deny our own essence, an essence rooted in a commitment to certain principles which we believe to be universal."[10] The credo would come to be tested sooner than Kagan anticipated.

ISLAMISM

Commentary magazine had been among the earliest to call attention to the pressing danger posed by Islamic militants. In a 1976 *Commentary* essay called "The Return of Islam," historian Bernard Lewis (the first to introduce the phrase "clash of civilizations") had put militant resistance movements such as the Muslim Brotherhood and Fatah—as well as the notion of jihad itself—into historical perspective and warned that the West remained blind to the gathering political force of "a resurgent Islam." *Commentary* had discussed "the surge in radical fundamentalist Islam" as early as 1988. Long before 9/11, it featured articles with titles such as "Can Democracy Defend Itself Against Terrorism?" (1978) and "Thinking About Terrorism" (1981). Frequent contributor Daniel Pipes (son of Richard Pipes), then a young historian of Islam at the University of Chicago and later director of the Middle East Forum, had weighed in on "The Politics of Muslim Anti-Semitism" (1981). Martin Kramer of the Moshe Dayan Center at Tel Aviv University (a student of Bernard Lewis) wrote on "Islam and the West (Including Manhattan)" (1993). After the first World Trade Center bombing in 1993, *Commentary* challenged the conventional wisdom that held that the bombing was an "isolated event," as *Foreign Affairs* called it, which only "frustrated cold warriors" sold on an "Islamic conspiracy theory" could tie to other terrorist attacks.

In short, the magazine, having long paid attention to militant Islam, had urged that the battle against the radicals should be waged more tenaciously.[11] It took the cold war—World War III as the Family called it—as the model for what it now deemed to be World War IV.[12] Against those who accused America of imperial overreach, it suggested that Osama bin Laden—like Ayatollah Khomeini and like the Soviet Union itself—was only emboldened by the decline of American power. *Commentary* cast Islamic fundamentalism as the new totalitarianism, the latest ideological enemy: first Communism, now Islamism. Radical Islam, the new "other," played the same role in the war on terror as Communism had played in the cold war. If Islamo-fascism was the new totalitarianism, the Family's experience as anti-Communist cold warriors would serve well. Needless to say, Islamism did not create concentration camps, nor did al-Qaeda—despite its yearnings for a caliphate—control a state apparatus. Nevertheless, Hannah Arendt had predicted that totalitarian tendencies would survive the death of totalitarian states. Certain members of the Family now looked through the lens Arendt had fashioned to see more clearly how the new jihadism bore the marks of the totalitarian impulse: a totalistic worldview that demanded from the individual total loyalty and achieved over him total domination; a retreat from the anxieties and resentments of modernity into an idealized past; a contempt for the "decadence" of the West; an obsessive anti-Semitism; a fetishized violence; a notion of a united, supranational *umma* where once there had been a racial *volk*; and, most of all, a will to annihilate human freedom. So when President George W. Bush called Islamic terrorists "successors to fascists, to Nazis, to communists and other totalitarians of the 20th century," the neoconservatives knew whereof he spoke. "The message of September 11 was loud and clear, allowing for no ambiguity," Daniel Pipes wrote in the January 2002 *Commentary*. "The enemy is militant Islam."

SADDAM

The enemy was also Saddam Hussein. The magazine's post-9/11 attention to Saddam's regime did not emerge from nowhere. Robert Tucker had warned in *Commentary* back in 1983 of "the need to have a credible Western presence in or proximate to the Gulf." Writing in 1990, Elliott Abrams had predicted in the magazine that one of the most pressing questions in coming years would be, "How should we react when Iraq threatens chemical warfare and advances in its search for nuclear weapons and the capability to deliver them?" After Iraq's invasion of the sheikhdom of Kuwait in August

1990 threatened American interests in the Persian Gulf, the magazine called for the United States to intervene. "Saddam Hussein is a man who must be stopped, his sword broken, and his plunder wrested from him," Elliot A. Cohen wrote in *Commentary*. To stop Saddam, President George H. W. Bush stitched an international coalition together with the largest mobilization of American troops since Vietnam and, with the authorization of a UN Security Council resolution, launched Operation Desert Storm in January 1991. "I can't remember when I last tasted such exhilaration," Norman Podhoretz said when he learned the aerial bombardment of Baghdad had begun. He called it a "great event."[13]

But the end of the Gulf war dampened Family spirits, for George H. W. Bush's equivocation had left Saddam in power. One *Commentary* piece compared Saddam's regime to "a bacterial infection that has been treated with enough antibiotics to make the patient feel better, but not enough to kill it."

Well before September 11, 2001, outraged by Saddam's massacres of Kurds, his flouting of Security Council resolutions, and his brazen violations of international law, the Family wanted to root out what it thought of as the Baathist infection. Four years before 9/11, Douglas Feith, who would serve as undersecretary of defense from 2001 to 2005, spelled out in *Commentary* what he thought that commitment entailed: the end of Saddam Hussein's regime. More than three years before 9/11, Joshua Muravchik again called in the magazine for the removal of Saddam.

This was not a uniquely "neoconservative" position. Recall that in 1998, President Bill Clinton had signed the Iraq Liberation Act, which announced that "it should be the policy of the United States to support efforts to remove the regime headed by Saddam Hussein from power." In December of that year, Clinton's national security adviser, Sandy Berger, had argued for regime change: "Saddam's history of aggression," Berger said, "and his recent record of deception and defiance, leave no doubt that he would resume his drive for regional domination if he had the chance." But the magazine worked to maintain the pressure. In June 2001, Daniel Pipes stressed to its readers "how urgently we need to move the question of Iraq to the very top of our foreign-policy agenda."

After the attacks of 9/11, these calls only intensified. It didn't require a deep mistrust of the United Nations to realize that the UN inspections regime had turned into a feckless charade. Removing Saddam, Frederick Kagan (brother of Robert and associate professor of military history at West Point) wrote in *Commentary* in late 2002, "is an extraordinary priority of this country. The only way to accomplish that task is by means of a large-scale ground and air invasion of Iraq." Containment—restraining Saddam in some way short of war—did not seem viable.

Better to confront Saddam and the possibility of "state-sponsored" terrorism before he went nuclear, Kozodoy's magazine maintained, rather than after. In the July–August 2001 issue, Gary Milhollin and Kelly Motz of the Wisconsin Project on Nuclear Arms Control had warned that Saddam "is on the way to having nuclear weapons, and the missiles that will deliver them." But on the question of weapons of mass destruction, editor-at-large Podhoretz set the tone: "It is by now no longer necessary to prove that Saddam is a sponsor of terrorism in order to consider Iraq a target of the war against it, since the President has already established a rationale in stating that, 'If you develop weapons of mass destruction [with which] you want to terrorize the world, you'll be held accountable.' There is no doubt that Saddam already possesses large stores of chemical and biological weapons." That was in the February 2002 issue. Three years later, with large stores nowhere to be found, Podhoretz defended the earlier claim: "When Bush charged Saddam Hussein with refusing to give up his weapons of mass destruction, he was relying in good faith on what the CIA—and every other intelligence agency in the world—assured him was the case."[14]

Although Podhoretz later admitted that he had predicted "that we would be greeted [in Iraq] with flowers and cheers," not every *Commentary* writer envisioned the postinvasion scene as blithely. Efraim Karsh, for instance, in the April 2003 issue, cautioned that democratization would not take place overnight. "This is certain to be a difficult process, one requiring an extensive American military presence (and, no doubt, occasional military operations) over a protracted period of time." Military historian Victor Davis Hanson referred in June to "the inevitably messy and protracted business of reconstruction." Nevertheless, Podhoretz himself harbored an optimism about the prospects for remaking the Middle East. The editor-at-large expressed the hope that in the aftermath of the reconstruction of Iraq, "a course might finally be set toward the reform and modernization of the Islamic religion itself."

After President Bush declared an end to major combat operations on May 1, the Family, flush with victory, felt vindicated. Not long thereafter, Syria's Bashar Assad withdrew his 14,000 troops from Lebanon after the assassination of Rafiq Hariri and the "Cedar Revolution." Libya's Muammar Qaddafi ended his bid for a nuclear bomb. Egypt's first multiparty presidential elections and elections in Afghanistan further encouraged the view that a wave of Arab democratization seemed imminent.

TWICE MUGGED

The tide of optimism soon receded. In Iraq, it was pushed back by the discovery that links between Saddam and terrorist networks were flimsier than had been thought, by inadequate postwar planning and bungled nation-building, by lawlessness and looting, by the appalling images from Abu Ghraib (David Brooks called the photos of prisoner abuse "weapons of mass morale destruction"), and, most of all, by a bloody insurgency that involved urban combat with the Shiite militias of the radical cleric Moqtada al-Sadr, beheadings carried out at the orders of Abu Musab al-Zarqawi, desecration of four American bodies in Fallujah, and Marines cut apart by "improvised explosive devices." The mounting resentment of America in the Arab world undermined America's reputation and deterrent power vis-à-vis Iran and Syria. Outside of Iraq, meanwhile, the rise of Islamist parties, coupled with Hezbollah's war against Israel, the fall of Gaza to Hamas, and Iran's nuclear brinksmanship all served to deflate hopes of remaking the Middle East.

George Orwell once said that American cold warriors drew a "picture of terrifying, irresistible power" threatening a world where everything was "expanding, contracting, decaying, dissolving, toppling, crumbling, crystallizing, and, in general, behaving in an unstable and melodramatic way."[15] Now many of those who had charged the Family with exaggerating the Soviet menace accused it of exaggerating the threat posed by Islamic terrorism. Critics charged that neoconservative ideas had been repudiated by the American campaign in Iraq, which was so disastrously conducted as to have compromised its aims (even though in September 2002 Bush's decision to invade Iraq received bipartisan congressional authorization). They accused neoconservatives of engaging in triumphalist overreaching, of not thinking through the postwar reconstruction. A number of traditional conservatives, such as William F. Buckley and George Will, conceded that the Bush Doctrine had dismally failed the test in Iraq. So it came as no surprise when after the Democrats swept to victory in the 2006 midterm elections, historian Douglas Brinkley became one among many to pronounce "the death of the neoconservative movement."

Critics concluded that the Family's old distrust of concentrated power and support of checks and balances inside America were nowhere evident in the neoconservatives' confidence in America's unchecked hegemony. These critics hastened to blame neoconservatives for a loss of American credibility abroad, though this, in truth, had been a common charge long before Iraq.[16] Finally, critics charged that *Commentary* had lost the very capacity for self-scrutiny and self-revision that made it what it was, that it had plowed under its own best political insight: namely, that overinflated ambitions to remake societies, at home or abroad, were doomed to tragic failure. They charged that neoconservatives had lost their skepticism about the belief in the perfectibility of man, that they were attempting in Iraq the very kind of ambitious social engineering they had rejected at home. The early tempering of expectations and insistence upon limits seemed to have vanished.

NOT ALL OF THE CRITICS were serious. In his book *Anti-Semite and Jew* (1946), parts of which had appeared in *Commentary*, Jean-Paul Sartre had explained that "the Jew is one whom other men consider a Jew. . . . It is the anti-Semite who makes the Jew." So it often seemed with the neoconservatives; long after they had assimilated into the larger conservative movement, the image of the neoconservative loomed large in the distorted vision of his enemies. After the American invasion of Iraq, "neocon" became a term of abuse, a euphemism for "warmonger," or worse. The "neocon cabal" figured as a reckless group of hawkish unilateralists who lured a weak-minded president into a war in Iraq they had long plotted. "Hatching vain Empires," to borrow Milton's phrase, they were seen as democratic imperialists, crude dogmatists driven by ideological hubris to impose on the world a Pax Americana.

Joshua Micah Marshall charged in the *New Yorker* that neocons took advantage of 9/11 "to espouse a world view that was unapologetically imperialist." They were perceived to be ubiquitous. "They have penetrated the culture at nearly every level from the halls of academia to the halls of the Pentagon," the *New York Times* whistled. "Will America's Superhawks Drag Us into More Wars Against Their Enemies?" was the subject of a BBC TV program on the neocons. Harvard's Stephen Walt, coauthor of *The Israel Lobby* (2007), complained that "publications like *Commentary* were beating the drum for war." Neoconservatives were said to be guided in all this by their philosopher-king, Leo Strauss, who had died in 1973—a "disguised

Machiavelli," according to the *Boston Globe*, "a cynical teacher who encouraged his followers to believe that their intellectual superiority entitles them to rule over the bulk of humanity by means of duplicity."[17]

A minor publishing industry spit forth titles such as *Where the Right Went Wrong: How Neoconservatives Subverted the Reagan Revolution and Hijacked the Bush Presidency* (2004); *Neo-conned! Again: Hypocrisy, Lawlessness, and the Rape of Iraq* (2005); and *Deadly Dogma: How Neoconservatives Broke the Law to Deceive America* (2006). Even the Rolling Stones got into the act. The group's 2005 album *A Bigger Bang* included a track called "Sweet Neo Con" about how wrong neocons were.

Not least, according to the stereotype, these notorious neocons were Jews! Jewish neocons quite often took this in stride. "Con is short for 'conservative' and neo is short for 'Jewish,'" David Brooks quipped. Some on the Left less humorously claimed that in calling for regime change in Iraq, the neoconservative Family had put Israel's interests before America's (not that Israelis by any means uniformly supported the war in Iraq), or believed in an illusory identity of interests between the two states. "These analysts," Stanley Hoffman of Harvard wrote in the *American Prospect* (January 13, 2003), "look on foreign policy through the lens of one dominant concern: Is it good or bad for Israel? Since that nation's founding in 1948, these thinkers have never been in very good order at the State Department, but now they are well ensconced in the Pentagon." "For years," Michael Lind fumed in the *Spectator* (April 24, 2004), "American neocons [have been] disseminating the propaganda of the Israeli Right."[18] George W. Bush "gave veto power to Israel's neoconservative supporters over U.S. government policy and appointees in the region," journalist Joe Klein charged in March 2009.

A curious thing, however: This frenzied flood from the Left rushed into canyons long before carved by the dual-loyalty canards of the old Right. America-firsters had scorned the Family as Likudniks who gave uncritical support to Israel. Scott McConnell, who had written for *Commentary* in the 1980s before turning toward the paleoconservatives and helping Pat Buchanan found the *American Conservative*, charged that Norman Podhoretz was "driven by a concern for Israel's needs, not America's."[19] "Not seldom it has seemed as if some eminent neoconservatives mistook Tel Aviv for the capital of the United States," Russell Kirk said. Pat Buchanan in 2003 described the Jewish tail wagging the American dog: "President Bush is being lured into a trap baited for him by these neocons that could cost him his office and cause America to forfeit years of peace won for us by the sacrifices of two generations in the Cold War. . . . Though few in number, they

wield disproportionate power through control of the conservative foundations and magazines, through their syndicated columns, and by attaching
themselves to men of power."

STAYING THE COURSE

When things went sour in Iraq, some Family neoconservatives were chastened. "The attempt to govern Iraq from Foggy Bottom and the Baghdad
'green zone' by thousands of American civil servants who knew nothing of
Iraq's history, language, culture, or politics," Richard Perle (assistant secretary of defense under Reagan) wrote in *Commentary* in 2005, "was a catastrophic mistake." "Maybe the moral of our experience with the Bush
administration is that we should stay in magazines and think tanks and not
in government," Joshua Muravchik conceded in late 2008.[20] A new question could be heard in Washington: If a neoconservative is a liberal mugged
by reality, what becomes of a neoconservative who is mugged by reality?

But for all its veers and tacks over the years, *Commentary* had never
been much given to exercises in self-criticism. From the loyal core of the
Commentary Family, there now came, not heart-searching mea culpa or
reexamination of first principles, but the opposite. Iraq's democratic elections in January 2005, Charles Krauthammer wrote in *Commentary*, confirmed two assumptions on which the Bush Doctrine rested: the universal
desire for freedom and the American commitment to democracy. Norman
Podhoretz—long practiced in the art of taking disparagement as a form of
tribute—likewise stuck to his guns with unrepentant vigor; he would not
repudiate or recant. The former editor regarded those who faltered, who
backed away from support for the war, as "summer soldiers and sunshine
patriots." Once more, he invoked the mantra of national greatness. "What
the United States has been doing in the Middle East is so charged with
greatness and so redolent of nobility," he insisted in November 2005, "that I
have lost all patience with its outright opponents. I find the haters of America among them to be morally contemptible and intellectually cretinous."[21]
In the September 2006 issue, Podhoretz measured the successes: "Iraq has
been liberated from one of the worst tyrants in the Middle East; three elections have been held; a decent constitution has been written; a government
is in place, and previously unimaginable liberties are being enjoyed. By what
bizarre calculus does all this add up to failure?" Three months later, Podhoretz paused to count "the great things that have happened as a result of
the Bush Doctrine: two countries liberated from monstrous tyrannies, one

religious and one secular, and then making extraordinary progress toward democratization—all done in the face of a relentlessly murderous opposition, in an amazingly short time, and at a very low cost (by any historical standard) in American lives." Declining to be swept into what he called the "panic over Iraq," Podhoretz feared a disaster if America were to pull out its troops too early. "In World War II and then in World War III," he said, "we persisted in spite of impatience, discouragement, and opposition for as long as it took to win, and this is exactly what we have been called upon to do today in World War IV." Waging the new war was just as necessary, and Podhoretz would defend it to the last.

AFTER IRAQ, Iran. In 1997, Joshua Muravchik and Jeffrey Gedmin had written for *Commentary* on "Why Iran Is (Still) a Menace." In a 2004 article called "Iran's Nuclear Card," Gary Milhollin and Valerie Lincy of the Wisconsin Project on Nuclear Arms Control in Washington described the Islamic Republic's violations of the Nuclear Nonproliferation Treaty. Alarmed by Iranian president Mahmoud Ahmadinejad's declared ambition to "wipe Israel off the map," and the likelihood that a nuclear-armed Iran would supply a nuclear bomb to terrorist militias it already armed, Podhoretz called for regime change in the Islamic Republic.

In his campaign for the Republican nomination for president, Senator John McCain suggested that the only thing worse than bombing Iran would be allowing Iran to get the bomb. "I wish you had been the first to say that," Podhoretz told Rudy Giuliani, on whose presidential campaign he was now serving as a senior foreign policy adviser. In *Commentary*, starting in 2007, Podhoretz would say so himself.[22] Over the course of several articles, he laid out the case for bombing a country he saw as the "main center of the Islamo-fascist ideology." Just as in the cold war, Podhoretz could summon little faith in diplomacy. "Since, to say it again, Ahmadinejad is a revolutionary with unlimited aims and not a statesman with whom we can 'do business,' all this negotiating has had the same result as Munich had with Hitler." For President Bush, therefore, Podhoretz saw no alternative to air strikes. "It now remains to be seen whether this President, battered more mercilessly and with less justification than any other in living memory, and weakened politically by the enemies of his policy in the Middle East in general and Iraq in particular, will find it possible to take the only action that can stop Iran from following through on its evil intentions both toward us and toward Israel. As an American and as a Jew, I pray with all my heart that he will."

During a forty-minute meeting on the subject at the White House with Bush and Karl Rove in April 2007, Podhoretz got the chance to deliver the prayer in person. At the end of the discussion, Podhoretz turned to Bush with special pleading. "Now I want to talk with you as a Jew," he said. "President Truman once declared: 'I am Cyrus.' You know the Bible, Mr. President. Cyrus was the only pagan king praised by the prophets. After he allowed the Jews to go home to Jerusalem and rebuild the Temple, in 538 BCE, Isaiah called the Persian king 'my anointed.'[23] You, Mr. President, must be the second Cyrus. You have the responsibility to prevent another Holocaust, and you're the only one with the balls to do it."

Several months later, Neal Kozodoy, sixty-six, announced his intention to retire as of the end of 2008. After forty-two years at *Commentary*, the last thirteen of which as editor, he would leave to serve as senior director in the gleaming Fifth Avenue offices of the Tikvah Fund, a philanthropy that had funneled the late Wall Street broker Sanford C. Bernstein's fortune to the Shalem Center, a Zionist think-tank in Jerusalem, but was now embarking on something momentous: establishing novel programs in Jewish thought for elite students at Princeton, New York University, and the Jewish Theological Seminary, and founding a new journal, the *Jewish Review of Books*.[24]

At Kozodoy's valedictory jamboree at the Metropolitan Club on Fifth Avenue, Bill Kristol praised the editor as an "exemplary Jew" and a "lover of excellence." "Neal saved my life, intellectually and spiritually," David Gelernter said in his toast. President Bush, himself about to retire from the White House, sent a note: "Under your guidance, *Commentary* has been at the center of our country's most important intellectual debates." To these encomia Kozodoy replied with characteristic self-effacement: "Anyone who had worked for so many decades as I did by the side of Norman Podhoretz would have had to be extraordinarily stupid not to have picked up a few tips about how to edit a magazine," he said.

The stewardship of *Commentary* was changing hands for the third time; the guard was changing and yet would remain the same, for Kozodoy appointed as his successor John Podhoretz, forty-six, the only son and youngest child of Norman and Midge. Before handing over the editorial reins, Kozodoy reminded the dauphin that *Commentary* still had plenty of work ahead. The cultural wars, Kozodoy told him, are real wars, and the battles against "the depredations of educated philistines" are far from over.

John Podhoretz once gave his father a bronze relief of Teddy Roosevelt, with the inscription: "Aggressive fighting for the right is the noblest sport the world affords." As a teenager, John had babysat several times a week for Kozodoy's three oldest kids. Unlike Kozodoy, his career in journalism took an itinerant course. At the University of Chicago he started a magazine called *Midway* (later *Counterpoint*) with Tod Lindberg (who himself would go on to edit *Policy Review*). He worked as a researcher at *Time*. He wrote a column at the *Washington Times*, where editor Arnaud de Borchgrave introduced him so often as "John Podhoretz, Norman's son" that the newspapermen took to calling him "John P. Normanson." He served as executive editor of *Insight*, did a brief stint at *U.S. News & World Report*, worked in the White House at the end of Ronald Reagan's second term, and served on the staff of George H. W. Bush's drug czar, Bill Bennett. Together with Bill Kristol's brains and Rupert Murdoch's cash, he helped found the *Weekly Standard* in Washington in 1995, and spent two and a half years as deputy editor. Then he edited the *New York Post*'s editorial page, blogged for *National Review Online*, and served as a consultant to *The West Wing*. A compulsive watcher of television, John won *Jeopardy!* five times, and took as his second wife a producer at *Saturday Night Live*. He reviewed movies for the *Weekly Standard*. Before 2008, his only articles for *Commentary* were on Groucho Marx and on reality TV. He had written three books. *Hell of a Ride: Backstage at the White House Follies 1989–1993* (1993) described the administration of the first President George Bush (the *Commentary* review praised it as both "very funny" and "unexpectedly dispassionate"). *Bush Country: How Dubya Became a Great President While Driving Liberals Insane* (2004) hailed the second President George Bush ("the best presidential speaker since Franklin Delano Roosevelt"). His third book was *Can She Be Stopped?: Hillary Clinton Will Be the Next President of the United States Unless . . .* (2007), which *Commentary* called "a virtuoso lesson in how to conduct the new, tribal brand of politics that, for better or worse, has now become our common lot." As for John's literary style, Andrew Ferguson of the *Weekly Standard* once described it as "*Mad* magazine meets *Foreign Affairs*."

After taking over in January 2009, John Podhoretz executed what he called a "dramatic redesign." He added pull quotes, color, and ornamentation (one dismayed longtime contributor called them "mauve *fleurs de lys* and la-la scrolls"); instituted a monthly Jewish jokes department; and retired the "Books in Review" section. Yet he valued continuity, and in his first fundraising letter to readers, Podhoretz Jr. explained how he saw his own editorship in relation to the magazine's past:

The challenge I accepted two years ago is now so much more than a challenge: It is a mission. It is a calling. What happens over the next few years is going to tell the tale of the 21st century—whether the United States will remain the confident, proud, and moral leader of the world, or whether, as many of our self-flagellating elites are proposing, we will accept our rightful decline into merely one nation among the many.

The fate of the United States, the fate of Western civilization, and the fate of democracies great and small—especially the miraculous, vibrant, and besieged democracy called Israel—all hang in the balance. Right now. We can tip the balance. We can help win this battle.

Why am I so confident? Because there's something I know in my marrow. I know the outsized role that little magazines can play both in sharpening minds and in strengthening hearts and convictions. I know because they have done this before—and one magazine in particular. Its name was *Commentary*.

I think back to a time nearly four decades past when the array of dangers facing the United States was, if anything, far worse—and the possibility of reversing the tide and setting the country and the world on the right path far more difficult. Vietnam was on its way to being lost. A conservative Republican president was working to accommodate the Soviet Union and had instituted government controls on wages and prices. There was a regulatory frenzy in the air. The media landscape was dominated by a few towering behemoths determined to block and silence voices of opposition to the prevailing Establishment consensus.

And yet this little magazine, with a readership dwarfed by that of the newspapers and the newsmagazines and the audience for the television networks, kept pounding away every month. On issue after issue, *Commentary* exposed the fallacies that dominated thinking in those perilous days. The restoration of national self-confidence and a proper sense of moral balance—these were the causes of the time. And they would not have been reasserted and reestablished as they were, with victory in the cold war and 25 years of prosperity, had it not been for the brave, lonely, fierce, and world-changing work of *Commentary*.

The decision to give *Commentary*'s crown to John Podhoretz had elicited some bewilderment. The *New York Times*, which might be expected to know something about Jewish publishing dynasties, greeted the appointment with an article about nepotism. John's "crude op-eds for the New York

Post didn't measure up to *Commentary*'s intellectual past," George Packer of the *New Yorker* said. The choice showed that neoconservatives excelled at "getting their children cushy jobs, no matter how far the fruit has fallen from the proverbial tree," said Eric Alterman of *The Nation*.

Kozodoy, however, was a man who kept his own counsel, and whatever inner reckonings determined his decision were never revealed. Thus, the appointment caught even those inside the magazine off guard. Senior editor Gabriel Schoenfeld—who had earlier dedicated his book *The Return of Anti-Semitism* (2004) "To Neal Kozodoy, brilliant editor, true friend"—now questioned the friendship of the man who passed him over and left the magazine before John took over to write a book about secrecy and national security. Managing editor Gary Rosen quickly landed a job as spokesman for the Templeton Foundation. Norman Podhoretz himself said he knew nothing of the choice until the day before it became public, though he conceded it was "a brilliant stroke." "I was absolutely amazed," John's father said. "It would never have occurred to me in a million years."

The choice of successor, then, was entirely Kozodoy's idea, and in all likelihood the reason for it had everything to do with his relationship with his lifelong mentor. Norman Podhoretz had steered the magazine through a double apostasy, first to the mildly radical Left, then to the staunchly neoconservative Right, twice asserting his independence against Elliot Cohen's powerful influence. But as Podhoretz's heir, Neal Kozodoy faithfully and lovingly preserved Podhoretz's legacy. As the book of Genesis (26:18) says: "And Isaac dug again the wells of water which they had dug in the days of Abraham his father. . . . He called them by the names which his father had called them." With filial piety, the loyal son deviated not one whit from the will of the head of the Family, who on several occasions called Kozodoy "my right hand, my left hand, and all the fingers thereof." More than a gesture of reciprocating love, then, Kozodoy's election of Podhoretz's son was a final fidelity.

Epilogue

Exile Language

In my beginning is my end.
—T. S. Eliot, "Four Quartets"

FROM THE WORLD OF THEIR FATHERS

John Podhoretz's assumption of the editorial chair, which happened to coincide neatly with his almost exact contemporary Barack Obama's inauguration in January 2009, made it seem undeniable that *Commentary* had become an inheritance, a dynastic succession.

Once a magazine's mind is settled, once it brooks fewer challenges to its certainties, its momentum flags. *Commentary* remained consistently well edited, but it would be futile to deny that the magazine's style seemed more cramped and crabbed than before, the pages less commodious. The magazine's deepest chords had already been struck. Even titles of articles bore signs of repetitiveness. After Norman Podhoretz's "My Negro Problem— and Ours," for example, came "Indian Art—and Ours"; "Gorbachev's Strategy, and Ours"; "Salman Rushdie's Delusions, and Ours"; "Iraq's Future—and Ours"; "Milton Avery's Art, and Ours"; and "Nixon's Fate, and Ours."[1] Editorial capaciousness and margins for disagreement had narrowed. Every magazine has its own shibboleths, but the more they were filled with liberal-bashing adamancy, the more *Commentary* pieces sounded as if they were written to order, like speeches intended to buck up the troops or self-congratulatory sermons to the faithful.

Clearly, the magazine was no longer at its high tide. Its intellectual charge surged into brilliance less often. The more settled its views became, the less was it talked about and heeded. There was a time, ex-leftist writer Christopher Hitchens said, in which a copy of *Commentary* on a coffee table was a dangerously loaded thing, "like a revolver in a Chekhov play." By the time John Podhoretz took hold of it, the magazine had lost some of its fearsome firepower. It was no longer what people in the magazine trade call a "hot book."

Some of the causes for this can be attributed to larger forces: an *embourgeoisement* and academic specialization of American intellectuals; a quickening tempo of journalism, a faster metabolism that made things harder for monthlies that took a longer view of political affairs; a vulgarization of political discourse; a growing indifference to critical writing; and a dwindling audience for opinion magazines, whose golden age drifted ever farther into the obscurities of cultural amnesia. "I think the life of significant contention no longer exists," Diana Trilling told *New York* magazine in 1995. "We have enormous division in our society on sectarian or ideological lines. But we don't have any discourse." There was also a sense of intellectual fatigue on the Right. "Republicans have been reprising Nixon's 1972 campaign against McGovern for a third of a century," said conservative journalist and *Commentary* contributor David Frum in his book *Comeback: Conservatism That Can Win Again* (2008). "As the excesses of the 1960s have dwindled into history, however, the 1972 campaign has worked less and less well."[2]

At the end of the day, however, *Commentary* changed, as it had all along, because the Family changed. The Family that had loosely knit itself together in the 1930s from dangling, marginal, free-floating, disinherited men free of the entanglements of power now defended the virtues of capitalist bourgeois democracy. Once unknown outside the Family, now their names resounded in important corridors. Their forerunners had scorned middle-class respectability; now the descendents counted themselves its most ardent defenders. The Family that had originally thrilled to the universalist dream of a secular classless society now defended particularism. The espousers of universal love, who had sought in it the pleasures of disincarnation, now spoke of Jewish interests. The fathers had once questioned Jewish nationalism and the prospects of a Jewish state; the sons now numbered themselves among Israel's staunchest defenders. The sons of those who had labored to create a home for Jews in America now, to lift a phrase James Nuechterlein used in *Commentary*, constructed "an intellectual home for those already at home in America." Those who had understood politics as a feature of culture now regarded culture as a feature of politics. Once the Family had argued that values, far from being entrusted to the government, had to be rescued from its interference; now, in recasting the role of

American power, the Family was persuaded that American government and military must forcefully promote the country's values abroad. Those who had once expressed skepticism about the prospects of exporting democracy now championed democratization. Those who had felt judged by American culture now appointed themselves its judges. The deracinated outsiders had become insiders; under their own centripetal force they had thrust themselves from the margins to the innermost hubs of American politics and letters. They had come far indeed from the world of their fathers.

THIS AGE OF CONFORMITY

Naturally, the Family's latest generation, or what was left of it, saw these transfigurations as virtues. Blazing paths from alienation to affirmation, from marginality to power, and from dislocation to integration, an immigrant community, seeking a sense of permanence, had learned how to be for itself—and this was an achievement to be celebrated.

But legion were those who insisted that Family virtues were merely vices disguised. Just as the vulgar Marxists worshipped the proletariat, the Family neoconservatives were said to have paid uncritical obeisance to America. They were attacked as "all rightniks"—bombastic flag-waving apologists for America. ("It is the self-imposed assignment of neoconservatives," Irving Kristol once wrote, "to explain to the American people why they are right, and to the intellectuals why they are wrong.") Shouting hurrahs, they were alleged to have let their love of country slip into self-satisfaction and sanctimony. In the eyes of its ideological opponents, the Family had lost sight of the fact that Hillel's teaching had two perfectly balanced parts: "If I am not for myself, who will be for me? And if I am for myself alone, what am I?" The Family's love affair with America was looked upon as somehow illicit. *Commentary* writers sometimes stood accused—both as intellectuals and as Jews—of loving America not wisely but too well, of falsely gilding the object of their affections, of falling upon the country with shrill devotion. They had proclaimed their love rather too loudly. ("That love is merchandized whose rich esteeming / The owner's tongue doth publish every where," said William Shakespeare in one of his sonnets.) They had cloaked self-interest in the rhetoric of national interest.

Some of the ill will came in the form of ad hominem opprobrium that had rained down on Norman Podhoretz's head ever since his neoconservative turn. Former *Commentary* contributor Alfred Kazin referred in his journal to "the brutal little mind of Norman Podhoretz." Podhoretz "was merrier in the old days," Norman Mailer, another ex-friend, caviled. "Today he couldn't stand up without having his arms around a missile." In *his* journal in 1982, Arthur Schlesinger Jr. called his ex-friend "odious and despicable." The following year, Christopher Hitchens referred to Podhoretz as the "sort of well-heeled power worshipper who passes for an intellectual these days." "As I read Mr. Podhoretz," Conor Cruise O'Brien commented in a review for the *New York Review of Books* of Podhoretz's collection of essays, *The Bloody Crossroads: Where Literature and Politics Meet* (1986), "that phrase of Edmund Burke came to mind: 'Those who have nothing of politics save the passions they excite.'" O'Brien added that Podhoretz "is not so much an authority on 'the bloody crossroads' as another of the romantic and power-infatuated victims with whom that crossroads is bestrewn." This sort of accusation would dog Podhoretz for the rest of his days. Podhoretz, ex-*Commentary* contributor Leon Wieseltier of the *New Republic* wrote in the *New York Times Book Review* in 2009, "has a completely axiomatic mind that is quite content to maintain itself in a permanent condition of apocalyptic excitation."

But most of the criticisms of the new *Commentary* pertained more generally to the Family's relation to power. Sociologist Lewis Coser, a socialist who wrote some twenty pieces for *Commentary* before cofounding *Dissent* with Irving Howe, once discussed the possible relationships of intellectuals to power. Intellectuals can criticize the powerful, Coser said, as did the biblical prophets; they can lend legitimacy and justification to men of power, as did Napoleon Bonaparte's *idéologues*; they can advise men of power, as did the Fabians in England; or they can actually exercise power, as did the early Bolsheviks. Ever since the magazine's neoconservative turn, the *Commentary* corps had been charged with abandoning the role of the prophet in order to provide rationales for the ruling elite, with siding with the haves against the have-nots. "They will find that the noble tradition that they readily bartered away for power and pottage," black writer Orde Coombs wrote in a 1976 *New York Times* op-ed piece, "was worth more than a grudging invitation to William Buckley's *pied-à-terre*."[3] Podhoretz and his house were said to have made themselves valets of the ruling ideology, ideological gendarmes, cheerleaders for the capitalist elite, janissaries for oligarchic America, flouters of the psalmist's admonishment: "Put not your trust in princes."

Or else they were regarded as elitists themselves, as self-appointed guides leading their fellow Americans toward secular redemption. With the old liberal elite doddering and in disarray, it was said, these flatterers of the powers-that-be who had let their old idealism wither had set out to form a new elite. According to a growing chorus of critics, some more scurrilous than others, the *Commentary* neoconservatives, having made it, too zeal-ously guarded both their own hard-won gains and the system by which they had earned them. Having identified with those in power, they had compro-mised their commitments and surrendered their values—in other words, they had sold out.

Their enemies further accused the neoconservatives of false intellectual courage.[4] They were opportunists, ex-Communists who had fashioned a career out of anti-Communism—only they had kept the old Marxist heresy hunters' concern with doctrinal purity. Their zeal in atoning for past enthu-siasms was excessive; their political penance had gone too far. They were said to have become at least as smug as their opponents on the Left.[5]

The neoconservatives were in other quarters perceived as belligerent alarmists who could not help reducing everything to friends and foes, us versus them. They were crisis-mongers, needful of antagonists, who had long since retreated into ideological bunkers. "Relax, *Commentary*," histo-rian Ronald Steel counseled in 1975. "Just because the U.S. has not bombed or invaded anyone this week does not mean that Western civilization is tot-tering on the brink of ruin."

IDEOLOGY AND IDOLATRY

The Family was hardly unfamiliar with the portrait lines its antagonists so acidly sketched. Much of the censure aimed at ex-liberal neoconservatives, after all, merely reprised the disapproval aimed in the 1950s at ex-radical liberals. Recall Irving Howe's dissent from "conformity." The *Commentary* crowd countered the charges old and new with the conviction that weakness may corrupt no less than power. Powerlessness is no virtue, the neoconserv-atives now understood, nor is the wishful, simpering refusal to credit the reality that the country has enemies.[6] Yet the defense of defending one's own, fundamental though it was to the magazine, can be nuanced by a look, not at *Commentary*'s political trajectory alone, but at the parallel paths of *Commentary*'s political and literary imaginations.

An hypothesis: Any work of fiction worthy of the name takes the full measure of human variousness, fathoms the contradictions of experience, and creates a web of meaning supple enough to capture uncertainty, incon-sistency, paradox. "Every novel says to the reader: Things are not as simple as you think," the Czech master Milan Kundera wrote. Another way of put-ting the point is to suggest that the imagination cannot be forced or fet-tered; it observes its own commandments. "Artistic creation has its own laws," said Leon Trotsky. Hence the long distrust of imagination among the rabbinic jurists, codifiers, theologians, and commentators, a wariness rooted in the Second Commandment's prohibition of graven images; God cannot be imagined. The devotees of Law refused to countenance those who would claim for literature complete autonomy. Stories formed an integral part of traditional Jewish literature (as in midrashic and aggadic writing), but until a body of Hebrew fiction came into being in the late nineteenth century, Jewish stories did not exist for their own sake; they served higher moral, exegetical, liturgical, or didactic purposes. They were commentaries in the guise of narratives. Never free-standing, they served to embroider a biblical text, to illustrate a point of law, to expound a moral doctrine, to hold up hagiographical example. And although there flourished at times a distinguished Jewish tradition of secular poetry and belletristic prose, there was also a strain of contempt for narrative—even biblical narrative—as a base literary form. "Woe to that man," the mystical masterwork the *Zohar* quotes Rabbi Shimon bar Yochai as saying, "who asserts that the Torah came to show us mere stories and profane matters. For if this were so, we too could compose a Torah today, one that would deal with profane matters, a Torah of even greater praise." In fact, until the time of the great medieval Jewish sage Maimonides, Hebrew furnished no word for imagination. Despite the utopian visions of the Prophets—"the wolf and lamb shall graze together" and other anticipations of messianic peace—there is no "imagination" in the Bible. Needless to say, Maimonides, who thought of imagination and intellect as antagonists (the former, though associated with prophecy, being sensual; the latter, capable of abstraction), did not try his hand at writing fiction.[7]

To come back to the present day, we might say that if imaginative literature involves openness to enigma and the evocation of the particular, if it prefers ambiguity and John Keats's "being in uncertainties, mystery, doubts," then its imperviousness to ideology is foreordained. If ideology is to ideas what the prefabricated house is to architecture, if it explains the world through general principles, then it cannot easily fit into art's attires. It can try. Apparatchiks on the Left, not to mention Soviet commissars, used to urge writers to produce novels that were "socially responsible." But that way lies tendentiousness. Stendhal was right to compare introducing politics in a novel to firing a pistol during a concert. Partisan political commitment— Right or Left—has proved inimical to the free play of imagination.

At first, the Family made little distinction between writing-as-imagination and writing-as-cognition. To illustrate the point, Saul Bellow reported a conversation he once had with frequent *Commentary* contributor Sidney

Hook. The scholar of Marxism suggested to the novelist that William Faulkner, though an excellent writer, would be better off if he had certain ideas. "I'd be glad to give him some," Hook said. "It would make a tremendous difference. Do you know him?"

With Cynthia Ozick, however, the illusion of a détente between politics and literature fell away. "Politics begins with premises, imagination goes in search of them," she wrote. For Ozick, this was a reason to fear the imagination. Ozick was far from the first in the *Commentary* circle to fear the destructive, destabilizing power the liberties of art unleash. The novelist, observed the young Lionel Trilling, "is subversive of dominant morality."[8] In his *Commentary* review of *Invisible Man* in the June 1952 issue, Bellow wrote that Ralph Ellison's masterpiece put to rest the notion that "family and class, university, fashion, the giants of publicity and manufacture, have had a larger share in the creation of someone called a writer than truth or imagination." The writer transcends the determinations of family and class. Indeed, this fear informed the Family's reverence for literature's power. But Ozick, remarking on the deep union between imagination and freedom, characteristically gave this idea its sharpest expression. "It might be said," she wrote in *Commentary*, "that Hitler carried the Enlightenment to its inevitable resolution, bringing *liberté* to its highest romantic pitch: the liberty, with no brake of tradition or continuity, to imagine everything, hence to do anything" ("Bialik's Hint," February 1983). (Recall Hilton Kramer's fear of the liberal uses of "unrestricted freedom.") "Fiction is liberty at its purest," Ozick wrote in another *Commentary* essay ("The Rights of History and the Rights of Imagination," March 1999). But "the free imagination, by virtue of its very freedom, tends to undermine Jewish imperatives," she added. Thus, fiction-making appeared to her as a kind of idolatry.

"The arts insist that a man shall dispose of all that he has," T. S. Eliot wrote in 1919, "even of his family tree, and follow art alone. For they require that a man not be a member of a family or of a caste or of a party or of a coterie, but simply and solely himself."[9] At the very moment the Family was becoming a coterie, this was a demand it could not entertain. The Family at large could not ultimately accede to literature's demands. In a 1950 *Commentary* piece, the then-liberal Gertrude Himmelfarb had listed as an "ineradicable" stamp of the conservative "the distrust of the completely free person, the man beholden to no one but himself. . . . What is the idea of presumptuous man that so exercises conservatives but the fear that the free use of man's reason, his intelligence, will undermine society?" This distrust had now made itself felt among the neoconservatives. If, as Ozick observed, there exists a sharp distinction between politics and the imagination, then one might say *Commentary* chose politics. Norman Podhoretz himself, once a literary man, had long since made of himself a *homo politicus*. "He drove his first passions mainly along literary lines," Ozick said, "and only later took on political heat." (Daphne Merkin, writing in the *New Yorker*, observed that "somewhere along the line the young man who was 'Trilling's favorite student' abandoned the still backwaters of literary prestige for the bustling corridors of political power.") In a *Commentary* piece called "Lolita, My Mother-in-Law, the Marquis de Sade, and Larry Flynt" (April 1997), Podhoretz registered discomfort with writers who turn away from "any and all obligations other than those imposed by the laws of his art." There were higher laws than the aesthetic.

From Elliot Cohen to Norman Podhoretz to Neal Kozodoy, members of the Family loved freedom and defended it with all their might. As beneficiaries of American freedoms, the *Commentary* crowd was well placed to discern them especially clearly and to defend them especially vigorously. "Over many years now," Senator Joseph Lieberman said in 2008, "*Commentary* has been a north star for Democrats and Republicans alike in formulating and advocating an American foreign policy that understands that America's cause is freedom, and that preserving, protecting, and defending freedom is the responsibility and destiny of every American leader—indeed, every American. *Commentary* has been and continues to be a great intellectual fighter in that cause." And yet in the very effort to conserve freedom, the Family also feared some of its manifestations—in literature as in morals.

END OF THE UNENDING

As it draws to a close, the story of *Commentary* leaves us with several other ironies. As a serious journal of opinion, *Commentary* acted as an agent of renewal that not only articulated a confident and comprehensive critique of Communism but also invigorated American conservatism—enlarged its palatability and powers of attraction and brought to it a new élan and intellectual respectability. In a sense, the magazine's neoconservatives, so firm in purpose, became better conservatives than the conservatives.

Yet the Jewish embrace of conservatism was not always warmly returned; many traditional conservatives spurned the newcomers. The true-blue, old-stock, country-club conservatives sometimes saw themselves as a Christian old guard beleaguered by Jonathans-come-lately, power-hungry interlopers, sons of Jewish immigrants who had insinuated themselves into positions of power, acted as though they were gentlemen to the manner born, and had managed to attract disproportionate patronage. Some traditional conservatives felt upstaged by a band of upstarts, crowded out by what Russell Kirk called a "little sect" of usurpers who had undergone a sham conversion to conservatism. They bitched like Esau complaining that his birthright had been stolen by Jacob. "Our estate has been taken over by an impostor, just as we were about to inherit," one paleoconservative complained. With no small envy, traditional conservatives often accused the neoconservatives—"revolutionary conservatives" as they called the converts—of attenuating conservatism, of corrupting the true faith.[10] The editor of *Modern Age* dismissed neoconservatism as a "tinsel, opportunistic, and hedonistic conservatism." "It is splendid when the town whore gets religion and joins the church," a traditionalist at the University of Michigan named Stephen Tonsor wrote in *National Review* (June 20, 1986). "Now and then she makes a good choir director, but when she begins to tell the minister what he ought to say in his Sunday sermons, matters have been carried too far."

A decade later, paleoconservative columnist Samuel Francis harped on the same theme. "Old conservatives who welcomed the neocons into their ranks soon found that their new allies often displayed the habit of telling them what was and what was not 'permissible' to say and how to say it" (*The New American*, August 5, 1996). A couple of years after 9/11, Francis wrote in *Chronicles* magazine (September 2003), "The neocons are essentially of the Left themselves and, thus, provide a fake opposition against which the rest of the Left can shadowbox and thereby perpetuate its own political and cultural hegemony unchallenged by any authentic Right." And still more: "Whatever you might say about the flaws of the Old Right," Francis wrote in *Chronicles* in January 2004,

> it never placed the interests of foreign states above those of its own country. . . . What neoconservatives have done is to design an ideology . . . that offers ostensible and plausible rationalizations for the perpetual war in which Israel and its agents of influence in the U.S. government and media seek to embroil the United States (and which all too many American conservatives, out of a foolishly misplaced patriotism, are eager to support) without explicitly invoking the needs and interests of Israel itself.

Another irony underlies the story of *Commentary*: Sons of the Family loved the Jews and defended them with all their soul. They forged an imagined community and led Jews into a fruitful appreciation of both an American and a Jewish tradition from which they had felt estranged. Before *Commentary*, matters had been very different. Consider, by way of example, a pamphlet Harvard professor Harry Wolfson wrote for the Menorah Society in 1922 in which he counseled Jewish students to accept their marginal, disadvantaged fate. "Because of our Judaism we must be prepared to give up some of the world's goods even as we must be prepared to make sacrifices because of other disadvantages with which we may happen to be born," he wrote. "All men are not born equal. Some are born blind, some deaf, some lame, and some are born Jews." Thus, Wolfson concluded, "to be isolated, to be deprived of many social goods and advantages, is our common lot as Jews."[11] Yet, by 2008 American Jews had held the presidencies of Harvard (Lawrence Summers), the fifteen-campus University of California system (David Saxon, Mark Yudof), Columbia (Michael Sovern), Yale (Richard L. Levin), the University of Pennsylvania (Martin Meyerson, Judith Rodin, Amy Gutmann), Princeton (Harold Shapiro), Dartmouth (John Kemeny, James O. Freedman), Cornell (Jeffrey Lehman), Bard (Leon Botstein), Swarthmore (Alfred H. Bloom), MIT (Jerry Weisner), Carnegie Mellon University (Jared L. Cohon), and so on.[12]

By teaching that there need be no contradiction between Jewish particularism and full participation in the larger culture, *Commentary* showed Jews how to weave the strands of Jewishness into the texture of American life. The magazine's editors, writers, and critics anticipated and then brought into being a culturally confident Jewishness, harvested its best fruits, brought them to the public square, and immeasurably enriched American Jewish life. From the beginning, they touched the matters that mattered most to American Jews and in doing so forged a new idiom of Jewishness by changing how Jews spoke about things Jewish and general both. They fostered a healthy self-respect. In ways previously unimaginable, they defended the Jews' right to defend themselves and to pursue their own interests. As an essay in *Dissent* acknowledged, "*Commentary* established itself as our mail-order polity; one could, it seemed, be actively Jewish just by reading about the Jews' history, debating the place in culture of Jewish ritual law, or discerning the American 'emancipation' in the elegance of the magazine's prose."[13] By reshaping Jewish culture into a distinctively American idiom, *Commentary* reversed the cultural isolation in which many Jews had lived before World War II.

And yet from Franklin Roosevelt, who garnered 90 percent of the Jewish vote in 1940, to Barack Obama, who got 78 percent in 2008, Jews remained the most consistently liberal religious group in the country. "If you scratch an American Jew," sociologist and *Commentary* contributor Earl Raab said, "you will find a Democratic voter." After 67 percent of American Jews voted for Walter Mondale's losing presidential bid in 1984, historian Lucy Dawidowicz expressed her bewilderment in *Commentary*. "The lopsided Jewish voting pattern," she wrote, "resembled that of the blacks, the unemployed, and persons in households earning under $10,000 a year, even though Jews in no way resemble those groups or share their social and political interests." Irving Howe once called liberalism the "secular religion" of American Jews. Nathan Glazer noted that Jews "remain the only white ethnic or religious group that is consistently liberal in its political attitudes and heavily Democratic in its voting." On issues such as school prayer, gay marriage, and euthanasia, Jews were far more likely than non-Jews to take on liberal colorations.[14]

Since its swing away from the Left, then, *Commentary* remained ever more out of sympathy with the near-universal liberal reflexes of American Jewish life. This was a source of some puzzlement for the Family, as Nathan Glazer made clear in *Commentary* in 1980: "Jews have been, disproportionately, businessmen and self-employed professionals. . . . They should have been against higher taxes and government spending, for tax breaks to business, against government regulation of business. But whatever the promptings of their *economic* interests, Jews have supported the party that wants to increase government spending, expand benefits to the poor and lower classes, impose greater regulations on business, support the power of organized labor."

The *Commentary* neoconservatives could not help but conclude that in their political habits the majority of American Jews lagged behind or were inauthentic somehow, that they fled from themselves, that their consistent support for liberal ideas and candidates represented an irrational refusal to act on self-interest. In an essay called "On the Political Stupidity of the Jews" (1999), Irving Kristol blamed the problem on an addled mentality cultivated by centuries of Jewish political powerlessness. Against such stupidity even he could not contend. But the truth of the matter is that this refusal grated so much because it represented American Jews' persistent view of themselves as outsiders. It seemed that their votes were motivated not by self-interest, but by their identification with the underdogs—blacks and immigrants, for instance—and by their self-identification as a marginal group, the very self-identification that *Commentary* had for its entire life sought to overcome.

President George W. Bush once asked Norman Podhoretz why the country's Jews seemed on the whole so set against him. "I tremble for my people when I reflect that God is just," Podhoretz replied, paraphrasing Thomas Jefferson. Podhoretz felt the behavior in question was a case of rank ingratitude. Nevertheless, he was prepared to wait. (The messianic idea in Judaism, as Gershom Scholem once said, had deeply instilled—or compelled—habits of patience and deferment.) Perhaps feeling himself to be among the most profoundly American of America's Jews, Podhoretz hoped that the deaf would be made to hear and the blind to see. "I cannot for the life of me," he admitted in 2009, "give up the hope that the Jews of America will eventually break free of their political delusions, and that they will then begin to recognize where their interests and their ideals both as Jews and as Americans truly lie."

In modern history, the distinction between what men think is in their interest and what is really in their interest, along with talk about individuals alienated from their true interests, calls to mind Lenin. In his pamphlet *What Is to Be Done?* (1902), Lenin explained that dominant classes use ideology to mislead lower classes as to their true interests; this is why the proletariat, though it suffers exploitation, does not begin the revolution itself but must instead rely on an elite "vanguard" that acts in the name of workers. Marxists insisted that the Communist Party discerned the true interests of workers better than workers did. It might be said that Podhoretz believed that the neoconservatives discerned the true interests of American Jews better than the Jews did—that in their political patterns the American Jewish masses suffered from what Marxists used to call "false consciousness."

Be that as it may, the *Commentary* Family's readiness to stand in solitary opposition to America (from the Left) had prepared it to stand in opposition to the Jews (from the Right). As radicals in the 1930s, the Family had defiantly stood apart from America; as neoconservatives in the 1980s and after, it stood as defiantly apart from the mainstream of American Jews.

A FINAL IRONY: Jews were not among the American Founders. No Jew signed the Declaration of Independence. But members of the *Commentary* Family came to love America, admire the justness of its cause, and defend it with all their hearts. Many Jewish lovers of America suffered at first a sense of apartness. In coming to grasp just how alien to American soil were the twin terrors of fascism and Communism, they learned to cling to that soil and to feel it as their own. As their passions for the country deepened, they identified with America and ardently wished to protect it from those who would do the nation harm. Declaring their love with full-throated cries, they joined their fate with America's. Sensing that their interests were consonant with the country's, they were enraptured by America and found special affinity with it.[15] In their lovesickness, they made a religion of the country (recall David Gelernter's Americanism) and thought themselves among its most ardent apostles. They toiled in the quarries of their magazine to mine what was best in the country, assimilate its values, codify its principles, and understand its heritage. Ever since World War II, they worshipped America as a sanctuary of culture and freedom. Smitten by their country, they became interpreters and celebrants of America, converts to the national faith, defenders of American power, advocates of the American Way. They looked at America, and their very looking became part of America. It was, as we have seen, a transformative love. For contrary to Shakespeare, sometimes love does alter when it alteration finds.

And yet at the very moment they arrived at the center, the sons of *Commentary* were regarded as arrivistes, as overanxiously Americanized Jews, as hyperacculturated, overidentified, overzealous converts to America who proclaimed their love of country rather too loudly. Their faith in the country, it was sometimes said, was as flawed as it was fervent. What they saw as successful assimilation, others saw as accommodationism. They curried favor, it was said. They truckled, they traded alienation for blind affirmation, they worshipped power and success, they strained too hard to prove their patriotism—in short, they were seen as the *hofjuden*, the "Court Jews," of America.

DIASPORA

On one level, this has been a tentative history of *Commentary*; not the official portrait, but one view of a journalistic institution in transition. It is first of all a family drama about three generations of an uncommonly articulate and uncommonly opinionated group of New York intellectuals who stood astride what Lionel Trilling, one of their number, called the bloody crossroads where politics and literature meet.

Yet this book has attempted to illustrate how the story of *Commentary* lies coiled within a larger story about how Jews over the last half-century embraced America and how they were changed by that embrace. It is no stretch at all to say that by reading *Commentary* as a single, multivolume text, a kind of American Talmud, a record of a decades-long give-and-take, one can trace the whole postwar history of the American Jewish experience. The magazine's history is, among other things, a story of belonging—with its profits and perils—to a society unparalleled in the history of the Diaspora, in which the protagonists were busy, with hammering self-consciousness, defining themselves and their relation to the new country. (George Orwell, an early contributor to the magazine, once interrupted his perusal of an issue of *Commentary* to ask his friend T. R. Fyvel why American Jews seemed so damn preoccupied with defining themselves.) The magazine acted as a new American vessel into which poured age-old Jewish wine.

The literary and political trajectories of *Commentary*'s story, to put it another way, opened onto the story of the often tumultuous Jewish love affair with America—an astonishingly successful postwar immigrant experience and one that remained vividly present for the children and grandchildren of those immigrants whom America had saved from tyranny and who in time willed their way from the periphery into the very heart of American political and cultural life. Historian George Nash put it this way: "In 1945, *Commentary* had been born into a marginal, impoverished, immigrant-based subculture and an intellectual milieu that touted 'alienation' and 'critical nonconformity' as the true marks of the intellectual vis-à-vis his own culture. Two generations later, *Commentary* stood in the mainstream of American culture, and even of American conservatism, as a celebrant of the fundamental goodness of the American regime. . . . It was a stunning achievement."[16] The outsiders had become insiders.

The magazine gave voice to a growing appreciation among Jews of certain American democratic principles and freedoms—and of the urgent necessity to conserve them when they were threatened. In doing so, *Commentary* hosted the Americanization of the Jewish mind, which, in turn, released potent forces that continue to shape American literature and politics today. By demonstrating that Jewish matters could be talked about with the same rigor as any serious subject, *Commentary*—its posture stiffened by the conviction that Jews could fully participate in American life *as Jews*—made itself home to the best writing in English on Jewish literature, history, sociology, and theology.

To be an American may be a complex fate, as Henry James said, but to be a Jew in America—to be a member of the most ancient of peoples in the most modern of countries—proved doubly so. *Commentary*'s founding editor made a startling declaration in the inaugural issue in 1945: "*Commentary* is an act of faith in our possibilities in America." His magazine soon seized those possibilities. Elliot Cohen predicted as much in 1947: "We Jews in America will live very deeply immersed in the culture of our general American society," he said. "This is not only unavoidable—it is eminently desirable." According to his successor, this credo represented the magazine's grand design: "to lead the family out of the desert of alienation in which it had been wandering for so long and into the promised land of democratic, pluralistic, prosperous America where it would live as blessedly in its Jewishness as in its Americanness."

Politically and Jewishly both, the neoconservatives gathered around *Commentary* were both chosen and reviled, both vanguard and anomaly. For all their prominence, they found themselves isolated, a minority of a minority. Here we return to the unlikely fact that the same magazine that would host the neoconservatives' ascendancy and would make itself almost their holy writ was founded by the American Jewish Committee "to meet the need for a journal of significant thought and opinion on Jewish affairs and contemporary issues." Who are the neoconservatives? And who are American Jews? The two questions, it turns out, may be intimately related, in which case the unembellished truth holds far more interest than any conspiratorial imagining. The Jewishness of neoconservatism may rest not in Jewish ancestry or in dark fantasies of a secretive cabal,[17] but in dual inclination to be both different and the same, and the awkward space between acceptance and rejection. It is a not-yet-requited love, but for all that a love that enlarged the hearts and refined the minds of those sunk in its reveries. Neoconservatism, in its heart of hearts, was not only a heresy that came from deep within the Left, but also a culmination of the love affair between America and its Jews.

IN THE JEWISH TRADITION, exile, one of the Bible's great themes, is a God-ordained state, a divine affliction. The condition of exile, as the Jewish tradition understood it, is nothing if not a bitter suffering, an anomaly, a not-yet-home, a temporary tarrying, an aberration of disinheritance and displacement.[18] Contrary to the forecasts of the Zionists, after the rebirth of Israel the Jews of the American exile flourished beyond measure, so much so that they could not feel themselves in exile. "The fact of its hiddenness is hidden from them," Gershom Scholem said of them. American Jews did not face political servitude or religious persecution or forced conversion or Inquisition, as in exiles past; they were not even the country's most oppressed group. They sought no deliverance. In a 1948 *Commentary* essay, Israel Knox declared, "Of all the lands in our long itinerary, none has been as much home as is America." In a 1954 issue, a writer named Benno Weiser honored the new country by reversing for its sake an old piece of Yiddish folk wisdom: "It is not *shver tsu zein a Yid* (hard to be a Jew) in America today."[19] American Jews, unlike those two dozen refugees who had set foot in New Amsterdam in 1654, were no longer disoriented strangers in a strange land. They did not feel unhoused.

Recall how the unprecedented possibilities of American Jewish flourishing fired Elliot Cohen's mind as he founded *Commentary*. "We may well see the Jewish intellectual-religious tradition flower in ways that will stand comparison with Spain, Germany, Eastern Europe, and elsewhere," he had said. In the magazine's first issue, he had expressed the hope that such a flowering would "harmonize heritage and country." Because it is unfinished, the American Jewish exile, the most comfortable exile ever, cannot yet be summed up; we stand too close to its still roiling crucible. Yet for better or worse, in speaking to the deepest concerns of that exile, *Commentary* during the formative years voiced the *galus-shprakh*, the exile language, of the "outsider-insiders" of the American Diaspora.

Acknowledgments

It is a pleasurable duty to acknowledge the deep debts of gratitude I've accrued in writing this book:

To my family—Judy, David and Liz, and Ilana—for the steadfastness of their love.

To Mem Bernstein and Arthur Fried of Keren Keshet and to Bob Guzzardi for generous grants that made this book possible.

To those who read and commented on drafts of the manuscript: gentlemen-editors Meir Persoff, formerly of the (London) *Jewish Chronicle*, and Gabriel Schoenfeld, formerly of *Commentary*; Stephanie Saldaña, luminous writer and true friend; Judy Heiblum of Sterling Lord Literistic, literary agent extraordinaire and steadfast supporter; and Yehudah Mirsky, about whom it was said by an authority greater than me that he put the *Mensch* back into *Luftmensch*.

To the indispensable Lisa Kaufman of PublicAffairs for her exceedingly deft editorial touch and to copy editor Jan Kristiansson for her punctiliousness.

To friends whose unstinting encouragement buoyed me more than they can know, including Edward Alexander, Karen Brunwasser, Werner Dannhauser, Anthony David, Rachel Donadio, Daniel Doneson, Mark and Lina Elsner, Natalie Fainstein, Eli M. Greenbaum, Eliana Harvey, Shai Held, Bill Hesse, Ory Holtzman, Aharon Horwitz, Rachel B. Kahan, Solomon Kalkstein, Daniele Kaplan, Mark Kuzmack, Bill Meyers and Nahma Sandrow, Isaac Meyers (of blessed memory), Sandra Milkovic, Johanna M. Mueller, Alex Orwin, Francoise Ouzan, Tova and Walter Reich, Ben Reis, Rory Schacter, Daniel Septimus, and Max and Suzanne Singer.

To Neal Kozodoy, who allowed me to examine the *Commentary* archives; to Cynthia Ozick, Norman Podhoretz, Philip Roth, and the estates of Saul Bellow and Irving Howe for generous permission to quote from letters in that archive; and to Maura Spiegel for sharing Ted Solotaroff's unfinished memoir.

To Shalom Carmy and the late Walter Wurzburger of Yeshiva University for their early guidance and example.

And finally to the librarians at the Van Leer Institute in Jerusalem, Rita Reiderman and Pinchas Maurer; to Michele Ben Ami, librarian of the American Jewish Committee's Israel office; to Charlotte Bonelli of the American Jewish Committee Archives in New York; and to the staff of the Hebrew Union College library in Jerusalem.

Notes

1. "American Power—For What?" January 2000. The symposium's last contributor, Paul Wolfowitz, about to be appointed deputy secretary of defense, hewed to a more careful line: "When it comes to putting American soldiers in harm's way, there is a big difference between protecting freedom where it exists and spreading it. . . . When it comes to armed intervention, similarly, there is a difference between giving others the means to fight for themselves, as we should have done in Bosnia, and fighting for them. And when it comes to promoting democracy, there is a difference between defending it where it is established, as on Taiwan, and promoting it where it has not yet taken root."

CHAPTER 1

1. A third wave of immigrants, those fleeing Hitler, added to the Orthodox ranks. Some of Eastern Europe's most brilliant rabbis and Talmudists arrived in the 1930s and 1940s: Joseph B. Soloveitchik of Yeshiva College came in 1932; Jacob Ruderman founded the Ner Israel Rabbinical College in Baltimore in 1933; Isaac Hutner, of the Chaim Berlin Yeshiva in Brooklyn, arrived in 1935; Moses Feinstein, born in Belarus, settled on the Lower East Side in 1936; Aaron Kotler, who arrived in 1941, founded an influential yeshiva in Lakewood, New Jersey; and Joseph I. Schneerson, head of the Lubavitch Hasidic movement, set down roots in Crown Heights in 1940.

2. See Norma Pratt, *Morris Hillquit: A Political History of an American Jewish Socialist* (Westport, CT: Greenwood Press, 1979).

3. Another graduate, Abraham Cahan, later the founding editor of the *Forward*, called City College "the synagogue of my new life." Nine alumni—more than from any other public college in the world—would win Nobel prizes.

4. The invocation of the Book of Esther in a 1927 letter of appreciation from former CCNY president John Finley to Professor Cohen is perhaps redolent of the time: "What more can I say except that you have put yourself by your merit in the class with the man of your own race, Mordecai, whom King Ahasuerus delighted to honor?" For fuller portraits of Morris R. Cohen, see Leonora Cohen Rosenfield, *Portrait of a Philosopher: Morris R. Cohen in Life and Letters* (New York: Harcourt Brace, 1962); M. R. Cohen, *A Dreamer's Journey*

(Boston: Beacon Press, 1949); and Israel Knox, "Odyssey of a Jewish Sage," *Commentary*, June 1949.

5. In this, once again, the Family took its cues from Trotsky himself. In 1938, Trotsky advocated "a parallel struggle by the workers of each country against their own imperialism, as their primary and most immediate enemy." In July of the next year, he wrote: "In the long run the imperialists are distinguished from one another in form—not in essence."

6. Greeting Schlesinger's 1949 book of that name, the October 1949 *Commentary* admired "the precision, vitality, and emotional power of his restatement of commonly accepted views."

7. See Gertrude Himmelfarb, *The Jewish Odyssey of George Eliot* (New York: Encounter, 2009). "By the time the state was established," Himmelfarb noted, "Israel's three largest cities, Jerusalem, Tel Aviv, and Haifa, had streets named after George Eliot."

8. Other winners of the prize included Thorstein Veblen, Harold Bloom, and Richard Ellmann.

9. *Der Jude* published a range of work: from novelists Franz Kafka and S. Y. Agnon, to philosophers Hermann Cohen and Franz Rosenzweig, to scholars Gershom Scholem and Leo Strauss. See Arthur A. Cohen, *The Jew: Essays from Martin Buber's Journal, Der Jude, 1916–1928*, trans. Joachim Neugroschel (Tuscaloosa: University of Alabama Press, 1980).

10. On the *Menorah Journal*, see Robert Alter, "Epitaph for a Jewish Magazine: Notes on the 'Menorah Journal,'" May 1965; Lewis Fried, "The *Menorah Journal*: Yavneh in America, 1945–50," *American Jewish Archives Journal*, 1998; Lewis Fried, "Creating Hebraism, Confronting Hellenism: The *Menorah Journal* and Its Struggle for the Jewish Imagination," *American Jewish Archives Journal*, 2001; Daniel Greene, "'Israel! What a Wonderful People!': Elliot Cohen's Critique of Modern American Jewry, 1924–1927," *American Jewish Archives Journal*, 2003; Elinor Grumet, "The Menorah Idea and the Apprenticeship of Lionel Trilling" (Ph.D. diss., University of Iowa, 1979); Louis Harap, "The *Menorah Journal*—a Literary Precursor," *Midstream*, October 1984; Mark Krupnick, "The Menorah Journal Group and the Origins of Modern Jewish Radicalism," *Studies in American Jewish Literature*, Winter 1979; Lauren Straus, "Staying Afloat in the Melting Pot: Constructing an American Jewish Identity in the *Menorah Journal* of the 1920s," *American Jewish History*, December 1996; and Alan Wald, "The Menorah Group Moves Left," *Jewish Social Studies*, Summer–Fall 1976.

11. Elliot Cohen did not invent such boasts. Consider, to take a later example of such claims, this sentence from Irving Howe's *World of Our Fathers* (New York: Simon and Schuster, 1976): "Samuel Silverman, beginning as a sweatshop worker, became a cloak manufacturer with a fortune estimated at $500,000."

12. In 1934, together with Lionel Trilling, Elliot Cohen appended his signature to an open letter protesting the Communist party's disruption of a socialist rally at Madison Square Garden.

13. At first, the *Contemporary Jewish Record* was under the joint editorship of Morris Waldman, Harry Schneiderman, and Sidney Wallach.

14. The *Contemporary Jewish Record* also featured a rich book review section. Reviews included Abraham Halkin on Meyer Waxman's *A History of Jewish Literature from the Close of the Bible to Our Own Days*; Harold Rosenberg on Ben Hecht's *A Guide for the Bedevilled*; Saul Bellow on two novels about black anti-Semitism in Harlem (*The Dark Stain*, by Benjamin Appel and *The White Face*, by Carl R. Offord); Isaac Rosenfeld on *The Ten Commandments: Ten Short Novels of Hitler's War Against the Moral Code*, edited by Armin Robinson, and on Morris R. Cohen's *A Preface to Logic*; Clement Greenberg on Saul Bellow's *Dangling Man*; Delmore Schwartz on the poetry of Karl Shapiro and A. M. Klein; and Nathan Glazer on Henrik Infeld's *Cooperative Living in Palestine*.

15. For useful histories of the AJC, see Marianne Sanua, *Let Us Prove Strong: The American Jewish Committee, 1945–2006* (Waltham, MA: Brandeis University Press, 2007); and an earlier book by Naomi Cohen, *Not Free to Desist: The American Jewish Committee, 1906–1966* (Philadelphia: Jewish Publication Society, 1972). The AJC's Europe office published *Commentary* counterparts *Evidences* in French, *Comentário* in Portuguese, and *Comentario* in Spanish.

16. The *New Leader* was founded in 1924 as a weekly newspaper "devoted to the interests of the Socialist and Labor movements," but it became a home of liberal anti-Communists starting with Sol Levitas's editorship in 1940. (Walter Goodman called it "a temple of premature anti-Stalinism.") Along with the work of Russian émigrés, it published Family writers such as Daniel Bell, Lionel and Diana Trilling, and Hans Morgenthau and printed Martin Luther King Jr.'s "Letter from a Birmingham Jail" (June 24, 1963). The *New Leader* switched to a magazine format in 1950, to a biweekly in 1961, and ceased print publication in 2006.

Warshow translated from the German eminent historian Fritz Baer's classic book on the Jewish idea of exile: *Galut* (New York: Schocken, 1947). See Milton Himmelfarb's review in the May 1948 *Commentary*.

17. The volumes published in 1949 and 1950 in the AJC's Studies in Prejudice series under Horkheimer's direction included Theodor W. Adorno and R. Nevitt Sanford, eds., *The Authoritarian Personality* (New York: Harper and Row, 1950); Bruno Bettelheim and Morris Janowitz, *Dynamics of Prejudice: A Psychological and Sociological Study of Veterans* (New York: Harper and Row, 1950); and Nathan Ackerman and Marie Jahoda, *Anti-Semitism and Emotional Disorder* (New York: Harper and Row, 1950).

18. Leslie Fiedler, whose piece in the January 1951 *Commentary* on Simone Weil ("Simone Weil: Prophet Out of Israel") gave him one of his first tastes of

literary acclaim among New York intellectuals, called Kristol the best magazine editor he had ever worked with.

19. Another of Elliot Cohen's secretaries in those years was Mae Wechsler Jurow, who would later gain some renown as an abstract painter.

20. Exceptions included five drawings by Saul Steinberg accompanying a piece in the October 1947 issue about the artist ("As comedy followed tragedy on the Attic stage, so Steinberg comes after the great documents of modern isolation: Marcel Proust, James Joyce, and Franz Kafka have given birth to this ludicrous postlude"); a hand-drawn map illustrating Israel's 1956 Sinai campaign; and Maurice Sendak's illustrations for three children's stories by Isaac B. Singer about the village of Chelm (in the July 1966 issue).

21. Some of the few *Commentary* articles to bear footnotes were H. R. Trevor-Roper's piece on Heinrich Himmler's doctor (April 1957); Gerald Reitlinger's essay on the Germans' systematic murder of Russian prisoners of war in 1941 (July 1959); Guenter Lewy's "Pius XII, the Jews, and the German Catholic Church," which exhaustively chronicled the Vatican's silence during World War II (February 1964); and Theodore Draper's long report on the Six-Day War (August 1967).

22. The disappearing act continued after the war, too. A piece by Henry Popkin in the July 1952 *Commentary* called "The Vanishing Jew of Our Popular Culture" ended with a plea: "If the creators of our popular culture believe in a world in which the Jew exists, let them show such a world. Let the Jew come back, not as apologist or walking object lesson, not as a generalized focus for sentiments of tolerance or as a public-relations representative of his people, but the man himself in all his concreteness—his strengths and his weaknesses."

23. Part of the problem was lingering Jewish anxiety about anti-Semitism. James Rorty reported in *Commentary*'s inaugural issue on "would-be American Fuehrers," including one reverend who railed against "Communist and radical and Jewish opposition to the Christian American crusade" ("American Fuehrer in Dress Rehearsal," November 1945).

24. This might explain the Family fascination with Franz Kafka, the archetype of alienation, the writer about whom Auden said that it was fitting he was a Jew, "for the Jews have for a long time been placed in the position in which we are all now to be, of having no home." ("What have I in common with Jews?" Kafka wrote in his journal. "I have hardly anything in common with myself.") William Phillips reviewed Kafka's *The Great Wall of China* in the June 1947 *Commentary*. Guenther Anders, Hannah Arendt's ex-husband, wrote for the magazine on "Kafka: Ritual Without Religion" (December 1949). Clem Greenberg, who had translated Kafka for *Partisan Review* and Schocken Books, suggested in a *Commentary* essay, "The Jewishness of Franz Kafka" (April 1955), that Kafka's Jewish distrust of Gentile history made him a kind of anti-Marx: "Marx and other emancipated Jews tried to hurry the Messiah by looking for him in Gentile history and

foreseeing the imminent conversion of the Gentiles—not exactly to Judaism, but to a kind of humanity to which Jews could assimilate themselves. Kafka, the Jew of Prague, could not be so disloyal to what his immediate experience told him." See also F. R. Leavis's reply to Greenberg in the letters columns of the June 1955 issue.

25. This paragraph draws on Jerome Karabel, *The Chosen: The Hidden History of Admission and Exclusion at Harvard, Yale, and Princeton* (Boston: Houghton Mifflin, 2005); and Susanne Klingenstein, *Jews in the American Academy: 1900–1940* (New Haven, CT: Yale University Press, 1991).

26. Rostow's *Commentary* articles included "America, Europe, and the Middle East," February 1974; "The American Stake in Israel," April 1977; "The Case Against Salt II," February 1979; "Why the Soviets Want an Arms-Control Agreement, and Why They Want It Now," February 1987; and "A False Start in the Middle East," October 1989.

27. Yale College did not appoint a Jewish tenured professor until 1946.

28. See Schapiro's reviews in *Commentary* of *The Face of Benedictus Spinoza,* by Simon L. Millner (August 1947) and of two books by Bernard Berenson (December 1949).

29. Trilling accused Clem Greenberg of accusing Trilling of Jewish self-hatred after reading a letter in which Trilling had declined to join the *Commentary* staff; Greenberg denied it.

30. Once again, the Family cannot be blamed entirely for this attenuation, for American Judaism was in those days suprisingly barren. Jewish studies programs at universities were as yet unimagined. Serious Jewish books were uncommon. Schocken Books, for instance, began publishing in the United States only in 1945.

31. See Daniel Bell, "A Parable of Alienation," *Jewish Frontier,* November 1946.

32. At a second meeting a month later, Nathan Ohrbach, founder of Ohrbach's department store on Union Square, offered to fund *Commentary* subscriptions for the entire staff of the National Conference of Christians and Jews.

33. The piece, by a returning G.I. named Aaron Frankel, had appeared in the August 1946 issue.

34. "The Americanism of Adolph S. Ochs," January 1947.

35. A year earlier, Isaac Rosenfeld had ventured a similar view in his *Commentary* review of *Treasury of Jewish Folklore,* in which he discussed the fecal associations of kreplach ("Kreplach," November 1948). Forty-five years later, the magazine would publish an earnest defense of *kashrut* (kosher laws) by Leon Kass (June 1994), which could not be farther removed from Rosenfeld's piece. Rosenfeld's other *Commentary* pieces included a story called "Bazaar of the Senses," February 1946; "Gandhi: Self-Realization Through Politics," August 1950; and "Life in Chicago: The Land and the Lake," June 1957.

36. See Theodor Gaster's review of *A Partisan Guide to the Jewish Problem*, November 1946; and Irving Kristol, "How Basic Is 'Basic Judaism'?" January 1948.

37. Tensions would crop up periodically in subsequent years. According to the minutes of the AJC Steering Committee meeting of February 5, 1952, for example, Edward A. Norman, an heir to the Sears, Roebuck fortune who founded what was to become the American-Israel Cultural Fund, raised "the matter of the basis for selection of articles appearing in *Commentary*, questioning the extent to which these articles truly reflected the major purpose as well as the specific objectives of the AJC. He inquired as to whether it might not be possible and advisable to exercise greater editorial responsibility over the magazine."

CHAPTER 2

1. *Partisan Review*, for instance, had nothing to say in the late 1930s on Nazism or the persecution of Jews, even after the Nuremberg laws were enacted in 1935. The journalistic silence wasn't total, however; Philip Bernstein and I. F. Stone wrote about the slaughter of Europe's Jews for *The Nation* as early as 1942, and in December of that year Varian Fry described in the *New Republic* the "systematic extermination" of Jews, gypsies, and homosexuals. For a discussion of how American Jews responded after the war to the enormity of destruction, see Hasia Diner, *We Remember with Reverence and Love: American Jews and the Myth of Silence After the Holocaust, 1945–1962* (New York: New York University Press, 2009); and Harry Feingold, *Bearing Witness: How America and Its Jews Responded to the Holocaust* (Syracuse, NY: Syracuse University Press, 1995).

2. For an excellent account of how World War II changed Jews who had served in the American armed forces and "altered the terms of American Jewish life in general," see Deborah Dash Moore, *GI Jews* (Cambridge, MA: Harvard University Press, 2004).

3. "The Last Days of the Warsaw Ghetto" appeared in May 1947. In 2006, the author, Zivia Lubetkin, was made the subject of a documentary film directed by Ayelet Heller. Thirty years after her piece had appeared, the magazine ran another gripping account of the last days of the ghetto by one of the initiators of the Jewish Combat Organization (Yitzhak Zuckerman, "From the Warsaw Ghetto," December 1975), and a harrowing piece by Michael Checinski ("How Rumkowski Died," May 1979) one of the leaders of the resistance in the Lodz ghetto, about the fate of that ghetto's infamous Judenrat leaders. Later, the magazine would feature early Holocaust fiction, such as Tadeusz Borowski's story "This Way for the Gas" (July 1962). The story was later collected in *This Way for the Gas, Ladies and Gentlemen: And Other Stories* (New York: Viking,

1967). Borowski, who had been in Auschwitz and Dachau from 1943 to 1945, killed himself in Warsaw in 1951. See Czeslaw Milosz's chapter on Borowski in *The Captive Mind* (New York: Knopf, 1953).

4. "What Happened to Me in My Childhood," May 1950. The document was discovered and translated by Edwin Samuel, son of Sir Herbert Samuel. See also L. Holliday, *Children in the Holocaust and World War II* (New York: Pocket Books, 1995).

5. This project would culminate in Dawidowicz's book *The War Against the Jews, 1933–1945* (New York: Holt, Rinehart and Winston, 1975). Her *Commentary* pieces included "Yiddish: Past, Present, and Perfect," May 1962; "Belsen Remembered," March 1966; "Toward a History of the Holocaust," April 1969; "The Rise and Fall of Yiddish," November 1980; "Lies About the Holocaust," December 1980; "In Berlin Again," August 1986; and "How They Teach the Holocaust," December 1990.

6. Twenty-five years later, in 1977, the magazine would run two chapters of *The Periodic Table*, by chemist and Auschwitz survivor Primo Levi, eight years before that book made its first appearance in English.

7. For detailed accounts of American Zionism, see a pair of books by Melvin Urofsky: *American Zionism from Herzl to the Holocaust* (New York: Doubleday, 1975); and *We Are One: American Jewry and Israel* (New York: Doubleday, 1978). See also Naomi W. Cohen, *The Americanization of Zionism, 1897–1948* (Waltham, MA: Brandeis University Press, 2003); Mark Raider, *The Emergence of American Zionism* (New York: New York University Press, 1998); Samuel Halperin, *The Political World of American Zionism* (Detroit: Wayne State University Press, 1961); and Nathan Kaganoff, ed., *Solidarity and Kinship: Essays on American Zionism* (New York: American Jewish Historical Society, 1980). In *Commentary*, see Judd Teller, "America's Two Zionist Traditions," October 1955.

8. Nathan Glazer was the only exception. He had belonged to Avukah, the American Student Zionist Federation, and had edited its newspaper.

9. Minority opinions were sometimes heard. Another *Commentary* piece that year, for instance, suggested that "Jewish nationalism rests on the bedrock of ineluctable necessity, the necessity of millions of human beings to live." Alfred Ivry, a scholar of medieval Jewish and Islamic philosophy, remembered that a counselor in his Zionist youth movement warned him in the early 1950s to beware of *Commentary*, "because it couldn't make up its mind vis-à-vis Zionism."

10. "There is one ray of hope," *Commentary* argued in November 1946. "Normalization of the Jewish economy in Palestine has transformed the bulk of Jews into working-class people who thereby have a common ground and can initiate cooperation with the Arab lower classes."

11. Arendt's piece was "The Jewish State: Fifty Years After," May 1946. In a 15,000-word *Menorah Journal* essay from October 1944 called "Zionism

Reconsidered," Arendt had written: "Nationalism is bad enough when it trusts in nothing but the rude force of the nation. A nationalism that necessarily and admittedly depends upon the force of a foreign power is certainly worse. . . . The Zionists, if they continue to ignore the Mediterranean peoples and watch out only for the big faraway powers, will appear only as their tools, the agents of foreign and hostile interests. Jews who know their own history should be aware that such a state of affairs will inevitably lead to a new wave of Jew-hatred."

12. David Horowitz, "Founding the New State." Horowitz was chief economic adviser to the Jewish Agency.

13. "To Save the Jewish Homeland: There Is Still Time," May 1948. In the September 1948 issue, in his first article in an American magazine, diplomat Abba Eban (soon appointed Israel's first ambassador to the United Nations) sounded the death knell for binationalism: "High minded people, cherishing the hope of peace, beguiled themselves for years with the pretence that Israel and the Arabs were or could be one people." But it was now clear, Eban said, "that between two national entities so organically distinct the ideal relationship is cooperation, not unity."

14. Tractate Ketubot 110b.

15. "Can We Stay Jews Outside 'the Land'?" September 1953. As late as December 1960, at the Twenty-fifth Zionist Congress, Ben-Gurion announced that Judaism outside of Israel "faces the kiss of death, a slow and imperceptible decline into the abyss of assimilation."

16. Those pleas also fell on deaf ears; there was no exodus. Only a trickle of American Jews—some five hundred a year out of 5 million—moved to the reborn Jewish state.

17. "Israel, Human Rights, and American Jewry: New Roles in the Centuries-Old Struggle," April 1950.

18. There was the matter of theological dependence, too. *Commentary* also noticed the irony that, as Israeli historian J. L. Talmon put it ("Uniqueness and Universality of Jewish History," July 1957), despite the blood-soaked history of Jews in Christendom, "Zionism would never have had a chance of success if centuries of Christian teaching and worship, liturgy and legend had not conditioned the Western nations to respond almost instinctively to the words 'Zion' and 'Israel,' and thus to see in the Zionist ideal not a romantic chimera or an imperialistic design to wrest a country from its actual inhabitants, but the consummation of an eternal promise."

19. Indeed, so critical could the early *Commentary* be of the fate of culture in Israel that the Hebrew Opera sued the magazine for libel, charging that a 1952 article called "Culture in Tel Aviv and Environs" spread anti-Zionist slander. It read, in part:

Miss [Edis] de Philippe and Mr. Simcha Even-Zohar, former secretary-general of the Histadrut, then organized the "Hebrew National Opera," taking in with them the veteran Mr. Golinkin. A dictatorial policy, not to speak of the absence of any artistic enterprise, has characterized the operation of this private—and not in any sense national—institution ever since. . . . The press was unanimous in demanding certain reforms and in deploring the depths to which opera had sunk in Israel. Thus there came the day of a certain opera premiere when no journalist had received a ticket; the secretary of the Journalists' Association called the company's office, to be told that only a single press critic had been invited and all the others were "unwanted." The critics then bought tickets for the performance, but ushers barred their way into the theater. The critics appealed to the police, whereupon Miss de Philippe called the Minister of Police at his home and he ordered his officers on the scene to send the critics home rather than allow a scandal. . . . The "Hebrew National Opera" is still going strong. Its standards have not improved, but audiences flock to it because no other opera is available at the moment.

The author of the piece, Peter Gradenwitz, a composer and music critic, was obliged to publish a retraction.

CHAPTER 3

1. In June 1956, a *Time* magazine cover story ran under the title "America and the Intellectual: The Reconciliation." The article quotes Lionel Trilling: "For the first time in the history of the modern American intellectual, America is not to be conceived of as *a priori* the vulgarest and stupidest nation of the world."

2. "Park Forest: Birth of a Jewish Community," April 1951. Six years later, Gans, who had worked at the Chicago Housing Authority, returned to write a follow-up ("Progress of a Suburban Jewish Community: Park Forest Revisited," February 1957). One study cited by historian Jonathan Sarna found that "between 1945 and 1965, about a third of all American Jews left the big cities and established themselves in suburbs."

3. This upward mobility would become especially evident on American campuses. According to Yuri Slezkine, *The Jewish Century* (Princeton, NJ: Princeton University Press, 2004), "By 1969, Jews (less than 3 percent of the population) made up 27 percent of all law faculties, 23 percent of medical faculties, and 22 percent of biochemistry professors. In the seventeen most prestigious American universities, they accounted for 36 percent of law professors, 34 percent of sociologists, 28 percent of economists, 26 percent of physicists, 24 percent of political scientists, 22 percent of historians, 20 percent of philosophers, and 20 percent of mathematicians. In 1949, there was one Jewish professor on the faculty of Yale College; in 1970, 18 percent of Yale College professors were Jews."

4. Nor, by the same token, is it a coincidence that the two greatest students of American immigration, Marcus Hansen and Oscar Handlin, wrote for *Commentary* in these years.

5. "The Situation of the Jew: Reflections on the Jewish Question," April 1948; "Portrait of the Inauthentic Jew," May 1948; "Gentile and Jew," June 1948. Sartre's book was originally published as *Réflexions sur la Question Juive* (Paris: Paul Morihien, 1946). See also Harold Rosenberg, "Does the Jew Exist? Sartre's Morality Play About Anti-Semitism," January 1949.

6. Taubes's contributions to *Commentary* were "The Issue Between Judaism and Christianity: Facing Up to the Unresolvable Difference," December 1953; and a review of Karl Barth's *Against the Stream,* September 1954. Taubes also influenced Susan Sontag, who studied with him at Harvard.

7. Boorstin's contributions to *Commentary* included "A Dialogue of Two Histories: 'Jewish Contributions to America' in a New Light," October 1949; "Our Unspoken National Faith: Why Americans Need No Ideology," April 1953; "Selling the President to the People," November 1955; and "The Puritan Tradition: Community Above Ideology," October 1958.

8. Chaired by Oscar Handlin, the first Jew appointed to Harvard's History Department, the meeting was attended by, among others, Hannah Arendt, Dan Bell, Nathan Glazer, Irving Kristol, Richard Clurman, Sidney Hook, Arthur Schlesinger, and poet Charles Reznikoff.

9. Grinstein, author of *The Rise of the Jewish Community of New York, 1654–1860* (Philadelphia: Jewish Publication Society, 1945), may have been thinking of the work of Werner Sombart, soon to publish *The Jews and Modern Capitalism* (Glencoe, IL: Free Press, 1951), which identified Judaism as a forerunner of capitalism.

10. The deli piece brought in a great many reader letters, including this one from Orson Welles: "We get a good deal of Jewish delicatessen in Hollywood. Without pastrami sandwiches there could be no picture-making. . . . My view on Jewish delicatessen in general is that it is far too good for the goyim, and the Jews are fools not to keep it to themselves. . . . Salami Aleichem."

11. There were isolated exceptions, though usually in Semitics, not in history or philosophy departments. Starting in the 1830s, for example, Joshua Seixas instructed on Hebrew at Oberlin and Western Reserve College, but he had converted to Christianity. The same decade, Isaac Nordheimer lectured on rabbinics at New York University (NYU, then the University of the City of New York). Abram Isaacs taught Hebrew at NYU starting in 1886, and beginning in 1885 Morris Jastrow taught Semitics at the University of Pennsylvania. Richard Gottheil taught Judaic studies at Columbia from 1886 to 1936. (One of his graduate students was a Russian immigrant named Abraham Halkin, who taught Jewish literature and history at the Jewish Theological Seminary and whose son Hillel would become a frequent *Commentary* contributor.) See Frederick Greenspahn,

"The Beginnings of Judaic Studies in American Universities," *Modern Judaism*, May 2000.

But as Harvard scholar Isadore Twersky wrote in 1976, Harry Wolfson's appointment at Harvard marked a turning point: "Actually, Wolfson's life-work at Harvard marks the emergence of Judaica in great universities as a respectable, self-sufficient discipline with its own integrity, autonomy, and comprehensiveness. In the past—and that means up to very recent times—the study of Judaica was ancillary, secondary, fragmentary, or derivative. . . . The establishment of the Littauer chair at Harvard for Harry Wolfson gave Judaica its own station on the frontiers of knowledge and pursuit of truth, and began to redress the lopsidedness or imbalance of quasi-Jewish studies" ("Harry Austryn Wolfson," *American Jewish Year Book*, 1976). The Association of Jewish Studies would come into being with forty-seven members only in 1969.

12. The only other magazines to carry Jewish theology in English were *Judaism: A Quarterly Journal of Jewish Life and Thought*, which the American Jewish Congress began publishing only in 1952, and *Tradition: A Journal of Orthodox Jewish Thought*, brought to life by the Rabbinical Council of America in 1958. For a brief history of the former, see Robert Gordis, "The Genesis of *Judaism*: A Chapter in Jewish Cultural History," *Judaism*, Fall 1981. As for books, almost the only example of an early stab at Jewish theology in America is Kaufmann Kohler, *Jewish Theology, Systematically and Historically Considered* (New York: Macmillan, 1918).

13. Kristol himself had a year earlier taken to the magazine to charge that Jewish thought had been scandalously indifferent to the questions of evil raised by the war. A Judaism that failed to address such matters, he said, was "catastrophically narrow."

14. Reinhold Niebuhr had the lead piece in the second issue, for instance. Paul Tillich wrote for *Commentary* on Martin Buber, and Mircea Eliade wrote on Gershom Scholem.

15. Rackman was perhaps the first to bring Soloveitchik's thought to a popular audience. See "Orthodox Judaism Moves with the Times," June 1952.

16. See, for example, "Can We Believe in Judaism Religiously?" December 1948; and "The Modern Jew's Path to God," May 1950.

17. *Commentary* also ran Robert Gordis's new translation of Ecclesiastes and the first appearance in English of some of the Dead Sea Scroll psalms. For a more detailed treatment, see Robert Goldy, *The Emergence of Jewish Theology in America* (Bloomington: Indiana University Press, 1990).

18. Bluefarb's own books include *The Escape Motif in the American Novel: Mark Twain to Richard Wright* (Columbus: Ohio State University Press, 1973); and *The Dubious Benefits of Nostalgia and Other Stories* (Berkeley, CA: Creative Arts Books, 2003).

19. Selections from Buber's *Tales of the Hasidim* (New York: Schocken, 1947) appeared in the January 1947, February 1947, and October 1948 issues. In a

review of three of Buber's books in the February 1949 *Commentary*, Leslie Fiedler remarked that Buber's Hasidic tales came at a moment when, "disinclined to choose between available avenues of accommodation and alienation for its own sake, we are casting about for a new way." Buber's other contributions to *Commentary* included "The Man of Today and the Jewish Bible: How the Modern Can Recapture Faith," October 1948; "Myth in Judaism," June 1950; and "Interpreting Hasidism," September 1963. See also Harold Rosenberg's review of *Tales of the Hasidim*, May 1947; Paul Tillich on "Martin Buber and Christian Thought," June 1948; Emil Fackenheim's review of *The Prophetic Faith*, April 1950; Will Herberg's reviews of *Paths in Utopia*, September 1950, and *Eclipse of God* and *At the Turning*, December 1952; Walter Kaufmann's omnibus review, October 1958; and Gershom Scholem on "Martin Buber's Hasidism," October 1961. A bimonthly series of personal commentaries by Norman Mailer on selections from *Tales of the Hasidim* appeared in *Commentary* between December 1962 and October 1963.

20. See Irving Kristol's review of A. J. Heschel's *The Earth Is the Lord's*, May 1950; Marvin Fox's review of Heschel's *Man Is Not Alone*, August 1951 ("In the fundamentally secular environment of contemporary American Judaism, in which almost every conceivable kind of activity is given precedence over Torah and worship, Professor Heschel has written a profoundly moving religious book"); and Will Herberg's review of *The Sabbath*, June 1952. See also Jacob Petuchowski, "Faith as the Leap of Action: The Theology of Abraham Joshua Heschel," May 1958. Heschel's own contributions to *Commentary* were "The Two Great Traditions: The Sephardim and the Ashkenazim," May 1948; and "Between Civilization and Eternity," October 1951.

21. Milton Steinberg wrote that Herberg's essay "indicates that Judaism has not lost the power to win souls from among free and uncommitted men. And it gives further evidence in support of certain old propositions whose very antiquity conceals their never failing pertinence: the truth that social idealism requires a religious faith on which it may stand, by which its purity shall be preserved." For a critical response, see Harold Rosenberg, "Pledged to the Marvelous: An Open Letter to Will Herberg," February 1947.

22. As it happens, five of the editors on *National Review*'s original masthead were born Jewish (though two came to embrace the Catholic faith): Frank Chodorov, Eugene Lyons, Frank S. Meyer, Morrie Ryskind, and William Schlamm.

23. Herberg's other contributions to *Commentary* included "Has Judaism Still Power to Speak?" May 1949; "Rosenzweig's 'Judaism of Personal Experience': A Third Way Between Orthodoxy and Modernism," December 1950; "What Happened to American Socialism?" October 1951; "Communism, Democracy, and the Churches," April 1955; "The Triple Melting Pot," August 1955; and "America's New Religiousness: A Way of Belonging of the Way of God?" September

1955. The very terms "melting pot" and "cultural pluralism," incidentally, were coined by Jewish writers Israel Zangwill and Horace Kallen, respectively.

24. Such stereotypical characters can be found in Sholem Asch, *East River* (New York: Putnam's, 1946); and Ludwig Lewisohn, *The Island Within* (New York: Harper and Brothers, 1928), for example. When Irving Howe criticized *The Island Within* in *Commentary* ("The Stranger and the Victim: Two Jewish Stereotypes of American Fiction," August 1949), Lewisohn wrote in to say: "Mr. Howe has no notion of the fact that in a dozen languages that book helped to sustain and comfort Jews. It was in the luggage of refugees; it was in the DP camps."

25. "The Prison," September 1950; "The Bill," April 1951; "The Loan," July 1952; "The Angel Levine," December 1955; and "Behold the Key," May 1958.

26. Norman Podhoretz, however, in his first *Commentary* piece after returning from Cambridge (in the October 1953 issue), felt more ambivalent about the novel: "Mr. Bellow has the very genuine distinction of giving us a sense of what a real American idiom might look like. It is no disgrace to have failed in a pioneer attempt."

27. Roth's short story bears similarities with "A Yeshiva Comes to Westchester," by Herrymon Maurer, a writer for *Fortune*, which appeared in the magazine in April 1949.

28. So was the magazine's poetry, which included the first publication of W. H. Auden's "Pleasure Island"; a cycle of Mark Van Doren's poems based on the Bible; the first appearance in English of Paul Celan's "Death Fugue" (in a translation by Clem Greenberg); and poems by Delmore Schwartz, Charles Reznikoff, Yehuda Amichai, and Harvey Shapiro.

29. The story, published in November 1953, was translated by Milton Himmelfarb and adapted for the screen in 1991 by David Brandes and Joseph Telushkin.

30. *Commentary* also ran a heartfelt memoir of Yiddish writer Sholem Asch (1880–1957) by his son Nathan (1902–1964), who died as it was coming to press. William Barrett, Irving Howe, and Norman Podhoretz each wrote for the magazine on the great Yiddish writer Sholom Aleichem ("who taught us to laugh with one eye and cry with the other," as Abba Kovner put it).

Translations from other languages also appeared frequently in *Commentary*. Italian Jewish writer Giorgio Bassani (author of *The Garden of the Finzi-Continis* [1965]) made his first appearance in America in the magazine ("A Plaque on the Via Mazzini," October 1958). *Commentary* hosted the first appearance in English of seven Isaac Babel stories ("The Awakening," February 1947; "First Love," September 1947; "In the Cellar," January 1948; "Froim Grach," and "Kolyvushka," February 1964; and "The Deserter," and "The Quaker," January 1968).

31. "On Not Being a Jew," April 1968.

32. In *The Victim* (New York: Vanguard Press, 1947), Bellow has Allbee say: "Last week I saw a book about Thoreau and Emerson by a man named

Lipschitz. . . . A name like that? . . . It seems to me that people of such background simply couldn't understand." Bellow used to quote from Goethe's *Wilhelm Meister's Apprenticeship* (1796): "We do not tolerate any Jew among us, for how could we grant him a share in the highest culture the origin and tradition of which he denies?"

33. "The Jewish Writer and the English Literary Tradition: A Symposium" appeared in the September and October 1949 issues. As for the Bollingen Prize, managing editor Clement Greenberg shared Cohen's displeasure. In a piece on the Pound controversy for *Partisan Review* (May 1949), he remarked: "I am sick of the art-adoration that prevails among cultured people, more in our time than in any other: that art-silliness which condones almost any moral or intellectual failing on the artist's part as long as he is or seems a successful artist. Psychopathy has become endemic among artists and writers, in whose company the moral idiot is tolerated as perhaps nowhere else in society."

34. Outside the magazine: Alfred Kazin, *On Native Grounds* (New York: Harcourt, Brace, 1942); Lionel Trilling, *The Liberal Imagination* (New York: Viking, 1950); Irving Howe, *Politics and the Novel* (New York: Horizon, 1957); Leslie Fiedler, *Love and Death in the American Novel* (New York: Criterion Books, 1960; rev. ed. New York: Stein and Day, 1966).

35. Midge Decter called Leon Uris, author of *Exodus* (New York: Doubleday, 1958), a book that held the top place on the *New York Times* best-seller list for nineteen weeks, "a gifted writer of hard-core trash" who indulges in "a pornography of the feelings."

36. *Commentary* also covered the nonliterary arts. This, too, began in a tentative, parochial key. The magazine's early music criticism, for example, included Kurt List's appraisals of twenty-seven-year-old Leonard Bernstein's *Jeremiah*, February 1946; of Arnold Schoenberg's *A Survivor in Warsaw*, November 1948; and of Jewish music, September 1946, December 1947, and November 1949. The magazine's early treatment of painting amounted to running a memoir by Marc Chagall ("My Beginnings," April 1946) and an appreciation of Chaim Soutine (Alfred Werner, "Soutine: 'Dedicated Traditionalist,'" May 1948).

Before long, however, Elliot Cohen—with the occasional help of Clem Greenberg and Harold Rosenberg, the two most influential critics of postwar American art and champions of the abstract expressionists—was publishing some of the best pieces in the country on mass art. (Rosenberg, a tall, husky man with a stiff leg and a cane, and a dazzling talker, coined the phrase "action painting.") American art was in these years jettisoning its dependence on Europe. It no longer reflexively held up European painting as more sophisticated. In this liberation the *Commentary* critics had a hand. Cohen also ran drama criticism. Robert Brustein, for example, later dean of Yale Drama School and longtime theater critic for the *New Republic*, made his first appearance in print in *Commentary*.

In the magazine's later neoconservative phase, *Commentary* would by no means neglect the nonliterary arts. William Pechter and then Richard Grenier wrote on movies, and Jack Richardson covered theater from 1966 to 1980. The unabashedly highbrow Sam Lipman, a piano prodigy and one of the country's finest music critics, wrote for the magazine starting in 1976. (Diana Trilling had introduced him to Norman Podhoretz.) The prolific Terry Teachout covered music for the magazine starting in the 1990s.

CHAPTER 4

1. Fineberg wrote a brief against the Rosenbergs for *Readers Digest*, later expanded into a book called *The Rosenberg Case: Fact and Fiction* (New York: Oceana, 1953).

2. Lucy Dawidowicz, "'Anti-Semitism' and the Rosenberg Case: The Latest Communist Propaganda Trap," July 1952; Robert Warshow, "The 'Idealism' of Julius and Ethel Rosenberg," November 1953. See also Leslie Fiedler's piece on the Rosenbergs, "Afterthoughts on the Rosenbergs," *Encounter*, October 1953, which reprises Warshow's main themes.

3. Buckley considered Macdonald's piece "unbalanced."

4. In a September 1948 *Commentary* article ("What the Nazi Autopsies Show"), Irving Kristol wrote: "The application of the term 'totalitarian' to both Stalin's Russia and Hitler's Germany seems to me a source of confusion. True, the effects of both systems on the free individual are similar. But in its ideology, motives, and mainsprings of power, there is an essential difference between Communism and Nazism. Communism can claim a certain continuity with significant aspects of Western civilization—which may possibly make it a more profound and enduring menace to freedom and liberty."

5. Arendt's biographer, Elisabeth Young-Bruehl, contends in *Why Arendt Matters* (New Haven: Yale University Press, 2006) that Arendt would today be troubled by totalitarian temptations within America. After 9/11, Young-Bruehl writes, "The secret services began to operate like a shadow government, that is, in ways that Arendt had identified as proto-totalitarian." For much of this, Young-Bruehl blames the "cadre of neoconservatives," adding that anti-Communists of Norman Podhoretz's stripe "distorted and exploited" Arendt's views. "Victory for democracy over totalitarianism, they held, justified any means for promoting democracy—including totalitarian means." For another view of Arendt's contemporary relevance, see Samantha Power's introduction to the latest edition of *The Origins of Totalitarianism* (New York: Schocken, 2004).

6. See Warshow's two *Partisan Review* essays: "Monsieur Verdoux," July–August 1947; and "A Feeling of Sad Dignity," November–December 1954. Both are reprinted in Sherry Abel, ed., *The Immediate Experience* (New York: Doubleday, 1962).

7. In one *Commentary* piece, Borkenau concluded: "None of the men who now lead the Communist movement, inside and outside the USSR, intends anything but the total destruction of Western society" ("World Communism Shifts Its Line: Making Room for Mau and Tito," January 1956).

8. Over the next decades, the magazine would remain attentive to Soviet Jewry. It ran Elie Wiesel's enormously influential report of a trip to Moscow's main synagogue for Simchat Torah in 1966, where some forty thousand celebrated the one night they were permitted to express their Jewishness openly. In the magazine's neoconservative phase, the attention continued. *Commentary* supported the Jackson-Vanik Amendment (part of the 1974 Trade Act), which linked freedom of emigration for Soviet Jews with granting the Russians most-favored-nation status. In the 1970s, *Commentary* published a memoir by Efim Davidovich, a refusenik, hero of World War II, and leading advocate of Soviet Jews' rights; and Simon Markish, son of murdered Soviet Yiddish writer Peretz Markish, who wrote on the psychology of Soviet Jewish émigrés. In the 1980s, see Allan Kagedan, "Gorbachev and the Jews," May 1986; and Edward Alexander, "Shcharansky's Secret," October 1986.

9. Examples include Harry Schwartz, "Has Russia Solved the Jewish Problem?" February 1948; three articles by Peter Meyer: "The Jewish Purge in the Satellite Countries," "Stalin Follows in Hitler's Footsteps," and "Soviet Anti-Semitism in High Gear," in July 1952, January 1953, and February 1953, respectively; George Lichtheim, "Will Soviet Anti-Semitism Teach the Lesson," March 1953; and Franz Borkenau, "Was Malenkov Behind the Anti-Semitic Plot?" May 1953. Some of these were collected in Elliot Cohen, ed., *The New Red Anti-Semitism* (New York: Beacon Press, 1953).

10. Dewey's own *Commentary* pieces were "The Crisis in Human History," March 1946; "Liberating the Social Scientist," October 1947; "William James' Morals, and Julien Benda's," January 1948; and "Philosophy's Future in Our Scientific Age," October 1949.

11. Barrett's report is "Culture Conference at the Waldorf," May 1949. Barrett's other contributions to *Commentary* included "What Existentialism Offers Modern Man," July 1951; "The Twentieth Century in Its Philosophy," April 1962; "The Truants: *Partisan Review* in the 40s," June 1974; "Delmore: A 30s Friendship and Beyond," September 1974; "Our Contemporary, William James," December 1975; "On Returning to Religion," November 1976; "Portrait of the Radical as an Aging Man," May 1979; and "The Authentic Lionel Trilling," February 1982.

Elliot Cohen joined the American Committee for Cultural Freedom board, Irving Kristol served as its first executive director, Sidney Hook as its first chairman, and Daniel Bell, Diana Trilling, and Nathan Glazer became members. With help from the Congress (which was later revealed to have received CIA funds), anti-Communist magazines on the *Commentary* model sprung up all over the world: *Encounter* in England (coedited by Kristol), *Preuves* in France, *Der Monat* in Germany, *Tempo Presente* (edited by Nicolà Chiaromonte and Ignazio Silone) in Italy, *Forum* in Austria, *Cuadernos* in Spain, *Quadrant* in Australia, and *Quest* in India. (*Commentary* itself never received covert funds.)

12. "The well-warranted hostility to Russia and to Communists generally was of course a factor in many contests, but in furthering the myth that McCarthy won a kind of endorsement, in recognizing him as a force, in talking solemnly about his ambitions for a vice-presidential nomination in 1952, Washington correspondents, liberals included, are certainly doing their best to inflate him beyond all reason or excuse." ("Has the American Voter Swung Right?" January 1951.)

13. *National Review* supported McCarthy even after his censure by his Senate colleagues in late 1954. *National Review* editors William F. Buckley and Brent Bozell defended the senator in their book *McCarthy and His Enemies* (Chicago: Regnery, 1954). There they argued that "on McCarthyism hang the hopes of America for effective resistance to Communist infiltration." McCarthy himself attended the book launch. Dwight Macdonald said the book gave "the general effect of a brief by Cadwalader, Wickersham and Taft on behalf of a pickpocket arrested in a subway men's room." See also Brent Bozell, "This Was a Man," *National Review*, May 18, 1957; and Frank Meyer, "The Meaning of McCarthyism," *National Review*, June 14, 1958. Frequent *National Review* contributor Forrest Davis authored McCarthy's infamous 1951 speech attacking George C. Marshall as a traitor.

14. A 1952 Gallup Poll found that 45 percent of Protestants disapproved of McCarthy's tactics, compared with 98 percent of Jews. The poll is cited in C. B. Sherman, *The Jew Within American Society* (Detroit: Wayne State University Press, 1960).

15. Glazer's review of *Dissent* appeared in the February 1954 *Commentary*. Diana Trilling was incensed at the violence with which *Dissent* attacked the idea that American democracy, for all its faults, deserved to be defended. *Dissent's* polemic, she said, "is based not upon intellectual cogency but upon the emotional intimidation of its readers."

16. On American Communists, see Theodore Draper, *The Roots of American Communism* (1957, rpt. Chicago: Ivan R. Dee, 1985); Theodore Draper, *American Communism and Soviet Russia* (1960, rpt. New York: Vintage, 1986); Nathan Glazer, *The Social Basis of American Communism* (New York: Harcourt Brace, 1961); Irving Howe and Lewis Coser, *The American Communist Party* (New York: Praeger, 1962); Harvey Klehr, *The Heyday of American Communism: The Depression Decade* (New York: Basic Books, 1984); Harvey Klehr

et al., *The Secret World of American Communism* (New Haven, CT: Yale University Press, 1995); and Guenter Lewy, *The Cause That Failed: Communism in American Political Life* (New York: Oxford University Press, 1990).

17. Unbeknown to Kristol, the magazine was subsidized by the CIA through Julius Fleischmann's Farfield Foundation. For a sense of the magazine's extremely high quality, see Melvin Lasky, Irving Kristol, and Stephen Spender, eds., *Encounters: An Anthology from the First Ten Years of* Encounter *Magazine* (New York: Basic Books, 1963).

18. The magazine's longtime circulation manager, Jean Rogers Anstey, died suddenly in 1959.

CHAPTER 5

1. Podhoretz himself had written in the April 1960 issue, "It is an issue that our society still lives by success, conceived in terms of status or money, and that the pursuit of success encourages the development of the worst human qualities and strangles the best."

2. Years later, Mailer told the *Paris Review* (Summer 2007): "He went into a depression and stayed there for about a year . . . just didn't do much. Worked on his magazine and listened to music and hardly saw anyone. And by the end of that time, he'd moved over to the right. "

3. After leaving *Commentary* when she and Norman started seeing each other in 1956, Decter would work at the Zionist journal *Midstream*, for the futurist and nuclear strategist Herman Kahn at the fledgling Hudson Institute, and as executive editor of *Harper's*.

4. Earlier, during Cohen's tenure, J. Edgar Hoover wrote in to criticize a piece called "The Day the FBI Came to Our House" (January 1952). Another letter (by Phillip Abbott Luce, editor of the *American Sentinel*) began, "As a former Marxist-Leninist political terrorist . . . "

5. See, for example, Neusner's "Zionist Revival on the Campus?" February 1955. Not everyone minded the change. Irving Howe had complained back in 1947 that *Commentary* was "given to the unwarranted attempt to discover a 'Jewish angle' in everything."

6. Magid's five pieces for *Commentary* included "The Innocence of Tennessee Williams," January 1963; "Auteur! Auteur!" March 1964; and a review of Wallace Markfield's *To An Early Grave*, November 1964.

7. Dienstfrey would later found the journal *Advances in Mind-Body Medicine*.

8. In Saul Bellow's last novel, *Ravelstein* (New York: Viking Penguin, 2000), the novelist would turn Dannhauser into the character Morris Herbst.

9. Walter Goodman of the *New York Times* once characterized the early *New York Review*'s editorial style as "cocktail-party revolutionary." Remarking on the magazine's weakness for the faddish, *Commentary* contributor Ruth Wisse pre-

ferred to call it "the *Women's Wear Daily* of the American intelligentsia." Podhoretz's first and last contribution to the *New York Review* was in 1965 ("The Old New Republic," April 8). Midge Decter wrote for it on Murray Kempton ("A Good Man Is Hard to Find," October 31, 1963), and on David Riesman ("Riesman in the Sixties," May 14, 1964).

10. Hayden, then a community organizer in Newark, did drop by the *Commentary* office. Podhoretz rejected a piece on "the crisis of liberalism," which Hayden had offered *Commentary* in 1962.

11. The most articulate of the symposium's thirty-one participants was Philip Roth, who used his reply to question the idea of chosenness. Roth insisted that until he could connect with the God of the Jews, "there will continue to exist between myself and those others who seek his presence, a question, sometimes spoken, sometimes not, which for all the pain it may engender, for all the disappointment and bewilderment it may produce, cannot be swept aside by nostalgia or sentimentality or even by a blind and valiant effort of the will: how are you connected to me as another man is not?"

12. Podhoretz persuaded his friend Jason Epstein at Random House to publish Goodman's book after more than a dozen publishers had declined it.

13. "On Paul Goodman," August 1963. Goodman's sexual omnivorousness was frequent fodder for Family jokes. One partygoer asks another, "Where's Paul Goodman?"

"I left him at the buffet."

"You mean you left him alone with the chopped liver?"

14. After *Commentary* editors complained about his piece's opacity, Marcuse wrote to Dannhauser: "I have neither the time nor the qualification to rewrite my review of Norman O. Brown's book so that it may become 'more accessible to the general reader.'" The magazine published it unedited. See Herbert Marcuse, "Love Mystified: A Critique of Norman O. Brown," February 1967; and Norman O. Brown, "A Reply to Herbert Marcuse," March 1967.

15. Podhoretz "was as valuable an editor as any I've ever worked with," Kateb said four decades later.

16. "The Imagination of Disaster," October 1965.

17. Baldwin's *Commentary* essays included "The Harlem Ghetto," February 1948; "Life Straight in De Eye," January 1955; and a beautiful memoir called "Equal in Paris," March 1955. His short stories "Previous Condition" and "The Death of the Prophet" appeared in the magazine in October 1948 and March 1950, respectively.

18. Broyard, himself an "inauthentic Negro" of the kind he described, kept a copy of that issue of the magazine by the dinner table for years, his daughter Bliss recalled. Broyard was inspired by Jean-Paul Sartre's "Portrait of the Inauthentic Jew," which had appeared in *Commentary* a couple of years earlier (May 1948).

19. *National Review* considered the desegregation decision an act of judicial usurpation from "a Supreme Court obsessed with an egalitarian ideology." According to a 1957 editorial in the magazine: "The central question that emerges . . . is whether the White community in the South is entitled to take such measures as are necessary to prevail, politically and culturally, in areas where it does not predominate numerically? The sobering answer is *Yes*—the White community is so entitled because, for the time being, it is the advanced race" ("Why the South Must Prevail," *National Review*, August 24, 1957).

20. Some young members of the Family were personally involved in the struggle for civil rights. Joseph Epstein had in his late twenties directed an antipoverty program in Little Rock. A twenty-five-year-old civil rights activist named Hillel Halkin had spent a year in the mid-1960s teaching at a small-town black college in the South.

21. "From Protest to Politics: The Future of the Civil Rights Movement," February 1965. In a piece on "black power" a year later, Rustin reminded *Commentary* readers that "Negroes today are in worse economic shape, live in worse slums, and attend more highly segregated schools than in 1954" ("'Black Power' and Coalition Politics," September 1966). See also Rustin's report in the October 1967 issue, "The Lessons of the Long Hot Summer."

22. "The American Crisis: Political Idealism and the Cold War."

23. "The Impotence of American Power," November 1963. Morgenthau's other contributions to Podhoretz's *Commentary* included "Prospect for a New Foreign Policy," February 1961; "The End of an Illusion," November 1961; "The Perils of Political Empiricism," July 1962; "Peace in Our Time?" March 1964; and "Goldwater—the Romantic Regression," September 1964.

There are plenty of other examples of anti-anti-Communism in the *Commentary* of those years. Ted Draper argued in the magazine that "the anti-Communism which has made a paranoid cliché or a political racket of the terms 'infiltration' and 'softness' has led us onto the path of disgrace and disaster" ("The Dominican Crisis," December 1965). Economist Robert Heilbroner charged those who regarded Communism as an irredeemable evil with "lurking fundamentalism" and urged them to abandon their obsolete ideological battle ("Counterrevolutionary America," April 1967).

For examples of cold war revisionism in that decade, see Denna F. Fleming, *The Cold War and Its Origins, 1917–1960* (New York: Doubleday, 1961); David Horowitz, *Free World Colossus: A Critique of American Foreign Policy in the Cold War* (New York: Hill and Wang, 1965); Michael Parenti, *Anti-Communist Impulse* (New York: Random House,1969); and Lloyd Gardner, *Architects of Illusion: Men and Ideas in American Foreign Policy, 1941–1949* (Chicago: Quadrangle Books, 1970).

24. See Bogdan Raditsa's early entry, "Beyond Containment to Liberation," September 1951. William Henry Chamberlin developed the theme in *Beyond*

Containment (Chicago: Regnery, 1953), as did James Burnham in *Containment or Liberation?* (New York: John Day, 1953).

25. Nisbet added, "To suppose that the United States can long maintain a political and military machine of containment dimensions without destroying the localism, pluralism, and free enterprise in all spheres that are the true basis of American freedom and creativity, is to suppose utter fantasy" ("Foreign Policy and the American Mind," September 1961).

26. In October 1963, President Kennedy had suggested to Arthur Ochs Sulzberger that perhaps Halberstam was too close to the story. When the *Commentary* piece came out, JFK sent his liaison with the Jewish community, Meyer Feldman, to register protest with the AJC.

27. "The World Politics of Responsibility," December 1965. Gass applauded Lyndon Johnson's April 1965 pledge to "remain as long as necessary, with the might required, whatever the risk and whatever the cost." On one occasion when Podhoretz refused to print a piece in which Oscar Gass took a hawkish line on Vietnam, Werner Dannhauser declared he would resign if it was turned down. Podhoretz finally changed his mind, but not before Gass, annoyed by the delay, had withdrawn the piece. Other writers took a different view. "There are far worse governments than Ho Chi Minh's," Paul Goodman wrote in *Commentary*'s September 1967 symposium "Liberal Anti-Communism Revisited," "which cause us no qualms; and there are few governments as bad as those we have supported in the South."

28. In Februrary 1978, Podhoretz published a piece by Guenter Lewy, the product of five years of examining the record on Vietnam, including classified documents never before studied. Lewy concluded that "while the charges of American political and military ineptitude in Vietnam can be sustained by all the available evidence . . . the charges of officially condoned crimes and grossly immoral conduct are without substance."

Most of the Family also dismissed those who blamed liberal anti-Communism for creating the climate that gave rise to the misbegotten war. In a 1967 symposium, "Liberal Anti-Communism Revisited," Sidney Hook rejected that charge as "myth" and "fantasy." "I cannot give even the beginning of credence to the idea that my views as a liberal anti-Communist helped bring about the war," Lionel Trilling added.

29. McCarthy arrived in Hanoi in a Chanel suit. Her first report, in the April 20, 1967, issue of the *New York Review of Books*, began: "I confess that when I went to Vietnam early in February I was looking for material damaging to the American interest and that I found it, though often by accident or in the process of being briefed by an official." Sontag averred that North Vietnam was "a place which, in many respects, deserves to be idealized."

30. "On Cowardice," June 1967. His friend V. S. Naipaul helped Theroux revise the essay through more than ten versions. "I think it's an important

statement," Naipaul said when it was done, "though you might have revealed too much of yourself." Theroux collected the essay in *Sunrise with Seamonsters* (New York: Houghton Mifflin, 1985).

31. "The Draft Card Gesture," February 1968.

32. The more personal parts of Mailer's book, which was most of it, appeared in *Harper's*.

CHAPTER 6

1. See, for example, Irving Howe, "Culture and Radicalism," a review of *The Democratic Vista*, by Richard Chase, May 1959; and Andrew Hacker, "The Rebelling Young Scholars," November 1960.

2. In a *Commentary* piece from February 1958 ("America's New Culture Hero: Feelings Without Words"), the same year as Podhoretz's attack, Robert Brustein denounced the new popular music: "Beginning by ignoring language, rock and roll is now dispensing with melodic content and offering only animal sounds and repetitive rhythms."

3. See also Norman Podhoretz, "My War with Allen Ginsberg," August 1997.

4. This was when Susan Sontag, who called the white race "the cancer of humanity," wrote her infamous "Some Thoughts on the Right Way (for Us) to Love the Cuban Revolution" (*Ramparts*, April 1969).

5. The *New American Review*, a paperback magazine issued three times a year starting in September 1967, would showcase innovative writing by Philip Roth, Grace Paley, Mordecai Richler, and many others. Solotaroff announced that his publication would avoid "the tendency toward cult and coterie by which literary magazines usually define their particular territory and assert their standards." He declined to impose his ideas on writers and chose instead a policy of "wise passiveness." "Behind some of our more 'topical'—and predictable— magazines," he wrote in the review's seventh issue, "lurks an editor's routinized megalomania." At its peak, the review reached a circulation of more than 100,000, but it wasn't a magazine in the normal sense. "Unlike a magazine," Richard Locke remarked in the *New York Times Book Review*, "NAR has no apparent sense of continuing obligation to go on record on an issue or event, to offer 'coverage.' . . . For the Sturm und Drang of Kulturkampf, for the excess and excitements of holy wars and political and cultural debates, we have to turn to *Commentary* and the *New York Review of Books*" ("The Last Word: New American Review," August 1, 1971).

6. "The On-Coming Generation Views the American Scene," *Journal of Jewish Communal Service*, Fall 1967.

7. The magazine endorsed the recommendation of the 1970 Scranton Report (officially called *The President's Report on Campus Unrest*) that perpetrators of violence on American campuses be vigorously prosecuted.

8. Harold Rosenberg, "The Trial and Eichmann," November 1961; Elie Wiesel, "Eichmann's Victims and the Unheard Testimony," December 1961. *Commentary* had reported on Eichmann in May 1949 (editor's note: "No one knows whether he is now alive or dead"). See also Avner Less, "Interrogating Eichmann," May 1983. Less was the Israeli police captain who had questioned the prisoner.

9. Remarkably, just over a year earlier, eminent Oxford historian H. R. Trevor-Roper, in his *Commentary* review of Raul Hilberg's landmark *The Destruction of the European Jews* (New York: Quadrangle, 1961), came to the "inescapable" conclusion that the Jewish victims, "obedient to their leader and to their own habits of mind, collaborated in their own destruction."

10. Ted Solotaroff thought this was Podhoretz's "finest hour as a writer, before or after," and Irving Howe remarked that Podhoretz had spoken "the most judicious words in the whole debate." There were several favorable reviews of Arendt's book, most prominently Bruno Bettelheim's in the *New Republic* and George Lichtheim's in the *New York Review of Books*.

11. The symposium appeared in book form in *The Condition of Jewish Belief* (New York: Macmillan, 1966).

12. Similarly, in the magazine's 1961 symposium on "Jewishness and Younger Intellectuals," only two of the thirty-one intellectuals in question mentioned the Holocaust as important to their thinking.

Gershom Scholem meanwhile gave *Commentary* his classic essay on the Sabbatian heretics, followers of the seventeenth-century false messiah Sabbetai Zevi. "The Holiness of Sin" (included under the title "Redemption Through Sin" in Scholem's book *The Messianic Idea in Judaism and Other Essays on Jewish Spirituality* [1971]) made its first appearance in English in January 1971. It was translated from the Hebrew by Hillel Halkin. Explaining the significance of *Commentary*'s publication of that essay, Podhoretz said: "How can one fail to be reminded in reading about these people of the type of revolutionists in America today who declare that the authority of this society is illegitimate and that the law must therefore be resisted and indeed violated if it is to be truly fulfilled?"

Commentary also introduced American readers to learned essays on Zionism, anti-Semitism, and the Jewish emancipation in Western and Central Europe by Jacob Katz, professor at Hebrew University in Jerusalem and one of the first historians to draw on rabbinic literature in the writing of Jewish social history. Katz's contributions to *Commentary* included "Emancipation and Jewish Studies," April 1974; "Zionism and Jewish Identity," May 1977; "Zionism vs. Anti-Semitism," April 1979; "Israel and the Messiah," January 1982; "German Culture and the Jews," February 1984; and "Leaving the Ghetto," February 1996.

13. "A Literary Approach to the Bible," December 1975; "Biblical Narrative," May 1976; "Character in the Bible," October 1978; "Joseph and His Brothers," November 1980; "The Voice from the Whirlwind," January 1984;

and "Scripture and Culture," August 1985. Some of these later served as the basis for Alter's books: *The Art of Biblical Narrative* (New York: Basic Books, 1981); and *The Art of Biblical Poetry* (New York: Basic Books, 1985). Alter's literary approach to the Bible did have precursors outside the American Jewish context, such as Richard Moulton's *The Literary Study of the Bible* (1895), and the essays on biblical translation of Martin Buber and Franz Rosenzweig, collected in *Die Schrift und ihre Verdeutschung* (1936). The very phrase "the Bible as literature" had been coined by Matthew Arnold. For a full discussion, see volume 2 of David Norton, *A History of the Bible as Literature* (Cambridge: Cambridge University Press, 1993); David Sperling, *Students of the Covenant: A History of Jewish Biblical Scholarship in North America* (Atlanta: Scholars Press, 1992); and the special issue of *Prooftexts* (Spring 2007) edited by Steven Weitzman, "Before and After *The Art of Biblical Narrative*."

14. In critical articles, *Commentary* would continue to introduce readers to literature in Hebrew. See, for example, Alan Mintz, "New Israeli Writing," January 1978, and "A Major Israeli Novel," July 1989; Ruth Wisse, "Aharon Appelfeld, Survivor," August 1983; Robert Alter, "Israeli Writers and Their Problems," July 1962, "New Israeli Fiction," June 1969, and "Inventing Hebrew Prose," March 1988; and Leon Wieseltier's review of *Songs of Jerusalem and Myself*, by Yehuda Amichai, May 1974. Under Podhoretz, the magazine also featured first-rate Israeli fiction: Amos Oz's novella "Crusade," August 1971, his first experiment with historical fiction, and his stories "Stefa and Pomeranz," August 1974, and "The Hill of Evil Counsel," April 1978; A. B. Yehoshua's novella "Early in the Summer of 1970," March 1973; and short stories by Yehuda Amichai ("Nina of Ashkelon," July 1967) and Shulamith Hareven ("Loneliness," September 1979).

15. In the 1990s, Alter moved away from the magazine; he sensed it had become "a dedicated soldier in the neocon political wars."

16. "The Vanishing Jews," September 1963; "On Leo Strauss," August 1974; "No Hitler, No Holocaust," March 1984.

17. "Is American Jewry in Crisis?" March 1969. Himmelfarb's essays are collected in *The Jews of Modernity* (Philadelphia: Jewish Publication Society, 1973); and *Jews and Gentiles*, ed. Gertrude Himmelfarb (New York: Encounter, 2007).

18. See Mark Bauman and Berkley Kalin, eds., *The Quiet Voices: Southern Rabbis and Black Civil Rights, 1880s to 1990s* (Tuscaloosa: University of Alabama Press, 1997); and Clive Webb, *Fight Against Fear: Southern Jews and Black Civil Rights* (Athens: University of Georgia Press, 2001).

19. For fuller accounts, see Murray Friedman, *What Went Wrong: The Creation and Collapse of the Black-Jewish Alliance* (New York: Free Press, 1995); and Jack Salzman and Cornel West, eds., *Struggles in the Promised Land: Toward a History of Black-Jewish Relations in the United States* (New York: Oxford University Press, 1997).

20. The war made Jewish intellectuals on the Left particularly uneasy. In an August 1967 piece ("Holy War") in the *New York Review of Books*, for instance, I. F. Stone contrasted the universalistic-minded Jew with the Israeli "concerned only with his own tribe's welfare."

21. "Jewishness and the Younger Intellectuals," April 1961. The same year, the magazine greeted rumors that Israel was secretly building an atomic reactor in the Negev by insisting that insofar as this represented atomic proliferation, "an Israeli atomic bomb would indeed be a terrible thing." In 1975, Robert Tucker defended the benefits of Israeli nuclear deterrence but also welcomed the end of its nuclear monopoly in the region: "Far from proving destabilizing, a nuclear balance between Israel and the major Arab states would have a stabilizing effect" ("Israel and the United States: From Dependence to Nuclear Weapons," November 1975).

22. In a 1970 letter to the magazine, Steiner wrote: "Anyone visiting Israel becomes more painfully aware with each visit of the pressures which the all-embracing job of armed survival are putting on intellectual and moral life. . . . The defeat of Israel would be a great disaster, a human tragedy which would affect the life of every Jew where he might be, however alien he might feel to the ideals of Zionism. But it could well be an even worse disaster if Israel grew into no more than a small fortified enclave."

23. See, for example, Amos Elon, "The Israeli Occupation," March 1968; and Shlomo Avineri, "The New Status Quo," March 1968.

24. Nor would the magazine shy away from criticizing Israeli leaders. In a 1974 issue, Lev Navrozov, a Russian Jewish émigré who had published a number of pieces in *Commentary* on Soviet affairs, alleged that in 1948 Golda Meir (then Israel's representative in Moscow) was "asked by Stalin . . . to draw up a list of all those Soviet Jews who wished to serve in the Israeli War of Independence. . . . Mrs. Meir complied, and Stalin duly handed the lists over to his secret police, who arrested the proposed volunteer army and sent the volunteers off to concentration camps for extermination by hunger, labor and frost" ("Notes on American Innocence," August 1974). The former prime minister filed a $3 million damage suit against *Commentary*: "I find it almost superfluous to state that there is not even one grain of truth in this story. Never, during my tenure in Russia was I put in a position where my 'innocence,' as Mr. Navrozov has it, was put to a test. No such request was ever presented to me, either by Stalin or by anyone else; therefore, naturally, I did not hand over such a list." Navrozov, acting as his own attorney, stood by his claim and said that he had supporting testimony in the form of interviews with an Israeli Embassy official and survivors of Soviet concentration camps. A short while later, *Commentary* received a letter from one such survivor, a Michael M. Solomon: "While a detainee of the 19th Lag-Otdelenie of Magadan, in Far-East Siberia, I came upon, during the fall of 1949, a group of Jewish intellectuals recently arrested in

cities like Moscow, Leningrad, Kiev, Odessa, etc., all of whom told me the same story, namely that their arrest followed the presentation of a list containing 400 names which was forwarded to Stalin at the latter's request, during the 9th November state banquet, by 'Israel's ambassador to the USSR, Mrs. Golda Meir.'" In the end, the AJC apologized, but not the magazine, and the former prime minister dropped the suit. It wasn't Golda's first tangle with the magazine. In 1964, Meir, then foreign minister, described as "slander" a piece (July 1964) that alleged she had cut younger leaders Shimon Peres and Moshe Dayan "down to size."

25. "The Intellectual and the Jewish Fate," *Midstream*, Winter 1957.

26. Yuri Slezkine reported, "In the first half of the 1960s, Jews (5 percent of all American students) made up between 30 and 50 percent of SDS (Students for a Democratic Society) membership and more than 60 percent of its leadership. . . . In a 1970 nationwide poll, 23 percent of all Jewish college students identified themselves as 'far left' (compared to 4 percent of Protestants and 2 percent of Catholics)."

27. In a November 20, 1969 speech at the Alabama Chamber of Commerce in Montgomery, Agnew cited a line from Walter Laqueur's June 1969 *Commentary* article "Reflections on Youth Movements": "The cultural and political idiocies perpetuated with impunity in this permissive age have gone clearly beyond the borders of what is acceptable for any society, however liberally it may be constructed." After a transcript of the speech appeared in the *New York Times*, Podhoretz sent in a letter to the editor (it was never published):

To the Editor:

It would be most unfortunate if the Vice President's approving reference to *Commentary* in his speech of November 20 were taken as implying that the magazine is in agreement with the general line of attack on the news media which Mr. Agnew appears to be pursuing. Moreover, by quoting Walter Laqueur's *Commentary* article out of context, the Vice President made it appear that Mr. Laqueur was entirely hostile to the student movement of today, whereas in fact the article's tone was distinguished by a quality of critical sympathy and a complexity of political judgment altogether foreign to the spirit of Mr. Agnew's own remarks about the radical young.

Norman Podhoretz

In a January 1972 speech in Cleveland, Agnew made another approving reference to the magazine: "The editor of *Commentary* magazine recently examined the charge that we are living in a repressive society and concluded, as others have, that the charge is totally absurd. In analyzing this rhetorical attack on America, he [Podhoretz] wrote: 'Never has there been so much talk of repression, but never has there been so great a degree of civil freedom, probably in the in history of the world, as exists in the U.S. today.'"

CHAPTER 7

1. For that matter, the names "Tory" and "Whig" also originated as slurs.

2. Francis FitzGerald, "The Warrior Intellectuals," *Harper's*, May 1976.

3. See Robert W. Tucker, "Behind Camp David," November 1978; and Alan Dowty, "In Defense of Camp David," April 1980. For a later treatment, see Rael Jean Isaac, "The Real Lessons of Camp David," December 1993, which took a somewhat darker view of the "cold peace" that transpired.

4. Resolution 465 determined "that all measures taken by Israel to change the physical character, demographic composition, institutional structure or status of the Palestinian and other Arab territories occupied since 1967, including Jerusalem, or any part thereof, have no legal validity and that Israel's policy and practices of settling parts of its population and new immigrants in those territories constitute a flagrant violation of the Fourth Geneva Convention relative to the Protection of Civilian Persons in Time of War and also constitute a serious obstruction to achieving a comprehensive, just and lasting peace in the Middle East."

In his 1980 defeat, Carter carried only 45 percent of the Jewish vote, thus becoming the first Democratic presidential candidate since 1924 to earn less than a majority of Jewish voters.

5. See Gertrude Himmelfarb, "The Prophets of the New Conservatism," January 1950.

6. Viereck argued in his book for a conservatism grounded in "the four ancestries of Western man: the stern moral commandments and social justice of Judaism; the love for beauty and for untrammeled intellectual speculation of the free Hellenic mind; the Roman Empire's universalism and its exaltation of law; and the Aristotelianism, Thomism, and anti-nominalism included in the Middle Ages."

In his book, Kirk reported his conviction "that civilized society requires orders and classes."

7. In the *Commentary* review of Trilling's book (August 1950), Stephen Spender wrote that such a view remained "very puzzling to a European like myself, firstly because, from three thousand miles away, America often appears the most conservative country in the world."

8. In 1988, Russell Kirk, author of the 1954 classic *The Conservative Mind* (New York: Faber and Faber), ventured a forecast-cum-wish: "I predict that within a very few years we will hear no more of the neoconservatives: some will have fallen away, and others will have been merged with the main current of

America's conservative movement, and yet others' pert loquacity will have been silenced by the tomb." The same Kirk, in the Catholic weekly *Commonweal,* had in 1956 called *Commentary* "the only intelligent monthly journal of opinion founded in recent years."

9. The first *Commentary* piece openly critical of Moynihan appeared in the June 1986 issue (Glenn Loury, "The Family, the Nation, and Senator Moynihan").

10. Bickel, the son of a Yiddish journalist who had immigrated from Romania, studied at City College and Harvard Law, clerked for Supreme Court justice Felix Frankfurter, taught constitutional law at Yale Law, and successfully defended the *New York Times* in the Pentagon Papers case in 1971. His *Commentary* articles included "The Civil Rights Act of 1964," August 1964; "The Failure of the Warren Report," October 1966; "The Constitution and the War," July 1972; and "Watergate and the Legal Order," January 1974.

"I am of the firmest belief that he would never have become a neoconservative," Diana Trilling wrote of her late husband in her memoir *The Beginning of the Journey* (New York: Harcourt Brace, 1993). "Nothing in his thought supports the sectarianism of the neoconservative movement. Everything in his thought opposes its rule by doctrine."

11. Abrams's piece argued that the Equal Employment Opportunity Commission was acting to remedy underrepresentation of minorities in hiring in ways that were "making it all but impossible for an employer to escape charges of discrimination if he attempts to hire on the basis of individual merit" ("The Quota Commission," October 1972).

12. A couple of years later, Sol Stern's outrage took on similar dimensions: "*Commentary*'s monthly fulminations against every movement for social change from women's liberation to the counterculture might be dismissed as the sour grapes of a bunch of West Side New York intellectuals hankering for the golden age of the 1950s when they were *de rigeuer* and traveled around the world on CIA credit cards. On the questions of the Jews, however, their combination of Sammy Glick and Spiro Agnew homilies ('listen kid, don't knock this country, it's been good to us') reflect a widespread sense of fear and isolation."

CHAPTER 8

1. Carl Gershman, "The Andrew Young Affair," November 1979.

2. Irving Kristol insisted in the January 1989 *Commentary* that "the 'politics of compassion,' which so dominates American Jewish thinking today, so far from being a natural extension of the Jewish moral-religious tradition, is a perversion of this tradition."

3. Max Boot, Bill Kristol, and Robert Kagan, for instance, were too young to have migrated from the Left.

4. Decter regarded even the Jonestown suicide of some nine hundred cult members in 1978 as "an outgrowth of 1960s radicalism."

5. "I have learned from experience," Podhoretz would write in the December 2006 issue, "that the more a given idea gets to be accepted as a self-evident truth by my fellow intellectuals, the more likely it is to be wrong."

6. Later, the neoconservative persuasion also developed in the *Weekly Standard*, the inside-the-Beltway magazine started in 1995 by Irving's son Bill Kristol.

7. See, for example, Aaron Wildavsky, "Government and the People," August 1973. *Commentary* also opposed compulsory school busing programs intended to achieve racial integration (Nathan Glazer, "Is Busing Necessary?" March 1972).

8. James Nuechterlein, "Neoconservatism and Irving Kristol," August 1984.

9. "Looting and Liberal Racism," September 1977. In his report for *Commentary* on the Crown Heights riots of 1991 ("The Crown Heights Riot and Its Aftermath," January 1993), Philip Gourevitch wrote, "So deep is the American predisposition to perceive blacks as the victims of racism that when they explode in the role of racists, we lack even the vocabulary to describe it."

10. "Many neoconservatives marched for racial justice thirty years ago," Glenn Loury said at a conference at Harvard marking *Commentary's* fiftieth anniversary. "Then the demons were clear. They are less so now. But you cannot tell me that what now transpires in ghetto America does not constitute a great injustice to those tens of thousands of youngsters who never get a chance. Is there no longer room within the intellectual edifice of neoconservatism for moral outrage in the face of such injustice?"

11. See, for example, William Bennett and Terry Eastland, "Why Bakke Won't End Reverse Discrimination I," September 1978 (which appeared in expanded form as William Bennett and Terry Eastland, *Counting by Race: Equality from the Founding Fathers to Bakke and Weber*, ed. Midge Decter [New York: Basic Books, 1979]); Nathan Glazer, "Why Bakke Won't End Reverse Discrimination II," September 1978; Thomas Sowell, "Are Quotas Good for Blacks?" June 1978; Carl Cohen, "Why Racial Preference Is Illegal and Immoral," June 1979; and Carl Cohen, "Justice Debased: The Weber Decision," September 1979.

12. See, for example, Walter Berns, "Let Me Call You Quota, Sweetheart," May 1981; Chester Finn, "'Affirmative Action' Under Reagan," April 1982; Carl Cohen, "Naked Racial Preference," March 1986; Terry Eastland, "Toward a Real Restoration of Civil Rights," November 1989; and Thomas Sowell, "'Affirmative Action': A Worldwide Disaster," December 1989.

13. "The Exposed American Jew," June 1975. Glazer's influential book *Affirmative Discrimination: Ethnic Inequality and Public Policy* (New York: Basic Books), one of the first full-length discussions of the issue, came out in 1975.

See also William Petersen's welcoming review in the May 1976 *Commentary*: "*Affirmative Discrimination* as it stands demonstrates once again that Nathan Glazer is one of the country's best social analysts. Intelligence, his first and most important working tool, shines through in every discussion and lights up every conclusion."

14. The first affirmative action case to be heard by the Supreme Court, *DeFunis v. Odegaard* (1974), was brought by a Jewish student from Seattle whose application to the University of Washington Law School had been rejected, though thirty-six less qualified "minority" applicants—who had scored lower than DeFunis on the LSAT and maintained lower grade-point averages—were admitted.

15. Abigail Thernstrom, "On the Scarcity of Black Professors," July 1990; Frederick Lynch, "Surviving Affirmative Action (More or Less)," August 1990; Chester Finn, "Quotas and the Bush Administration," November 1991; Timothy Maguire, "My Bout with Affirmative Action," April 1992; Arch Puddington, "What to Do About Affirmative Action," June 1995; Arch Puddington, "Will Affirmative Action Survive?" October 1995; Carl Cohen, "Race, Lies, and 'Hopwood,'" June 1996; Stephan Thernstrom, "The Scandal of the Law Schools," December 1997; "Is Affirmative Action on the Way Out? Should It Be?—a Symposium," March 1998; Justin Danilewitz, "Counting Noses at the *Harvard Crimson*," April 1998; Stephan Thernstrom and Abigail Thernstrom, "Racial Preferences: What We Now Know," February 1999; Jason Riley, "The 'Diversity' Defense," April 2001; Carl Cohen, "Race Preference and the Universities—a Final Reckoning?" September 2001.

16. Here was another province disproportionately peopled by Jews: Betty Friedan, author of *The Feminine Mystique* (1963) and founder of the National Organization for Women; Gloria Steinem of *Ms.* magazine; Bella Abzug of the National Women's Political Caucus; Shulamith Firestone of New York Radical Feminists and *The Dialectic of Sex* (1970). *Commentary*'s barrage only intensified in the 1980s and after. See, for example, Michael Levin, "Feminism, Stage Three," August 1986; Ruth Wisse, "Living with Women's Lib," August 1988; Carol Iannone, "Sex and the Feminists," September 1993; and Elizabeth Powers, "A Farewell to Feminism," January 1997.

17. Clive James, in the December 1973 issue ("Auden's Achievement"), had praised the influence of homosexuality on W. H. Auden's poetry, an influence that had forced the poet "to find a language for indirection." But the magazine had not since been kind to gays. Joseph Epstein, in a 1977 essay on Gore Vidal ("What Makes Vidal Run," June 1977), asked: "Is nihilism built into a certain strain of homosexuality? Many of the Pied Pipers of the youth rebellion of the late 60s were homosexuals." Samuel McCracken, in the lead piece of the January 1979 issue, attacked from a different direction: "The fact is that homosexuality

generally entails a renunciation of responsibility for the continuance of the human race and of a voice in the dialogue of the generations."

See also Norman Podhoretz, "Culture of Appeasement," *Harper's*, October 1977, where he wrote: "The homosexual ethos in England between the wars was anti-English: English society had been criminal in sending the flower of its youth off to war; it was bourgeois and dull. The writers who were propagating these attitudes did a good deal to undermine the feelings of confidence and belief in the legitimacy that there was something to defend in England. . . . The American homosexual literary world has been saying the same kinds of things about this society. This is an absolutely important element in the culture of appeasement."

Other *Commentary* treatments of the subject included Marjorie Rosenberg, "Inventing the Homosexual," December 1987; E. L. Pattullo, "Straight Talk About Gays," December 1992; Midge Decter, "Homosexuality in the Schools," March 1993; James Q. Wilson, "Against Homosexual Marriage," March 1996; Norman Podhoretz, "How the Gay-Rights Movement Won," November 1996; and Stanley Kurtz, "What Is Wrong with Gay Marriage," September 2000. In a *Commentary* piece on Vikram Seth's first novel, *The Golden Gate* ("Yuppies in Rhyme," September 1986), Carol Iannone denounced the author's breezy portrayal of homosexuality as, in her paraphrase, "life-enhancing and spiritually expansive."

18. In a piece called "Pink Triangle and Yellow Star" (*The Nation*, October 14, 1981), Vidal wrote: "For sheer vim and vigor, 'The Boys on the Beach' outdoes its implicit model, *The Protocols of the Elders of Zion*. . . . Not even the authors of *The Protocols of the Elders of Zion* ever suggested that the Jews, who were so hateful to them, were also hateful to themselves. So Decter has managed to go one step further than the *Protocols'* authors; she is indeed a virtuoso of hate, and thus do pogroms begin." (The piece is included in Jay Parini, ed., *The Selected Essays of Gore Vidal* [New York: Doubleday, 2008].)

19. David Robinson Jr., "Sodomy and the Supreme Court," October 1986.

20. "AIDS: Are Heterosexuals at Risk?" November 1987; "Are We Spending Too Much on AIDS?" October 1990; "AIDS So Far," December 1991.

21. *The De-Moralization of Society: From Victorian Virtues to Modern Values* (New York: Knopf, 1995). Many of Podhoretz's literary heroes were Victorians, whom he preferred over the later Bloomsbury writers. His teacher Lionel Trilling had written his first book on Matthew Arnold and had greatly admired E. M. Forster.

22. In 1982, Gilder had criticized the neoconservatives in *National Review* (March 5, 1982) for not sufficiently endorsing conservative views on social issues such as abortion, sex education, school prayer, and pornography. Midge Decter edited two of Gilder's books.

23. "A Ladies' Room of One's Own," August 1995. Shalit's other contributions to *Commentary* included "A Feminist Seder," January 1995; "Daughters of the (Sexual) Revolution," December 1997; and "Among the Gender Benders," January 1999. Allan Bloom of the Committee on Social Thought at the University of Chicago had earlier argued in *Commentary* that the feminist project suppressed modesty ("Liberty, Equality, Sexuality," April 1987).

24. See, for example, Joseph Epstein, "A Case of Academic Freedom," September 1986; and Stephen Balch and Herbert London, "The Tenured Left," October 1986.

25. See, for example, Frederick Crews, "Criticism Without Constraint," January 1982.

26. As in Terry Eastland, "In Defense of Religious America," June 1981.

27. The exceptions are: Magda Denes, "Performing Abortions," October 1976; Margaret Liu McConnell, "Living with *Roe v. Wade*," November 1990; James Q. Wilson, "On Abortion," January 1994.

28. In one *Commentary* article, for instance, Robert Bork urged a permissive interpretation of the First Amendment's establishment clause to allow religious speech on public property ("What to Do About the First Amendment," February 1995).

29. Lino Graglia, "How the Constitution Disappeared," February 1986; Walter Berns, "Government by Lawyers and Judges," June 1987; Stanley Brubaker, "Rewriting the Constitution: The Mainstream According to Laurence Tribe," December 1988; Wallace Mendelson, "Brennan's Revolution," February 1991. *Commentary* never went so far as *First Things*, which in a symposium called "The End of Democracy?" (November 1996) suggested that the "judicial usurpation of politics" put into question the legitimacy of the American "regime."

30. Leslie Lenkowsky, "Funding the Faithful: Why Bush Is Right," June 2001.

31. "The Future of American Jewry," August 1991. Daniel Pipes later made a parallel claim in *Commentary*. "The real and present danger," he wrote, "is by no means the pro-Israel Christian Coalition but the rabidly anti-Semitic Muslim Arab Youth Association; not Jerry Falwell but Sheikh Omar Abdel Rahman." In both cases, the enemy was said to pose a threat to the Judeo-Christian West ("America's Muslims Against America's Jews," May 1999).

32. See, for example, Howard Singer, "The Rise and Fall of Interfaith Dialogue," May 1987.

33. "Should Jews Fear the 'Christian Right?'" *New York Times*, July 23, 1994. Podhoretz's *Commentary* article is "In the Matter of Pat Robertson," August 1995. For more on the Robertson controversy, see Michael Lind, "Rev. Robertson's Grand International Conspiracy Theory," *New York Review of Books*, February 2, 1995; and Gustav Niebuhr, "Pat Robertson Says He Intended No Anti-Semitism in Book He Wrote Four Years Ago," *New York Times*, March 4,

1995. For more on Jerry Falwell, see Merril Simon, *Jerry Falwell and the Jews* (Middle Village, NY: Jonathan David, 1984). For another neoconservative defense of Evangelical Christians from the standpoint of Jewish interests, see Elliott Abrams, *Faith or Fear: How Jews Can Survive in a Christian America* (New York: Free Press, 1997).

34. Compare with Daniel J. Boorstin on page 48 above and with the anti-Semitic Reverend Gerald L. K. Smith, who said, "Christian character is the true basis of real Americanism." David Gelernter expanded his argument in *Americanism: The Fourth Great Western Religion* (New York: Doubleday, 2007).

35. In a much earlier *Commentary* essay on philo-Semitism, Edmund Wilson described how the American Puritans settling the new Canaan "identified George III with Pharaoh and themselves with the Israelites in search of the Promised Land" ("Notes on Gentile Pro-Semitism: New England's 'Good Jews,'" October 1956).

36. See, for instance, Reinhold Niebuhr, "Will Civilization Survive Technics?" December 1945; John Dewey, "Philosophy's Future in Our Scientific Age," October 1949; and Karl Jaspers, "Is Science Evil?" March 1950.

37. Richard John Neuhaus also weighed in, expressing alarm at "The Return of Eugenics," April 1988.

38. Other writers weighed in on evolution, too. In a *Commentary* piece called "The Deniable Darwin" (June 1996), David Berlinski, a fellow of the Discovery Institute in Seattle, called evolutionary theory a "secular myth." And Kass's student Eric Cohen argued in *Commentary* that the "Darwinian reduction of man to the beasts," as he put it, threatened the biblical idea of man as the only animal created in the image of God. A portent of the Family's criticism of Darwin's theory of natural selection can be found in Gertrude Himmelfarb, *Darwin and the Darwinian Revolution* (Chicago: Elephant Paperbacks, 1996 [1959]). *Commentary*'s discussions of evolution were often surprisingly technical for a general-interest magazine. See, for example, David Berlinski's attack ("A Scientific Scandal," April 2003) on a paper about the evolution of the eye from a patch of photoresponsive cells, authored by Dan-E. Nilsson and Susanne Pelger. Berlinski claimed Richard Dawkins had misrepresented the paper. The magazine also published Richard Herrnstein on the hereditary nature of IQ two decades before *The Bell Curve* made its splash ("In Defense of Intelligence Tests," February 1980).

39. "The Crisis of the Individual," December 1945.

40. See Rudolf Klein, "Growth and Its Enemies," June 1972; B. Bruce-Briggs, "Against the Neo-Malthusians," July 1974; and later pieces such as Peter Huber, "Reverend Malthus, Meet Doctor Faustus," November 1998.

41. *Commentary* also derided what it called the "apocalypse soon" school of environmentalism with its exaggerated fears of global warming. One writer argued that no evidence supported the theory that global warming was caused

by greenhouse gases. Another wrote that energy conservationism is "a popular political rallying cry not because of its intrinsic merit as an instrument of public policy but because it expresses the anti-bourgeois ideology of the dominant intellectual class" (Eugene Bardach, May 1976). Yet another decried the "misanthropic concepts that lie at the heart of environmentalist thought" (Jeffrey March, August 1995). Later, the magazine defended Bjorn Lomborg's book *The Skeptical Environmentalist* (Cambridge: Cambridge University Press, 2001), which challenged the scientific credibility of some parts of environmentalist dogma (see Kevin Shapiro's review in the November 2001 issue; and David Schoenbrod, "The Mau-Mauing of Bjorn Lomborg," September 2002).

42. P. T. Bauer, "Western Guilt and Third World Poverty," January 1976; P. T. Bauer and B. S. Yamey, "Against the New Economic Order," April 1977; P. T. Bauer and John O'Sullivan, "Foreign Aid for What?" December 1978; P. T. Bauer and B. S. Yamey, "East-West/North-South," September 1980; and P. T. Bauer and B. S. Yamey, "Foreign Aid: Rewarding Impoverishment?" September 1985. Related criticisms were taken up by Nick Eberstadt in articles such as "The Perversion of Foreign Aid," June 1985.

43. In a June 1982 review, Samuel McCracken called Novak's book "a stunning achievement . . . an argument of immense weight."

44. For examples, see George Gilder, "In Defense of Capitalists," December 1980; Tod Lindberg, "Four Cheers for Capitalism," April 1985; André Ryerson, "Capitalism and Selfishness," December 1986; Michael Novak, "Boredom, Virtue, and Democratic Capitalism," September 1989; Paul Johnson, "Blessing Capitalism," May 1993; and Joseph Epstein, "Culture and Capitalism," November 1993 (which argued that capitalism is better for art and creativity than socialism is).

45. They admitted that the eighteen-century inventors of laissez-faire capitalism favored the absolute monarchy and that many modern authoritarian regimes enjoyed free-market economies.

46. James Toback, "Norman Mailer Today," October 1967. Mailer first appeared in the magazine after the publication of *The Naked and the Dead* (New York: Rinehart, 1948), his novel about the war in the South Pacific. "His detonating outburst," *Commentary* exulted in its July 1948 review, "huge, acrid, and raspingly uncouth, comes as a relief—a whiff of the actual—after the pussyfooting of his contemporaries." But his "awkward, muscle-bound prose" was "terrible." (The review was by assistant editor Raymond Rosenthal, later esteemed for his translations into English of the works of Primo Levi.)

47. See Peter Shaw, "Portnoy and His Creator," May 1969; Irving Howe, "Philip Roth Reconsidered," December 1972; Norman Podhoretz, "Laureate of the New Class," December 1972; and John Aldridge, "My Life as a Man, by Philip Roth," September 1974. For subsequent treatments of Roth in *Commentary*, see Pearl Bell, "Philip Roth: Sonny Boy or Lenny Bruce?"

November 1977; Ruth Wisse, "Reading About Jews," March 1980; Ruth Wisse, "Philip Roth Then and Now," September 1981; Joseph Epstein, "What Does Roth Want?" January 1984; Robert Alter, "Defenders of the Faith," July 1987; Neal Kozodoy's review of *Patrimony*, May 1991; Hillel Halkin, "How to Read Philip Roth," February 1994; and Norman Podhoretz, "The Adventures of Philip Roth," October 1998. ("Roth's great contribution," Podhoretz wrote, "[was] to bring masturbation, up to then one of the dirtiest and most secret of dirty little secrets, into the realm of serious fiction.") See also John Podhoretz, "Philip Roth, the Great American Novelist," *American Spectator*, September 1981.

48. The *Commentary* review of *Humboldt's Gift* by Jack Richardson, calling it "a sad, shallow book, a statement of intellectual and artistic surrender," bore the title "A Burnt-Out Case."

49. "Socialism and Its Irresponsibilities: The Case of Irving Howe," December 1982.

50. In *Commentary*, Wieseltier wrote on Emil Fackenheim, Mordechai Kaplan, and Arthur Cohen (December 1973); Elie Wiesel (January 1974); Yehuda Amichai (May 1974); Hilton Kramer (June 1974); and Harry Wolfson (April 1976).

51. In a *Harper's* essay on George Orwell, for example, Podhoretz wrote: "I am convinced that if Orwell were alive today, he would be taking his stand with the neoconservatives and against the Left" ("If Orwell Were Alive Today," January 1983).

52. Edelshtein is based on the Yiddish poet Jacob Glatstein, who once said to Irving Howe: "What does it mean to be a poet of an abandoned culture? It means that I have to be aware of Auden but Auden need never have heard of me." The title of the story was Podhoretz's; Ozick groused against it. The novella was collected in Cynthia Ozick, *The Pagan Rabbi and Other Stories* (New York: Schocken, 1976).

53. Unpleasant notice came from the Yiddish press, some quarters of which attacked the story's withering portrayal of literary backbiting. The editor of one Yiddish paper wrote an angry letter to *Commentary*: "Not since the days of Dr. Goebbels have we seen expressed in writing such hatred toward Jews, Yiddish, and Yiddish literature."

54. Associate Editor Maier Daishell had told Ozick that Podhoretz had compared her outlook with that of black nationalism. "The difference," Ozick replied, "is again the difference between pretense and naturalness: they invent a culture, I inherit one."

55. *Commentary* also featured the first appearance in English of Chaim Grade's classic short Yiddish novel "The Rebbetzin" (October 1982); and a story by Hanoch Bartov, translated from the Hebrew ("Son, Father, Judge," March 1986).

CHAPTER 9

1. James Madison addressed America's role in the great battle between "Liberty and Despotism." Franklin D. Roosevelt declared, "Let us say to the democracies: 'We Americans are vitally concerned in your defense of freedom.'" John Kennedy pledged "to pay any price, bear any burden, meet any hardship . . . to assure the survival and the success of liberty." Ronald Reagan announced a "global campaign for democracy" and a "crusade for freedom." Barack Obama asserted during the 2008 campaign that America's "larger purpose in the world is to promote the spread of freedom."

Nor was this a theme new to *Commentary*. In September 1951, an Eastern European exile urged the magazine's readers to adopt a "democratic idealism," steered by the knowledge "that the Soviet dictatorship in Russia and East Europe can be overthrown by the democratic forces within these countries, if these forces are properly encouraged and guided" (Bogdan Raditsa, "Beyond Containment to Liberation").

2. "Human Rights and American Power," September 1981.

3. I. F. Stone called the article's publication irresponsible. Hyman Bookbinder, the AJC's man in Washington, called it "a serious mistake" in that it advocated a "dangerous and irresponsible" policy.

4. "Making the World Safe for Communism," April 1976.

5. See, for example, Michael Ledeen, "How to Support the Democratic Revolution," March 1985.

6. Kissinger, in a speech to the Economic Club of Detroit on November 24, 1975, said: "I recommended that he be appointed to this position [of UN ambassador] after I had read an article of his in which he laid out in some considerable detail what he thought the appropriate strategy of the UN should be."

7. Although Podhoretz advised Moynihan's 1976 campaign, almost as soon as he was elected to the Senate the next year, Moynihan gravely disappointed Podhoretz's hopes in him, but that is another story. Nevertheless, several members of Moynihan's Senate staff—Elliott Abrams, Chester Finn, and Charles Horner—became *Commentary* contributors. Moynihan's other contributions to the magazine included "'Bosses' and 'Reformers': A Profile of the New York Democrats," June 1961; "The President and the Negro," February 1967; "The Professors and the Poor," August 1968; "The Presidency and the Press," March 1971; "Was Woodrow Wilson Right?" May 1974; "The Politics of Human Rights," August 1977; and "Imperial Government," June 1978.

8. Contemplating the revelations, poet Robert Lowell wrote in the *Commentary* symposium: "One is plagued by unhappy thoughts of gullibility, shallowness, and opportunism—are we the discredited generation?" In the same symposium, Philip Rahv wrote: "The people who accepted secret CIA subsidies without being clear in their own minds as to what was involved are in

many ways to be compared to the 'fellow-travelers' and 'stooges' of the 1930s, who supported Stalin's reading of Marxism and his murderous policies even as they spoke of the Russia he despotically ruled as a 'worker's paradise' and as a 'classless society.' But in contrast to the 'stooges' of yesterday, the 'stooges' of today are paid cash on the line for their pious declarations." "It goes without saying," Lionel Trilling added, "that the CIA's covert backing of cultural and political projects, many of which were admirable in themselves, was a disaster in our national life." Finally, Stephen Spender, recently resigned as coeditor of *Encounter*, wrote: "It is not just that the free were duped but that they were made to appear dupes, and sometimes unjustly made to appear hypocrites." See also Peter Coleman, *The Liberal Conspiracy: The Congress for Cultural Freedom and the Struggle for the Mind of Postwar Europe* (New York: Free Press, 1989).

9. The title upended that of Mailer's novel *Why Are We in Vietnam?* (1967) which was dedicated, among others, to Podhoretz. In a review of Podhoretz's book in the *New Republic*, Ted Draper, by now an ex-friend, retorted that this kind of "selective moralistic zealotry . . . opens the door to a viciously dangerous stab-in-the-back legend by inferentially blaming the horrors of the war on those who opposed it rather than on those who waged it." "Mr. Podhoretz's righteousness becomes as offensive as the righteousness of his enemies on the New Left," Arthur Schlesinger Jr. said. "He feels that the purity of our motives sanctified the wantonness of our acts."

10. For another instance of how neoconservatives began looking at history through a new lens consider *Commentary*'s charges, four decades after the Yalta conference of February 1945, that President Franklin Roosevelt, the old liberal hero, had been guilty there of wishful thinking with regard to Soviet intentions in Eastern Europe after World War II. In the November 1985 issue of *Commentary*, its fortieth anniversary issue, Robert Nisbet referred to "Roosevelt's credulity toward Stalin," and Lionel Abel informed readers that "Roosevelt was personally responsible for terrible foreign-policy decisions . . . which gave the Soviet Union control of Eastern Europe." For a response to these charges, see Theodore Draper, "Neoconservative History," *New York Review of Books*, January 16, 1986.

11. Bukovsky, who had spent twelve years in Soviet prisons and psychiatric hospitals, took the title from Oscar Wilde's 1891 essay of the same name. Bukovsky's other *Commentary* pieces included "The Peace Movement and the Soviet Union," May 1982; "Will Gorbachev Reform the Soviet Union?" September 1986; "What to Do About the Soviet Collapse?" September 1991; "Boris Yeltsin's Hollow Victory," June 1993; and "Secrets of the Central Committee," October 1996.

12. See, for example, Donald Kagan, "World War I, World War II, World War III," March 1987; and Williamson Murray, "Munich at Fifty," July 1988.

13. See, for example, Eugene Rostow, "Why the Soviets Want an Arms-Control Agreement, and Why They Want It Now," February 1987; Angelo Codevilla, "How Eminent Physicists Have Lent Their Names to a Politicized Report on Strategic Defense," September 1987; Mary Tedeschi Eberstadt, "Arms Control and Its Casualties," April 1988. In "Reagan's Rush to Disarm," March 1988, Patrick Glynn criticized Reagan's "unreserved embrace of arms control in the final months of his administration."

14. Robert Jastrow, "Reagan vs. the Scientists: Why the President Is Right About Missile Defense," January 1984; Robert Jastrow, "The War Against 'Star Wars,'" December 1984 (Jastrow founded NASA's Institute for Space Studies); Angelo Codevilla, "How SDI Is Being Undone from Within," May 1986; Robert Jastrow and Max Kampelman, "Why We Still Need SDI," November 1992.

15. T. S. Eliot's *Criterion* held an average circulation of about 500. *Commentary's* paid circulation in 1985 reached 39,000.

16. See also Norman Podhoretz, "The Reagan Road to Détente," *Foreign Affairs* 63, no. 3 (1985).

17. "The Old New Republic," *New York Review of Books*, April 8, 1965.

18. "Trop de Zèle," *New York Review of Books*, October 9, 1986.

19. "The Presidency and the Press," March 1971.

20. In January 1985, Edward Luttwak wrote a piece for the magazine called "Delusions of Soviet Weakness." Four years later, he warned that the Soviet Communist Party remained implacably intent on accumulating military power. In the March 1990 issue, Richard Pipes argued that "until and unless incontrovertible evidence of Soviet cutbacks in military production and foreign engagements are forthcoming," "it will be premature to conclude that a new era in international relations has dawned."

21. So, too, did one voice in *Commentary*. "Changes within the Communist world and the evolution of Communist mentality depend much less on factors within our power," Adam Ulam, a professor of government at Harvard, had said in the magazine in January 1973, "than on the configuration of events and forces within that world itself" ("The Cold War According to Kennan").

22. Obviously, not everyone agreed. According to John Judis, a senior editor of *New Republic*, neoconservatives "laid the basis for the massive and at least partly unnecessary American arms buildup, which may have accelerated the decline of the Soviet Union but also contributed to the decline of the American economy—leading, among other things, to the crippling deficits of the 1980s."

23. Comintern archives, moreover, vindicated the claim that American Communists were by and large funded and directed by Moscow. In October 1996, Vladimir Bukovsky reported for the magazine ("Secrets of the Central Committee") on declassified documents showing that in the last two decades of the cold war, Moscow had funneled some $35 million to the Communist Party of the USA.

24. A May 1997 piece by two military historians at West Point (Frederick Kagan and David Fatua, "Could We Fight a War if We Had To?") noted that American military spending had dropped 24 percent in the previous six years.

25. Two notable exceptions: Bush's vice president, Dan Quayle, made Bill Kristol his chief of staff, and at about the same time Paul Wolfowitz was appointed under secretary of defense for policy.

26. "Against the Independent Counsel," February 1993. Bork's other contributions to *Commentary* included "What to Do About the First Amendment," February 1995; and "Civil Liberties After 9/11," July–August 2003.

27. In *An Old Wife's Tale: My Seven Decades in Love and War* (New York: ReganBooks, 2001), Decter wrote that her son-in-law, "as a result of a monstrous injustice, would one day pay a heavy price for having loyally carried out Reagan's policy in Central America."

28. The 1973 war also led to a pronounced engagement with Israel and a growing curiosity about its cultural products. Witness, for example, Saul Bellow's *To Jerusalem and Back* (New York: Viking, 1976), a personal and profoundly involved account of the writer's three-month visit.

29. In the November 1975 *Commentary*, Robert Tucker observed that this dependence brought into question the legitimacy of the Jewish state. Echoing the magazine's old discomfort with Zionism, he wrote: "The basic idea of Zionism was not simply to create another small nation-state, but one in which the Jews would live without fear and one in which they could be masters of their own destiny rather than protected individuals. . . . In Israel's case, particularly, a dependence that has no readily discernable limits must place in question the very *raison d'être* of the state" ("Israel and the United States: From Dependence to Nuclear Weapons?"). But Tucker's effusions would turn out to be the last gasp of the magazine's old coolness to the Jewish state.

30. Several years later, Irving Kristol would make a similar point in *Commentary* about supporting American interventions: "Can anyone believe that an American government which, in righteous moralistic hauteur, refuses to intervene to prevent a Communist takeover of Central America, will intervene to counterbalance Soviet participation in an assault on Israel? . . . If American Jews truly wish to be noninterventionist, they have to cease being so concerned with Israel." And again: "We American Jews have, in addition to a normal American interest, a specifically 'Jewish interest' in seeing to it that the U.S. is not merely a great democratic power, but the strongest and most influential of the great powers. For the U.S. is the only power in the world that is committed to Israel's survival" ("The Political Dilemma of American Jews," July 1984).

31. The first time *Commentary* led the way in arguing that American self-interest required siding with Israel was after the Soviet-Egyptian arms deal in 1955. As a May 1956 piece put it: "Only a resolute confrontation of the Arabs will help America. One vital element of such a confrontation is American support of Israel's

right to security and peace. Not for Israel's sake, but for America's" (Hal Lehrman, "Western Self-Interest and Israeli Self-Defense: They Coincide").

32. Moynihan noted that "the counts read as if they could have come from the Nuremberg verdicts" ("The Politics of Human Rights," August 1977).

33. "J'Accuse" provoked an unusually heavy volume of correspondence—some two hundred letters to the editor—not all of them enthusiastic. One Robert Kohn, for instance, a doctor from Cleveland, wrote in to say: "During thirty-plus years as a subscriber I've seen *Commentary* change from a voice of enlightenment and humanism to a forum for increasingly narrow and rigid points of view. When I read Norman Podhoretz's strained efforts to blunt criticism of Israel's shameful and self-destructive behavior, I knew I'd had enough. . . . Please cancel my subscription." Replying to "J'Accuse" in *The Nation* (October 9, 1982), Christopher Hitchens wrote: "It takes a real fool to confuse the editor of *Commentary* with Emile Zola. Who the hell does Podhoretz think he is?" Podhoretz called Hitchens's editorial "a scurrilous piece."

34. "Literary Gangsters," March 1970.

35. "The Empire Lovers Strike Back," *The Nation*, March 22, 1986. Vidal had earlier attacked Commentary's views on homosexuals in a Nation piece called "Some Jews and the Gays." Commentary's distaste of The Nation, meanwhile, was not new. In an April 1951 *Commentary* piece called "The Liberals Who Haven't Learned," Granville Hicks greeted *The Nation*'s eighty-fifth anniversary by wondering what brought the liberals there to apologize for the deeply illiberal Soviet Union: "The *Nation*—and, unhappily, it is not alone in this respect among 'progressive' organs and organizations—has preserved what was weakest and blindest in the old liberalism, and has carried over attitudes that once were merely irresponsible but now are dangerous."

36. Podhoretz wasn't the only one to register protest. Irving Howe denounced Vidal's "racist diatribe." Arthur Hertzberg dismissed the essay as "the screaming rhetoric of American nativism, in the accents of patrician highhandedness and self-righteousness."

37. Podhoretz had his managing editor, Marion Magid, write to twenty-nine people who appeared on *The Nation*'s masthead: "In connection with a projected article, we are asking a number of friends and supporters of the *Nation* whether they have seen fit to protest against the contribution by Gore Vidal to the 120th anniversary issue ("The Empire Lovers Strike Back"). Could you let us know whether you have made such a protest, either in private or in a letter for publication?" Most never bothered to reply. Victor Navasky, *The Nation*'s editor, stood by his writer. "Gore Vidal is a satirist, an ironist. . . . When he suggested that Jewish neoconservatives like 'Poddy' should register as foreign agents for the state of Israel, either one could take his arguments literally, in which case they were anti-Semitic, or one could take them as his ironic way of commenting

on the folly of Jewish intellectuals making alliances with the Moral Majority (who were the real anti-Semites)."

38. "The Palestinians and the PLO," January 1975. Lewis's other contributions to the magazine included "The Return of Islam," January 1976; "Settling the Arab-Israeli Conflict," June 1977; "Is Peace Still Possible in the Middle East? The Egyptian Perspective," July 1978; "The Decline and Fall of Islamic Jewry," June 1984; "The Arab World Discovers Anti-Semitism," May 1986; and "Eurocentrism Revisited," December 1994. Lewis, befriended in the 1970s by Senator Henry Jackson, gained a measure of influence in Washington and became the neoconservatives' most admired and consulted scholar of Islam, especially after 9/11. In his book *From Babel to Dragomans* (New York: Oxford University Press, 2004), for example, Lewis remarked on the futility of negotiating with Islamic autocrats: "As with the Axis and the Soviet Union, real peace will come only with their defeat or, preferably, collapse, and their replacement by governments that have been chosen and can be dismissed by their people."

39. *Commentary* also ran a couple of articles in the mid-1970s by Joan Peters, soon to become notorious for her book *From Time Immemorial* (New York: HarperCollins, 1984), which drew on demographic data to show that many of those regarded as Palestinian refugees had themselves immigrated from neighboring Arab countries not long before 1948, attracted by the jobs and wealth Jewish immigrants to Palestine had created. One of those pieces, "An Exchange of Populations" (August 1976), would form part of the book, which aroused fierce controversy. Israeli historian Yehoshua Porath, for instance, called *From Time Immemorial* "a sheer forgery." In the July 1984 issue, Daniel Pipes gave the book a largely favorable review. Two years later, the magazine conceded evidence of "carelessness" but concluded that the book's thesis was "generally sound" (Erich Isaac and Rael Jean Isaac, "Whose Palestine?" July 1986).

40. Milson's other *Commentary* articles were "How Not to Occupy the West Bank," April 1986; and "A Great Twentieth-Century Novelist," June 1991 (on Egyptian writer Naguib Mahfouz).

41. Justus Reid Weiner, "'My Beautiful Old House' and other Fabrications by Edward Said," September 1999. See also Hillel Halkin, "Whose Palestine? An Open Letter to Edward Said," May 1980; and Edward Alexander, "Professor of Terror," August 1989. Outside of *Commentary* see Bernard Lewis, "The Question of Orientalism," *New York Review of Books*, June 24, 1982.

42. In 2002, Kozodoy edited a collection of *Commentary*'s pieces on the subject called *The Mideast Peace Process: An Autopsy* (New York: Encounter, 2002), which included contributions from David Bar-Illan, Doug Feith, Hillel Halkin, Daniel Pipes, Efraim Karsh, and Mark Helprin.

43. Like every family, this one had its share of feuds, of course. Clem Greenberg refused for five decades to speak to Saul Bellow. Bellow called critic Irving Howe "an old-fashioned lady." Robert Warshow feuded with Lionel Trilling

after aiming a devastating *Commentary* piece ("The Legacy of the 30's: Middle-Class Mass Culture and the Intellectuals' Problem," December 1947) at Trilling's novel of ideas, *The Middle of the Journey* (New York: Viking, 1947). During an argument about his wife, Diana's, politics, Trilling, in high dudgeon, nearly punched literary critic Alfred Kazin. (Kazin used to call Diana "Mrs. Cooking Spoon.") Midge Decter thought Diana was out of touch. "She hasn't read a book since 1957," Decter would say. Arendt resented Diana. Sidney Hook and Arendt were nemeses. Et cetera.

44. "The Old People's Socialist League," August 1998.

45. Leslie Farber, "I'm Sorry, Dear," November 1964.

46. Not everyone saw the divergence. Journalist Murray Kempton, for example, said in the early 1970s: "*Commentary* has a fake independence. The American Jewish Committee has no other function than to tell Jews to love the United States" (cited in Philip Nobile, *Intellectual Skywriting: Literary Politics and the New York Review of Books* [New York: Charterhouse, 1974]).

47. "Neoconservatism: A Eulogy," March 1996. See also Irving Kristol, "America's Exceptional Conservatism,'" *Wall Street Journal*, April 18, 1995; and John Judis, "Trotskyism to Anachronism," *Foreign Affairs*, July–August 1995, which asserted that "if neoconservatism exists in the 1990s, it is much the way the New Left survived into the 1980s—as cultural nostalgia rather than distinct politics." Earlier, Seymour Martin Lipset ("Neoconservatism: Myth and Reality," *Society*, July–August 1988) had concluded that "the concept of neoconservatism is irrelevant to further developments within American politics."

CHAPTER 10

1. The series, published by the Behrman House in New York, included Isadore Twersky, *A Maimonides Reader* (1972); Marshall Sklare, *The Jew in American Society* (1974); Robert Alter, *Modern Hebrew Literature* (1975); Lucy Dawidowicz, *A Holocaust Reader* (1976); and Robert Chazan, *Church, State, and the Jew in the Middle Ages* (1979).

2. In *Patrimony*'s climactic scene, Roth cleans up after his father has befouled himself: "There was my patrimony: not the money, not the tefillin, not the shaving mug, but the shit."

As for Dawidowicz, two years after her death, Kozodoy would edit a collection of her essays, *What Is the Use of Jewish History?* (New York: Schocken, 1992). Kozodoy also contributed to *Contentions*, the newsletter of the Committee on the Present Danger, but only because its editor, Midge Decter, assured him there would be no bylines.

3. Other *Commentary* contributors to have received the Medal of Freedom include Sidney Hook (1985), Jeane Kirkpatrick (1985), and Pat Moynihan (2000).

4. For the December 2003 *Commentary*, Kozodoy assigned Victor Davis Hanson to review Decter's book:

Consider: in little more than two years after the murder of 3,000 Americans on September 11, 2001, the United States military under Rumsfeld's direction has won two wars, overthrown the Taliban and Saddam Hussein, inaugurated consensual government for 50 million Middle Easterners, scattered al-Qaeda terrorists, put both allies and enemies on notice that the entire way the United States uses its military is now under review, and crafted a new, lighter, and more mobile style of fighting—all without suffering another catastrophic attack on our territory and at the cost of about 300 soldiers lost. What Decter's biography reminds us is that we need this seventy-one-year-old veteran far more than he needs us.

5. "It is exceedingly difficult, if not impossible," Michael Ledeen wrote in *Commentary* in March 1985, "to achieve a successful transition from dictatorship to democracy in the midst of a violent crisis" ("How to Support the Democratic Revolution").

6. "Johnson So Far: III: Foreign Policy," June 1965. Under Lyndon Johnson, who "has little background in foreign affairs," Goldbloom added, "we were also acting in a manner which was predictably certain to antagonize world opinion." The blame was not all Johnson's, however. "American intelligence agencies, whose reports are cited in justification of the policies adopted and presumably contributed significantly to their adoption, have not only been consistently wrong in their predictions as to developments in the Vietnamese war, but have been repeatedly taken by surprise by political developments in Saigon itself."

7. "An Agenda for American Liberals," June 1966.

8. The judgments of Goodman and Rosenberg appear in the *Commentary* symposium "Liberal Anti-Communism Revisited," September 1967. Former Green Beret William Pfaff (later a columnist for the *International Herald Tribune*) wrote in *Commentary* that "Special Forces, like, later, the Army itself, was put to work without an intellectually and politically rigorous definition of what could be expected in Vietnam. . . . Our tactics of 'nation-building' proved incompetent to change anything fundamental in Vietnamese hamlets which had experienced twenty or more years of politicized violence." He resented the way American soldiers had been asked "to impose 'security' upon a violently divided foreign population." ("Confessions of a Green Beret," January 1970).

9. It should be said that Fukuyama's "The End of History?" appeared in the *National Interest*, Summer 1989, not in *Commentary*, where Paul Johnson dismissed him as "a blinkered Hegelian." Fukuyama's *Commentary* articles included "A New Soviet Strategy," October 1979; "Immigrants and Family Values," May 1993; "Against the New Pessimism," February 1994; "Asian Values

and the Asian Crisis," February 1998; and "Can Any Good Come of Radical Islam?" (with Nadav Samin), September 2002.

10. "Democracies and Double Standards," August 1997.

11. A February 1949 article by S. D. Goitein mentioned the Muslim Brotherhood and worried that "Islamic fundamentalism, so strongly decried by enlightened Arabs only a short while ago is now openly encouraged." But the magazine subsequently looked at the subject either from a Jewish point of view—for example, Ronald Nettler, "Islam vs. Israel," December 1984; and Bernard Lewis, "The Arab World Discovers Anti-Semitism," May 1986—or through a cold war lens. Historian John Patrick Diggins took another view of the matter:

> Twenty years ago, *Commentary* dismissed "the Islamic revolution" as little more than a sideshow concealing the movement of the Soviet Union into the Mideast. Thus the fall of the shah in Iran in 1979 was alleged to be as ominous as the fall of the czar in Russia in 1917—not because it presaged a religious fundamentalism that one day would become America's mortal enemy but because it signaled the "prelude" to Communism's inevitable march into the oil states. With the stakes so high, *Commentary* saw nothing wrong with America arming Osama bin Laden and Saddam Hussein and establishing a covert alliance with the House of Saud, which would turn out to be the financial angel of al-Qaeda.

12. As early as 1947, ex-Communist James Burnham referred to the cold war as the Third World War (and, in fact, would take the term as the name of his column in *National Review*).

13. Pat Buchanan blamed Israel and its "amen corner" in Washington for dragging the United States into the first Gulf war. Saddam agreed: "This war that is being waged against us is a Zionist war," he said in January 1991.

14. Podhoretz pointed out that even Bill Clinton, Sandy Berger, and William Cohen believed Saddam possessed these weapons, as did (in 2002) Senator Ted Kennedy. President Clinton called Iraq "a rogue state with weapons of mass destruction, ready to use them or provide them to terrorists, drug traffickers, or organized criminals who travel the world among us unnoticed." A May 2003 Gallup Poll found that 79 percent of Americans considered the war justified with or without conclusive evidence that Saddam Hussein had possessed weapons of mass destruction.

15. The charge appears in his essay "Second Thoughts on James Burnham" (from the British anti-Communist magazine *Polemic*, May 1946).

16. "By persisting in their ideology," Sidney Blumenthal said back in 1988, "the neoconservatives had fostered the conditions by which America lost much of its international prestige and influence."

17. The Straussian gravitational pull on *Commentary*'s neoconservative turn was tangential. Gertrude Himmelfarb's brief discussions of Strauss's interpretation of Xenophon in the January 1950 ("The Prophets of the New Conservatism") and July 1951 issues ("Political Thinking: Ancients vs. Moderns") were the first to bring Strauss to the attention of a general readership. At the time Nathan Glazer sent her the book, she said, "no one had a notion of who Strauss was." Along with her husband, Irving Kristol, who in October 1952 reviewed *Persecution and the Art of Writing* (Glencoe, IL: Free Press, 1952) for the magazine, Himmelfarb was one of the first outside of Strauss's circle of students to take note of his work. Associate editor Werner Dannhauser had studied with Strauss. But contributing editor George Lichtheim thought little of Strauss and gave a negative review in the magazine (November 1963) to Strauss's book *On Tyranny* (New York: Political Science Classics, 1948). There was only one full-length article on Strauss in *Commentary*. It was by contributing editor Milton Himmelfarb ("On Leo Strauss," August 1974), and it said nary a word about foreign policy. (Strauss seldom weighed in on foreign policy, and explicitly warned that "we cannot reasonably expect that a fresh understanding of classical political philosophy will supply us with recipes for today's use.") Strauss himself contributed only one piece to the magazine: "Jerusalem and Athens," his essay on Judaism and Hellenism, made its first appearance there in 1967.

For more on the question of Strauss's influence on the neoconservatives generally, see Nathan Tarcov, "Will the Real Leo Strauss Please Stand Up?" *American Interest*, September–October 2006; Kenneth Weinstein, "Philosophic Roots, the Role of Leo Strauss, and the War in Iraq," in *The Neocon Reader*, ed. Irwin Stelzer (New York: Grove Press, 2004); Anne Norton, *Leo Strauss and the Politics of American Empire* (New Haven: Yale University Press, 2004); and Thomas G. West, "Leo Strauss and American Foreign Policy," *Claremont Review of Books*, Summer 2004.

18. In the early 1990s, as executive editor of *National Interest*, Lind contributed several pieces to *Commentary*, including "The Two Cultures (Continued)," August 1991; and "A Map of Modern Art," April 1992.

19. McConnell's articles in the magazine included "Homage to Raymond Aron," May 1984; "Vietnam and the 60s Generation: A Memoir," June 1985; "Resurrecting the New Left," October 1987; and "The Making of the Mayor 1989," February 1990.

20. For a useful sampling of the conversation among conservatives about the war in Iraq, see Gary Rosen, ed., *The Right War? The Conservative Debate on Iraq* (Cambridge: Cambridge University Press, 2005).

21. Some of the war's critics, Senior Editor Gabriel Schoenfeld added, "are opposed not only to the war in Iraq but to American purposes more generally, and to American success most of all."

22. "The Case for Bombing Iran," June 2007; "Stopping Iran: Why the Case for Military Action Still Stands," February 2008. In the May 2009 issue, Podhoretz wrote: "If there is a threat to Israel coming from Obama, it is that, having eschewed the use of force by the United States, he will follow through on his Vice President's declaration that the Israelis would be 'ill-advised' to attack the Iranian nuclear sites and will prevent them from doing the job themselves." Other *Commentary* writers chimed in, too. In the November 2006 issue, historian Arthur Herman wrote:

> In 1938, Britain and France could have joined forces with the well-armed and highly motivated Czech army to administer a crushing defeat to the German Wehrmacht and probably topple Hitler in the bargain. Instead they handed him the Sudetenland, setting in motion the process that in 1939 led to the most destructive war in world history. Do we intend to dither until suicide bombers blow up a supertanker off the Omani coast, or a mushroom cloud appears over Tel Aviv, before we decide it is finally time to get serious about Iran?

23. In 536 BCE, Cyrus, king of Persia, allowed those who wished to return to Zion and rebuild the Temple to do so. During a 1953 visit to the Jewish Theological Seminary in New York, Kansas City businessman Eddie Jacobson introduced his old friend Harry Truman as "the man who helped create the state of Israel." The former president said: "What do you mean 'helped create'? I am Cyrus. I am Cyrus!" (Jacobson and Truman had served together during World War I in the 129th Field Artillery, and after the war they opened the Truman and Jacobson haberdashery in Kansas City.)

24. The new journal was edited by Abe Socher—a professor at Oberlin who had reviewed in *Commentary* books by James Kugel (December 2007) and Cynthia Ozick (September 2008). Its editorial board included, among others, Robert Alter, Shlomo Avineri, Hillel Halkin, Leon Wieseltier, and Ruth Wisse.

EPILOGUE

1. The first in this line was Leon Trotsky's 1938 essay "Their Morals and Ours" (included by Irving Howe in *The Basic Writings of Leon Trotsky* [London: Mercury Books, 1964]).

2. Frum's contributions to *Commentary* included "It's Big Government, Stupid," June 1984; "What to Do About Healthcare," June 1985; "Colin Powell and the Conservatives," January 1996; and "What the Tories Have to Teach Us," November 2009.

3. "The Retreat of the Liberal Sages," *New York Times*, May 17, 1976.

4. "Under the unwritten and somewhat eccentric rules of American public discourse," Michael Kinsley has observed, "a statement that contradicts everything you have ever said before is considered for that reason to be especially sincere, courageous and dependable" ("In God, Distrust," *New York Times*, May 13, 2007).

5. "There is one vice of which ex-Communists are less likely to be guilty," Granville Hicks wrote in the March 1950 *Commentary*, "and that is smugness" (a review of Richard Crossman's *The God That Failed*). James Nuechterlein, writing in *Commentary* in August 1984, warned that neoconservatives "need to be careful that in combating the ideologues of the Left they do not turn themselves into mirror images of that which they oppose" ("Neoconservatism and Irving Kristol").

6. In October 1965, *Commentary* ran a piece criticizing the intellectual's involvement in politics: "The intellectual who engages in current politics is usually lost. . . . The intellectual cannot engage in current political discussion and hope, at the same time, to think deeply or precisely" (Henry Fairlie, "Johnson and the Intellectuals"). After it swung to the neoconservative direction, this was no longer the magazine's view.

7. See, for example, Moses Maimonides, *Guide of the Perplexed*, 1:73; Bahya ibn Paquda's preface to *Hovot Ha-Levavot* (Duties of the Heart); and Joseph Albo's *Sefer Ha-Ikarim* (Book of Principles) 3:8. The Hebrew term for "imagination," dating from the twelfth century, is *dimyon* or *koach ha-medameh*. The word *dimyono* in Psalms 17:12 means "likeness," not imagination.

8. "The America of John Dos Passos" (*Partisan Review*, April 1938), collected in Lionel Trilling, *The Moral Obligation to Be Intelligent*, ed. Leon Wieseltier (New York: Farrar, Straus and Giroux, 2000).

9. "A Romantic Aristocrat," collected in T. S. Eliot, *The Sacred Wood: Essays on Poetry and Criticism* (London: Methuen, 1920).

10. For more paleoconservative complaints along these lines, see Paul Gottfried and Thomas Fleming, *The Conservative Movement* (New York: Twayne, 1988); and "The State of Conservatism: A Symposium," *Intercollegiate Review*, Spring 1986.

11. *Escaping Judaism*, Menorah Society Pamphlet No. 2 (New York: Menorah Press, 1922).

12. Ernest Hopkins, president of Dartmouth in 1945, declared it "almost impossible for a Jew to be appointed to an administrative position at any university not sponsored by Jews." One view in *Commentary* of the transformation is Lawrence Bloomgarden, "Our Changing Elite Colleges," February 1960.

13. Bernard Avishai, "Breaking Faith: *Commentary* and the American Jews," *Dissent*, Spring 1981.

14. See Steven M. Cohen and Charles S. Liebman, "American Jewish Liberalism: Unraveling the Strands," *Public Opinion Quarterly* 61 (1997); Tom

Smith, *Jewish Distinctiveness in America* (New York: American Jewish Committee, 2005); and Lawrence Fuchs, *The Political Behavior of American Jews* (New York: Free Press, 1956). Norman Podhoretz draws on each of these in *Why Are Jews Liberals?* (New York: Doubleday, 2009).

15. For attempts to describe the Founders' debt to the principles of liberty in the Hebrew Bible, see Oscar Straus, *Origin of Republican Form of Government* (New York: Putnam's, 1901); and Daniel Elazar's four-volume study, *The Covenant Idea in Politics* (New Brunswick, NJ: Transaction, 1996–1998).

16. George Nash, "Joining the Ranks: *Commentary* and American Conservatism," in *"Commentary" in American Life,* ed. Murray Friedman (Philadelphia: Temple University Press, 2005.)

17. The non-Jewish branch of the neoconservative Family included Pat Moynihan, Jeane Kirkpatrick, Father Richard John Neuhaus, James Nuechterlein, Michael Novak, George Weigel, Bill Bennett, James Q. Wilson, and Peter L. Berger.

18. The most penetrating studies of the subject are Yehezkel Kaufmann, *Golah Ve-Nekhar* (Tel Aviv: Dvir, 1929 [Hebrew]); Yitzhak Baer, *Galut* (New York: Schocken, 1947); and Arnold Eisen, *Galut: Modern Jewish Reflection on Homelessness and Homecoming* (Bloomington: Indiana University Press, 1986).

19. *Shver tsu zayn a yid* (Hard to Be a Jew) is also the title of a play by Yiddish writer Sholom Aleichem.

Bibliography

Aaron, Daniel. *Writers on the Left*, reprint. New York: Columbia University Press, 1992 [1961].

Abel, Lionel. *The Intellectual Follies: A Memoir of the Literary Venture in New York and Paris*. New York: Norton, 1984.

Abrams, Nathan. *"Commentary" Magazine, 1945–59*. London: Vallentine Mitchell, 2007.

Alexander, Edward. *Irving Howe: Socialist, Critic, Jew*. Bloomington: Indiana University Press, 1998.

———. *Lionel Trilling and Irving Howe: And Other Stories of Literary Friendship*. New Brunswick, NJ: Transaction, 2009.

Atlas, James. *Saul Bellow*. London: Faber and Faber, 2000.

Ausmus, Harry J. *Will Herberg: From Right to Right*. Chapel Hill: University of North Carolina Press, 1987.

Barrett, William. *The Truants: Adventures Among the Intellectuals*. New York: Doubleday, 1982.

Bell, Daniel. *The End of Ideology: On the Exhaustion of Political Ideas in the Fifties*. Cambridge, MA: Harvard University Press, 2000 [1960].

Bell, Daniel, and Irving Kristol, eds. *Confrontation: The Student Rebellion and the Universities*. New York: Basic Books, 1969.

Berkowitz, Peter, ed. *Varieties of Conservatism in America*. Palo Alto, CA: Hoover Institution, 2004.

Blau, Joseph. *Judaism in America: From Curiosity to Third Faith*. Chicago: University of Chicago Press, 1976.

Bloom, Alexander. *Prodigal Sons: The New York Intellectuals and Their World*. Oxford: Oxford University Press, 1986.

Blumenthal, Sidney. *The Rise of the Counter-establishment: From Conservative Ideology to Political Power*. New York: Harper and Row, 1986.

Boorstin, Daniel. *The Genius of American Politics* (Chicago: University of Chicago Press, 1953).

Brightman, Carol, ed. *Between Friends: The Correspondence of Hannah Arendt and Mary McCarthy, 1949–1975*. New York: Harcourt Brace, 1995.

Caute, David. *The Fellow Travelers: Intellectual Friends of Communism*. New Haven, CT: Yale University Press, 1988.

Cohen, Elliot E., ed. *"Commentary" on the American Jewish Scene*. New York: Knopf, 1953.

Cohen, Steven M. *American Modernity and Jewish Identity*. London: Tavistock, 1983.

Coleman, Peter. *The Liberal Conspiracy: The Congress for Cultural Freedom and the Struggle for the Mind of Postwar Europe*. New York: Free Press, 1989.

Cook, Richard. *Alfred Kazin: A Biography*. New Haven, CT: Yale University Press, 2007.

Cooney, Terry. *The Rise of the New York Intellectuals: "Partisan Review" and Its Circles, 1934–1945*. New York: Harper and Row, 1985.

Coser, Lewis, and Irving Howe, eds. *The New Conservatives*. Chicago: Quadrangle, 1974.

Dash Moore, Deborah. *At Home in America: Second-Generation New York Jews*. New York: Columbia University Press, 1981.

Dawidowicz, Lucy. *On Equal Terms: Jews in America, 1881–1981*. New York: Holt, Rinehart and Winston, 1982.

Decter, Midge. *The New Chastity and Other Arguments Against Women's Liberation* (New York: Coward, 1972).

———. *An Old Wife's Tale: My Seven Decades in Love and War*. New York: Regan Books, 2001.

DeMuth, Christopher, and William Kristol, eds. *The Neoconservative Imagination: Essays in Honor of Irving Kristol*. Washington, DC: AEI Press, 1995.

Dickstein, Morris. *Gates of Eden: American Culture in the Sixties*. New York: Penguin, 1989.

Diggins, John Patrick. *The Proud Decades: America in War and Peace, 1941–1960*. New York: Norton, 1988.

———. *Up from Communism: Conservative Odysseys in American Intellectual History*. New York: Harper and Row, 1975.

Diner, Hasia. *The Jews of the United States, 1654 to 2000*. Berkeley and Los Angeles: University of California Press, 2004.

Dollinger, Marc. *Quest for Inclusion: Jews and Liberalism in Modern America*. Princeton, NJ: Princeton University Press, 2000.

Dorman, Joseph. *Arguing the World: The New York Intellectuals in Their Own Words*. New York: Free Press, 2000.

Dorrien, Gary. *Imperial Designs: Neoconservatism and the New Pax Americana*. London: Routledge, 2004.

———. *The Neoconservative Mind*. Philadelphia: Temple University Press, 1993.

Editors of *Commentary* Magazine. *The Condition of Jewish Belief*. New York: Macmillan, 1966.

Ehrman, John. *The Rise of Neoconservatism: Intellectuals and Foreign Affairs, 1945–1994*. New Haven, CT: Yale University Press, 1995.

Fein, Leonard. *Where Are We? The Inner Life of America's Jews*. New York: Harper and Row, 1988.

Fiedler, Leslie. *Fiedler on the Roof: Essays on Literature and Jewish Identity.* Boston: David R. Godine, 1992.

Forman, Seth. *Blacks in the Jewish Mind: A Crisis of Liberalism.* New York: New York University Press, 1998.

Friedman, Murray, ed. *"Commentary" in American Life.* Philadelphia: Temple University Press, 2005.

———. *The Neoconservative Revolution: Jewish Intellectuals and the Shaping of Public Policy.* Cambridge: Cambridge University Press, 2005.

Fukuyama, Francis. *America at the Crossroads: Democracy, Power, and the Neoconservative Legacy.* New Haven, CT: Yale University Press, 2006.

Gerson, Mark. *The Neoconservative Vision: From the Cold War to the Culture Wars.* Toronto: Madison Books, 1996.

Gilbert, James. *Writers and Partisans: A History of Literary Radicalism in America.* New York: Wiley, 1968.

Glazer, Nathan. *American Judaism,* 2d ed. Chicago: University of Chicago Press, 1989.

Goren, Arthur. *The American Jews.* Cambridge, MA: Harvard University Press, 1982.

Gross, John. *The Rise and Fall of the Man of Letters.* Chicago: Ivan R. Dee, 1992 [1969].

Guttmann, Allen. *The Jewish Writer in America.* Oxford: Oxford University Press, 1971.

Halper, Stefan, and Jonathan Clark. *America Alone: The Neoconservatives and the Global Order.* Cambridge: Cambridge University Press, 2004.

Handlin, Oscar. *The Uprooted: The Epic Story of the Great Migrations That Made the American People,* 2d ed. Philadelphia: University of Pennsylvania Press, 2002.

Hart, Jeffrey. *The Making of the American Conservative Mind: "National Review" and Its Times.* Wilmington, DE: ISI Books, 2005.

Hartz, Louis. *The Liberal Tradition in America* (New York: Harcourt Brace, 1955).

Heilbrunn, Jacob. *They Knew They Were Right: The Rise of the Neocons.* New York: Doubleday, 2007.

Hellman, Lillian. *Scoundrel Time.* New York: Bantam, 1977.

Hertzberg, Arthur. *The Jews in America: Four Centuries of an Uneasy Encounter.* New York: Simon and Schuster, 1989.

Higham, John. *Send These to Me: Jews and Other Immigrants in Urban America.* New York: Atheneum, 1975.

Hoffman, Fred, Charles Allen, and Carolyn Ulrich. *The Little Magazine.* Princeton, NJ: Princeton University Press, 1947.

Hook, Sidney. *Out of Step: An Unquiet Life in the 20th Century.* New York: Carroll and Graf, 1987.

Howe, Irving. *A Margin of Hope: An Intellectual Autobiography.* New York: Harcourt Brace Jovanovich, 1982.

———. *World of Our Fathers: The Journey of the East European Jews to America and the Life They Found and Made.* New York: Simon and Schuster, 1976.

Jacoby, Russell. *The Last Intellectuals: American Culture in the Age of Academe.* New York: Basic Books, 1987.

Jumonville, Neil. *Critical Crossings: The New York Intellectuals in Postwar America.* Berkeley and Los Angeles: University of California Press, 1991.

———. *The New York Intellectuals Reader.* London: Routledge, 2007.

Kadushin, Charles. *The American Intellectual Elite.* Boston: Little, Brown, 1974.

Kaplan, Dana Evan, ed. *The Cambridge Companion to American Judaism.* Cambridge: Cambridge University Press, 2005.

Karp, Abraham. *Haven and Home: A History of the Jews in America.* New York: Schocken, 1985.

Kazin, Alfred. *A Lifetime Burning in Every Moment: From the Journals of Alfred Kazin.* New York: HarperCollins, 1996.

———. *On Native Grounds.* New York: Harcourt Brace, 1942.

———. *Starting Out in the Thirties.* Ithaca, NY: Cornell University Press. 1989.

Kempton, Murray. *Part of Our Time: Some Ruins and Monuments of the Thirties.* New York: Simon and Schuster, 1955.

Kessner, Carole, ed. *The "Other" New York Jewish Intellectuals.* New York: New York University Press, 1994.

Kimmage, Michael. *The Conservative Turn: Lionel Trilling, Whittaker Chambers, and the Lessons of Anti-Communism.* Cambridge, MA: Harvard University Press, 2009.

Klingenstein, Susanne. *Enlarging America: The Cultural Work of Jewish Literary Scholars, 1930–1990.* Syracuse, NY: Syracuse University Press, 1998.

Klinghoffer, Judith A. *Vietnam, Jews, and the Middle East: Unintened Consequences* (New York: St. Martin's, 1999).

Kozodoy, Neal, ed. *The Mideast Peace Process: An Autopsy.* New York: Encounter, 2002.

———, ed. *What to Do About . . . : A Collection of Essays from "Commentary" Magazine.* New York: ReganBooks, 1995.

Kramer, Hilton. *The Twilight of the Intellectuals: Culture and Politics in the Era of the Cold War.* Chicago: Ivan R. Dee, 1999.

Kristol, Irving. *Neoconservatism: The Autobiography of an Idea.* New York: Free Press, 1995.

———. *Reflections of a Neoconservative: Looking Back, Looking Ahead.* New York: Basic Books, 1983.

Kuspit, Donald. *Clement Greenberg: Art Critic.* Madison: University of Wisconsin Press, 1979.

Lasch, Christopher. *The New Radicalism in America, 1889–1963*. New York: Knopf, 1965.

Laskin, David. *Partisans: Marriage, Politics, and Betrayal Among the New York Intellectuals*. New York: Simon and Schuster, 2000.

Lipset, Seymour Martin, ed. *American Pluralism and the Jewish Community*. New Brunswick: Transaction, 1990.

Lipset, Seymour Martin, and Earl Raab. *Jews and the New American Scene*. Cambridge, MA: Harvard University Press, 1995.

Macdonald, Dwight. *Memoirs of a Revolutionist*, 1957. Revised as *Politics Past*. New York: Viking Press, 1970.

———. *A Moral Temper: The Letters of Dwight Macdonald*, ed. Michael Wreszin. Chicago: Ivan R. Dee, 2001.

McCarthy, Mary. *The Company She Keeps*. New York: Harcourt Brace Jovanovich, 1970.

Morris, Willie. *New York Days*. New York: Little, Brown, 1993.

Mott, Frank L. *A History of American Magazines,* vol. 3. Cambridge, MA: Harvard University Press, 1960.

Murray, Douglas. *Neoconservatism: Why We Need It*. New York: Encounter, 2006.

Nash, George. *The Conservative Intellectual Movement in America Since 1945*, rev. ed. Wilmington, DE: Intercollegiate Studies Institute, 2006.

Navasky, Victor. *A Matter of Opinion*. New York: Farrar, Straus and Giroux, 2005.

Nobile, Philip. *Intellectual Skywriting: Literary Politics and the "New York Review of Books."* New York: Charterhouse, 1974.

Ouzan, Françoise S. *Histoire des Américains juifs*. Paris: Andre Versailles, 2008.

Patterson, Orlando. *Ethnic Chauvinism: The Reactionary Impulse*. New York: Stein and Day, 1977.

Pells, Richard. *The Liberal Mind in a Conservative Age: American Intellectuals in the 1940s and 1950s*. New York: Harper and Row, 1985.

Podhoretz, Norman. *The Bloody Crossroads: Where Literature and Politics Meet*. New York: Simon and Schuster, 1986.

———. *Breaking Ranks*. New York: Harper and Row, 1979.

———, ed. *The "Commentary" Reader*. New York: Atheneum, 1966.

———. *Doings and Undoings: The Fifties and After in American Writing*. New York: Noonday Press, 1964.

———. *Ex-Friends*. New York: Free Press, 1999.

———. *Making It*. New York: Harper and Row, 1967.

———. *My Love Affair with America: The Cautionary Tale of a Cheerful Conservative*. New York: Free Press, 2000.

———. *The Present Danger*. New York: Simon and Schuster, 1980.

———. *The Prophets: Who They Were, What They Are*. New York: Free Press, 2002.

————. *Why Are Jews Liberals?* New York: Doubleday, 2009.

————. *Why We Were in Vietnam*. New York: Simon and Schuster, 1982.

Powers, Richard Gid. *Not Without Honor: The History of American Anti-Communism*, rev. ed. New Haven, CT: Yale University Press, 1998.

Rubenfeld, Florence. *Clement Greenberg: A Life*. New York: Scribner, 1998.

Sachar, Howard. *A History of the Jews in America*. New York: Knopf, 1992.

Sarna, Jonathan. *American Judaism*. Oxford: Oxford University Press, 2004.

Seltzer, Robert, and Norman Cohen, eds. *The Americanization of the Jews*. New York: New York University Press, 1995.

Shapiro, Edward, ed. *Letters of Sidney Hook: Democracy, Communism, and the Cold War*. Armonk, NY: Sharpe, 1995.

Shechner, Mark. *After the Revolution: Studies in Contemporary Jewish-American Imagination*. Bloomington: Indiana University Press, 1987.

Silberman, Charles. *A Certain People: American Jews and Their Lives Today*. New York: Simon and Schuster, 1985.

Slezkine, Yuri. *The Jewish Century*. Princeton, NJ: Princeton University Press, 2004.

Smith, Adrian. *The "New Statesman:" Portrait of a Political Weekly*. London: Routledge, 1996.

Solotaroff, Ted, ed. *Alfred Kazin's America: Critical and Personal Writings*. New York: HarperCollins, 2003.

————. *First Loves: A Memoir*. New York: Seven Stories Press, 2003.

Sorin, Gerald. *Irving Howe: A Life of Passionate Dissent*. New York: New York University Press, 2002.

————. *Tradition Transformed: The Jewish Experience in America*. Baltimore, MD: Johns Hopkins University Press, 1997.

Staub, Michael E. *Torn at the Roots: The Crisis of Jewish Liberalism in Postwar America*. New York: Columbia University Press, 2002.

Steinfels, Peter. *The Neoconservatives: The Men Who Are Changing America's Politics*. New York: Simon and Schuster, 1979.

Stelzer, Irwin, ed. *Neoconservatism*. London: Atlantic Books, 2004.

Story, Ronald, and Bruce Laurie. *The Rise of Conservatism in America, 1945–2000*. New York: Bedford/St. Martin's Press, 2008.

Svonkin, Stuart. *Jews Against Prejudice: American Jews and the Fight for Civil Liberties*. New York: Columbia University Press, 1997.

Tanenhaus, Sam. *The Death of Conservatism*. New York: Random House, 2009.

Tebbel, John, and Mary Ellen Zuckerman. *The Magazine in America, 1741–1990*. Oxford: Oxford University Press, 1991.

Teres, Harvey. *Renewing the Left: Politics, Imagination, and the New York Intellectuals*. Oxford: Oxford University Press, 1986.

Trilling, Diana. *The Beginning of the Journey.* New York: Harcourt Brace, 1993.

Wald, Alan. *The New York Intellectuals: The Rise and Fall of the Anti-Stalinist Left from the 1930s to the 1980s.* Chapel Hill: University of North Carolina Press, 1987.

Warshow, Robert. *The Immediate Experience: Movies, Comics, Theater, and Other Aspects of Popular Culture.* Cambridge, MA: Harvard University Press, 2001.

Whitfield, Stephen. *In Search of American Jewish Culture.* Lebanon, NH: University Press of New England, 1999.

Widmer, Kingsley. *Paul Goodman.* New York: Twayne, 1980.

Wilford, Hugh. *The New York Intellectuals: From Vanguard to Institution.* Manchester, UK: Manchester University Press, 1995.

Winchell, Mark Royden. *Neoconservative Criticism: Norman Podhoretz, Kenneth S. Lynn, and Joseph Epstein.* New York: Twayne, 1991.

———. *"Too Good to Be True": The Life and Work of Leslie Fiedler.* Columbia: University of Missouri Press, 2002.

Wisse, Ruth. *If I Am Not for Myself: The Liberal Betrayal of the Jews.* New York: Free Press, 1992.

Wreszin, Michael. *A Rebel in Defense of Tradition: The Life and Politics of Dwight Macdonald.* New York: Basic Books, 1994.

Wyman, David. *The Abandonment of the Jews: America and the Holocaust 1941–1945* (New York: Pantheon, 1984).

Zipperstein, Steven. *Rosenfeld's Lives: Fame, Oblivion, and the Furies of Writing.* New Haven, CT: Yale University Press, 2009.

ARCHIVES

American Jewish Committee archives, New York.

Commentary magazine archives, New York.

Harvey Shapiro, transcribed oral history, taped January 11, March 4, and May 5, 1993, Dorot Jewish Division, New York Public Library.

INTERVIEWS/CORRESPONDENCE/E-MAIL

Robert Alter, Josiah Lee Auspitz, Bernard Avishai, Norman Birnbaum, Sam Bluefarb, Eugene Borowitz, Robert S. Brustein, Jerome Charyn, Werner Dannhauser, Midge Decter, Morris Dickstein, Harris Dienstfrey, John P. Diggins, Amos Elon, Joseph Epstein, Herbert J. Gans, James B. Gilbert, Nathan Glazer, Herbert Gold, Allegra Goodman, Tom Hayden, Edward Hoagland, Rael J. Isaac, Daniel Johnson, Paul Johnson, George Kateb, Stanley Kauffmann,

Neal Kozodoy, Irving Kristol, Edith Kurzweil, Walter Laqueur, Alison Lurie, Edward Luttwak, Norman Mailer, Daphne Merkin, Victor Navasky, Lev Navrozov, Hillel Neuer, Jacob Neusner, Alicia Ostriker, Richard Perle, William Pfaff, Norman Podhoretz, Philip Roth, Gabriel Schoenfeld, Harvey Shapiro, George Steiner, Michael Wyschogrod, and Chayym Zeldis.

Index

162, 163, 172, 182,
197
Reconstructionist Judaism,
5
Reform Judaism, 4, 33–34,
36
Reich, Tova, 152
Reitlinger, Gerald, 222n21
Republican Party, 8,
118–119, 123–124,
131–134, 208
Resolution 465, 245n4
"The Return of Islam"
(Lewis, B.), 187
Revel, Bernard, 5
Revel, Jean-Francois, 164
Revolutionary Age, 52
Revolutionary War, Jews in,
3–4
Reznikoff, Charles, 12,
228n8, 231n28
Ribicoff, Abraham, 87
Rice, Condoleezza, 185
Richardson, Jack, 232n36
Richler, Mordecai, 240n5
Riesman, David, 46, 47, 48,
50, 72, 93
Ringelblum, Emmanuel, 32
Robertson, Pat, 143
Roosevelt, Franklin D., 11,
63, 122, 123, 210,
254n1, 255n10
Roosevelt, Theodore, 196
Rorty, James, 71, 89–90,
222n23
Rosen, Gary, 181, 199
Rosen, Norma, 152, 183
Rosenberg, Ethel, 64
Rosenberg, Harold, 19, 30,
45, 70, 93, 102,
221n14, 229n19,
232n36
Rosenberg, Julius, 64
Rosenfeld, Isaac, 17, 27–28,
50, 61, 74, 85, 124,
221n14, 223n35
"Adam and Eve on
Delancey Street" and,
29–30

Rosenfeld, Paul, 54
Rosenman, Samuel, 123
Rosenthal, A. M., 177
"The Boys on the Beach"
and, 139
on Cohen, E. E., 74
"The Negro and the New
York Schools" and, 90
Rosenthal, Midge. *See*
Decter, Midge.
Rosenwald, Nina, 176
Rosenzweig, Franz, 51, 53,
179, 220n9
Rossiter, Clinton, 121, 122
Rostow, Eugene, 157, 168
Roth, Cecil, 31
Roth, Henry, 54, 57
Roth, Philip, x, 55, 56, 57,
58, 60, 86, 97, 146,
147, 148, 151, 152,
180, 237n11, 240n5,
260n2
Rothko, Mark, 23
Rousseau, Jean-Jacques, 121
Rove, Karl, 196
Rubin, Jerry, 87
Rudd, Mark, 101
Ruderman, Jacob, 219n1
Rumkowski, Mordechai
Chaim, 32
Rumsfeld, Donald, 184
Rushdie, Salman, 201
Rustin, Bayard, 90
Ryskind, Morrie, 230n22

The Sabbath (Heschel), 52
Sadat, Anwar, 120
al-Sadr, Moqtada, 191
Said, Edward, 173
Salanter, Israel, 113
SALT (Strategic Arms
Limitation Talks), 157
Samuel, Maurice, 35
Samuel, Ralph, 28, 29
Santayana, George, 12
Sarna, Jonathan, 227n2
Sartre, Jean-Paul, 47, 83,
192
Schechter, Solomon, 5, 34

Scheer, Robert, 242n19
Schiff, Jacob, 16, 34, 35
Schlamm, William, 230n22
Schlesinger, Arthur Jr., 11,
87, 93, 204, 220n6,
221n16, 228n8, 255n9
Schneerson, Joseph I.,
219n1
Schneiderman, Harry,
221n13
Schocken Books, 223n30
Schoenfeld, Gabriel, 181,
183, 199
Scholem, Gershom, x, 52,
84, 104, 215, 220n9,
229n14, 229n19,
241n12
Schultz, George, 170
Schwartz, Delmore, 3, 20,
24, 37, 46, 57, 221n14,
231n28
Schwerner, Michael, 108
Scoundrel Time (Hellman),
72
Scowcroft, Brent, 166
SDI. *See* Strategic Defense
Initiative
SDS. *See* Students for a
Democratic Society
Seale, Bobby, 109
Seixas, Joshua, 228n11
Selznick, David O., 23
Sendak, Maurice, 222n20
"The Sense of Alienation Is
Not Exclusively Jewish"
(Sartre), 47
September 11, 2001, ix, x,
183, 184, 186, 187,
189, 209, 233n5, 260n4
Shachtmanites, 6
Shakespeare, William, 59
Shalit, Wendy, 141
Shamir, Yitzhak, 173
Shapiro, Harvey, 74,
231n28
Shapiro, Karl, 221n14
Shapiro, Philip, 242n19
Sharansky, Natan, 164
Sharon, Ariel, 172, 176

Shaw, Peter, 147, 176
Shawn, William, 74
Sheed, Wilfrid, 82
Shelley, Percy Bysshe, 9
Shermanites, 6
Shneour, Zalman, 57
Shtenkler, Ephraim, 32
Shub, Anatole, 75
Silver, Abba Hillel, 35
Silvers, Robert, 85, 87
Simon, Ernst, 36–37, 42
Singer, I. J., 57
Singer, Isaac Bashevis, x, 57, 58, 127, 183, 222n20
Six-Day War, x, 109–113, 173
Slawson, John, 17, 28
Slesinger, Tess, 12, 25
Slezkine, Yuri, 244n27
Smelansky, Moshe, 36
Smith, Gerald L. K., 63
Snow, C. P., 83
Socher, Abe, 264n24
Socialism, 21, 134
  Jews and, 4
  rise and fall within Family, 6–11
  as synonymous with Judaism, 9
Socialist Labor Party, 5
Socialist Party, 4
Solomon, Michael M., 243n25
Solotaroff, Ted, 85, 86, 100, 147, 150, 175, 240n5, 241n10
Soloveitchik, Joseph B., 51, 219n1, 229n15
Sombart, Werner, 228n9
Sontag, Susan, 88, 95, 101, 110, 150, 228n6, 239n29, 240n4
South Korea, 154
Spectator, 193
Spender, Stephen, 245n7, 254n8
The Spirit of Democratic Capitalism (Novak), 145

"The Spiritual Reconstruction of European Jewry" (Baron), 179
Stalin, Joseph, 6, 9–10, 11, 65, 67, 68–69, 100, 160, 233n4, 243n25, 254n8, 255n10
Stein, Gertrude, 18
Steinberg, Milton (rabbi), 29, 230n21
Steinberg, Saul, 222n20
Steiner, George, 88, 111, 124
Steinfels, Peter, 127
Stendhal, 206
Stern, Fritz, 31
Stern, Sol, 115, 246n12
Stieglitz, Alfred, 23
Stone, I. F., 109, 224n1, 243n21, 254n3
Strasser, Adolph, 5
Strategic Defense Initiative (SDI), 159, 165
Straus, Nathan, 4, 35
Straus, Oscar, 16
Straus, Roger, 81
Strauss, Leo, 6, 86, 106, 175, 192, 220n9
Strauss, Levi, 4
Streicher, Julius, 29
Students for a Democratic Society (SDS), 97, 101, 111, 244n27
Der Stürmer, 29
Stuyvesant, Peter, 3
Sulzberger, Arthur Ochs, 239n26
Sulzberger, Mayer, 16
Swope, Gerard, 23
Symposiums, 17, 26, 111, 145, 248n15, 265n10
  "American Jews and Israel", 173
  "American Power—for What?", ix, 183, 219n1
  "Jewishness and the Younger Intellectuals", 88, 237n11, 241n12

"Liberal Anti-Communism Revisited", 93, 95, 156, 239nn27–28, 254n8, 261n8
"Liberalism and the Jews", 124, 131–132, 180
"The National Prospect", 141
"On the Future of Conservatism", 183
"The State of Jewish Belief", 105, 183, 241n11
"What Do American Jews Believe?", 183
"What Is a Liberal—Who Is a Conservative?", 119
Syria, 109, 120, 167, 190, 191
Szold, Henrietta, 34

Taft, Robert, 155
Tales of the Hasidim (Buber), 104
Talmon, Jacob, 112, 226n18
Talmud, 40
Taubes, Jacob, 48, 143, 228n6
Taylor, Maxwell (general), 94
"Teaching Jewish Teachers" (Alter), 106
Telushkin, Joseph, 231n29
Temple Emanu-El, 4
Theology, cultivation of Jewish, 50–54, 229n12
Thernstrom, Abigail, 142
Theroux, Paul, 95, 239n30
Thompson, Dorothy, 114
Thurber, James, 49
Tiananmen Square, 166
Tikkun, Lerner and, 172
Tillich, Paul, 229n14, 229n19
Time, 69, 109, 145, 197, 227n1
Times Literary Supplement, Solotaroff and, 85

"Writing About Jews"
(Roth, P.), 147
Wrong, Dennis,
125

Yeats, W. B., 59, 63
Yeltsin, Boris, 165
Yeshiva College, 5
Yezierska, Anzia,
54
Young, Andrew, 120,
132–133
Young People's Socialist
League (YPSL), 6, 8
Young-Bruehl, Elisabeth,
233n5

al-Zarqawi, Abu Musab,
191
Zionist Organization of
America (ZOA), 34, 35
Zionists, 9, 21, 23, 25, 26,
128, 225n7, 226n18,
241n12, 243n23,
257n29
AJC and, 34–36
America as home or place
of exile for, 33–38
anti-, 33–34, 36
Arendt on, 37, 39
Ben-Gurion and, 40–41
Commentary's view of,
36–39, 40–41

diaspora Zionism and,
38, 40–41
Family's views of, 37, 38,
42–43
non-, 34
as pro-American, 34–35
Reform movement's
denunciation of,
33–34
return to Zionism and,
38–41
writers, 35
See also Israel
Zola, Emile, 170
Zuckerman, Nathan,
148

Benjamin Balint is a fellow at the Hudson Institute. His articles and reviews have appeared in the *Wall Street Journal*, the *American Scholar*, the *Weekly Standard*, *Policy Review*, *Haaretz*, the *Claremont Review of Books*, and *Commentary*, where he served as assistant editor from 2001 to 2004. Originally from Seattle, Balint earned a master's degree in philosophy at the University of Washington. He now lives in Jerusalem.

PublicAffairs is a publishing house founded in 1997. It is a tribute to the standards, values, and flair of three persons who have served as mentors to countless reporters, writers, editors, and book people of all kinds, including me.

I. F. STONE, proprietor of *I. F. Stone's Weekly*, combined a commitment to the First Amendment with entrepreneurial zeal and reporting skill and became one of the great independent journalists in American history. At the age of eighty, Izzy published *The Trial of Socrates*, which was a national bestseller. He wrote the book after he taught himself ancient Greek.

BENJAMIN C. BRADLEE was for nearly thirty years the charismatic editorial leader of *The Washington Post*. It was Ben who gave the *Post* the range and courage to pursue such historic issues as Watergate. He supported his reporters with a tenacity that made them fearless and it is no accident that so many became authors of influential, best-selling books.

ROBERT L. BERNSTEIN, the chief executive of Random House for more than a quarter century, guided one of the nation's premier publishing houses. Bob was personally responsible for many books of political dissent and argument that challenged tyranny around the globe. He is also the founder and longtime chair of Human Rights Watch, one of the most respected human rights organizations in the world.

. . .

For fifty years, the banner of Public Affairs Press was carried by its owner Morris B. Schnapper, who published Gandhi, Nasser, Toynbee, Truman, and about 1,500 other authors. In 1983, Schnapper was described by *The Washington Post* as "a redoubtable gadfly." His legacy will endure in the books to come.

Peter Osnos, *Founder and Editor-at-Large*